Imperial Underworld

During a major overhaul of British imperial policy following the Napoleonic Wars, an escaped convict reinvented himself as an improbable activist, renowned for his exposés of government misconduct and corruption in the Cape Colony and New South Wales. Charting scandals unleashed by the man known variously as Alexander Loe Kaye and William Edwards, *Imperial Underworld* offers a radical new account of the legal, constitutional and administrative transformations that unfolded during the British colonial order of the 1820s. In a narrative rife with daring jail breaks, infamous agent provocateurs, and allegations of sexual deviance, Professor Kirsten McKenzie argues that such colourful and salacious aspects of colonial administrations cannot be separated from the real business of political and social change. The book instead highlights the importance of taking gossip, paranoia, factional infighting and political spin seriously to show the extent to which ostensibly marginal figures and events influenced the transformation of the nineteenth-century British empire.

KIRSTEN MCKENZIE is Associate Professor of History at the Department of History, University of Sydney.

Critical Perspectives on Empire

Editors

Professor Catherine Hall
University College London

Professor Mrinalini Sinha
University of Michigan

Professor Kathleen Wilson
State University of New York, Stony Brook

Critical Perspectives on Empire is a major series of ambitious, cross-disciplinary works in the emerging field of critical imperial studies. Books in the series explore the connections, exchanges and mediations at the heart of national and global histories, the contributions of local as well as metropolitan knowledge, and the flows of people, ideas and identities facilitated by colonial contact. To that end, the series not only offers a space for outstanding scholars working at the intersection of several disciplines to bring to wider attention the impact of their work; it also takes a leading role in reconfiguring contemporary historical and critical knowledge, of the past and of ourselves.

A full list of titles published in the series can be found at:
www.cambridge.org/cpempire

Imperial Underworld

An Escaped Convict and the Transformation of the British Colonial Order

Kirsten McKenzie
University of Sydney

CAMBRIDGE UNIVERSITY PRESS

CAMBRIDGE
UNIVERSITY PRESS

University Printing House, Cambridge CB2 8BS, United Kingdom

Cambridge University Press is part of the University of Cambridge.

It furthers the University's mission by disseminating knowledge in the pursuit of education, learning and research at the highest international levels of excellence.

www.cambridge.org
Information on this title: www.cambridge.org/9781107070738

© Kirsten McKenzie 2016

This publication is in copyright. Subject to statutory exception and to the provisions of relevant collective licensing agreements, no reproduction of any part may take place without the written permission of Cambridge University Press.

First published 2016

Printed in the United Kingdom by Clays, St Ives plc

A catalogue record for this publication is available from the British Library

ISBN 978-1-107-07073-8 Hardback
ISBN 978-1-107-68679-3 Paperback

Cambridge University Press has no responsibility for the persistence or accuracy of URLs for external or third-party internet websites referred to in this publication, and does not guarantee that any content on such websites is, or will remain, accurate or appropriate.

Contents

	List of illustrations and map	*page* vi
	Cast of main characters	vii
	Acknowledgements	ix
	Map	xii
	Introduction: 'A soul reared in the lap of liberty'	1
1	'Plausible and audacious frauds': The theatre of imperial politics and reform	25
2	'A Daemon behind the Curtain': Reputation, parliamentary politics and political spin	60
3	Green-bag-makers and blood-hunters: Information management and espionage	83
4	'In return for services rendered': Liberated Africans or prize(d) slaves?	103
5	'The dishonorable Court of Gothamites': Corrupting abolition	130
6	'Under the cloak of liberty': Seditious libel, state security and the rights of 'free-born Englishmen'	159
7	'Unruly subjects': Political removal and the problem of colonial constitutions	191
8	'A conspiracy of the darkest and foulest nature': The placard affair	213
9	Bring up the body: The many escapes of 'Alexander Edwards'	245
	Epilogue: An infamous end	276
	Bibliography	285
	Index	301

Illustrations and map

ILLUSTRATIONS

1. John Thomas Bigge, 1819. Thomas Uwins. State Library of New South Wales — *page* 7
2. 'A View of Somerset', Robert Dighton, 1811. Courtesy of the National Portrait Gallery, London — 40
3. Portrait of Ralph Darling, governor of New South Wales, 1825. John Linnell. National Library of Australia — 56
4. Henry Bathurst, third Earl Bathurst. William Salter, 1834. Courtesy of the National Portrait Gallery, London — 65
5. George Cruikshank, 'Conspirators; or, delegates in council', 1817. US Library of Congress — 90
6. 'The Theatre, Cape Town', H.C. de Meillon. Courtesy of Sydney Living Museums — 218
7. Copy of evidence from the Cape fiscal's enquiry into the placard scandal, 1824. Western Cape Archives Depot, Cape Town, Council of Justice 3352 — 220
8. Portrait of James Barry, in youth, bust; anon., no date. The RAMC Muniment Collection in the care of the Wellcome Library — 222
9. Convict Barracks, Sydney, New South Wales c. 1820. State Library of New South Wales — 257
10. Settlement, Norfolk Island, 1838. State Library of New South Wales — 283

MAP

1. The imperial world of William Edwards — xii

Cast of main characters

Edwards, William: Cape Town notary. Formerly convict Alexander Loe Kaye.
Barry, James: Army medical officer and inspector-general of hospitals at the Cape.
Bathurst, Henry, third Earl Bathurst: Secretary of state for war and the colonies between 1812 and 1827.
Bigge, John Thomas: Commissioner of inquiry in New South Wales and Van Diemen's Land, and (with William Colebrooke) Commissioner of Eastern Inquiry at the Cape of Good Hope.
Bird, William Wilberforce: Comptroller of Customs at the Cape and, along with Charles Blair, responsible for the assignment of prize slaves.
Blair, Charles: Collector of Customs at the Cape and, along with William Wilberforce Bird, responsible for the assignment of prize slaves.
Brougham, Henry: Radical Whig member of Parliament (MP) and parliamentary ally of Cape reformers.
Burnett, Bishop: British settler at the Cape, involved in frequent disputes with authorities, ally of William Edwards.
Cooke, Lancelot: Cape Town merchant and employer of the prize slave Jean Ellé.
Darling, Ralph: Governor of New South Wales, 1825–1831.
Denyssen, Daniel: Cape fiscal (a combination of chief of police and public prosecutor).
Donkin, Sir Rufane: Acting governor at the Cape, 1820–1821, during Somerset's leave. Subsequently embroiled in a prolonged feud with Somerset and his supporters.
Edwards, Elizabeth (neé Rens): Wife of William Edwards.
Ellé, Jean: Mauritian cook 'liberated' as a prize slave and forcibly apprenticed at the Cape.

Fairbairn, John: Co-editor with Thomas Pringle of the *South African Commercial Advertiser*, the colony's first independent newspaper. Later Cape politician.
Forbes, Francis: Chief justice of New South Wales, 1824–1837.
Greig, George: Printer and proprietor of the *Advertiser*.
Hall, Edward Smith: Political reformer and editor of the *Sydney Monitor* newspaper.
Hudson, Samuel: Cape Town diarist.
Hume, Joseph: Radical MP and ally of Cape reformers.
Jones, William Oliver, aka W. J. Richards, styled 'Oliver the Spy': Government spy and alleged agent provocateur.
Lee, Daniel: Irish indentured servant employed by William Edwards.
Meurant, Louis: Printer's apprentice to George Greig. Later journalist and member of the Cape Parliament.
Philip, John: Missionary and political ally of Pringle and Fairbairn.
Pringle, Thomas: Poet, journalist and philanthropist. Co-editor with John Fairbairn of the *Advertiser* at the Cape. Later secretary of the British Anti-Slavery Society.
Somerset, Lord Charles Henry: Governor of the Cape between 1814 and 1826.
Somerset, Lord Granville: Tory MP for Monmouthshire, nephew to Lord Charles Somerset.
Stephen, James (the younger): Legal advisor and later permanent undersecretary at the Colonial Office.
Truter, Johannes (John) Andreas: President of the Council of Justice, Cape Colony.
Wardell, Robert: Sydney barrister, colonial reformer and co-editor of the *Australian* newspaper.
Wentworth, William Charles: Sydney barrister, colonial reformer and co-editor of the *Australian* newspaper.
Wilmot-Horton, Robert: Parliamentary secretary, Colonial Office.

Acknowledgements

The debts for this book go back many years, for its origins can be traced across several previous projects. Rhiannon Davis first alerted me to the fact that William Edwards's story extended beyond South Africa. In one of his many inspiring conversations, Robert Ross made me realise that the topic deserved a book in its own right. The research was financed by Australian Research Council grant DP110103718, 'Personal Liberty, British Identity and Surveillance in the Antipodes, 1780–1830' and by grants from the Faculty of Arts and Social Science at the University of Sydney. During the course of the project, earlier versions of the findings appeared in *The South African Historical Journal*, *Journal of Imperial and Commonwealth History* and the *Australian and New Zealand Law & History E-Journal*.

At the University of Sydney, Dean Duncan Ivison, Head of School Barbara Caine and Heads of Department, Andrew Fitzmaurice and Penny Russell, all offered their personal support across every stage of the research. I particularly wish to acknowledge the warm friendship and encouragement provided by my fellow members of the Department of History.

Steering me through the very diverse fields touched by this investigation were countless people who were extremely generous with their specific areas of expertise. In many cases they also read sections of the manuscript. Bruce Baskerville guided me around the curious place that is Norfolk Island. Timothy Causer helped me with the island's records and provided me with copies of his detailed research on the same. Hamish Maxwell-Stewart and Helen MacDonald discussed practices of dissection. Patrick Harries, Christopher Saunders and Kerry Ward shared their knowledge of prize slaves. Antonia Malan helped me interpret household inventories. Lisa Ford's insights into the law, and indeed on countless other matters, were unfailingly sharp. Conversations with Alan Atkinson, Elizabeth Elbourne, Zoë Laidlaw and Alan Lester greatly enhanced my arguments. Hans Pols and Nigel Worden gave advice on translations. In all instances, of course, the remaining mistakes are my own.

I would like to pay a special tribute to the unfailing generosity of Peter Burbidge, legal scholar and descendant of Alexander Loe Kaye. Without his family research, significant proportions of this book could never have been written. He saved me from many mistakes, legal and genealogical. I would also like to thank Judy Buxton for sharing her family history research into William Edwards. One of the outcomes of this project was the pleasure of introducing these two family historians to one another. Although my protagonist would undoubtedly have disapproved, it was satisfying to see his two lines of descent finally reconnect.

The archivists and librarians at the institutions listed in the references were unfailingly courteous and helpful. I would not have been able to get through the vast source base generated by the scandals of William Edwards without my research assistants Rhiannon Davis, James Drown, Chris Holdridge and Maureen Rall. Chris also generously shared his personal researches into Edwards's time at the Cape. Martin Thomas kindly photographed material in the National Library in Canberra. James Drown, editorial ventriloquist, worked his magic on the drafts. Maria DenBoer prepared the index.

Robert Aldrich, David Andrew Roberts, Robert Ross and Nigel Worden were all brave and generous enough to read complete drafts of the manuscript. Their editorial advice and specialist knowledge were absolutely invaluable. Frances Clarke inaugurated the 'shut up and write' sessions that kept revisions going even through the most chaotic periods of the academic year. The dedicated members of the Alchemists writing group led by Ann Curthoys and Penny Russell were subjected to some of the most tortuous early versions of the narrative. Base metal undoubtedly remains, but it would be untempered without your efforts. I thank you all.

Sarah Mee, Kezia Lange and Rob Pavey hosted me during repeated research trips to the United Kingdom. I began writing this book at the European University Institute, Florence. Dirk Moses arranged my visiting fellowship there, and he and Natasha Wheatley also lent me their apartment in the Piazza del Carmine. To them and to all at the 'Repubblica Palmerino' my heartfelt thanks for this golden time.

My parents again offered the most useful gifts that anyone can give a writer – an isolated retreat with a view of the sea and a golden Labrador for company. Amber once more provided advice on solitary walks. Sebastian napped on the drafts. To all my family and friends I offer my thanks for their generous support across the project and my apologies for grumpy responses to polite enquiries about progress.

My profound thanks go to Michael Watson for his enthusiasm and astute advice, to the series editors, Catherine Hall, Mrinalini Sinha and

Kathleen Wilson, to Vicki Danahy for her meticulous copyediting and to all the production team at Cambridge University Press.

This book is dedicated to my teachers, students and mentors, whose work has connected three continents. Most especially it is for Nigel Worden, who first inspired me to explore the links between South Africa and Australia.

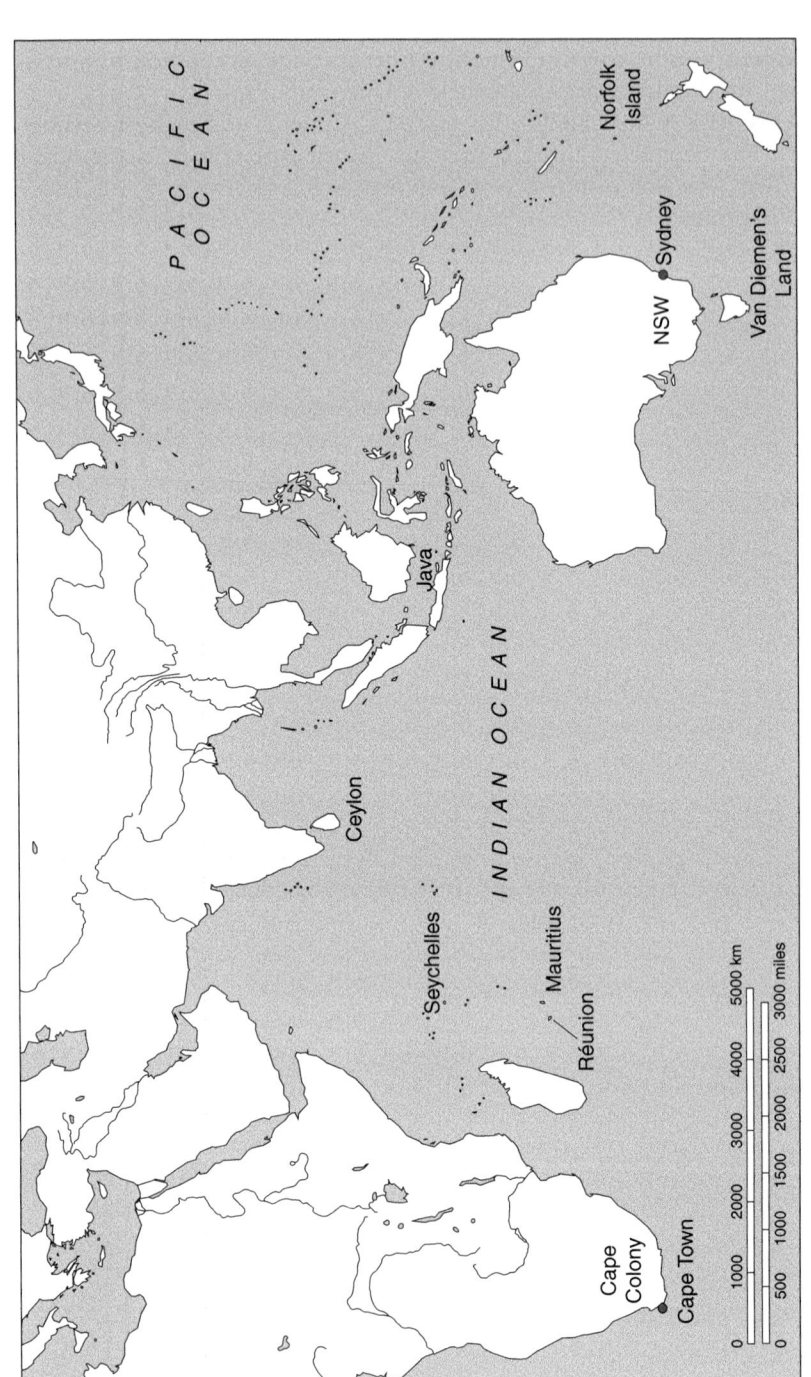

Map 1 The imperial world of William Edwards

Introduction
'A soul reared in the lap of liberty'

Norfolk Island, a tiny green speck upon the expanse of ocean that separates Australia and New Zealand, is now a place of somewhat improbable beauty. Ringed almost entirely by cliffs, the first European explorations dubbed it 'only a place fit for angels and eagles to reside in'.[1] Today the landscape is still dominated by the eponymous pine trees whose name belies their quintessentially Pacific appearance. They present an incongruous backdrop to the sound of imported blackbirds, the shops stocked with duty-free Royal Doulton and Crown Derby porcelain, and the Burne-Jones stained-glass windows of the mission church. If ever there were an edge of empire, this is it.

In 1825 British imperial reforms decreed that Norfolk Island become part of a system designed to render convict transportation, in the words of the secretary of state, 'an Object of real Terror to all Classes of the Community'.[2] A previous settlement on the island had been abandoned in 1814 as too remote and costly. Now this distance, 1700 kilometres east of the increasingly prosperous colony of New South Wales, would be put to new disciplinary use as part of a major transformation in penal governance. As the declared destination for reoffenders of the worst type, the outpost would be feared and despised as 'Norfolk's fell Isle' and, because all women would be banned, 'the modern Gomorrah'.[3] This dark history continues to figure prominently in the Gothic-inflected commentaries of tour buses and nighttime ghost walks. Convicts unlucky enough to end

---

William Edwards, conducting his own defence in *Fiscal v. Cooke, Edwards and Hoffman*, 20 February 1824, in G. M. Theal (ed.), *Records of the Cape Colony* (London: Clowes Printers, 1897–1905) (hereafter *RCC*), vol. 17, p. 185.

[1] The words of French explorer Jean-François de Galaup, Comte de La Pérouse, reported in Chief Surgeon White to Mr. Skill, 17 April 1790, *Historical Records of New South Wales* (*HRNSW*) (Sydney: Government Printer, 1892–1901), vol. 1, part II, p. 333.

[2] Earl Bathurst to Commissioner John Thomas Bigge, 6 Jan. 1819, *Historical Records of Australia* (*HRA*) (Sydney: Library Committee of the Commonwealth Parliament, 1914–1925), series 1, vol. 10, p. 7.

[3] *Monitor*, 20 Dec. 1828.

up on Norfolk Island, it is widely assumed, often chose death rather than endure its horrors. With suicide regarded as a crime against God, some would even cast lots to elect one of their number to the office of executioner. The man with the short straw would only await the hangman's noose before joining his murdered comrades in the afterlife.

Like much of what we know about transportation to Norfolk Island, this image of depravity and mass despair needs to be tempered with a more prosaic reality. Both the intentions of imperial policy and the lurid reputation of the island were undercut by the messy practices of actually running a penal system. From unlucky circumstance or bureaucratic bungling, a far wider variety of prisoner ended up there than the hardened criminals of legend.[4] If assumptions about the character of the inmates needs reassessment, so too do other commonly held beliefs. Despite their inclusion in a high-profile history of convict Australia, no incidents of Norfolk Island murder–suicide lotteries can be verified beyond hearsay, and there were in fact only two conventional suicides recorded during the thirty years of the second penal settlement there.[5]

About the first death we know almost nothing: only that an unidentified man threw himself over a cliff in 1826.[6] The second attracted far more official attention, as well as considerable public debate. On 9 June 1828 a man who began his life as Alexander Loe Kaye and ended it as William Edwards hanged himself from the rafters of the hut that he shared with three other convicts. He had barely arrived on the island. Sydney's *Monitor* newspaper mourned the loss of 'a man of literary talents, and of an unconquerable spirit of independence'.[7] In life Edwards had declared himself a 'patriot' and a 'soul reared in the lap of liberty'.[8] Contemporaries variously regarded him as a 'champion', a 'maniac' and a 'desperadoe'.[9] With some justification, opinions differed considerably

---

[4] The complexities of Norfolk Island's history and the arbitrariness of transportation there during the second penal settlement are convincingly demonstrated in the revisionist work of T. Causer: '"Only a place fit for angels and eagles": The Norfolk Island penal settlement 1825–1855', PhD thesis, University of London (2010).

[5] R. Hughes, *The Fatal Shore: A History of the Transportation of Convicts to Australia 1787–1868* (London: Collins, 1986), pp. 467–9. Hughes's account of suicide lotteries is based on the reminiscences of Foster Fyans, second-in-command on the island. Causer's meticulous research into the alleged incident casts serious doubt on its authenticity: no record exists of either the convicts involved or the trial for murder that would have followed. See Causer, 'Only a place fit for angels and eagles'; and M. Wolter, 'Sound and fury in colonial Australia: The search for the convict voice 1820–1840', PhD thesis, University of Sydney, 2014.

[6] Causer, 'Only a place fit for angels and eagles', p. 213.

[7] *Monitor*, 20 Dec. 1828.

[8] Letters received from Court of Justice, CA, CO, 214, no. 31; *RCC*, vol. 17, 185.

[9] Samuel Hudson, Diary, 11 March 1824, CA, A602, vol. 3; Somerset to Bigge, 12 May 1824, Rhodes House, MSS Afr 24, 126; T. Pringle, *Narrative of a Residence in South Africa* (London: Moxon, 1835), p. 198.

Introduction

as to his sanity. If his name is now largely forgotten, he was widely notorious across diverse localities when, as the Sydney press described it, he 'terminated his wretched existence by self-destruction, and thus satiated the vengeance of his enemies'.[10] The man who called himself Edwards went to his death claiming that his body would testify in his favour and clear his name, but in death he would prove no less controversial than he had in life.

Despite the obsession of both supporters and detractors over discovering the truth behind his multiple identities, *Imperial Underworld* is not a whodunit. There is arguably little mystery (though there was considerable subterfuge) involved in the question of whether Alexander Kaye and William Edwards were one and the same.[11] More intriguing is to consider how such an unlikely agent of change came to cause so much trouble across so many and such varied British imperial contexts and to ask how it came to be that by 1828 so many people knew his names. He was one amongst hundreds of convicts who used doubts over their identity as a tactical pressure point against an often-confused and inconsistent colonial legal apparatus. But he was also a fulcrum around which much larger changes in imperial administration would revolve.

The turn of the nineteenth century was a period of profound significance for the relationship between personal freedom and the exigencies of state security and imperial governance. Debates over their relative importance were given a heightened resonance in the circumstances of revolutionary wars in Europe and America, social unrest in Britain, and humanitarian activism over the abolition of slavery and the treatment of indigenous peoples across the globe. Britons were fond of claiming that, unlike their continental rivals, they had managed to reconcile the notions of freedom and empire. Their national identity, it was said, made them uniquely adapted to found an empire based upon just principles. The loss of the American colonies had compromised such assertions. The struggle against revolutionary and Napoleonic France would stretch Britain's internal cohesion to the limit. For a nation that premised its right to global domination on its ability to resolve what historian Peter Cochrane calls the 'marvellous paradox' of liberty and empire, the new colonies of the Southern Hemisphere offered the

---

[10] *Monitor*, 20 Dec. 1828.
[11] To avoid confusion I will name my protagonist as 'William Edwards' from the time he took on this persona in 1823, despite the fact that it was almost certainly an assumed name. Prior to that date I will refer to him as 'Alexander Kaye'. Given that his identity was contested, contemporaries continued to use one or the other depending on their position in the dispute.

possibility of a fresh start, a crucible in which the right kind of empire could be forged.[12]

Early nineteenth-century Southern Africa and Australasia share commonalities with other theatres of colonial expansion and dispossession. They witnessed their own distinct local variations on broader questions such as sovereignty, free trade, the cost of defence and relations with indigenous peoples (in particular their place under British law). Yet they also offered a set of peculiar challenges to delivering on the supposed promises of liberty and empire, challenges in which the life and death of William Edwards became embroiled. As such, they are especially suitable places to examine how the parameters of British imperial rule were tested and defined.

In the Antipodes, the operation of the rule of law in penal colonies with expanding free populations and a growing economy posed an increasing challenge. As New South Wales Governor Ralph Darling complained in 1827, 'the Papers' taught people 'to talk about the rights of Englishmen' when this concept had no relevance to the society he ruled.[13] Analogous conundrums were faced by the British at the Cape of Good Hope. It had been a slave colony, seized at the end of the eighteenth century just as a passionate commitment to abolishing the slave trade was reaching its climax. It possessed the further complication of its prior Dutch history that over the past century and a half had seen (to British eyes) a peculiarly foreign settler society emerge on the tip of the African continent. Like other colonies conquered during the Revolutionary and Napoleonic Wars, the Cape remained in constitutional limbo for decades, technically under temporary military occupation. The result was a thin veneer of British legal and administrative practice stretched over an entrenched and alien system of governance. As with the Australian penal colonies, problems in the judiciary were amongst the most acute of the challenges to effective governance faced at the Cape. Administration in both localities evolved on the ground with an often-blatant disregard for metropolitan niceties.

Faced with these problems, the British Parliament ordered a series of investigations into what were increasingly untenable systems of governance. The new disciplinary structures at Norfolk Island were but one iteration of a set of interconnected equations designed to generate a transformation in the colonial order. A major overhaul of imperial administration took place in the aftermath of the Napoleonic conflict.

---

[12] P. Cochrane, *Colonial Ambition: Foundations of Australian Democracy* (Melbourne University Press, 2006), p. 9.
[13] Darling to Hay, 9 Feb. 1827 (secret and confidential), *HRA*, 1:8, p. 99.

Introduction

The key mechanisms by which this overhaul was achieved were parliamentary Commissions of Inquiry. Massive and expensive undertakings that frequently took years to complete, they were part of a 'burgeoning culture of information collection which underwrote early nineteenth-century notions of good government'.[14] At the Cape and in the Australian colonies they were also led by the same man, John Thomas Bigge. Formerly chief justice of Trinidad, Bigge began his work in New South Wales and Van Diemen's Land in 1819.[15] He had barely completed his reports on these colonies before being ordered to lead another commission into the former French and Dutch possessions at the Cape, Mauritius and Ceylon. Together with Co-Commissioner William Colebrooke, Bigge's Commission of Eastern Inquiry arrived in Cape Town in July 1823. Pressure of work was such that the two men were joined by a third commissioner, William Blair, in 1825. Their final reports from this second inquiry were only completed a decade later. By the end of the process, few areas of colonial life remained untouched.

The commissions of Bigge and others constituted part of a vast imperial stocktaking prompted in part by growing public criticisms over reckless spending and the system of self-interested government known as 'Old Corruption'. First coined by radical pamphleteer William Cobbett, the term encompassed far more than just misappropriation of funds. Its key characteristics were parasitic: a malignant growth that fed on the nation's wealth, diverting it 'into the pockets of a narrow political clique whose only claim to privileged status was its proximity to the sources of patronage'.[16] Although prompted by public opinion and parliamentary criticism, the imperial Commissions of Inquiry were also an attempt to keep the direction of reform as far as possible under the control of the Colonial Office, for it was the secretary of state who appointed the commissioners and to whom they directly reported.[17] In the cut and thrust of parliamentary politics, such investigations could also act as useful delaying tactics.

The context in Britain itself is as important in understanding these investigations as the situation in the colonies. In circumstances of increasing social unrest, in which many saw the threat of outright revolution,

---

[14] Z. Laidlaw, 'Investigating empire: Humanitarians, reform and the Commission of Eastern Inquiry', *Journal of Imperial and Commonwealth History*, 40:5 (2012), 752.

[15] It was as a result of Bigge's investigations and recommendation that Van Diemen's Land became a separate colony in 1825.

[16] P. Harling, *The Waning of 'Old Corruption': The Politics of Economical Reform in Britain 1779–1846* (Oxford: Clarendon, 1996), p. 1.

[17] J. Ritchie, *Punishment and Profit: The Reports of Commissioner John Bigge on the Colonies of New South Wales and Van Diemen's Land 1822–1823 ~ Their Origins, Nature and Significance* (Melbourne: Heinemann, 1970), p. 29.

solutions were sought abroad to problems of crime, surplus population and economic stagnation at home. These domestic British concerns constantly ran up against vexed local debates that were playing out on the imperial periphery about the rights and responsibilities of settlers, convicts, slaves and indigenous peoples. The commissioners' investigations and recommendations thus became bound up in circuits of political contestation that linked Britain and its antipodean colonies.

Designed to acquire the necessary information on which to base widespread reforms, the investigations of the Cape and the Australian colonies would utterly recast the boundaries of colonial administration and direct policy in these regions for decades to come. They resulted in major changes in both the constitutions and the governance of Britain's antipodean colonies as they established new supreme courts, legislative councils and councils of advice that increasingly curbed executive power. These reform initiatives, however, were accompanied by sustained efforts to control the diverse groups and interests which challenged state authority.

Commissioner Bigge [Figure 1] exemplified a type of information-gathering bureaucrat who was transforming British imperial governance in this period. Historians have paid increasing attention to how such men, and the networks of information and surveillance they set up, bound the administration of formerly distinct localities together.[18] Bigge was one of a new breed of reforming administrators forging transnational networks by connecting men of literate and legal status across colonial borders and vast oceans. But there were also other far less conventional actors making similar links, making similar claims to expertise, and also seeking a part in the same unfolding dramas of imperial governance.

Alexander Kaye reluctantly stepped onto this stage when he was transported to New South Wales in 1819 for stealing a chestnut horse worth £30. It proved the first in an uncanny series of temporal and geographic connections between his travels and those of Bigge's various Commissions of Inquiry, which began work in the Australian colonies in the same year. So closely did their colonial itineraries seem to coincide with one another's that the man known variously as Kaye and Edwards would later be accused of acting as a covert agent for Bigge. Kaye escaped from Sydney in 1821 and made his way to the Cape Colony via Batavia in the Dutch East Indies and the Indian Ocean island of Mauritius. He landed

---

[18] For example, Z. Laidlaw, *Colonial Connections 1815–1845: Patronage, the Information Revolution and Colonial Government* (Manchester University Press, 2005); D. Lambert and A. Lester (eds.), *Colonial Lives across the British Empire: Imperial Careering in the Long Nineteenth Century* (Cambridge University Press, 2006).

Figure 1 Commissioner John Thomas Bigge in 1819, the year he began his investigations into the Australian colonies.

in Cape Town in 1823 under the name of William Edwards, just as Bigge was beginning his second set of colonial investigations there.

Kaye was born in 1791 to a provincial English family on the margins of gentility. As we learn in the following chapter, he was poorly regarded by certain members of his immediate circle before he fell foul of the law. His conviction for theft was the final act in a pattern of increasingly erratic behaviour, but he nonetheless managed to achieve some legal training before he was forced to leave England. Taking the name William Edwards, Kaye set himself up as a notary in Cape Town. In 1823 he was employed by Cape Town merchant Lancelot Cooke to draw up a memorial protesting official corruption in the assignment of 'Prize Negroes'. His exposé of the treatment of these former slaves, liberated by the Royal Navy following the banning of the slave trade, threatened to undermine the moral high ground of British abolition. It would unexpectedly catapult him into imperial notoriety. Edwards now joined a loose alliance of disaffected British emigrants at the Cape who had been galvanised by the presence of the Commissioners of Inquiry. More mainstream campaigners from the humanitarian lobby, however, regarded men like Edwards as 'desperadoes', and many commentators (not without reason) even judged him to be insane. His was very much the lunatic fringe of liberal reform.

Edwards's continued protests against the Cape administration ended with him sentenced to transportation to New South Wales under his new identity for seditious libel of the governor, Lord Charles Somerset. Widely recognised as escaped convict Kaye upon his return to New South Wales in 1824, he nonetheless continued to insist that he was Edwards, to protest against the illegality of his transportation from the Cape and to lambast the injustices of the convict system in Australia. He remained a thorn in the flesh of the imperial system until he was charged with absconding and transported to Norfolk Island in 1828. Committing suicide shortly after his arrival, his death coincided with significant transformations in the imperial structures of both New South Wales and the Cape, reforms he had played a role (part deliberate, part inadvertent) in bringing to fruition.

Placing a maverick outsider like William Edwards at the centre of a study of colonial governance may appear a curious decision. His colourful tale includes daring escapes, courtroom pyrotechnics, alleged cross-dressing, letters smuggled into jail in the collars of faithful dogs and even some really bad love poetry. It might then seem equally perverse to limit the audience of such a manifestly 'ripping yarn' by turning it into a book about constitutional law and transformations in colonial administration. In choosing to do so I want us to take a fresh look at how these changes were brought about.

As I argue, the view from the margins provides us with a different way of understanding the cultural history of imperial politics. However,

Introduction 9

it is also worth remembering that this approach is faithful to the events of the time. Politics on the imperial periphery set impressive standards for feuding and factionalism. Yet the two administrations in which Edwards played notable roles in the 1820s – one in New South Wales and one in the Cape Colony – rank highly within even this fractious company. Local attitudes to Ralph Darling, governor of New South Wales from 1825 to 1831, were evident in the celebrations at his departure, including a notoriously riotous party attended by a large proportion of the town's inhabitants. Illuminations in the window of Sydney's *Monitor* newspaper claimed 'He's Off! The Reign of Terror Ended'.[19] In the years immediately following the arrival of the Commission of Eastern Inquiry at the Cape, Governor Somerset's administration (1814–1826) was rocked by so many and such fruity scandals that it began to resemble, in the memorable description of historian Robert Ross, 'the more racy type of comic opera'.[20] Yet far from being separate from the real issues at hand, these seemingly frivolous disputes were considered central to the Commission's investigations and to parliamentary discussions more generally. An official's honour and reputation were acknowledged political resources, and interpersonal conflicts were inseparably bound up with broader policy debates. Accusations of misconduct made against colonial officials (by both settlers and rival administrators) were eagerly taken up in Commons debates, generating extensive press coverage and lengthy printed parliamentary papers. They absorbed significant quantities of the commissioners' time and energy, spawning large and numerous volumes of evidence (the one concerning Edwards ran to more than 800 double-sided manuscript pages) and significantly delaying the tabling of their final reports. This would spark criticism at the time, but it is abundantly clear that not only the commissioners but also their superiors in the Colonial Office felt it necessary to investigate these ostensibly frivolous matters. Smoothing away the more salacious elements in the controversies over colonial administrations, I argue, significantly distorts our understanding of them. These scandals were not regarded by contemporaries merely as distractions from the real business of enquiring into colonial governance, and we need to take them equally seriously.[21]

[19] B. Fletcher, *Ralph Darling: A Governor Maligned* (Oxford University Press, 1984), p. 292.
[20] R. Ross, *Status and Respectability in the Cape Colony 1750–1870: A Tragedy of Manners* (Cambridge University Press, 1999), p. 46.
[21] J. M. Bennett suggests the Bigge reports on New South Wales abounded with accusations of petty factionalism and a preoccupation with 'personalities', and that various investigations were simply irrelevant and 'satisfying the parliamentary taste for gossip': see 'The day of retribution: Commissioner Bigge's iniquities in colonial New South Wales', *American Journal of Legal History*, 85 (1971), 93, 97. As I argue repeatedly

As their sometimes-exasperated correspondence testifies, officials both in London and on the periphery were constantly bombarded by individual complainants seeking redress against the perceived injustices of colonial administrations. Although Edwards was by no means alone in this regard, as this book makes clear, his case became bound up in an array of vexed issues to which reformers were simultaneously directing their attention. That these important and far-reaching debates should be connected with ostensibly marginal, interpersonal disputes is the central proposition of my investigation into Edwards and his world.

C. A. Bayly's influential 1989 study *Imperial Meridian: The British Empire and the World* rightly emphasised the establishment of 'overseas despotisms' in the late eighteenth century as a response to the challenges presented by imperial expansion. This conservative reaction in the wake of revolutionary challenges in North America and Europe lasted from the 1780s until a liberal shift in the 1830s. It was a system that encouraged and supported 'viceregal authority' backed up by military rule and (where relevant) alliances with local elites from previous colonial regimes. Thus, in Bayly's view, colonial reform in the period between 1780 and 1830 was

> autocratic in style, tending to create or confirm social and racial hierarchies through the liberation of private property. Government remained militaristic and monopolistic in practice in spite of the softer protestations of constitutional and political theory.[22]

This climate allowed the controversial 'despots' who figure largely in this story to flourish – men like Somerset at the Cape and Darling in New South Wales.[23]

Yet it bears remembering that these *were* controversial figures, and not just with their colonial critics. Proconsular autocrats caused a great deal of difficulty for their political allies in London, even when both sides held outlooks on the same conservative end of the contemporary political spectrum. In the social and economic upheaval that followed the Napoleonic Wars, heightened public concern about fiscal responsibility and proper governance meant that complaints about imperial administration from the periphery gained political traction in the metropole.

---

across these pages, this is to fundamentally misread both the very real power and the proper place that such 'gossip' occupied in the workings of imperial politics and the elaboration of reform initiatives.

[22] C. A. Bayly, *Imperial Meridian: The British Empire and the World 1780–1830* (London: Longman, 1989), pp. 8, 162.

[23] As Brian Fletcher subtitled his biography of Darling, 'A Governor Maligned'.

Tory ministries not only reacted with repressive measures against perceived popular democracy; they also sought to prove to themselves and to their critics that they could govern with both frugality and rectitude.[24] If the periodic suspension of *habeas corpus* and notorious legislation like the Six Acts of 1819 expressed the former political imperatives, then the Commissions of Inquiry were the embodiment of the latter.

More recently, Bayly's pioneering work in reassessing this period has undergone some useful adjustment, including by Bayly himself.[25] Zoë Laidlaw emphasises how 'gradual, and often haphazard' was this transition from despotism to liberalism across the decades spanning the eighteenth and nineteenth centuries.[26] She dates it somewhat earlier than Bayly did originally, and I would concur, seeing in the 1820s a transitional decade in which the scandals instigated by figures like William Edwards played into a broader and more fractious debate over the nature of imperial governance than historians once recognised.[27]

Like Laidlaw and others, I place a due degree of emphasis on individuals and their interpersonal networks in explaining this process, one in which 'developments were more organic than programmatic, reflecting attitudes much tempered by uncertainty and pragmatism'.[28] The 'transnational' individual has lately garnered significant scholarly attention as a way of understanding connections between previously nationally focussed and disaggregated questions.[29] Moving away from a metropole-centred paradigm, historians have followed Tony Ballantyne in employing the metaphor of the web to better understand the reciprocal and multidirectional interconnections woven between metropole and colonies.[30] Edwards's 'imperial careering' and, even more, his self-conscious awareness that this was how the empire worked underscore the validity of these perspectives. He demonstrates the power of transnational biography to

---

[24] Harling, *The Waning of 'Old Corruption'*, p. 151; A. Lester, *Imperial Networks: Creating Identity in Nineteenth-Century South Africa and Britain* (London: Routledge, 2001), pp. 26–8.

[25] C. A. Bayly, *Recovering Liberties: Indian Thought in the Age of Liberalism and Empire* (Cambridge University Press, 2012).

[26] Laidlaw, *Colonial Connections*, p. 40.

[27] There are precursors to this view. In the 1960s, historian J.J. Eddy characterised the work of the Colonial Office in the 1820s as 'progress in disguise by statesmen in disguise': *Britain and the Australian Colonies 1818–1831: The Technique of Government* (Oxford: Clarendon, 1969), p. 6.

[28] Laidlaw, *Colonial Connections*, pp. 40–1.

[29] On the question of imperial history recast by transnational biography, see Lambert and Lester, *Colonial Lives across the British Empire*; C. Anderson, *Subaltern Lives: Biographies of Colonialism in the Indian Ocean World 1790–1920* (Cambridge University Press, 2012).

[30] T. Ballantyne, *Orientalism and Race: Aryanism in the British Empire* (New York: Palgrave, 2002); Ballantyne, *Webs of Empire: Locating New Zealand's Colonial Past* (Wellington: Bridget William Books, 2012).

In South Africa the controversy over establishing the freedom of the press is well-known territory in standard academic accounts.[35] The struggle was cast in heroic vein by histories that emphasised the contribution of English-speaking South Africans to the national story. Thomas Pringle's version of these events in his *Narrative of a Residence in South Africa* (1834) was a founding document in this tradition. Pringle, as I discuss in the following chapter, was involved in reform agendas far beyond the issue of press freedom. Nevertheless, the contest is a key episode in his book, presented as a struggle between 'Old Corruption' (exemplified by Somerset and his administration) and the forces of liberty and progress (in which Pringle, Fairbairn and their ally the missionary John Philip play the starring roles). For all the hint of melodrama with which Pringle occasionally flavours his account of what he called 'the Cape Reign of Terror', he had some justification in seeing it as a battle between two political worlds that were increasingly at odds in 1824.[36] What interests us here is how Edwards appears in Pringle's account of the Cape reformers. In his narrative of the press battle, Pringle dismisses Edwards in all but one line: 'one Edwards, a reckless and desperate adventurer' who had 'brought forward certain scandalous and libellous charges against the character of Lord Charles Somerset, both in his public and private capacity'. Edwards is classed as one of the 'desperadoes' of the colony.[37]

Pringle's assessment of 'Edwards the adventurer' would prove of lasting impact, and most historians have followed his lead. In the early twentieth century, George McCall Theal's monumental *History of South Africa* followed Pringle by skirting over the 1824 libel trials and their unsavoury

double identity is still historic mystery': *Daily Mirror*, 2 May 1977, BIOG, Biographical cuttings on Alexander Lockaye (also known as William Edwards), National Library of Australia.

[35] A.M.L. Robinson, *None Daring to Make Us Afraid: A Study of English Periodical Literature in the Cape Colony from its Beginnings in 1824 to 1835* (Cape Town: Maskew Miller, 1962); H.C. Botha, *John Fairbairn in South Africa* (Cape Town: Historical Publication Society, 1984); L. Meltzer, 'Emancipation, commerce and the rise of John Fairbairn's *Advertiser*', in N. Worden and C. Crais (eds.), *Breaking the Chains: Slavery and its Legacy in the Nineteenth-Century Cape Colony* (Johannesburg: Witwatersrand University Press, 1994); K. McKenzie, 'The Franklins of the Cape: The *South African Commercial Advertiser* and the creation of a colonial public sphere 1824–1854', *Kronos: Journal of Cape History*, 25 (1998/1999), 88–102; and J. M. MacKenzie, '"To enlighten South Africa": The creation of a free press at the Cape in the early nineteenth century', in C. Kaul (ed.), *Media and the British Empire* (Basingstoke, UK: Palgrave, 2006), pp. 20–36.

[36] At a personal level, Somerset's persecution of Pringle and his allies also resulted in Pringle's financial ruin and his eventual departure from the colony.

[37] T. Pringle, *Narrative of a Residence in South Africa* (London: Moxon, 1835), p. 198. The *Narrative* was first published as part of Pringle's *African Sketches* in May 1834, seven months before the author's death. It was reissued posthumously as a separate volume the following year. R. Vigne, *Thomas Pringle: South African Pioneer, Poet and Abolitionist* (Woodbridge, Suffolk, UK: James Currey, 2012), p. 226.

defendants. Edwards, for example, was dismissed as 'a noisy and turbulent individual, a rabid declaimer against the Tory party, and a constant boaster of his position and influence in England.'[38] In the 1920s W. M. Macmillan claimed that the pressure-cooker atmosphere of the period accounted for 'the countenance given to the uncontrolled extravagances of an adventurer like Edwards'. As the great chronicler of John Philip's struggles at the Cape, Macmillan dubbed Edwards 'a 'bounder'', a judgement with which we can imagine both Somerset *and* his evangelical critics in hearty agreement.[39]

Pringle may have written Edwards out of his published *Narrative*, but his private correspondence from the time reveals a more complex relationship. George Greig and his editors Pringle and Fairbairn had closed their own newspaper after supporting Edwards in his case against the government. The notary did command great interest and potential – at least up to a point – and his primary use was a tactical one. In Pringle's letters to his parliamentary ally, the Whig MP Henry Brougham, we can track not only the profound distaste that the former had for men like Edwards, but also his equally fundamental need to make political use of them. Pringle provided regular updates to Brougham from the Cape in his hopes that 'my pen might be of some little use in exposing the oppression and disgraceful character of this Colonial Administration.' To Brougham he situated his role firmly within the wider political context of Britain, and indeed of Europe:

since I came to this Colony I have fully felt and seen the necessity of Whig principles if England is to be preserved in any degree worthy of former times – or in any respect better than in the other countries subjected to the sway of the Holy Alliance.[40]

The key thrust of Pringle's correspondence was to provide colonial ammunition for the opposition in the House of Commons. Pringle was

---

[38] G. M. Theal, *History of South Africa from 1795–1872* (London: Allen & Unwin, 1915), vol. 1, p. 417. Less glib was the work of G. E. Cory, written around the same time: *Rise of South Africa: A History of the Origin of South African Colonisation and of its Development towards the East from the Earliest Times to 1857* (London: Longmans, Green, 1913). Edwards also attracted renewed interest in an excellent undergraduate thesis by Christopher Holdridge, 'The escape of William Edwards: Respectability, intrigue and invented identity in the early British Cape and Australia', BA (hons) thesis, University of Cape Town, 2008 (although we differ quite profoundly in our views on Edwards's character and motivation).

[39] M. W. Macmillan, *The Cape Colour Question: A Historical Survey* (London: Faber & Gwyer, 1927), p. 194.

[40] Pringle to Brougham, 18 and 20 Dec. 1824, *Letters of Thomas Pringle*, pp. 146, 152. The Holy Alliance was a reactionary Russian–Austrian–Prussian pact against revolutionary tendencies in post–Napoleonic Europe.

well aware that he needed to work on the party political self-interest of his allies. Writing to John Fairbairn he reported his concerns:

> the appointment of such a council and the dead set against Dr Philip [taken by Somerset's administration] do look as if Ministry intended to back him [Somerset] out through thick and thin. If they do it will render the Colony then at least a complete *party question* and we will have a chance of some effective support from the selfish as well as the generous sessions of our part of the House of Commons. It is so sad but I fear it is true that the former are most to depend on.[41]

Pringle was at pains to give Brougham all the details of the complaints against Somerset, though some, he feared were 'of too personal and peculiar a nature to be of much use to the general cause of the Colony'.[42] These included the case of Edwards and that of a disaffected British settler named Bishop Burnett.[43] Burnett immediately connected with Edwards after he came to Cape Town to pursue his own complaints against the authorities. The notary had made a name for himself as a critic of Somerset's administration, and Edwards's servant would testify that, 'as long as I have known Mr. Burnett, which is not very long, Mr. Edwards and Mr. Burnett always were talking together as two brothers'.[44]

In Pringle's view, the charges that Edwards had made against Somerset included 'many disgraceful crimes. Too much of it related however I fear to personal character – and Edwards I fear was a Blackguard – though that is no reason for the unjust condemnation and cruel punishment inflicted on him.' Yet, whatever Edwards's personal character, it was possible that he could be used by Brougham: 'His defence I presume must be upon record and may be called for in the House of Commons. Greig I dare

---

[41] Pringle to Fairbairn, 20 May 1825, *Letters of Thomas Pringle*, p. 184 (original emphasis). The 'council' is the Advisory Council, and here too Pringle demonstrates his accurate reading of the party political intent behind the secretary of state's introduction of the institution, a measure discussed in the following chapter.

[42] Pringle to Brougham, 18 and 20 Dec. 1824, *Letters of Thomas Pringle*, pp. 149, 151.

[43] Bishop Burnett was no cleric, as his misleading Christian name might perhaps suggest. Formerly a lieutenant in the Royal Navy, he arrived in Grahamstown in May 1820. His first action in Cape public life was to horsewhip an Army doctor. The attack was in vindication of the character of Landdrost [District Magistrate] Andries Stockenstrom of Graaff Reinet, who had clashed with Governor Somerset. It was a taste of things to come. For the next seven years Burnett would prove himself one of the most irritating thorns in the Governor's flesh, so much so that his entry in the *Dictionary of South African Biography* (vol. V, p. 105) describes him succinctly as 'British 1820 Settler and trouble-maker'. The papers eventually tabled before Parliament concerning Bishop Burnett's activities at the Cape ran to well over 200 pages. BPP 1826 (431), *Mr Bishop Burnett, Cape of Good Hope*.

[44] Evidence of Daniel Lee before the fiscal, 9 June 1824, *BPP* 1826 (431), p. 146.

say can inform you of the chief points of it though he never intended publishing it.'⁴⁵

Pringle was searching for ammunition that he could provide for the Whig cause, and this is the key thrust of his correspondence with Brougham. Even though Pringle's view of Edwards was dim, he was aware that the case might prove useful ('though the man himself may be a vagabond [the case] is one of flagrant cruelty and injustice'). In this regard, the cases of mavericks like Edwards were potentially powerful leverage, but they also offered the danger of being tainted by association. Pringle made it very clear to Brougham that the evangelical reformers 'have kept ourselves all along perfectly clear and aloof from these Radicals and Desperadoes – Edwards and Burnett'.⁴⁶

The disjunctures to be found between Pringle's published *Narrative* and his private correspondence are instructive. Not only do they provide us with a key to the tactical relationship that existed between men like Edwards and more mainstream reformers, they also anticipate a central element of my reappraisal of Edwards's place in the broader story of imperial reform by reminding us to be attentive to the relationship between published and manuscript sources. The vicissitudes of Lord Charles Somerset, in which Edwards loomed so large, received fulsome attention in Theal's *Records of the Cape Colony*, copied from the manuscripts of the Public Record Office (now The National Archives) in London and published from the end of the nineteenth century. Documents from the vexatious year of 1824 run across three of the thirty-six volumes that span the period from 1793 to 1831, roughly three times the average space per year. In choosing to include so much material in his collection, however, Theal has paradoxically obscured the fact that his selection is merely the tip of the archival iceberg.⁴⁷ Many of the questions in this book have been inspired by tracking the scandals of Kaye and Edwards through unpublished manuscript sources and by comparing confidential and public accounts of the same events and issues.

---

[45] Pringle to Brougham, 18 Dec. 1824, *Letters*, p. 150; Cory, *The Rise of South Africa*, vol. II, p. 246; *Dictionary of South African Biography*, vol. V, p. 105.
[46] Pringle to Brougham, 20 Dec. 1824, *Letters*, p. 152. After Pringle left the colony for London in April 1826 he continued to be very careful to disassociate himself from 'Burnet and his set'. Nevertheless, he considered that Burnett had been 'done up' by the Commissioners of Inquiry in connivance with the 'Home Govt' and saw some similarities in their respective situations. Pringle to Fairbairn, 30 September 1826, *Letters*, pp. 302–303.
[47] On Theal and his editorial practices see C. Hamilton, B. K. Mbenga and R. Ross, 'The production of preindustrial South African history', in Hamilton, Mbegna and Ross (eds.), *The Cambridge History of South Africa* (Cambridge University Press, 2010), pp. 20–1; K. Smith, *The Changing Past: Trends in South African Historical Writing* (Ohio University Press, 1988), pp. 35–6.

In the years between the defeat of Napoleon at Waterloo in 1815 and the Great Reform Act of 1832 (the first of the nineteenth-century transformations in British parliamentary structure) a series of interconnected social problems were playing out in Britain, the Cape and Australia. Understanding how they linked together is crucial to understanding not only the politics of reform but also how Edwards came to play a role amidst it. In the following chapter I track both the personal origins of the mysterious notary and the origins of the reform initiatives in which he took an unexpected part. My account of the colonial contexts in which Edwards came to prominence revolves around the sequential parliamentary Commissions of Inquiry that were sent out to make the necessary investigations to set the process of reform in motion.

Chapter 2 centres on the Colonial Office in London and tracks its response to the scandals initiated by Edwards through a maze of secret and confidential communications. Doing so not only underscores why such seemingly trivial disputes were taken so seriously, but also reveals the tactics employed to neutralise them. A designated Colonial Office was established in 1795, on the cusp between two centuries and at the very moment that the first British empire merged into the second. This transition was central to its character and had a profound impact on how it dealt with the problems detailed in this book. A nineteenth-century professional bureaucracy was emerging from an organisation that was still effectively run like an eighteenth-century gentleman's club. Although the Commissions of Inquiry were a harbinger of more formalised and empirical methods in information gathering, colonial governance continued to place a high value on insider knowledge, which, being intrinsically personal, also entailed a great deal of rumour and gossip. The system had distinct advantages in the way it allowed the secretary of state to manage hostile opinion in Britain's Parliament by techniques we would now call political spin. It also, however, had liabilities in a climate that was increasingly hostile to covert information techniques and espionage. Chapter 3 considers how this tactical use of unofficial information gathering, although useful to the strategies of oppositional politics, could also be discredited by accusations of spying.

It was at the Cape that Kaye (now Edwards) first burst onto the scene of colonial politics when he arrived in 1823 from Mauritius. Why did he take on this patently dangerous role? Influential early accounts dubbed Edwards an 'adventurer', and most narratives have left the explanation there. Contemporaries themselves differed as to whether he was mad or sane. As we shall see, there are grounds for suspecting that Edwards's attitude towards Somerset and his powerful family may have been influenced by the role that the Cape governor's brother, Lord Edward Somerset, played in the conviction and subsequent transportation of Alexander Kaye. There is also the fact that Alexander's younger brother, Thomas, was killed in Canada serving in a regiment that had been raised by Lord Charles Somerset.

In the midst of the Cape controversies, John Thomas Bigge and William Colebrooke, as Commissioners of Eastern Inquiry, tried to get a straight answer out of Edwards as to why he had attacked Somerset so vehemently. 'Mr Edwards gave us to understand', they wrote privately to Bathurst, 'that Lord Charles Somerset's former conduct to his Brother in England on some military question had laid the foundation of the resentment that he felt towards him.' This, however, must be set against the many and varied claims that Edwards made about his identity in the same exchange, none of which could be verified, and some of which we can discount as untrue. He frequently claimed, for example, to possess brothers and other close relatives in positions of authority in both Britain and the Cape who could not be connected to him since they 'did not retain the family name'.[48]

Although it is difficult to pin down prior resentment against Somerset and the Cape authorities with any precision, it is certainly easy to see how their treatment of him at the Cape pushed Edwards into further reckless behaviour. Initially, however, Edwards was extremely respectful in his dealing with the authorities. The most likely explanation is that Edwards initially got sucked into controversy unwittingly through routine legal work. From then on he appears to have been prompted by a complex amalgam of personal and political motivations.

Edwards was working as a notary in Cape Town when he was employed by a local merchant, Lancelot Cooke, who had become embroiled in a public argument with the Collector of Customs about the distribution of slaves seized by the British Navy. Around 2000–3000 of these men and women, known variously as 'Prize Slaves', 'Prize Negroes' and 'Liberated Africans', were captured as prizes from foreign vessels and landed at the Cape after the British abolished the slave trade in 1807. In the context of the Cape labour market these are small numbers, yet the liminal position of prize slaves throws several of the paradoxes of imperial liberty into especially sharp relief. Their treatment also highlights the many and contradictory ways in which concepts of honour and gentlemanly status were employed in the quotidian operation of imperial power.

It was the responsibility of Collector of Customs Charles Blair to apprentice prize slaves for fourteen years in order that they might be prepared for the responsibilities of freedom. The right to distribute this

---

[48] Colebrooke and Bigge to Bathurst, 14 July 1824, BL, Bathurst Papers, 57/87, no. 6.

free labour source to masters was used as a source of patronage and power by Blair and his cronies. Cooke was at odds with Blair over the assignment of a valued Mauritian cook named Jean Ellé, and the result was a public altercation in which Cooke deemed himself insulted. Seeking legal redress, he employed Edwards as a notary. Subsequently, however, the two men decided to bring the matter to the attention of the authorities, and Edwards assisted Cooke in drawing up a memorial of complaint to the Lords Commissioners of the Treasury. Rather than transmitting the memorial, however, the governor ordered Edwards and Cooke to be arrested and put on trial for criminal libel.

The abolition of the slave trade had become an emblem of British virtue, more especially in the context of war with Napoleon (who had reopened the trade in 1802). Slaves rescued from foreign ships were held up as a symbol of national honour, a sign that right was on Britain's side, and a powerful justification of divinely ordained victory over rivals. The fourteen-year apprenticeships that followed their rescue were intended to bring forth a suitably devout and industrious class of working people from the ranks of the 'liberated Africans'. In practice, the system by which prize slaves were assigned and controlled at the Cape opened up rampant opportunities for personal gain. Edwards charged that the honourable intentions of an abolitionist nation had been ruthlessly perverted by the corruption of dishonourable officials. Yet, ironically, we can see how it was personal honour – a right to respect based on elite status – that acted as the basis upon which an alliance of officials and favoured colonists rested. Patterns of reciprocity and patronage, particularly amongst elite men, enabled this oligarchy to bypass the system of regulations put in place to protect the prize slave system from abuse. When these interpersonal arrangements broke down, personal honour also became the unexpected catalyst that exposed the prize slave system to official scrutiny.

In Chapters 4 and 5, I explore the prize slave scandal as exposed and subsequently orchestrated by Edwards at the Cape. In the first instance I consider the place of liberated Africans in Cape society, the ways in which these men and women negotiated their position between slavery and freedom, and the difficulties they faced in distinguishing themselves from chattel slaves. Stacked against them were the ways that colonial officials and the Cape elite used patterns of patronage and unstated 'gentleman's agreements' to circumvent the rules ostensibly in place to protect against the erosion of liberated African rights. I then turn in more detail to the case of Jean Ellé and the trial of Edwards and Cooke. What began as a case of affronted honour on the part of Jean Ellé's master spiralled into a lengthy defamation action in the courts and finally an extensive official investigation. Last, I address the question of national honour and the way that rhetoric about abolition was employed by Edwards and other critics of the Somerset regime in an attempt to extricate themselves from its persecution.

Cooke and Edwards were acquitted of charges of criminal libel against Blair, but Edwards spent a month in jail for contempt of court. Shortly after being released he allegedly sent two libelous letters to Lord Charles Somerset and was arrested on criminal charges once more. This time he was found guilty and sentenced to transportation to New South Wales for seven years under Roman–Dutch law, a controversial decision in the light of both English law and wider British colonial practice. The actions of the government against Edwards attracted the attention of the group of Radical- and Whig-orientated British settlers who had recently founded the Cape's first independent newspaper and who were in increasingly vocal opposition to the Somerset regime and its Tory backers in London. Despite promises to keep away from political matters, the *South African Commercial Advertiser* had given a full account of the prize slave libel trial. Because Edwards had used that trial to make a broader attack on government 'tyranny', the result had been a great deal of unwanted publicity for a regime already facing extended criticism both locally and in the House of Commons. With Edwards coming up for trial once more, this time for a highly personal attack upon the Governor, the authorities were eager to prevent a repeat performance of newspaper publicity. Confrontation between the colonial government and the *Advertiser*'s editors and printer saw the paper suppressed and printer George Greig banished from the colony by executive order.

If William Edwards is known to historians for his role in the suppression of South Africa's first independent newspaper, the legal and constitutional implications of these actions remain unexplored, as does their wider imperial significance. The contrast between Somerset's actions against the Cape press and the contemporaneous struggles of Governor Darling in New South Wales, for example, highlights the broader context of debate over the relationship between judicial and executive power, and the legal definitions of, and the remedies for criminal libel. In Chapter 6, I consider how questions of defamation and freedom of expression came head to head in Edwards's transportation for criminal libel. It threw into sharp relief the legal pluralism of a colony caught between Roman–Dutch and English judicial systems.

In acting against the Cape newspaper that was giving publicity to Edwards's charges of tyranny by publishing his court proceedings, the governor exercised the right of banishment by executive order without judicial process. In Chapter 7, I demonstrate how this unleashed a storm of protest that the Colonial Office was keen to defuse. Much legal wrangling ensued between officials in London and the Cape as to the constitutional grounds upon which this action rested and the transition from a Dutch to a British imperial system. The question of how far the state should go in ensuring stability by protecting the reputation of its functionaries thus threw up the vexed question of sovereignty in conquered territories. Finally, I demonstrate how debate over these trials spilled out of the courtroom onto the streets of Cape Town, into the pages of the British and Australian press, and onto the floor of the House of Commons. The local circumstances of the Cape proved useful ammunition in a much broader debate about the relationship between liberty and security in both the metropole and in widely differing colonial contexts, from Australia to India.

In an attempt to contain the spread of an unfolding public relations disaster, Somerset had shut down the *Advertiser* in the wake of the prize slave trials. Public opinion in Cape Town may have found it more difficult to make the jump from local to global, but it was by no means silenced. The city was plastered with broadsheets commenting on the criminal libel cases and the government's actions. In Cape Town diarist Samuel Hudson's words they were 'truly expressive of the indignation of the generality of the people'.[49] As William Edwards lay in jail awaiting a ship to transport him to the Australian colonies, he was accused of conspiring with a series of accomplices to put up a paper accusing Governor Lord Charles Somerset of 'buggering Dr Barry', the British army surgeon whose sex remains a topic of unresolved debate. My account of the placard scandal in Chapter 8 does not attempt to uncover the truth behind alleged sexual improprieties of Somerset and Barry. Nor does it seek either to prove or disprove that Edwards was the author of the placard. An extensive official investigation into his involvement proved inconclusive, whatever Somerset (and indeed Barry) may have believed about the erstwhile notary's guilt. Instead, I argue in this chapter that the placard scandal's explanatory power lies in teasing out the webs of information that were spun together by both sides in seeking to bring the act home to their political enemies.

The final chapter of *Imperial Underworld* returns us to Norfolk Island in 1828 and the death of the man known variously as Alexander Loe Kaye and William Edwards. Giving the authorities the slip en route to his convict transport in 1824 had seen him at large for several days at the Cape. He attempted suicide both during his recapture there and shortly after his arrival in Sydney. As Alexander Kaye, William Edwards

---

[49] Hudson, Diary, 25 Feb. 1824. Hudson Papers, CA, A602, vol. 3.

was finally sent to Norfolk Island after allegedly making plans to jump ship from New South Wales yet again, seven years after his first success. Ending his life was the final act of escape for a man who had made repeated attempts to flee the shackles of state authority.

The repeated investigations made into the escapee's identity, during his life and after his death, underscore both the nature of imperial information gathering in this period and the paradoxical consequences of the Bigge reports in the Australian colonies. An emphasis on 'objective' and measurable physical characteristics was becoming increasingly important, but gossip and interpersonal information networks remained vital to the business of government. Similarly, the harsher disciplinary context of convict punishment enacted in the wake of the Bigge reports did not entirely negate the wider opportunities for legal challenges that were opened up by the same reforms. This chapter concerns the mechanisms used by the state to control and track those deemed to pose a threat to its security, the manner in which the state sought (often in vain) to fix identity and track movement through a variety of surveillance and punishment initiatives and the ways in which convicts sought to use the same legal apparatus to challenge their subjection to the system.

The endless interpersonal controversies that marked imperial governance can all too easily be dismissed as tempests in the colonial teapot. But individuals like Edwards matter because of the role they played in the functioning of an oppositional parliamentary system that was bound together by networks of influence that extended far beyond the corridors of Whitehall. Although their immediate motives were undoubtedly self-interested, Edwards and his ilk were astute enough to link their personal ambitions and vendettas to highly charged contemporary debates about imperial liberty and despotism. As a result, they set in train a series of events that would have an important impact on the changes already under way in these antipodean colonies. Contemporary circumstances secured them a wide-ranging audience for what might look at first glance like trivial and localised personal disputes, for the Commissions of Inquiry were operating in a highly volatile political context which tied British domestic politics and colonial disputes together. Settler discontent proved useful for the opposition press in Britain and for Whig and Radical politicians criticising the Colonial Office in the House of Commons as part of their wider agenda of parliamentary reform and fiscal responsibility. Tracking the extensive investigations made into Kaye/Edwards' case, and the various types of political capital to be made from it, helps us to understand how party politics and reform initiatives interacted through this period. It also throws up important implications for understanding debates over how individual liberty and security could be reconciled in an imperial situation. As increasing numbers of free British settlers arrived in convict colonies and in colonies recently conquered from foreign powers, the stage was set for a struggle over their social and political organisation. The Antipodes would become a laboratory where a specifically British idea of imperial power could be developed. This transformation, and the unexpected yet instrumental role played by ostensibly marginal figures and the scandals they instigated, is the subject of this book.

1 'Plausible and audacious frauds'
The theatre of imperial politics and reform

Within days of one another in the winter of 1823, two men disembarked at the port of Cape Town. Having narrowly avoided shipwreck after the *Lady Campbell* lost a rudder crossing the Bay of Biscay, John Thomas Bigge arrived on 12 July, accompanied by his fellow commissioner, William Colebrooke. Governor Lord Charles Somerset welcomed Bigge warmly and immediately offered rooms in Government House as his headquarters. Bigge would soon move from these, writing confidentially to the Colonial Office in London that the location might intimidate those who came to give testimony critical of the Cape administration.[1] Bigge's investigations in Australia a few years before had seen increasingly bitter divisions between the commissioner and Governor Lachlan Macquarie. At the Cape, personal relations between the commissioners (Bigge particularly) and Somerset would remain surprisingly cordial.[2] Shifting the location of the Commission's activities was nevertheless symbolic. The colony was about to enter into an increasingly vexatious state of divided authority. An administration already riven by internal division and attracting growing external criticism would be pushed to breaking point as deeply divided political interests sought opportunities to gain

Report by Robert Hay (14 Oct. 1830) to Sir George Murray on despatch from Darling, 23 Nov. 1829, TNA, CO 201/203.

[1] Bigge to Wilmot Horton, 25 Sept. 1823 (private and confidential), Catton Collection, Derbyshire Record Office, D3155/WH 2751. The letter is eloquent on the need to keep the provision of official documents to the Commission independent of the governor as well as of the importance of negotiating the shoals of factionalism in the Cape administration.

[2] The Commission of Eastern Inquiry was effectively put in place to dismantle the system by which Somerset governed. Yet this did not stop Somerset both calling on Bigge's legal advice and confiding in him to an often startlingly candid degree. Somerest and Bigge engaged in an extensive private correspondence during the latter's absences from Cape Town. Although we have only the governor's side by which to judge, the letters suggest that friendly relations existed between them throughout the Edwards controversies. Bigge–Somerset correspondence, MSS Afr, series 24, Bodleain Library, Rhodes House, University of Oxford.

the upper hand. As those in the Australian colonies had already discovered, 'the Commissioner of Inquiry came amongst us as an Angel of Discord.'[3]

Five days before the Commission's arrival, a man who would play an increasingly central role in this upheaval slipped into the colony with far less fanfare. Hailing from Mauritius, the English brig *Hero* arrived with a cargo of sugar, rum and coffee, plus a passenger calling himself William Edwards. It was common knowledge that the Commission was charged with investigations that all expected would see a comprehensive overhaul of Cape officialdom. From the highest official to the most marginalised slave, its arrival presented possibilities of all kinds. There was the hope of circumventing the established chains of authority by appealing directly to British officials in the metropole. There was the chance of directing policy and influencing public opinion in the mother country. More prosaically, with years and years of paperwork ahead of it, the arrival of the Commission raised hopes of clerical employment. Three days after Bigge's arrival, the commissioner received a letter from William Edwards, detailing his past history and asking for a job as a 'copying clerk'.

In the yarn that Edwards spun for the commissioners, he claimed to have held 'the situation of English clerk to the Resident of Java'. He admitted spending time in New South Wales (and alluded to seeing Bigge during the commissioner's time there), but in this version of his story he had been 'obliged by ill health' to travel from Java to Sydney in 1820 'in order to avail myself of a better climate and the assistance of your [Bigge's] friend Dr Bowman'. A relapse later prompted him to leave Java for Mauritius, where he was employed in the offices of the British administration. Recurrent bouts of 'Java fever' led him eventually to abandon Mauritius for the more temperate climate of the Cape. There he hoped to remain, finding in the colonies a not-uncommon solution to loss of caste: 'I would not return to England (from a reluctance to live in a humble situation amongst my early associates) if I could obtain employment to eke out a decent living here with a small annuity I possess at home'. Having justified his claim to employment on the basis of the 'character' he had earned in Java and Mauritius, 'a solicitousness whilst here to have an honest occupation; and a full reliance that you will never find me unworthy of the favor', he ended by asserting his genteel social credentials:

---

[3] Edward Eager to Wilmot Horton, 12 Nov. 1822, quoted in J. Ritchie, *Punishment and Profit: The Reports of Commissioner John Bigge on the Colonies of New South Wales and Van Diemen's Land 1822–1823 ~ Their Origins, Nature and Significance* (Melbourne: Heinemann, 1970), p. 105.

My Father being a Captain in a Regiment of Dragoons, and my Mother a relative of Mrs Burton the Lady of General Christie Burton formerly the Member for Beverley nothing but a want of economy earlier in life could have reduced me to the necessity of thus supporting myself by the labour of my hands.[4]

Two weeks later Edwards wrote again, this time to the commissioners' secretary, enclosing several letters intended to prove the legitimacy of his connections in Mauritius where (as the commissioners later received independent confirmation) he had indeed worked as a clerk.[5] Edwards later explained that he had left Mauritius for the Cape upon hearing that the Commission of Eastern Inquiry was due to arrive there. Much of the information he would give to authorities, for obvious reasons, was false: this, however, seems plausible. Given both his legal expertise and his experience working on the fringes of colonial administration, it was not unreasonable that he hoped to find work with them.

We know about the existence of these job requests because copies are to be found enclosed in a letter written almost exactly a year later (14 July 1824) from Bigge and Colebrooke to Secretary of State Lord Bathurst. By this time the obscure would-be copying clerk William Edwards had become arguably the most notorious man in the Cape Colony and a significant source of concern for the Colonial Office in London. Seeking as much information as could be gleaned about his mysterious background, what were once banal requests for employment soon gained new importance for the authorities in Britain, the Cape and New South Wales. Accordingly these copies arrived at the Colonial Office with marginalia ('I have no recollection of having seen Mr Edwards, during my residence in New South Wales. J. T. Bigge.'); they were followed by copies of the two letters to Governor Somerset for which Edwards had been recently been sentenced to transportation for criminal libel; and they were proceeded by a lengthy report.

'Bred to the Law'

How had Alexander Kaye, the man transported in 1819 for stealing a chestnut gelding, really come to turn up at the Cape some four years later as the notary William Edwards? In the 1820s the authorities' interest in this question was precisely defined. For their purposes it was necessary to prove only that Kaye and Edwards were one and the same. Having done

---

[4] William Edwards to Bigge, 15 July 1823, encl. in Colebrooke and Bigge to Bathurst, 14 July 1824, Bathurst Papers, BL, 57/87, no. 6.
[5] Bigge, Colebrooke and Blair to Hay, 14 July 1827, *RCC*, vol. 32, p. 199.

so, they had no further investment in the matter.[6] Since then, scholars have shown scant interest in investigating Kaye's past.[7] Yet it remains significant. Like the commissioners and the secretary of state, we need to track (as far as we are able) the journey that the one had taken into the life of the other. If I have argued that Edwards has proved difficult to fit into existing historical explanations of imperial policy and reform, then one reason emerges by examining his life prior to his sentence of transportation to New South Wales.

Baptised on 29 May 1791, Alexander Kaye was the second child and eldest son of Margaret and Thomas Kaye of Bolton, Lancashire. He was given the second Christian name of Loe to honour his mother's wealthy aunt, Margaret Loe. And so began, perhaps fittingly for a man determined to keep his origins mysterious, more than two centuries of confusion. In convict records, newspaper accounts and later in the writings of historians, Alexander Loe Kaye appears in the guise of Lockaye, Lookaye, Lockage, Lukay, and Loo Kaye, to name but five of the variants on his surname. His actual surname, Kaye, is the exception rather than the rule in both the primary sources and the secondary literature, perhaps because Alexander lent himself distinction by customarily including his second name in his signature and always referring to himself as 'Loe Kaye'. Margaret Loe thus unwittingly muddied the archival waters of her grand-nephew's life, but we also have reason to be grateful to her. Her decision to leave money to Alexander Kaye's family, and in particular the lengthy case in Chancery that resulted from disputes over this legacy, give us our most detailed look into his family background.[8] Like the famous case in Charles Dickens's novel *Bleak House*, wrangling in the case of *Kaye v. Folds* rumbled on interminably. What concerns us here are less the legal machinations than the unwitting light that the documents it assembled shed on the relationships within the fractured Kaye household.

As well as acting as an attorney and, from 1796, a money-scrivener (part notary, part investment manager), in the 1790s Thomas Kaye was involved in extensive property speculation. By 1808 the marriage between

---

[6] Although I outline the key events here, the investigations that authorities made to prove this dual identity (and the rebuttals attempted by Kaye/Edwards) are discussed extensively in Chapter 9.

[7] Here I must pay grateful tribute to the meticulous sleuthing and to the generosity of Peter Burbidge of the School of Law, University of Westminster, a direct descendant of Alexander Loe Kaye. Most of the following discussion of Kaye's English background is based either directly upon his as-yet-unpublished research or upon following up his suggestions.

[8] The following discussion is based on *Kaye v. Folds*, in Records of the Chancery Court, Palatinate of Lancaster: Chancery Court: Pleadings, Miscellanea, TNA, PL 14/84.

Margaret and Thomas Kaye had broken down, and the couple separated. Four years later Thomas was declared bankrupt and also suffered a period of imprisonment when he refused to cooperate with the proceedings. In 1815 Margaret Kaye swore an affidavit before the Chancery Court that 'she receives no Support whatever from her husband who lives separate [sic] and apart from her neither does he contribute to the maintenance and support of her family who are maintained by this deponent'. The following year Alexander's sister Mary (his elder by two years) wrote to lawyer Thomas Shuttleworth about her mother's difficulties in relation to securing the interest from Margaret Loe's legacy held in trust. Her letter speaks eloquently of estrangement between what Mary evidently considered two halves of her family: The virtuous half (herself, her mother, her brothers Thomas and Charles and the younger siblings) and the vicious half (her father and her twenty-five-year-old eldest brother Alexander Loe Kaye). 'Perhaps Sir', she wrote to Shuttleworth, 'you are not aware that having given up all intercourse with the unworthy members of my family, *that sum trifling as it is*, is all that my mother and her 3 young children have to exist upon'. Mary sought to protect her mother from a degree of poverty 'which might be a means of making her return to her unworthy husband, and by so doing not only ruin the principles of her young children, but banish for ever all hope of respectability for them'.[9]

Mary's younger brother Thomas Kaye had joined the 103rd Foot and died a soldier's death at Fort Erie, Canada, in the British–American War in 1814. Charles Kaye (born 1797) was safely training for the law. Alexander, however, had already cast himself beyond the pale in Mary's view:

Viewing as I do the conduct of my father & eldest brother with disgust & abhorrence is it to be wondered at that I almost rejoice in the *honorable* death of one brother and exert every nerve to prevent the other 3 and my *sister*, having the smallest contact with them, you Sir I am sure as an honourable man & a Gentleman will do all in your power to save them being driven to the necessity of seeking refuge with their unhappy father, who would in all probability teach them to follow *his own* and his son Alexander's example – whereas if they are kept apart from him, they may become, as well as their brother Charles *honest* & respectable members of society.[10]

Mary did not stipulate exactly why Alexander and his father were held in such poor regard by the self-declared '*honest* & respectable' members of his family. The 1812 bankruptcy and associated imprisonment of

---

[9] Mary Kaye to Thomas Shuttleworth, 17 Feb. 1816 TNA, PL 14/84, original emphasis.
[10] Mary Kaye to Thomas Shuttleworth, 17 Feb. 1816, original emphasis.

Thomas Kaye, which swept away the family's financial security, are the most likely sources of her resentment.

Alexander had begun his training for the law as an articled clerk to Samuel Humphreys, who acted as Margaret Kaye's solicitor and also was deputy prothonotary (principal clerk of the Court) at Chester. In 1812 Kaye relinquished these articles, and they were taken up instead by his brother Charles. Alexander apparently saw more prospects in small-time banking in Flint, North Wales. He held licenses for the Flint Bank between 1812 and 1814 and, as Kaye & Co., for the Flintshire Bank from 1814 to 1815.[11] Later reports of his trial emphasised 'the strange vicissitude of fortune: not many years ago, Mr Kay was living in considerable repute, as a banker and a merchant, at Flint, in North Wales; and at one time, many thousands of his notes were in circulation'.[12] On 6 May 1811, Alexander, then still resident in Chester, married Susanna Shackfield. The groom was barely 20, the bride three years older. Her father, Edward Shackfield, was a substantial landowner in Flint, and Alexander and Susanna's first three children would be born there.

In the period of two decades that separated the death of Margaret Loe in 1805 and the winding up of the trust in 1826, the expectation of the legacy would be used as security by the Kaye siblings amongst themselves and with others. Each could expect the substantial sum of £500, increased by interest. Charles Kaye borrowed against it from his eldest sister Mary, probably in order to fund his legal training in London (where he moved after a year with Humphreys in Chester). The investment justified the faith of both parties, for Charles became a successful solicitor, just as his sister had predicted in her 1816 letter to Shuttleworth.

Alexander, however, used the security for much less responsible purposes. By 1815 he, Susannah and their young family were also in London, with Alexander writing to Shuttleworth concerning the Loe inheritance from '3 Middle Temple Buildings'.[13] Although the address, apparently in the heart of the barristers' Inns of Court, carries the aura of legal prestige, it may actually have had no basis in reality.[14] By means of an indenture dated 24 April 1816, Alexander signed over his share in the inheritance to Charles Goldsmith, a coffeehouse keeper in Blackfriars, London, probably in lieu of paying his debts. At this time Alexander was

---

[11] R. Outing, *The Standard Catalogue of the Provincial Banknotes of England and Wales* (Honiton, UK: Token Publishing, 2010). My thanks to Peter Burbidge for this reference.

[12] *Hull Packet and Original Weekly Commercial, Literary and General Advertiser*, 27 April 1819.

[13] Alexander Loe Kaye to Shuttleworth, 24 Oct. 1815. TNA, PL 14/84.

[14] Peter Burbidge, a genuine member of the Middle Temple (unlike his less-respectable ancestor) has tried and failed to locate the address through the organisation's records.

practising as a solicitor (despite his incomplete qualifications) and meeting his clients at Goldsmith's establishment, the York Hotel. Goldsmith, in turn, used the prospective legacy to pay off William Charouneau, a Marylebone silversmith.[15]

Relations between Kaye and his in-laws, if they had ever been good, may have soured by the time the family lived in London. When the couple had married in 1811, Kaye had seemed to have prospects in the law. He had abandoned these a year later for a brief career as a small-time banker. This failed when it became caught up in his father's bankruptcy proceedings. He had even spent a few weeks in King's Bench Prison in November 1816 as the result of a dispute over a fuel bill. In September 1817 Kaye's father-in-law Edward Shackfield drew up a will that explicitly left his property in trust to his daughter Susannah 'for her own sole and separate use and benefit without being in any manner subject to the control, debts or engagements of her husband'.[16] Alexander was thereby specifically excluded from any access to the inheritance. This means of protecting a married woman's property had also been employed in Margaret Loe's bequests to Margaret Kaye, from which Alexander's father Thomas was similarly excluded. Edward Shackfield's decision to ensure his daughter's financial security followed the birth of his grandson, Edward Shackfield Kaye, in July 1817. Alexander's precarious financial situation was probably also significant. Sadly, the child would be dead within six months, and grief may have been yet another factor in Alexander Loe Kaye's downfall.

On 31 March 1819, at the Gloucester Lent Assizes, Alexander Loe Kaye was convicted of stealing a chestnut gelding worth £30 from 'Thomas Evans... Gentleman' in the nearby village of Deerhurst on the river Severn.[17] The chair of the bench of judges was the famous law reformer William Garrow. The president of the grand jury that indicted him was Lord Edward Somerset, brother to Lord Charles Somerset, Cape governor, the man who would find himself locked in conflict with the crusading notary calling himself William Edwards five years later. In a taste of things to come, Kaye appeared within the court records as 'Alexander Loo Kaye... otherwise called Alexander Lowe Kaye otherwise called Alexander Kaye'.[18] The trial marked the culmination of a series of run-ins with the law in the preceding months, for Kaye had

---

[15] Indenture on Alexander Loe Kaye share, 24 April 1816, enclosed in Newcomb to Shuttleworth, 24 April 1816, TNA, PL 14/84. Charouneau never appeared to claim his debt, and the money eventually went to Susannah Kaye and her children.
[16] Welsh Probate Records, Parish of Flint, Flintshire, Diocese of St Asaph, National Library of Wales, SA/1820/39.
[17] Gloucester Archives, Gaol Calendar, Q/Gc 5/2.
[18] Office copy of Alexander Loe Kaye's conviction, 31 March 1819. TNA, PL 14/84.

also been indicted for an alleged assault against one Robert Collier on 9 October 1818 at Cheltenham. He was committed for trial in the Michaelmas Assizes in late 1818, but because he was subsequently arrested for stealing Evans's horse the charges of assault were never pursued. The Gloucestershire Gaol Calender also notes the charge of having 'in the month of Dec[ember] last feloniously stolen and driven away a gig of the value of £30 the property of... Thomas Hughes', a 'porter merchant' of Cheltenham.[19] This charge was also never tried, perhaps because the theft of the chestnut gelding was the easiest to prove and, as a capital offence, carried the heaviest penalty.

The *Times* newspaper reported that the case had 'excited considerable interest in Cheltenham and its vicinity'. According to its report, Kaye obtained a chestnut horse from Evans in November 1818 'on condition of returning or paying for it the same evening'. Neither the money nor the horse was forthcoming. A few days later Kaye sent a draft to Evans drawn on the firm of 'John Birnie and Co. of London', but no such firm was found to exist. Evans traced his horse to Oxford, where Kaye had sold it to a dealer.[20] The *Gloucester Journal* described Kaye as 'a very gentlemanly respectable looking young man' who 'conducted his own defense'. Anticipating his later dramatic performances in colonial courts, he 'cross-examined the prosecutor for upwards of two hours without being able however to invalidate that gentleman's testimony in the smallest degree'. Although the paper noted that Kaye had served a clerkship to a respectable attorney in Chester, 'we entertain some doubts whether this case would have borne a better complexion with the jury had he employed counsel or submitted himself to the humane interposition of the judge'.[21] He seems not to have learnt this lesson, as choosing to represent himself in court would prove to be Kaye/Edwards's undoing more than once in the future. Having been found guilty, the death sentence, according to the *Times*,

was received by the Court with evident symptoms of surprise. The prisoner, a young man of prepossessing appearance and peculiarly fascinating manners, had also to boast of a liberal education, and was endowed by nature with talents of a very superior order. In the early years of his life he was articled to an attorney. Whatever property he possessed was early dissipated, and for the last eight or ten years he has lived by sheer contrivance and his wits.[22]

---

[19] Quarter Sessions Indictment Book 1808–1819, Gloucester Archives, Q/SIB 3; Quarter Sessions Indictment Rolls, Q/SI (a), 1818 D; Gaol Calendar, Q/Gc 5/2.
[20] *Times*, 14 April 1819.   [21] *Gloucester Journal*, 2 April 1819.
[22] *Times*, 14 April 1819.

Capital sentences such as Kaye's (unlike those for murder) were mostly commuted to transportation in this period. Petitions for mercy might sway judicial recommendations, but no record of any petition on Kaye's behalf has been traced. Nor do we know whether he had any contact with his family in England after he was transported to New South Wales. There are curious anomalies in the Chancery investigations into the Loe inheritance in the years that followed. Everyone, from the attorney general down to his own wife and family, repeatedly testified, quite wrongly, that Alexander Loe Kaye had been sent to Van Diemen's Land. Does this suggest that no contact was maintained by either Susannah or the Kaye family? Certainly once he escaped and took on the identity of William Edwards it was imperative that Alexander break any traceable connection with this previous life in order to maintain his new role.

Kaye becomes Edwards

Alexander Kaye embarked upon the convict transport *Atlas* bound for Sydney in May 1819. According to the ship surgeon's journal, the voyage to Sydney was largely uneventful until 23 June, when plans for a mutiny were uncovered, and a familiar name makes an appearance:

At 10 00 P.M. several of the Prisoners were overheard laying plans for taking the Ship. Two were Handcuffed for being found out of bed. At 10 00 P M Punished Alex^r L. Kaye, Edward Mills, and Jno White Prisoners with one dozen lashes each for having broke through the Prison into the Hospital, and having two Steel Saws in their possession.[23]

The surgeon made no further comment on this bald entry, and it is to be assumed that the affair was neatly nipped in the bud.[24]

Kaye arrived in Sydney on the *Atlas* in October 1819. His conduct on the voyage out saw him immediately sent by Governor Macquarie to Newcastle for twelve months, a penal settlement then being used as an ad hoc site of secondary punishment.[25] An account later provided by William Hutchinson (principal superintendent of convicts in 1819) presents an image of a persistent troublemaker: Kaye was 'received from

---

[23] *Atlas* surgeon's journal, TNA, ADM 101/6/2.
[24] As the research of Hamish Maxwell-Stewart into convict mutiny attempts shows, such incidents were far more common and had a far greater impact on convict management techniques than their almost total absence of success would suggest: '"Those lads contrived a plan": Attempts at mutiny on Australia-bound convict vessels', *International Review of Social History*, 58 (2013), 177–96.
[25] L. Ford and D. A. Roberts, 'Legal change, convict activism and the reform of penal relocation in colonial New South Wales: The Port Macquarie penal settlement 1822–1826', *Australian Historical Studies*, 46: 2 (2015), 174–91.

Newcastle with a bad Character on the 26 February 1821, and employed at Head Quarters as an Overseer of light workers, in consequence of having received a hurt while at the penal Settlement'. He did no better in this role, but 'abused the confidence reposed in him, in consequence of which he was dismissed and put to work in a labouring gang'. Subsequently Kaye was assigned to the solicitor Thomas Wylde, father of the colony's judge advocate, Sir John Wylde, the man who would later preside over a reformed Cape judiciary as chief justice. It was 'generally believed', wrote Hutchinson, that Kaye had robbed Thomas Wylde before absconding. What was certain is that he was 'advertised accordingly in the Sydney *Gazette* as a Runaway on the 8th December 1821'. A postscript to Hutchinson's letter noted 'This Said Alexander Lockaye appears to have been the cause of several of the better Class of convicts having been sent to this Country, having connected himself with them in England'.[26]

By 1825, when this information was transmitted to the secretary of state, Lord Bathurst, the man in Hutchinson's narrative had made himself widely notorious. How much of this later history retrospectively coloured the authorities' account of Kaye's time in New South Wales between 1819 and 1821 is therefore difficult to quantify. In this regard, Hutchinson's postscript is particularly interesting, for although the movements of Kaye within the convict system of New South Wales can indeed be verified, his alleged role in broader associations of 'elite' criminality is mere supposition. The postscript speaks to the broader concerns about 'gentleman convicts' that are explored in the final chapter of this book. Whether it has any basis in fact is more doubtful in the absence of any corroborating records. It may well tell us more about Edwards and attitudes towards him in 1824 and 1825 than it does about Kaye's time in New South Wales between 1819 and 1821.

Thomas Wylde died on 4 December 1821, his death listed in the same issue of the *Sydney Gazette* that advertised 'Alexander Lookaye' amongst a long list of 'Prisoners having absented themselves from their respective Employments, and some of them at large with false Certificates'. Principal Superintendent Hutchinson warned in the notice that 'Any Persons harbouring, concealing, or maintaining any of the said Absentees, will be prosecuted for the Offence'.[27] The same issue noted the departure on Wednesday 5 December of the *Jane* for Batavia. The brig had been in

---

[26] Somerset to Bathurst, 27 Aug. 1825, incl. letters from T. Ovens and W. Hutchinson, 20 Nov. 1824, *RCC*, vol. 23, pp. 24–6.
[27] *Sydney Gazette*, 8 Dec. 1821.

Sydney since October, arriving from Batavia via Hobart with a cargo of rum and gin.[28]

Although we do not know for certain that Kaye escaped on board the *Jane*, he did (as we have seen) admit to time in Batavia (Java), and the route was a logical one for an escaping convict to take. As the work of Clare Anderson suggests, Sydney was essentially a hub on the Indian Ocean shipping network that connected the east coast of Australia to Europe.[29] Until recently, the emphasis in convict escape historiography has been mostly on dramatic group escapes (such as that of Mary Bryant and family in a cutter stolen from Governor Arthur Phillip in 1791) and on the oft-repeated stories of convicts trying to escape overland through the Australian bush to China.[30] In fact, individual escapes by sea were more the norm and more common than the regulations to prevent them might lead one to expect.

From the very beginning of the convict settlement, it was recognised that the penal settlement's isolation would be continually undercut by the existence of an expanding maritime world. Governor Phillip's instructions banned colonial boat building and contact with Asian settlements.[31] Yet persistent local regulations regarding boats proved largely unworkable.[32] Bigge's 1822 report on New South Wales noted frequent escapes, 'often with the connivance of sailors'.[33] His report on the judicial establishments recommended that more regulations were required to prevent the escape of convicts in ships because such practices were increasing with the increase of trade in the colony.[34]

Bigge's report noted the precautions required at the departure of every vessel, precautions that Kaye evidently evaded. All those taking passage

---

[28] *Hobart Town Gazette*, 6 Oct. 1821; *Sydney Gazette*, 27 Oct. 1821; *Bataviasche Courant*, 2 and 9 June 1821, 28 July 1821, 23 Feb. 1822, 2 and 9 March 1822.

[29] C. Anderson, 'Multiple border crossings: 'Convicts and other persons escaped from Botany Bay and residing in Calcutta''', *Journal of Australian Colonial History* 3:2 (2001), 1–22.

[30] W. Hirst, *Great Convict Escapes in Colonial Australia*, rev. edn (Sydney: Kangaroo Press, 2003); D. Levell, *Tour to Hell: Convict Australia's Great Escape Myths* (Brisbane: University of Queensland Press, 2008); G. Karskens provides a historiographical survey in a special issue on convict escapes: '"This spirit of emigration": The nature and meanings of escape in early New South Wales', *Journal of Australian Colonial History*, 7 (2005), 1–34.

[31] C. McCreery and K. McKenzie, 'The Australian colonies in a maritime world', in A. Bashford and S. Macintyre (eds.), *Cambridge History of Australia* (Cambridge University Press, 2013), vol. I, p. 561.

[32] Karskens, '"This spirit of emigration"', p. 30.

[33] *Report of the Commissioner of Inquiry into the State of the Colony of New South Wales*, 1822, p. 33.

[34] *Report of the Commissioner of Inquiry on the Judicial Establishments of New South Wales and Van Diemen's Land*, 1823, p. 79.

on a vessel apart from the crew were required to obtain certificates from the judge advocate's office, in part to prove that they were not attempting to escape outstanding debts in the colony. Their names, ages and places of abode were all recorded at the secretary's office. If previously a convict, records of pardon must be checked. All of this took time and presented considerable inconvenience as sailors took the opportunity to abscond either temporarily or permanently. Ships leaving the harbour were searched by the chief constable, and if any suspicion existed of convicts being concealed on board, the vessel was smoked with brimstone.[35] Any stowaways were thereby forced to reveal themselves or risk suffocation.

To stop convicts from joining vessels under weigh, the ships were required to proceed straight out of the heads, unless in cases of 'necessity or of stress of weather'. But in many cases this proved not practicable so that government vessels with constables on board were usually ordered to accompany outward-bound ships and to remain near them until they had cleared the harbour. Preventing convict escape by sea was perceived to have a serious negative impact on the conduct of colonial commerce. Deputy Judge Advocate Bent compared the 'peculiar circumstances' of port regulations in the colony in respect to the escape of convicts 'to His Majesty's plantations in the West Indies in respect to the escape of their Negroes'.[36] In his testimony to Bigge, Superintendent of Convicts William Hutchinson agreed that the captains of merchant vessels complained of the 'restraints and regulations necessary to prevent the concealment of convicts on board their ships' and that 'they object strongly to the smoking their ships or any minute search of them'.[37]

Evading these precautions was clearly more than possible, making convict escape by sea a significant problem for the authorities. By Bigge's calculation (and he admitted that this was likely the tip of the iceberg), 255 convicts had attempted to escape between 1803 and 1820 by concealing themselves on board vessels or attempting to seize ships by violence. Of these, he claimed, 194 had been retaken and 9 had died. 'Their usual object in making escape is to land in India; or, in taking possession of vessels, to make their passage to Timor or Batavia'.[38] Clare Anderson's work on convicts who escaped Australia for India underlines the broader Indian Ocean context in which these individual acts, and official response to them, should be analysed. Escaping convicts not only eroded

---

[35] Bigge, *Judicial Establishments*, p. 79.   [36] *HRA*, 4:1, p. 123.
[37] Attempted and actual escapes from settlement in NSW, Evidence of William Hutchinson, 10 Nov. 1819, State Library of New South Wales, Bonwick Transcripts, BOX 1, pp. 161–6.
[38] Bigge, *Judicial Establishments*, p. 79.

legal and punishment regimes; their presence in non-settler colonies like Bengal and Mauritius also challenged local definitions of respectability and racial hierarchy.[39]

As a convict who successfully escaped and changed his identity, therefore, Alexander Kaye was hardly unusual. It was his subsequent activities that set him apart. When Kaye arrived in Cape Town in 1823, there was nothing in his story thus far to suggest that this heralded a career as a political activist or colonial reformer. His emergence as such is far more difficult to explain than his transformation into the notary William Edwards.

In October 1830, two years after the death of the man who called himself William Edwards, Undersecretary of State Robert Hay sat down to pen what would be the Colonial Office's last substantive word on this troublesome subject. Those who had never lived in a 'convict settlement', Hay wrote, could not even 'imagine the possibility of such plausible and audacious frauds as are daily practised there'. In his rich career of duplicity and imposture, Edwards ranked as a consummate performer even within 'that strange system of artifice'. It was indeed a pity, commented Hay, 'that a man possessing so much dramatic power should not have used it to a better purpose'.[40]

Even with his jaundiced view of penal colonies, Hay was clearly baffled by the enigma presented by William Edwards. We might similarly ask why Edwards chose to challenge corrupt behaviour on the part of the Cape authorities, particularly in circumstances in which, as an escaped convict, it might have been more prudent to lay low. Can we find some kind of answer in his background? There is nothing to suggest that he or any of his connections had links to reformist politics. No clues exist to suggest that he might fit within recent scholarly accounts that have uncovered the networks that Britain's radical underworld extended into the colonial world in this period.[41] As I argue in later chapters, suggestions made by those who knew him that Edwards was insane cannot easily be discounted, but are equally hard to assess. He persistently resists categorisation, one reason why his activities have been so difficult to incorporate properly into existing understandings of imperial reform. Whatever the political views he expressed in the colonies (and this is not to argue that they

---

[39] Anderson, 'Multiple border crossings'; *Subaltern Lives: Biographies of Colonialism in the Indian Ocean World 1790–1920* (Cambridge University Press, 2012).
[40] Report by Hay (14 Oct. 1830) to Sir George Murray on despatch from Darling, 23 Nov. 1829, TNA, CO 201/203.
[41] J. Epstein, 'The radical underworld goes colonial: P. F. McCallum's *Travels in Trinidad*', in M. T. Davis and P. Pickering (eds.), *Unrespectable Radicals? Popular Politics in the Age of Reform* (Aldershot: Ashgate, 2008).

were insincere), Alexander Loe Kaye was not transported for any form of action against tyranny or 'Old Corruption'. His crimes cannot be easily linked to either poverty or protest.

One theme we can trace from his previous life into his later career as an activist is his insistence on his identity as a lawyer. In the description made of Kaye at Gloucestershire Gaol, the record note 'says he was bred to the Law'.[42] As a convict he ensured that 'Solicitor' and 'Educated for the Bar' were recorded under the information collected as to 'calling'. On the *Atlas* convict transport, his native place was listed as 'Dublin'. We can speculate that one reason for this may have been to mask his failure to qualify when he was practising in London, because credentials from Ireland would have been more difficult to check. Kaye may never have finished his legal training, but he not only practised the law but also ensured that it was listed in his convict records. This may all have had a merely pragmatic purpose, but he would make much of this identity in his contests with colonial authorities in the guise of William Edwards. His adversaries, he claimed at the Cape, should have 'known there was something in the free, honest, unbending spirit of an English lawyer, not to be insulted with impunity'.[43] Supporters would take up the same image: 'Edwards will attack them with his own weapons and conquer them by good sense and sound Law proceedings'.[44]

In years to come it would also be reported to authorities in Cape Town that William Edwards had boasted that

money is no object to me. I have been at Van Diemen's Land where I kicked up a rough; at the Isle of France [Mauritius], where I did the same & from thence I came to the Cape; which after I have set in fire, Shall leave for another place, to start a similar agitation.[45]

As we shall see, this information came from a paid informer against Edwards and a man who was widely regarded as an unreliable witness. We must also recognise the hyperbole to which Edwards undoubtedly was prone. If Edwards indeed made these claims, then he did so in the context of a self-reinvention that I chart over the following chapters. Tempting as it might be to see him as setting out on his travels in the role of global revolutionary, the reality was undoubtedly more complex.

How are we to understand the peculiarities of the theatre upon which Edwards was able to exert such 'dramatic power'? Edwards's insistence

---

[42] Gaol Calendar, Gloucester Archives, Q/Gc 5/2.   [43] *RCC*, vol. 17, p. 185.
[44] Hudson, Diary, 30 April 1824.
[45] Testimony of Daniel Shee, CA, CJ 3352, Inquiry into Placard scandal, 1824, 222.

upon his legal credentials, like his attempt to find work with the Commission of Eastern Inquiry, is emblematic of the broader transition in imperial governance with which this book is concerned. In the rest of this chapter I seek to lay a path for the reader through the entangled problems that bound together the three contexts within which Edwards's drama played out. Only by demonstrating the connections in imperial policy and reform that existed amongst Britain, the Cape and the Australian colonies can we understand why Edwards and his challenges to authority were able to secure the far-reaching impact that they did.

If imperial governance was transformed in the period following the Napoleonic Wars, then the key institutional mechanism for achieving this was an intensive phase of parliamentary Commissions of Inquiry. Tracking their investigations and the consequences that flowed from them is a key path towards understanding how the colonial order was recast in this period. For the Cape and the Australian colonies the relevant investigations are those associated with John Thomas Bigge in the 1820s, enquiries that Edwards's own travels would mimic in almost uncanny ways. Bigge was sent out first to the Australian colonies (1819–1821) and later, together with William Colebrooke, to the Cape (1823–1826). Edwards, however, first came to prominence in imperial debate at the Cape, only later making his mark in New South Wales. Because it is Edwards' political trajectory that I follow in *Imperial Underworld*, I deal with the commissioners' investigations in reverse order here.

Cape of Torments: Reforming a Dutch colony[46]

When Edwards arrived at the Cape in 1823, he joined an improbably eccentric cast of characters that was headed by the governor himself. Second son of the fifth duke of Beaufort, with his colourful background (direct descent from the Plantagenets, a scandalous elopement from a masked ball), his autocratic rages, his passion for the hunt and for horse racing, and his tendency to treat the Cape like a private fiefdom, Somerset [Figure 2] can easily approach caricature. Perhaps unsurprisingly, this highest of high Tories remains one of the few British colonial administrators to live on in popular memory in South Africa.[47] His time at the

---

[46] The phrase *Cabo das Tormentas* (Cape of Storms) was used by the Portuguese explorers in the fifteenth century. Amongst the foundational histories of Cape slavery is that of R. Ross, *Cape of Torments: Slavery and Resistance in South Africa* (London: Routledge, 1983).

[47] K. Millar, *Plantagenet in South Africa: Lord Charles Somerset* (Oxford University Press, 1965), p. 1. Millar's book is an overt, unapologetic (and largely unsuccessful) attempt to 'rehabilitate his subject': see J. Butler's 'Review of Anthony Kendal Millar, *Plantagenet in South Africa*', *American Historical Review*, 71:2 (1966), 638–9.

Figure 2 Lord Charles Somerset in 1811, three years before taking up his position as governor of the Cape Colony.

Cape spanned (with one interruption) the period from 1814 to 1826. Historians have long argued, as did contemporaries, that he was possibly the least suitable choice for the times in which he found himself. Yet if Somerset had departed the colony permanently in January 1820 (when he left for Britain on a period of home leave) he might not have become, as one scholar has described him, 'one of the villains of South African history'.[48] Upon his return in November 1821, Somerset embarked upon bitter feuding with all those functionaries who had been favoured by Acting Governor Sir Rufane Donkin during his absence. The colonial secretary, Colonel Christopher Bird, was a particular target. This paranoid factionalism, which reached almost absurdist heights, did much to poison Somerset's second term. He was also faced, after 1820, with a settler population that was rapidly changing its composition as an influx of new British emigrants arrived in the colony. These new arrivals were far outnumbered by the existing Cape Dutch inhabitants (and even more so by slaves and indigenous people). But they could punch above their weight in colonial disputes not only through their connections to high-status individuals in Britain itself, but also through the influence of British public opinion on parliamentary decisions.

The governor was immensely popular with the Cape Dutch elite of the colony, with whom he ironically shared far closer political and social sympathies than with most of the fellow countrymen who began arriving at the colony from 1820. He was the last of the Cape governors to possess the almost unhindered autocratic powers that were so congenial to his personality and background and so increasingly out of kilter with the spirit of the reformist age. He was obliged to play host to a Commission of Inquiry sent out to dismantle the system by which he ruled, a system whose fundamental principles of patronage and self-enrichment he had taken to with such alacrity. The growing mismatch between Somerset and the circumstances in which he was expected to rule, together with his poor handling of this situation, proved a significant liability to the Tory administration in the House of Commons and a magnet for opposition attacks.

Although the criticisms made of Somerset, even by his supporters, were for the most part richly deserved, it is hard not to accord him at least a modicum of sympathy for being the victim of bad timing. If he had taken up the same post and handled it in the same way even a decade earlier, he would have proved far less controversial.

In 1826, shortly before Somerset returned to London to answer changes against him in the House of Commons, Dudley Perceval – son of the assassinated British Prime Minister Spencer Perceval – wrote from the Cape:

a good Tory, like myself, observing that his foes are Englishmen & Radicals here, & supported by Radicals at home, will judge quite as favourably of his Character

---

[48] Butler, 'Review of *Plantagent in South Africa*', 639.

from contemplating who they are that attack him, as from the knowledge of what part of the community are satisfied with & well disposed to him.[49]

In both governance and social structure, the colony where Edwards arrived in 1823 was still Dutch rather than British, for the latter had conquered it from the Dutch East India Company (Vereenigde Oostindische Compagnie [VOC]) as recently as 1795. Of those estimated to live within the colony's borders in 1820, around 43 000 were designated Europeans or 'Christians'. The vast majority of these were Cape Dutch rather than British settlers, though the census did not differentiate between them.[50] Over 33 000 were slaves whose ethnic heritage was mixed (including what was later known as Madagascar, India, Indonesia and Malaysia, for example), a heritage of Dutch dominance in the Indian Ocean. Some 2000 might be termed 'free blacks', including not only manumitted slaves but also those descended from political prisoners exiled from Batavia and other Dutch colonial possessions, almost entirely confined to Cape Town and increasingly forging a distinct Islamic identity there. More than 25 000 were indigenous Khoekhoen (Hottentots, as Europeans referred to them) or 'Bastaards' (those with a Khoekhoe mother and a slave father).[51] Nearly a quarter of the colonial population lived in Cape Town. A full half were to be found in the mere 5 per cent of the total land area of the colony that comprised the city's immediate surrounding districts. These were the areas of intensive agricultural production, particularly in wheat and wine. The rest of the inhabitants were spread out increasingly thinly towards the frontier, primarily engaged in pastoralism.[52]

---

[49] D. M. Perceval to Countess Bathurst, 19 Jan. 1826, D. M. Perceval, Letters written from the Cape of Good Hope 1825–1828, Library of Parliament, Cape Town, class a. 916.87, no. 9202.

[50] The Cape Dutch should not be equated with the metropolitan Dutch, despite their common language (at least in formal contexts). A much broader constituency of Europeans was drawn into the orbit of the Dutch East India Company over the previous century and a half. The creolised Dutch language from which Afrikaans would emerge had not yet attained respectability amongst white elites.

[51] The figures and categorisations are those of R. Elphick and H. Giliomee, 'The origins and entrenchment of European dominance at the Cape 1652–c. 1840', in R. Elphick and H. Giliomee (eds.), *The Shaping of South African Society 1652–1840*, 2nd edn (Cape Town: Maskew Miller Longman, 1989), p. 524. The term 'free black' was a fluid one and presents complexities of definition, particularly by the 1820s when manumissions were on the rise. It is generally employed by Cape historians to mean free persons of whole or part African (though not Khoekhoen) and Asian descent, which was roughly how it was used during the VOC (Vereenigde Oostindische Compagnie: Dutch East India Company) period. R. Elphick and R. Shell, 'Intergroup relations: Khoikhoi, settlers, slaves and free blacks, 1652–1795' in R. Elphick and H. Giliomee (eds.), *Shaping of South African Society*, p. 184.

[52] J. E. Mason, *Social Death and Resurrection: Slavery and Emancipation in South Africa* (University of Virginia Press, 2003), p. 17.

For reasons of financial and political expediency, an alliance had been forged between the conquering British administration and the Cape Dutch gentry, one that reached its climax under the Somerset administration. Somerset, who behaved very much as the past colonial experience of the Cape elite would lead them to expect of a ruler, had a great deal to offer. He dispensed lavish hospitality and generous patronage to those who were loyal to him. He agitated to keep the preferential access of Cape wines to the British market, a highly significant development for Cape trade and labour to which I return in Chapter 4. The Cape Dutch dominated the ranks of European colonists not only demographically, but also financially and in terms of access to power and patronage. Key posts in the administration, above all in its judicial branch, remained filled by leading members of the Cape Dutch elite who were members of (or connected by marriage to) the wealthiest families in the colony. Amongst them were many who had held office between 1803 and 1806, during the period that Britain returned the colony to the Batavian Republic under the terms of the Treaty of Amiens. Despite increasingly loud criticism of 'Old Corruption' in Britain, similar sentiments had failed to penetrate very far into Cape Dutch society or governance, which was likely one reason why Somerset felt so at home there.[53] At least at first, the British conquerors played entirely by the established Cape rules of patronage and reward. The price of switching loyalty, argues historian Wayne Dooling, 'probably paled in comparison with the opportunities for outright theft that continuity in office allowed the Dutch elite'.[54]

Amongst the men who embodied this colonial two-step were those who played important parts in the fate of William Edwards at the Cape: Johannes Andreas Truter,[55] a tireless supporter of Somerset and the colony's president of the Council of Justice (chief justice), and Daniel Denijssen, the last man to hold the unpopular office of fiscal. Truter

---

[53] This is not to imply that criticism of state corruption at the Cape had to await the arrival of British settlers. It was a significant theme across a series of eighteenth-century protests by Cape Dutch burghers against oligarchical rule under the VOC. The culmination of these may perhaps be seen in what has been termed 'the Cape Patriot movement' in relation to protests from 1778 and into the 1780s. Interpretations of these events have differed widely, however. Afrikaner nationalist historians saw in them a proto-Afrikaner struggle for political liberation from VOC tyranny. In more recent work, Teunis Baartman has argued convincingly that the events emerged from a dispute between rival gentry factions over political and economic advantage. As such he sees a greater degree of continuity between the late eighteenth-century protests and the periodic patronage-network disputes that preceded them across the previous century: see his 'Fighting for the spoils: Cape burgerschap and faction disputes in Cape Town in the 1770s', unpublished PhD thesis, University of Cape Town (2011).

[54] W. Dooling, *Slavery, Emancipation and Colonial Rule in South Africa* (Scottsville, South Africa: University of KwaZulu-Natal Press, 2007), p. 74.

[55] From 1820 Sir John Truter, the first South African to be knighted.

exemplified the parasitical forces of 'Old Corruption' in a Dutch colonial idiom. As president of the Orphan Chamber during the Batavian interregnum of 1803–1806,[56] he had lent himself and his family the vast sum of 51 000 rixdollars, a figure he knew he could never repay. But because he was also president of the Council of Justice, 'and thus empowered to deliver the final judgement on any case that might be brought against himself', he had reason to rest easy.[57] Somewhat akin to an attorney general, the Cape fiscal combined the duties of public prosecutor and chief of police. In a city where illegal trading was a way of life, the fiscal also prosecuted all matters of revenue and breach of customs duties.[58] He was arguably the most hated man in the colony, partly because one third of any fines he imposed went by law into his own pocket. As a contemporary wrote, 'The acuteness of a lawyer, whetted by a prospect of gain, and aided by the greedy watchfulness of an officer of customs, appear to be dreadful odds against a defendant'.[59] The office was so despised that it has lived on in the popular identification of the species *Lanius collaris*. Not only its black-and-white legal plumage but also its habit of impaling its (often-still-living) prey upon convenient thorns for later consumption has given this southern African bird the common name of fiscal shrike.

Denijssen (or Denyssen as he tended to anglicise it for the new administration) was born in Amsterdam in the late 1770s. Trained at the University of Leiden, Denyssen had been appointed to the Cape Council of Justice during the Batavian interregnum. In 1812, when the previous fiscal, Johannes Andreas Truter, was appointed president of the Council of Justice, Denyssen took on the role. As a Crown prosecutor tasked with tackling critics charged with seditious libel, Denyssen faced ridicule both inside and outside court because of his switch in loyalties, from William Edwards's rhetoric, which dubbed him one of the 'renegadoes of Amsterdam',[60] to scrawls on the city's walls in the guise of 'Dog Dan'. A placard posted after the fiscal had refused to fight a duel (by reason of his office) may have started the nickname:

---

[56] Between 1803 and 1806 the French-Allied Batavian Republic in the Netherlands regained control of the Cape from the British as a result of the Treaty of Amiens. The British conquered the Cape for a second time when the hostilities of the Napoleonic Wars broke out once more.

[57] J. B. Peires, 'The British and the Cape' in R. Elphick and H. Giliomee (eds.), *The Shaping of South African Society*, p. 491. In fact Truter would be embarrassed by one of his slaves, Marie, who made sure the matter came out during the British period. Dooling, *Slavery, Emancipation and Colonial Rule*, pp. 76–7.

[58] Anon. [William Wilberforce Bird], *State of the Cape of Good Hope in 1822*, facs. edn (Cape Town: Struik, 1966), pp. 16–17.

[59] Anon. [Bird], *State of the Cape*, p. 17.

[60] William Edwards to the secretary of the Court of Justice, 26 May 1824, Letters received from Court of Justice, CA, CO 214, no. 31.

Lost, stolen, or strayed, a white-livered Dog, answering to the name of 'Dan'. Whoever will bring the said dog to the African Society House, with a rope round his neck, will be well rewarded – N.B. This dog is of no use to any Sportsman, as he does not stand fire.[61]

As we shall see, Denyssen was eager both to defend the attacks that Edwards had made on his service to the 'revolutionaries' of the Batavian Republic and to assert his loyalty to the British administration.

Denyssen was a man of undoubted abilities, very far from the tyrannical buffoon that Edwards and his allies alleged. For all his professions of loyalty to the British in the face of his critics' courtroom arguments, petitions to Parliament, and scurrilous placards, he clearly saw quite another kind of writing on the wall. In 1826 he requested permission from Lord Bathurst, secretary of state for the colonies, to retire on a full pension. After protracted negotiations as to the return of a portion of the fines he had collected as fiscal, his plea was ultimately granted. Denyssen retired in 1828, the year a new legal system was established at the Cape. The office of fiscal was replaced by that of attorney general, and Irishman William Porter was brought out to fill the post.

Denyssen resumed the private practice of an advocate (barrister) and would later become an outspoken opponent of anglicisation. The 1830s would find him publicly urging the importance of asserting what was becoming an increasingly 'Afrikaner' (as distinct from Cape Dutch) identity.[62] Truter was similarly excluded from the new regime and went into retirement after being succeeded by a new chief justice, Sir John Wylde. The removal of such officials and their replacement by British equivalents was part of a wider transformation of the Cape colonial administration following the Commission of Eastern Inquiry, particularly in the realm of the law. The transformation was wide ranging, but it lagged behind the actual conquest of the colony by more than two decades, one reason for the frustration voiced by the increasing numbers of recently arrived British settlers with whom Edwards allied himself.

Somerset had come to the Cape an autocratic conservative by reason of birth and upbringing, but his natural antipathy to those he stigmatised as 'Radicals' was only exacerbated by recent events in Britain itself. The years since Waterloo had seen a series of political upheavals in which many of Somerset's class and political outlook, as well as those of more

---

[61] L. H. Meurant, *Sixty Years Ago; or Reminiscences of the Struggle for the Freedom of the Press in South Africa*, orig. publ. 1885, facs. edn (Cape Town: Africana Connoisseurs Press, 1963), p. 26.
[62] *Dictionary of South African Biography*, vol. III, p. 208.

moderate views, saw the sparks of revolution. The anti-machinist Luddite attacks of 1812–1815 were followed by the Spa Fields riots of 1816, the Blanketeers March and the Pentrich uprising of 1817. The 1819 'Peterloo' massacre of unarmed men, women and children attending an open-air meeting at Manchester calling for parliamentary reform was succeeded the following year by the exposure of the Cato Street conspiracy to blow up the prime minister and cabinet. These represented only the most prominent moments in an all-pervading climate of class-based anxiety felt amongst the elite, an anxiety prompted by an equally class-based resentment amongst the lower orders.[63] It would have important implications for the thrust of reform initiatives in both colonial Australia and at the Cape.

At the Cape an urgent overhaul of the administration seemed necessary not only to bring colonial governance into line with demands for greater probity in administrative practice, but also to make the colony more attractive to British immigration. In an economy shifting under the forces of industrialisation, those who found themselves on the more precarious rungs of the gentry in Britain were to be encouraged to make homes elsewhere by various schemes of colonial emigration. These emigration initiatives played out in different ways in distinct colonial contexts. In the Australian colonies, as we shall see, they dovetailed with an overhaul of the convict system designed to combat crime rates by making transportation a greater deterrent to the criminally inclined poor. In New South Wales and Van Diemen's Land this meant changing policies of land grants and convict assignment in order to favour free emigrants with capital over emancipated felons. The same British problems with regard to population pressure and social upheaval sought solutions at the Cape Colony in a subsidised emigration scheme that substantially increased the number of British settlers. Landing at the Cape across the first half of 1820, around 4000 people were to be established on an eastern frontier that was in the midst of heightened tension and episodic full-scale warfare with the amaXhosa.[64]

---

[63] The classic account remains that of E. P. Thompson, *The Making of the English Working Class* (London: Penguin, 1980), first published 1963.

[64] The settlers' role as a projected 'buffer zone' between expanding Cape Dutch pastoralists and the amaXhosa has been much debated by South African historians. The consensus now places more emphasis on metropolitan social problems as a motivation for the emigration scheme. By contrast the establishment of a Khoekhoen farming community in the Upper Kat River Valley of the Eastern Cape from 1829 was deeply implicated in the strategies of frontier warfare. For an account of the settlement and its tragic betrayal see R. Ross, *The Borders of Race in Colonial South Africa: The Kat River Settlement, 1829–1856* (Cambridge University Press, 2014).

This group of new arrivals, who would become known as the '1820 Settlers', developed as one of the biggest thorns in Governor Somerset's flesh, though ironically he had initially promoted the idea of assisted emigration. The scheme proved an unmitigated disaster, planned as it largely had been more as a way for the Tory government in Britain to show its concern for postwar unemployment than with due regard for circumstances on the ground.[65] The raft of problems contributing to its failure included the ecological (infertile soil, crop diseases and natural disasters), strategic (escalating frontier warfare with the amaXhosa) and social (most settlers lacked the capital, experience or inclination to succeed as farmers). Adding to this potent mix of dissatisfaction was the fact that amongst the 1820 settlers, and amongst the increasing numbers of British emigrants arriving in the colony in general, were a number of highly articulate and well-connected Whigs and Radicals. They would prove to be significant players in the debates over colonial reform heightened by the arrival of the Commission of Eastern Inquiry in 1823.

Prominent amongst the 1820 settlers was Thomas Pringle. Poet, journalist and evangelical reformer, Pringle was a product of both the Scottish Enlightenment and of concomitant transformations in the Scottish economy that saw his extended family pushed into circumstances that were sufficiently precarious for them to join the Cape assisted emigration initiative. Having moved from the eastern frontier to Cape Town, he was quick to see a potential role for men of letters in the colony. He wrote urging his friend John Fairbairn to join him in various publication and education schemes. The advantages were not only material: 'I am projecting a magazine to enlighten South Africa'.[66] In 1824, Pringle, who had served as co-editor of the celebrated literary review *Blackwood's Edinburgh Magazine*, would, together with Fairbairn, a contributor to the same publication, take on the editorship of George Greig's *South African Commercial Advertiser*. A detractor would later sniff, 'I have no doubt that Mr Pringle conceived himself to be a very great Man, quite a Dr Johnson in his way, among the Cape people most of whom I take it are as well qualified to read as he may be to write'.[67]

Fairbairn and Pringle's editorship of the *Advertiser* was a carefully guarded secret. The public face of the paper was Greig, its printer and proprietor. The presses upon which it was produced were the property of

---

[65] Peires, 'The British and the Cape', 474–5; A. Lester, *Imperial Networks: Creating Identity in Nineteenth-Century South Africa and Britain* (London: Routledge, 2001), pp. 48–50.
[66] Pringle to Fairbairn, 24 November 1822, Randolph Vigne (ed), *The South African Letters of Thomas Pringle* (Cape Town: Van Riebeeck Society, 2011), p. 82.
[67] Lockhart to Hay, 30 Oct. 1826, Private Correspondence of Robert Hay, TNA, CO 323/144.

the 'upheaval' in South Africa that followed Bigge's and Colebrook's Commission within a liberalising and reforming framework, for all that it was cast in the mould of fundamentally racialised imperial interests.

In Australia these same interests have been viewed in a very different register and the contrast with how Bigge is remembered there – indeed, the fact that he is remembered at all – is profound. Far from being a faceless bureaucrat, in Australia Bigge occupies 'a pre-eminent place in the annals of Australian infamy'.[80] He is the man who ended the egalitarian rule of Lachlan Macquarie (1810–1821) the governor who, in this version of events, was 'The Father of Australia' and one of the earliest embodiments of the national values of a 'fair go' for all.[81] Macquarie looms large in the popular imagination. His name is affixed to landmarks and institutions country-wide, and his extravagant building projects (whose cost was so deplored by Bigge) still dominate what survives of Sydney's colonial townscape. Macquarie's downfall at the hands of an alliance of imperial bureaucrats and ambitious colonial 'exclusives' is still mourned, and Bigge easily fits the bill of villain. The 'Bigge reports' – that is, the three reports of Bigge's first Commission of Inquiry – rate a chapter in Martin Crotty and David Andrew Roberts's 2009 collection *Turning Points in Australian History*. Here they are cast in a provocative essay by Raymond Evans as an imperial hatchet-job on colonial egalitarianism and 'a decisive break in the erratic evolution of Australian colonial society towards democracy'.[82] A few months before Australia celebrated the 200th anniversary of Macquarie's assumption of office, the New South Wales Annual History Lecture was delivered by the then chief justice of New South Wales on 'The Macquarie Bicentennial: A Reappraisal of the Bigge Reports'. It is impossible to think of a high-profile public lecture in South Africa being devoted to the same subject, nor to there

and its extensions 1800–1854' in that collection. In the *Cambridge History of Australia* (A. Bashford and S. Macintyre (eds.), 2013), both Bigge and his Commission appear as (multiple) index entries. Exhaustive survey volumes such as these are inevitably faced with vexed choices as to what to include and emphasise. My point is not to praise one choice above the other but to indicate that popular knowledge about Bigge and his Commissions loom so much larger in Australia than they do in South Africa that it would have been difficult for the editors of either volume to do otherwise than make the choices they did.

[80] J. J. Spigelman, 'The Macquarie Bicentennial: A reappraisal of the Bigge reports'. History Council of New South Wales Annual History Lecture 2009 (Sydney: History Council New South Wales, 2009), p. 5.

[81] Both phrases are to be found in publicity material for *Lachlan Macquarie: The Father of Australia* (Ronin Films, 2010), http://www.roninfilms.com.au/feature/6093/lachlan-macquarie-father-of-australia.html, viewed 17 Jan. 2014.

[82] R. Evans, '19 June 1822: Creating "an object of real terror" ~ The tabling of the first Bigge Report', in M. Crotty and D. A. Roberts (eds.), *Turning Points in Australian History* (University of New South Wales Press, 2009), p. 61.

being sufficient foreknowledge amongst the audience for it to be framed as a 'reappraisal'. There are of course a number of reasons for this, of which the far more recognisably postcolonial situation of South Africa after apartheid is perhaps the most obvious. British imperial governors, and even less, obscure bureaucrats, do not rate highly in national commemoration there. In Australia, where power remains concentrated in the hands of the descendants of European emigrants (convicts amongst them), the political imperatives of public commemoration are unsurprisingly different. But Bigge's greater visibility in Australian compared with South African memory and historiography also points us to important differences in the intention, content and consequences of his original reports.

In understanding the motives behind the Bigge Commission of Inquiry in Australia, we must start with the same British circumstances that had seen emigrants like Pringle and family arrive in the Cape amongst the 1820 settlers. The social upheaval at the end of the Napoleonic Wars saw a dramatic rise in convict transportation. In the six years after 1815 the free emigrant population of New South Wales more than doubled also, from 12 911 to 29 783.[83] It is worth remembering how much smaller the Australian settlement still was than the Cape in this period, the non-indigenous Cape population being almost double that of New South Wales at around 75 000. Bigge arrived in Sydney on 26 September 1819, coincidentally a month after the Peterloo Massacre. His instructions from the secretary of state included the warning that by 'ill considered Compassion for Convicts... their Situation in New South Wales be divested of all Salutary Terror'. If so:

Transportation cannot operate as an effectual example on the Community at large, and as a proper punishment for those Crimes against the Commission of which His Majesty's Subjects have a right to claim protection, nor as an adequate Commutation for the utmost Rigour of the Law.[84]

This emphasis on 'salutary terror' was taken up by Commissioner Bigge in his investiture speech upon arrival and has garnered the most attention in historical assessments of his reports.[85]

---

[83] G. Karskens, 'The early colonial presence 1788–1822', in A. Bashford and S. Macintyre (eds.), *Cambridge History of Australia* (Cambridge University Press, 2013), vol. I, pp. 116–18. Indigenous population levels are far harder to calculate. Numbers had declined substantially by the 1820s although Aboriginal people remained a significant and visible presence in the public spaces of central Sydney, at least until the middle of the decade.

[84] Bathurst to Bigge, 6 Jan. 1819, *HRA*, 1:10, pp. 7–8.

[85] Spigelmann, 'Reappraisal', 5, 12.

Macquarie considered the Australian colonies to be places of 'reclamation as well as punishment' and he sought to balance the needs of former convicts (emancipists) with those who were dubbed the 'exclusives' – free settlers who considered that political rights and socio-economic advantage should remain restricted to their ranks. Yet at the time of Bigge's arrival in the Australian colonies, these free settlers were overwhelmingly outnumbered by convicts and their descendants, a group that also controlled about half the wealth in New South Wales and had grown in confidence under Macquarie's patronage.[86] As with the Cape, the colony of New South Wales was highly centralised. In 1821 around 94 per cent of the colony's population, 97 per cent of its cultivated land and more than 70 per cent of its livestock were located within a 70-kilometre radius of the town of Sydney.[87]

The key outcomes of the Bigge reports on New South Wales and Van Diemen's Land, tabled before the British Parliament in 1822 and 1823, were a reduction in public spending, a tightening up on the severity of convict punishment, a restriction on the rights and social opportunities of former convict 'emancipists' and a corresponding expansion in the horizons of their rivals, the free settlers. The central premise, in the phrase of historian John Ritchie, was to connect 'punishment and profit'.[88] As I discuss at length in the final chapter of this book, regulation and surveillance over convicts were substantially increased. Large-scale agriculture and pastoralism would be encouraged by preferential import duties, the provision of land and the assignment of convict labour. This new elite would also gain preferential access to land, patronage and political rights.

By the time Governor Ralph Darling arrived in New South Wales in 1825, migrants and emancipists constituted some 45 per cent of a population of 36 366.[89] Under Bigge's recommendations, convicts would be removed from the pernicious influence of vice-ridden towns and redistributed to the redemptive isolation of frontier districts. As pastoralism began spreading over increasing areas of prime hunting land, consequences for the Indigenous people of this massive expansion in the colony's economy and geographical extent would be catastrophic. Heightened frontier warfare was paralleled by increased coercion and disciplinary violence against perceived convict troublemakers. These individuals were to be removed from the settlement itself and consigned to newly established (or re-established in the case of Norfolk Island) sites of

---

[86] S. Macintyre, *Concise History of Australia* (Cambridge University Press, 1999), pp. 50–1.
[87] L. Ford and D. A. Roberts, 'Expansion 1820–1850', in A. Bashford and S. Macintyre (eds.), *Cambridge History of Australia* (Cambridge University Press, 2013), vol. I, p. 122.
[88] Ritchie, *Punishment and Profit*.   [89] Fletcher, *Ralph Darling*, p. 80.

'secondary punishment'. Far from increasing social order, many of these initiatives instead exacerbated resistance from convicts and Indigenous people while the growing geographical extent of the colonies stretched disciplinary measures to the limit.[90] Such developments would have a direct impact upon the life and ultimately death of William Edwards once he returned to New South Wales in 1824.

Yet, for all the 'terror', both intended and unintended, that they unleashed, Bigge's recommendations also contained the seeds for far greater colonial rights in the future. Nor, for all the disciplinary thrust of the reports, would these rights ultimately be confined to those who had come to the colonies as free men. In both the Australian and Cape colonies, the recommendations of the Commissions of Inquiry established new supreme courts, restrictions on the executive power of governors and greater legislative responsibility. Such measures were not intended to favour settler autonomy, but to reassert a centralised *metropolitan* control over unlicensed gubernatorial despotism on the periphery. Yet these very provisions paradoxically opened up spaces for constitutional developments in the following decade that would see greater colonial legislative and judicial responsibility. The New South Wales Act of 1823, a direct consequence of Bigge's recommendations, ended gubernatorial despotism by establishing an appointed legislative council and a supreme court. Significantly for a colony run as a penal settlement, it required that the chief justice certify that any proposed legislation was not 'repugnant to English law'. It also raised the possibility of locally overriding the operation of English laws if they were deemed in contradiction to the particular – or as many said, peculiar – context of the colony. These arrangement gave the courts in New South Wales 'the power to nullify government policy on the basis of their interpretation of colonial circumstances',[91] a political influence far in advance of that exerted by the courts in England itself, and they could become a powerful force for pushing governance in a more liberal direction.

The governor most directly affected by these changes in the constitution of New South Wales would be Ralph Darling, arguably another unfortunate choice for a time of administrative transition. Although from a very different social background to that of Lord Charles Somerset at the Cape, Darling [Figure 3] bore some similarities to his aristocratic counterpart. In their defence, both men were put under considerable strain by relentless factional opposition, but neither would be well served

---

[90] Ford and Roberts, 'Expansion', 124–8.
[91] D. Neal, *The Rule of Law in a Penal Colony: Law and Power in Early New South Wales* (Cambridge University Press, 1991), p. 87.

Figure 3 Ralph Darling in 1825, the year he became governor of New South Wales.

by their inflexible impatience with local protests against alleged gubernatorial despotism. In Darling's case this related to his insistence that New South Wales was a penal colony in which the 'free institutions of Great Britain' were 'extremely inapplicable to the inhabitants of New South Wales though born in England'. In a sentiment that Somerset might have echoed at the Cape in relation to the new Whig and Radical arrivals, Darling concluded that 'the evil of this place is the passion which exists that New South Wales should be the counterpart of England'.[92]

They may have had similar political allegiances, but Somerset and Darling were operating in extremely different constitutional circumstances and with very different men at the helm of their judiciaries. The Cape was a conquered colony and, until the recommendations of the Commission of Eastern Inquiry took effect in 1828, it remained under a Roman–Dutch legal system – with Somerset's close ally Johannes Andreas Truter as president of the Council of Justice. In tactical terms it would have made more sense, at least in London's eyes, for Somerset to have anticipated the reforms that were clearly coming by exercising his authority in a less dogmatic and more flexible way. Technically, however, he generally operated within the confines of the law in some of the less politically astute decisions we will see him make across the chapters that follow. The administrative overhaul at the Cape would come only after the end of Somerset's tenure as governor. For Darling, however, the constitutional landscape had already changed. The Commission of Inquiry into the Australian colonies predated that into the Cape, and the New South Wales Act of 1823 that resulted placed Darling in a far less secure position than Somerset with regard to their shared assumptions about the proper operation of colonial governance. One stark example of particular relevance to the case of William Edwards is in the battles that both governors fought against a newly independent colonial press, established in New South Wales and the Cape Colony in the same year, 1824.

New South Wales and Van Diemen's Land were judged to be colonies of settlement rather than conquest, an idea now widely notorious in its dismissal of rights held by Indigenous Australians. In relation to questions of sovereignty, the two Australian colonies were considered 'uninhabited' prior to European arrival. This meant very different legal parameters to those of the Cape. As Blackstone's *Commentaries on the Laws of England* expressed it, 'if an uninhabited colony be discovered and planted by English subjects, all the English laws then in being, which are the birthright of every subject, are immediately there in force'.[93] The presence of convicts and former convicts in the colony nevertheless profoundly complicated this assumption. The legal paradox presented by the penal system in the Australian colonies was evident almost from the

---

[92] Darling to Hay, 9 Feb. 1827 (secret and confidential), *HRA*, 1:13, p. 99.
[93] W. Blackstone, *Commentaries on the Laws of England*, first published 1765; facs. of 9th edn, 1783 (New York & London: Garland, 1978), vol. I, p. 107; Neal, *Rule of Law*, p. xii.

start. Within months of the British occupation of New South Wales in 1788, two convicts successfully brought a civil action against the master of the *Alexander* for the recovery of their missing luggage. Henry and Susannah Kable had both been sentenced to hang,. As such, according to the British legal doctrine of 'felony attaint', they were immediately dead in law. They could not give evidence or sue in court, and their goods were forfeit to the Crown. David Collins (a marine officer acting as judge-advocate of the fledgling colony) ignored felony attaint, however, and the court awarded the Kables £15 for the loss of their goods. From the very outset, therefore, convicts had rights in New South Wales that they did not possess under English law. The eventual reconciliation of English law and colonial practice would unfold through two decades of controversy in the wake of the Bigge reforms.[94]

Its 'character as a Penal Settlement', as James Stephen of the Colonial Office put it in 1828, was the 'great anomaly in the condition of this Colony'.[95] Blackstone's comments on the legal 'birthright' of 'English subjects' had a crucial caveat: 'But this must be understood with very many and very great restrictions. Such colonists carry with them only so much of the English law, as is applicable to their own situation and the condition of an infant colony'.[96] How then, should this 'situation' be defined? And at what moment did a colony's 'infancy' end and this 'planting' be said to have occurred? For the new chief justice, Francis Forbes, this transition was confirmed by the New South Wales Act of 1823, and Forbes would do all he could to hold Governor Darling to his own interpretation of these new constitutional parameters. This ushered in a period of profound conflict in the relationship between, and the disputed powers of, the executive and judiciary.[97] If the rights of convicts and of former convicts were by no means supported by the judicial reorganisation that followed the Bigge Commission, it nonetheless opened up

---

[94] B. Kercher, *An Unruly Child: A History of Law in Australia* (Sydney: Allan & Unwin, 1995), pp. 22–3, 36–8; also Kercher, *Debt, Seduction and Other Disasters: The Birth of Civil Law in Convict New South Wales* (Sydney: Federation Press, 1996).

[95] J. Stephen, annotated commentary on amendments to the New South Wales Act of 1823, TNA, CO 201/195 Offices: House of Commons, Admiralty, Crown Agents, King's Agent, Commander-in-Chief, Board of Trade, East India Company, Foreign, Home and Law Officers.

[96] Blackstone, *Commentaries*, vol. I, p. 107.

[97] C. H. Currey, *Sir Francis Forbes: The First Chief Justice of the Supreme Court of New South Wales* (Sydney: Angus & Robertson, 1968); Fletcher, *Ralph Darling*; Brendan Edgeworth, 'Defamation law and the emergence of a critical press in colonial New South Wales 1824–1831', *Australian Journal of Law and Society*, 6 (1990–1991), 50–82; J. M. Bennett, *Sir Francis Forbes: First Chief Justice of New South Wales 1823–1837* (Sydney: Federation Press, 2001); L. Ford, *Settler Sovereignty: Jurisdiction and Indigenous People in America and Australia 1788–1836* (Harvard University Press, 2010).

possibilities for a free society that would ultimately benefit far more than just the 'exclusives'. In the short term, these constitutional problems led to inconsistencies in authority and governance that would be ruthlessly exploited by William Edwards and his political allies, particularly those within the colonial press.

The distinct circumstances of the Cape and the Australian colonies that Edwards encountered necessitated variation in the content and emphasis of the imperial Commissions of Inquiry, one reason why they have been viewed so differently by historians and in popular memory. Yet they were not fundamentally contradictory. Ordered by the same secretary of state and led by the same individual, they were also part of the same metropolitan mindset and representative of the shift in thinking on imperial governance in this period. The Commissions were the instruments of broader forces of transformation, at once liberal and disciplinary. It was these forces with which Edwards was to contend as he embarked upon his unconventional career as a colonial reformer.

2 'A Daemon behind the Curtain'
Reputation, parliamentary politics and political spin

When Bigge and Colebrooke presented the secretary of state with their investigations into Edwards's background in July 1824, they did so in the knowledge that the notary's recent accusations against the governor's 'private character' carried serious political implications for the progress of their Commission of Inquiry. In particular, they wrote to Bathurst, 'we are apprehensive, that they may become the subject of public observation in England, before we shall be able to notice the connexion in which they stand with some of the most important objects of our public inquiry'. The care they took into investigating such a seemingly unimportant personage underlines how ostensibly marginal figures like Edwards could do real damage to entrenched political interests when their causes were joined to opposition voices in the British Parliament. As their report acknowledged, the secretary of state needed to be armed against the public debate that was looming by 'a very brief & early notice of the sources from whence these violent attacks have proceeded'.[1] To do so, Bigge and Colebrooke deliberately made use of unofficial conduits of information. Marking their letter 'private' kept it outside the view of Parliament, where attacks on Somerset's Cape administration (and by implication on the Tory government in Britain with which he was allied) were becoming increasingly heated.

Somerset's period at the Cape during his second term as governor (1821–1826) was more than usually vexatious. In part this was unavoidable, a function of the problems described in the previous chapter. Frontier conflict, debates over unfree labour and tension between British and Dutch settlers were a volatile mix. The context would undoubtedly have proved a challenge to any colonial administration. In this instance, however, interpersonal frictions seriously hampered the government's ability to deal with the situation facing it. Following his return to the colony in

---

Somerset to Bigge, 27 May 1824, Bigge–Somerset correspondence. Rhodes House, University of Oxford, MSS Afr s. 24.

[1] Colebrooke and Bigge to Bathurst, 14 July 1824. Bathurst Papers, BL, 57/87, no. 6.

'A Daemon behind the Curtain' 61

November 1821, Somerset and the acting governor, Sir Rufane Donkin, embarked upon a bitter and long-standing feud in which the colonial secretary, Colonel Christopher Bird, became embroiled. Somerset was convinced that Bird had gathered around him a set of conspirators ('the Aviary' as he called them in letters to Bigge[2]) who were devoted to undermining the governor at every point. The inability of the governor and his colonial secretary to work together seriously compromised both the unity and effectiveness of the administration.[3]

The specific allegations made against the administration, and Somerset personally, were protean in nature. Although William Edwards was not the sole instigator of these scandals, he was front and centre of their most powerful phase. There was extensive criticism of the administration's handling of the frontier situation and the problems of the 1820 settlers. The governor's son, Colonel Henry Somerset, was a particular cause of complaint. Somerset himself was accused of taking bribes for fraudulent land grants under the cover of horse trading. The infamous sale of the 'Sorcerer' colt (it changed hands for the enormous sum of 10 000 rixdollars) prompted a lengthy investigation by the Commissioners of Eastern Inquiry into the governor's personal conduct.[4] The scandals reached their climax in 1824 with the events that form the subject of this book: accusations of corruption in distributing liberated Africans, attacking the liberty of the press and deportation without trial. The suggestion that Somerset was engaged in sexual relations with the surgeon James Barry further tainted an administration already mired in charges of using draconian punishments, dirty tricks and espionage against British colonial subjects. All of this was unfolding in the midst of the Commission of Eastern Inquiry, whose presence only added to the glare of parliamentary scrutiny.

If the troubles of the Somerset regime in this period were unusually colourful in their specifics, ongoing controversies were more the rule than the exception in the imperial system. Parliamentary Commissions of Inquiry were one response to the systemic problems of colonial governance in this period. Dealing with such matters was also part of the routine business of the Colonial Office in London. Bigge and Colebrooke's report into Edwards's allegations against Somerset's 'private character' is a representative example of both the dangers anticipated from such scandals and the tactics employed to neutralise them. It demonstrates

---

[2] Somerset to Bigge, undated, 1824, Bigge–Somerset correspondence.
[3] Bigge to Wilmot Horton, Cape Town, 25 September 1823. Wilmot Horton Papers, Derbyshire Record Office. Catton Collection D3155/WH 2751.
[4] D'Escury and Lord Charles Somerset, TNA, CO 48/89.

the commissioners thoroughly investigating personal attacks made on colonial governors by even obscure individuals, doing so in order to provide the Colonial Office with ammunition against opposition in Parliament, and making use of private conduits of correspondence as their method. As several historians have emphasised, imperial bureaucrats in this period made (often highly effective) tactical use of a dual system of private and public information exchange to ward off the consequences of parliamentary scrutiny.[5] Tracking these practices highlights the role that marginal troublemakers could play in the relationship between oppositional politics and reform initiatives. It also underscores the importance of reputation management and political spin in the mechanics of imperial policy changes.

There were both opportunities and liabilities to such methods. Despite their strategic utility, relying on informal intelligence networks that were deliberately kept away from public scrutiny was a double-edged sword. It inspired a profound degree of paranoia on the part of colonial officials. The factionalism of the Somerset regime is an extreme example of a much wider phenomenon. The petty infighting of colonial regimes, what Lady Anne Barnard (wife to the Cape's colonial secretary in the 1790s) called 'the little politicks of our *Lilliput* court',[6] has been well recognised. The gossipy letters that were exchanged between private individuals (as well as public individuals acting deliberately in their private capacity) had an overtly strategic purpose. Such correspondents were essentially informing upon the activities of their neighbours and close associates and were being encouraged to do so in the interests of their political 'party'. As Zoë Laidlaw has demonstrated, the influence of such practices was increasingly seen as disruptive. As a result, private correspondence between colonial officials and anyone other than the secretary of state was banned in October 1835. Private information dispersed through interpersonal networks was largely replaced by a reliance on more statistical forms of information in the practice of imperial governance.[7] In the time of William Edwards, however, this lay in the future. Tracking the Colonial Office response to the Cape scandals provides us with a window into a particular moment in imperial governance and highlights the

---

[5] Eddy, *Britain and the Australian Colonies*; N. D. McLachlin, 'Bathurst at the Colonial Office 1812–1827: A reconnaissance', *Historical Studies: Australia and New Zealand*, 13 (1967–69), 477–502; Laidlaw, *Colonial Connections*.

[6] Lady Anne to Henry Dundas, 14 Dec 1799, in A. M. Lewin Robinson (ed.), *The Letters of Lady Anne Barnard to Henry Dundas from the Cape and Elsewhere 1793–1803, Together with her Journal of a Tour into the Interior and Certain other Letters* (Cape Town: Balkema, 1973), p. 209.

[7] Laidlaw, *Colonial Connections*, pp. 169–70, 178.

relationship between individual troublemakers and parliamentary politics, and the reform iniatives that flowed from this.

Inside the Colonial Office

By the time William Edwards arrived at the Cape in July 1823, he had spent eighteen months at large in the colonial networks that stretched across the Indian Ocean. He had experience on the fringes of British judicial administration in the formerly French colony of Mauritius, now marked for investigation by the Commission of Eastern Inquiry. In seeking employment as a clerk with the Commission at the Cape, Edwards hoped to become the smallest of cogs in the mechanism upon which imperial administration ran.

The engine of this great machine was the Colonial Office at No. 14 Downing Street, conveniently close to the Houses of Parliament. Despite its imposing position in the heart of Whitehall, it was a distinctly underwhelming locale. The basement was damp (to the point that it had to be periodically pumped out), the building was in ill repair and space was at a premium. By 1822 circumstances had become so cramped that the mounds of paper created by the occupants' responsibilities threatened to overwhelm them. Parliamentary Under-Secretary Robert Wilmot Horton opened negotiations for the Colonial Office to take over the house next door, 13 Downing Street, but their neighbour, the judge-advocate general, did not take kindly to the suggestion. Wilmot Horton sent the chancellor of the exchequer a graphic description of the overcrowding in 1826. With only one waiting room, visitors were herded promiscuously together: 'every person, whatever his Rank or Station may be, from a Governor General down to a Lascar', was not only forced to wait there, but also to overflow into the passages when the room became too crowded. The officials themselves were so much on top of one another, continued an exasperated Wilmot Horton, that undersecretaries did not have individual offices but were forced to squeeze in with their private secretaries. If a visitor wished to speak to him confidentially, Wilmot Horton complained, he either had to get rid of his secretary or (to stop the 'business of the day' being disrupted) conduct a sensitive conversation 'upon the Staircase'.[8] Matters moved slowly, but in 1827 a change of government finally ensured that the judge-advocate general lost both his position and his occupation of No. 13. The two houses were knocked together. Everyone got a lot more space, but the renovations failed to

---

[8] Robert Wilmot-Horton to J. C. Herries, Treasury, 15 December 1826, TNA, CO 324/146. Letters from Secretary of State (domestic).

solve the persistent damp problems, and the buildings continued to gently subside into the alluvial soil of the ancient watercourse upon which they were built.[9]

Responsibility for war and the colonies as well as internal affairs had previously fallen under the Home Office. A designated Colonial Office was established in 1795, consisting of a secretary of state, his private secretary, one undersecretary, six clerks, a housekeeper and two office-keepers. Two porters were hired from the start, and additional clerks were added to the household in time.[10] The office expanded in the nineteenth century, with the appointment of a parliamentary undersecretary in 1812 and a permanent undersecretary in 1825.[11]

For decades this would remain a small group of people working closely together in claustrophobic conditions. Even by 1830 those carrying real responsibility for decision-making across the vastness of the British empire numbered only around ten individuals.[12] Thinking about the spaces in which administration actually happens, and about the people who inhabit this space, is invariably instructive. It helps us to understand the transition going on within the Colonial Office from eighteenth- to nineteenth-century cultures of bureaucracy. It reminds us that politics in this period was still overwhelmingly individual rather than institutional, bound together by interpersonal connection, patronage and mutual obligation.[13]

Although established almost twenty years earlier, the Colonial Office that would emerge into the nineteenth century was above all the creation of one man: Henry Bathurst [Figure 4], third Earl Bathurst, secretary of state from 1812 to 1827. Bathurst's father had been lord chancellor, and he came from a family of government servants. In public he did not cut a charismatic figure. He addressed Parliament seldom, and with reluctance. Charles Greville, Bathurst's private secretary from 1812 to 1821, retrospectively summed him up in an oft-quoted assessment as

a very amiable man with a good understanding, though his talents were far from brilliant, a High Churchman and a High Tory, but a cool Politician, a bad speaker,

---

[9] D. M. Young, *The Colonial Office in the Early Nineteenth Century* (London: Longmans, 1961), p. 146.

[10] Young, *Colonial Office*, p. 14.

[11] Like the secretary of state, parliamentary undersecretaries were political appointments and could change according to who held power in Parliament. Permanent undersecretaries were non-political civil service appointments.

[12] Laidlaw, *Colonial Connections*, p. 41.

[13] J. M. Bourne, *Patronage and Society in Nineteenth-Century England* (London: Edward Arnold, 1986). For those wishing to understand the workings of the period, Young's *Colonial Office* remains an exemplary study.

Figure 4 Henry Bathurst, third Earl Bathurst, secretary of state for war and the colonies, 1812–1827.

a good writer, greatly averse to changes, but acquiescing in many. He was nervous and reserved, with a good deal of humour, habitually a jester.[14]

[14] Charles Greville, diary entry of 24 July 1834 (on hearing news of Bathurst's death), in P. Morrell (ed.), *Leaves from the Greville Diary: A New and Abridged Edition* (London: Eveleigh Nash & Grayson, 1929), pp. 236–7. Greville went on to complain that by

66   Imperial Underworld

It was said of Bathurst that he was the last man in London to wear a pigtail. He supposedly cut it off and sent it round in an official box to ministerial colleagues after losing office. It is a fitting image of changing times, but the story probably says more about Bathurst's public image than about the man himself.[15] It is certainly belied by portraits from at least a decade earlier in which Bathurst, sporting a suitably modish crop, was painted by Sir Thomas Lawrence.

In fact the secretary of state was far more complex than this anecdote of his coiffure suggests. Greville's somewhat acid thumbnail sketch recognises the contradictions that lay at the heart of his former employer but fails to do justice to their subtlety in the effective running of the Colonial Office. Bathurst's personal views may indeed have turned towards the conservative, but he was a skilful pragmatist. He had no patience with those who behaved like throwbacks to an earlier era. Understandably, Somerset frequently exasperated him. Entertaining the Cape governor at his country house, he reported: 'Lord Charles was much less boring & unreasonable than I expected. Indeed I did not give him time to be the first, and I suppose he thought it better policy not to appear the other.'[16] Above all, Bathurst sought to protect his office from the hostile attention of critics in Parliament. He was no rousing orator. He sent his subordinates into public battle in the House against the likes of Henry Brougham and Joseph 'Economy' Hume ('a post-box for colonial complaints', in the words of historian J. J. Eddy).[17] But he had a keen eye for political spin and a genius for managing people. Henry Taylor, who joined the Colonial Office as a clerk in 1823, was full of admiration for Bathurst's skill in this regard, remembering some forty years later how

I could not have fallen in with any man in whose official style there was more of the dignity of good-nature. He could be severe when necessary; but in his severity there was generally a parental tone; and to the severest of his rebukes he could contrive to give a colouring of consideration for the culprit.[18]

Greville classed Bathurst as a 'habitual jester', and his dry sense of humour is certainly sprinkled liberally through his private correspondence. Bathurst believed in delegation (to the point of sending blank

the 'mistaken kindness' of appointing him private secretary but giving him little real employment, Bathurst 'abandoned' him to a life of 'idleness and dissipation'.

[15] E. Cokayne et al. (eds.), *The Complete Peerage of England, Scotland, Ireland, Great Britain and the United Kingdom, Extant, Extinct or Dormant*, new edn, 6 vols. (Gloucester, UK: Alan Sutton, 2000), vol. II, p. 30. The source is the author and memoirist Lady Louisa Stuart.
[16] Bathurst to Hay, 13 Sept. 1826, Bathurst papers, BL, 57/58.
[17] Eddy, *Britain and the Australian Colonies*, p. 59.
[18] H. Taylor, *Autobiography of Henry Taylor* (London: Longmans, 1885), vol. I, p. 69.

sheets of writing paper into the office bearing his signature[19]) and relied heavily on his subordinates. He was not above poking fun at his own habits, particularly in correspondence with Permanent Under-Secretary Robert Hay, with whom he forged an especially close relationship. Writing from Brighton, he admitted: 'I shall be in Town on Saturday, but not time enough, or with disposition enough (to speak more correctly) to go to the Office.'[20]

Bathurst spent significant amounts of time running matters away from Downing Street, particularly at Cirencester Park, his country estate in Gloucester, eighty-eight miles to the west of London. Official business followed him around the country, not always successfully. As Bathurst explained to Hay: 'Ten hours after I sent off the express, the Box was found in the Butler's Pantry. I did not send another express after the first, as I thought it would be too late to rectify the mistake.'[21] It was by no means an isolated case of misplaced paperwork. Correspondence from the commissioners about Somerset's troubles 'has been found in looking for some other papers, in a drawer of Lady Bathurst's table, having given it her nearly two years ago to show to the D[uche]ss of Beaufort'.[22] When in London, however, No. 14 Downing Street doubled as the secretary of state's official residence. In both its domestic organisation and its business operations, in many ways the Colonial Office was like a private house. The same housekeeper, Maria Caldwell (later Pillochody), was in residence between 1795 and 1837, on a salary of £100 a year. Female servants were kept for housekeeping duties, male servants doubled as porters and messengers and could thus supplement their income.[23] Additional clerks were added to the household in times of extra copying.

The organisation was moving out of *ancien regime* patronage and into modern bureaucratic efficiency, but the process was slow, and marked by idiosyncrasies. Deadlines and the demands of professionalism jostled uneasily with a culture that assumed that social status was based upon the possession of leisure. The lives of Colonial Office clerks exemplified this contradiction. It was they who kept the wheels of bureaucracy turning. Although printing and lithography were available, they were uneconomic for daily business. The paperwork was immense, and clerks went through quills at a tremendous rate: witness the 6000 pens ordered between April 1795 and January 1796 when there was a staff of only nine.[24] Every overseas dispatch, for example, needed to be hand-copied three times. An

---

[19] McLachlin, 'Bathurst', 494.
[20] Bathurst to Hay, 1 Feb. 1827, BL, 57/59; also Bathurst to Hay, 6 Sept. 1826, BL, 57/58; Bathurst to Hay, 26 Sept. 1825, BL, 57/57.
[21] Bathurst to Hay, 31 March 1826, BL, 57/58.
[22] Bathurst to Hay, 14 Aug. 1826, BL, 57/58.   [23] Young, *Colonial Office*, p. 131.
[24] Young, *Colonial Office*, p. 135.

original was sent immediately, a second by a later mail to guard against accidents such as shipwreck or piracy, with the third duplicate kept as a record. Yet Colonial Office clerks during this period kept leisurely hours (eleven to four, when necessary extending into the evening but never in the early morning). The arrival and departure of suitable vessels nevertheless prompted an abrupt change of pace. Clerks descended into a vortex of overtime copying, with huge bursts of activity required to make the eight o'clock mail coach for Falmouth. There was much quarrelling, and an endless blame game played out amongst different government departments over clerks and messengers who took their deadlines down to the wire. Holding up the mail was a dire administrative sin. If correspondence was late, or delivered late to the mail coach, it could miss the sailing of the required vessel. Being late by even a few minutes could mean a delay in communication of weeks or even months. The assumption that clerks needed time outside the office to pursue the social lives of gentlemen was nonetheless slow to erode. The demands of gentility meant that extra costs were incurred for heating and lighting in winter. Even in the midst of a mania for economy, it was more important that clerks follow the daily rhythm of men of social status than that they be tied to natural daylight hours.

Bathurst's man in the House of Commons during the Edwards scandals was Robert Wilmot Horton. Born Robert Wilmot, he added his wife's surname to his own in 1823. The change was a condition of his father-in-law's will, whereby the couple inherited the family estate of Catton Hall in Derbyshire. Anne Beatrix Horton's financial assets were more than matched by her appearance. Lord Byron immortalised her in the poem 'She walks in Beauty, like the night'. The poet was less enamoured of her bureaucrat husband, who also happened to be his own cousin. Byron famously penned an acid thumbnail sketch of 'Wilmot the small wit' in a rhyming letter to his publisher in 1818.[25] For all Byron's jaundiced views, Wilmot Horton would prove invaluable to the Colonial Office. If Bathurst was the 'bad speaker' that Greville claimed, then Wilmot Horton was an eloquent one and highly effective as the Colonial Office's designated defence-dog on the floor of the House of Commons.

James Stephen Jun., legal advisor to the Colonial Office (later permanent undersecretary) was an equally important asset and would play a similarly prominent part in the events associated with William Edwards's career in the colonies. Quite unlike the secretary of state, Stephen found it so impossible to delegate that he was prone to periodic collapse. Initially employed on a contract basis, he kept up his private work as a barrister,

---

[25] Young, *Colonial Office*, pp. 49–50.

but the demands of the Colonial Office on top of trying to sustain his practice proved so much that he suffered a breakdown in 1822. From 1823 Stephen moved permanently to the Colonial Office, inspired in part by his belief that he could gain some influence there over the great question of slavery. His arrival on a permanent basis, together with the appointment in 1825 of a second undersecretary, Robert William Hay, eased the burden of work somewhat. James Stephen's son Leslie would later claim that his father, an ardent evangelical, had enjoyed his first cigar so much that he vowed never to smoke another one. The gashes that periodically marred his face came from an insistence on being clean shaven coupled with a refusal to pander to vanity by looking into a mirror.[26] Stephen complained that the insistence that clerks be gentlemen made for too much informality and undermined office discipline. As a chronic workaholic, he found it unacceptable to employ men who needed to sandwich their official business into a window between morning rides and afternoon dinners. By the 1830s Stephen's view had prevailed, and he was presiding over a far greater degree of professionalisation, with clerks required to work until 6 pm and copyists hired on a piecework basis.[27]

During the time of William Edwards, however, the Colonial Office's amalgam of gentleman's club and official civil service was most clearly manifested in the way in which all correspondence (and therefore all administration) took place simultaneously on two levels: one public, the other private. This was absolutely fundamental to how Bathurst operated. Undersecretaries Wilmot Horton and Robert Hay were both willing participants, and Hay would become particularly associated with the practice. Stephen, on the other hand, deplored it, and his was the view that would ultimately prevail as Stephen eased out and eventually replaced Hay as permanent undersecretary in 1836.[28] Historian N. D. McLachlin goes to the heart of the matter when he describes the 'dual system of administration' developed by Bathurst: 'despatches announced official decisions and ostensible reasons for them, private letters went to the heart of the matter'.[29] The practice has been much criticised by reformers and historians alike. J. J. Eddy judged it an 'invidious and subversive' system that 'encouraged the reporting of gossip which was often unfounded'.[30] McLachlin called it 'the most serious flaw in Bathurst's whole administration',[31] even as he recognised it for what it

---

[26] E. T. Williams, 'The Colonial Office in the Thirties', *Historical Studies, Australia and New Zealand*, 2:7 (May 1943), 154.
[27] Young, *Colonial Office*, pp. 254–5.   [28] Laidlaw, *Colonial Connections*, pp. 52–3.
[29] McLachlin, 'Bathurst', 501.   [30] Eddy, *Britain and the Australian Colonies*, p. 33.
[31] McLachlin, 'Bathurst', 502.

was – the political *habitus* of the eighteenth century. It rode roughshod over public accountability and would not outlast the transition to a modern bureaucracy, but as a management tool it did possess particular (if self-interested) advantages. Nothing, indeed, proves its effectiveness more than the way in which the Colonial Office was able to successfully weather the storms in public opinion in which Edwards played so prominent a part. That it was marshalled against these controversies simultaneously underlines their importance in the relationship between the workings of the Colonial Office and the operation of parliamentary politics and the British public sphere.

'There are few assemblies more unjust': managing parliamentary politics

Amongst Bathurst's key concerns were to keep the workings of his office outside the scrutiny of the House of Commons, where debate was hard to control and outcomes were unpredictable. The publication of parliamentary proceedings from the early nineteenth century and the growing influence of newspapers and periodicals had shifted and widened the domain of debate in Britain even before the parliamentary reforms of the 1830s. Bathurst recognised the fact that the Colonial Office was subject to public opinion and was impatient with Somerset's very different political sensibilities. In September 1826 he saw fit to reprimand the Cape governor (in a letter carefully marked 'Private and Confidential') on this issue. In dealing with the Commission of Eastern Inquiry's investigations, it had come to the secretary of state's attention that Somerset evidently considered it 'degrading' to his 'rank and station' to summon witnesses in his own defence. Bathurst pointed out that this rested on a fundamental misreading of the current political climate:

> You must allow me to say that we do not consider in this country that rank & station make any man less amenable to public opinion, and that all subjects servants of the Crown are alike bound to vindicate themselves, when their conduct, in the service of the public is impeached.... Pretentions of this kind are rarely urged with a good grace by public men; and you must forgive me for adding that this was one of the last occasions where it was judicious to introduce them.[32]

Barthurt's reprimand speaks to the very heart of how ideas regarding the conduct and accountability of administrators were transforming in this period, shifting the proper notions of public masculinity into a more bourgeois and less aristocratic idiom. For all he has been regarded as

---

[32] Bathurst to Somerset, 4 Sept. 1826 ('Private and Confidential'), BL, 57/65. Strikethrough in original.

a conservative, Bathurst saw the nature of his changing times far more clearly than did Somerset. If, as I argued in the last chapter, proconsular despotism was still the dominant flavour of colonial governance in the 1820s, the private correspondence of Colonial Office officials demonstrates that it was becoming an increasing liability.

Bathurst's 1826 insistence on the importance of public opinion was not an isolated remark. It was part of a carefully orchestrated campaign to manage this most troublesome of colonial governors. The campaign is most clearly demonstrated in the unofficial correspondence being carried on between Robert Wilmot Horton and Lord Granville Somerset (the governor's nephew, junior treasury lord and MP for Monmouthshire). Running between late 1824 and late 1825, it tracks their response to the scandals instigated by Edwards and others at the Cape and their management of the political fallout that resulted in Britain.

This exchange is important for three reasons. First, it illuminates both men's recognition of the generational shift then happening as eighteenth-century notions of governance and public-sphere scrutiny were succeeded by nineteenth-century ones. Second, it recognises how much and how wide-ranging was the damage that someone like Edwards could do to the Tory alliance and helps us to understand why such seemingly obscure colonial misfits were taken so seriously. Finally, because it was 'most private and confidential' (and punctuated with repeated urgings to secrecy) it exhibits an almost startling degree of candour on the tactics of political spin that the Colonial Office employed to neutralise such scandals in the face of hostile elements in the House of Commons.

Having received copies of all the relevant documentation on William Edwards's anti-government crusade at the Cape, in December 1824 Lord Granville Somerset wrote a detailed letter of advice to Wilmot Horton on how he should handle the matter in Parliament. Lord Charles Somerset had clearly opened a flank to the opposition in press and Parliament by a series of tactical errors that I explore at some length across the following chapters. The main thrust of the letter from Lord Granville was therefore damage control:

It would... certainly be advantageous to all parties to stand off any thing like a pitched battle upon the subject of the Cape of Good Hope... But at the same time if these attacks enter in the Papers & if the Question is mooted in the House of commons I do not see how without abandoning Lord Charles altogether you can do otherwise than boldly support those parts of his conduct turning as much as possible the debate upon these, which are justifiable & palliating the others by existing circumstances.[33]

---

[33] Granville Somerset to Wilmot Horton, 5 Dec. 1824, Wilmot Horton Papers, Derbyshire Record Office, Catton Collection, D3155/WH 2876.

Almost a year later, Lord Granville Somerset recognised both the immediate and the wider problems raised for the Colonial Office and the Tory government by the growing chorus of critics:

> If the attention of the opposition is not diverted by matters of more importance, I fear the Cape of Good Hope affairs will cause no inconsiderable trouble in the H. of Commons this year. There is every reason to dislike such investigations, & there is on the other hand no possibility of eluding them. There are few assemblies more unjust in accusations of *detail* than that honourable House. And members are very apt to think that numerous accusations are equivalent to conviction of guilt. Nor are they often inclined to hear the defence, if the accusations do but bear the semblance of truth.[34]

Allowing attacks on Somerset free reign would only open the way to attacks on the Tories at home. Regardless of what the Colonial Office might think of how his relative had behaved, Lord Granville Somerset insisted that it was in the interest of the government to back him. 'To criminate an Aristocratist Governor when in office is most agreeable to [Joseph] Hume & Co' and unless the Tories were willing to cut his uncle loose entirely they would inevitably be tainted by association:

> Besides which I am convinced if Lord Charles were to be recalled upon this account, he would moot the Question in such a way as to put Government in a more awkward position than they can find themselves in if they support Him; I do not mean this as a *Threat*, but I think the Government can never go so far as to approve of all the attacks made upon Lord Charles, & that they would find it a very difficult course to steer when called upon to explain their motives for his recall.[35]

Lord Granville Somerset was perfectly aware that the course he was suggesting presented 'considerable inconvenience' for the Colonial Office, for the Tory administration and personally for Wilmot Horton, but he nevertheless insisted that it was the 'most expedient' course of action. There was a solution, he went on, if only Bathurst's office would pursue the right tactics: 'if Government moot the Question boldly blinking thru parts that are not tenable by want of information & relying upon them wherein there is no difficulty, they will not be left in the lurch by the H. of C. nor diminish their reputation.' All of this advice, of course, was to be strictly off the record: 'You may rely on my secrecy & I must beg yours for my letters.'[36] Even Lord Charles Somerset's brothers (Lord

---

[34] Granville Somerset to Wilmot Horton, 13 Nov. 1825 ('Most private and confidential'), Wilmot Horton Papers, D3155/WH 2876.
[35] Granville Somerset to Wilmot Horton, 5 Dec. 1824, Wilmot Horton Papers, D3155/WH 2876.
[36] Granville Somerset to Wilmot Horton, 5 Dec. 1824.

'A Daemon behind the Curtain'   73

Granville's father the sixth duke of Beaufort, and his uncle Lord Edward Somerset) were to be kept out the arrangements, in part because Lord Granville Somerset realised they did not truly appreciate the difficulties under which the Colonial Office was labouring in relation to the forces of public opinion.[37]

Wilmot Horton was clearly increasingly exasperated at having to defend Lord Charles before Parliament, particularly when rumours had reached him 'from very good though unofficial authority' that the Beaufort family and Governor Somerset himself regarded him as a 'liberal' who had not taken up the governor's case with sufficient vigour. He wrote a stringent rebuttal of such rumours to Lord Granville Somerset that also lays out the tactics he was using in the House to undercut the legitimacy of the accusations being made. In addition it delivered a stinging rebuke of Governor Somerset's failure to recognise the changing political climate in which they all necessarily now operated. In 1826, Bathurst would make much the same point, writing to the governor himself in the letter I have already quoted. Wilmot Horton reminded Lord Granville Somerset that he had repeatedly defended Lord Charles 'on the ground that there was a conspiracy against him, & that it was most unfair to trust to accusations without defence'. He did not need to remind Lord Granville that in the context of the House of Commons it would be 'utterly ineffectual' to be seen to be ducking investigation in 'a case which involved the questions of liberty & despotism'. What Lord Charles needed to realise, wrote Wilmot Horton, was that 'his tenure of the Cape Government is not only under the Colonial Department, but under Public Opinion as expressed in the House of Commons.' Colonial administration was a battleground, explained Wilmot Horton, with British public opinion a weapon that needed strategic deployment:

unless a Governor will impregnate his mind with the constant recollection of what may be said in Parliament upon any thing that he does, it is perfectly impossible but that he should get into scrapes from which it may be very difficult to extricate him:- and when he is surrounded by all the provocations of a factious party, he should remember that it is his interest not to play their game, but his own, & by temper & caution, to lead them into scrapes rather than the reverse.[38]

Lord Granville Somerset was born in 1792, a decade after Wilmot Horton. He was of the younger generation and well aware that the behaviour

---

[37] Granville Somerset to Wilmot Horton, 20 Dec. 1824, Wilmot Horton Papers, D3155/WH 2876.
[38] Wilmot Horton to Granville Somerset, 8 Nov. 1825 ('Private and Confidential'), Wilmot Horton Papers, D3155 /WH 3028.

of the older Beauforts was out of step with the times. Liaising between them and the Colonial Office clearly put him (Lord Granville) in what he considered 'rather a delicate situation' in the matter of his Uncle Charles's affairs at the Cape.[39] Lord Granville's reply to Wilmot Horton's somewhat fractious complaint was therefore conciliatory, and in a letter marked 'most private and confidential' he admitted that Lord Charles's brothers were urging a more vehement course of action in his defence, 'not knowing the House of Commons quite so well as myself'. Lord Granville Somerset was apologetic in recognising that his elders might 'think he [Lord Charles Somerset] is not defended with sufficient anxiety by the *Ministers* in the H. of Commons, because they do not reject all investigation when attacks are made upon him by Individuals of infamous Character'.[40] The emerging public sphere in which obscure men like Greig and Edwards could exert a real influence by holding public officials to account was clearly galling to a family such as the Beauforts.

Lord Granville declared himself cognisant, as his uncles were not, of the tactical nature of parliamentary politics and the importance of allowing for public opinion in devising stratagems. He assured Wilmot Horton that he did not agree with accusations made by Lord Charles and the Beauforts that the Colonial Office was unduly influenced by the ideologies of 'Liberalism' in failing to come to the governor's defence. Instead he recognised that 'to resist Investigations is not possible' and that it was necessary for government ministers to be motivated by larger questions than an individual family's 'Character & Feelings'. Unlike his father and uncles, Lord Granville was only too aware that Lord Charles's character and attitudes made him a political liability:

I go also still further as you must be aware & feel that there are certain points of attack, on which it will be difficult to make a triumphant parliamentary defence. I give Lord Charles full credit for ability, but I am also acquainted with the vehemence of his temper when roused & the indiscretions it will lead him into, I also know that in his amusements he is not so cautious, & does not take such precautions to remove himself from suspicion of making an unfair use of his situation as I should say was desirable.

Seeking to reassure an obviously chagrined Wilmot Horton, Lord Granville assured him that the sentiments of his father, the sixth duke of Beaufort were 'those of obligation rather than the reverse' for the way the Colonial Office had defended Lord Charles Somerset:

[39] Granville Somerset to Wilmot Horton, 13 Nov. 1825 ('Most private and confidential'), Wilmot Horton Papers, D3155/WH 2876.
[40] Granville Somerset to Wilmot Horton, 13 Nov. 1825.

'A Daemon behind the Curtain' 75

For tho' he may feel annoyed at the attacks & may not view Lord Charles's conduct so impartially as I do, he is nevertheless aware of the difficulties in which the Colonial Office, & you (its H. of Commons representative) are placed by these continued accusations.

Signing off, he reiterated that 'I need not add that I trust these communications may be strictly confidential.'[41]

I have quoted this correspondence at some length because it sheds so much light on the way an eighteenth-century British empire was transforming into its nineteenth-century iteration. If Lord Granville Somerset and Wilmot Horton could feel a wind of change blowing through the corridors of imperial governance, they still needed to devise strategies to deal with those like Governor Somerset and the elder Beauforts, who patently could not. By outlining exactly how and why 'Individuals of infamous Character' like Edwards were deemed important to both the Colonial Office and the Tory interest, the private correspondence of Bathurst and his staff demonstrates why it is worth looking at the operation of politics and reform from this angle. Finally, these clear articulations of the tactics of political spin cut the Gordian knot on an old controversy in South African historiography. In 1951 Michael Roberts published a detailed refutation of the then-current assumption that Lord Charles Somerset had been protected from impeachment by the powerful 'Beaufort Influence'.[42] Roberts ranked the Beaufort influence as small and dismissed the influence of Cape affairs: 'colonial questions were not questions upon which governments resigned, or significant damage could be done; at any rate, not before 1832.' Thus 'the suggestion that Liverpool's government was nervously cowering before the storm of indignation at Lord Charles's misdeeds is simply ludicrous.'[43] Although the once-heated debate about the 'Beaufort influence' is now unquestionably dated, the issue regains significance in the light of more recent arguments over the interconnected nature and the mechanisms of imperial politics. Historians have differed widely on how significant colonial issues were in metropolitan politics and society.[44] In this book I would argue that

---

[41] Granville Somerset to Wilmot Horton, 13 Nov. 1825.
[42] M. Roberts, 'Lord Charles Somerset and the "Beaufort Influence"', *Archives Year Book for South African History*, 2 (1951). His key target was Isobel Edwards's *The 1820 Settlers in South Africa: A Study in British Colonial Policy* (London: The Royal Society, 1934).
[43] Roberts, 'Somerset and the "Beaufort Influence"', 28–9.
[44] Eddy's view in the 1960s was that interest in colonial matters was 'fitful, intermittent, and secondary' (*Britain and the Australian Colonies*, p. 51). With the advent of new approaches to imperial history two decades later, a wider debate was ignited with Bernard Porter and John MacKenzie amongst the key protagonists. See J. M. MacKenzie, *Propaganda and Empire: The Manipulation of British Public Opinion 1880–1960* (Manchester University Press, 1984), J. M. MacKenzie (ed.), *Imperialism and*

seemingly obscure and local scandals on imperial peripheries did in fact have real implications for power relations at home and provided tactical advantage on questions and relationships that were much closer to the power plays of metropolitan politics than the original offence might suggest. Questions about the 'Beaufort influence' and the broader issue of attention to colonial matters in metropolitan public debate should be sought not just in crunching the numbers of how people were likely to vote publicly in the House of Commons, nor in considering published debate or the press, but also by looking into private correspondence. It was through this interplay between private and public methods of governance and sources of information that we can get a more accurate sense of the situation on the ground at the Colonial Office. It is here that we find Bathurst circumventing the obstacles presented by the new political landscape in which he was forced to operate.

Thus for all that Bathurst reprimanded Somerset for standing on his 'rank and station', concern about gubernatorial reputation pervaded the secretary of state's private correspondence. A private letter to Governor Thomas Brisbane of New South Wales in 1824, outlining a long series of criticisms of the New South Wales administration, invokes the concept:

I cannot close this private letter without bringing before you the representations which more or less officially are perpetually coming before me. . . . You will I trust attribute to its true motive whatever may be unpleasant in this long letter, – I have always considered and as long as I continue in this office, I shall always consider that the honor of an absent Governor is in my custody, and when I see perpetual attempts made to impeach it, I am bound to apprise him of it, and enable him to put me in possession of his vindication.

I feel myself more particularly called upon to do so now, as I foresee that there will be an attack upon both you and Major Goulburn [colonial secretary] in the course of the next session, and you will believe that my apprehensions are not without a foundation, when you see that the opposition papers have begun upon the subject.[45]

Three key elements of how Bathurst managed the interpersonal relations of colonial governance are laid clearly before us here: his judicious combination of circuits of information designated 'private' and 'official', the manner in which he justified personal criticisms by the duty to protect his correspondent's reputation, and the constant need to pre-empt the hostile attentions of Parliament and the opposition press. The Colonial

Popular Culture (Manchester University Press, 1986) and B. Porter, *The Absent-Minded Imperialists: Empire, Society and Culture in Britain* (Oxford University Press, 2004).
[45] Bathurst to Brisbane, 23 Aug. 1824, Bathurst Papers, BL, 57/64.

Office response to the Edwards scandals at the Cape should be considered one example of a much wider phenomenon.

Bathurst certainly felt as much exasperation as did Wilmot Horton about how Somerset was dealing with the unfolding situation at the Cape. In private notes to his undersecretaries, with whom he habitually enjoyed jesting, the secretary of state could be devastatingly candid.[46] He once described Somerset to Wilmot Horton as a 'Jockey'.[47] Writing of a forthcoming dinner he would be forced to endure with a Somerset clearly morose at stings from his critics, Bathurst teased Hay that 'I mean to give as a toast after dinner The Bees – Bird, Bigge, & Bishop of Burnett.'[48] Yet even in his most critical correspondence with this most troublesome of governors, Bathurst was careful to pay him due deference in their correspondence. A governor, as Laidlaw has emphasised, was in an inherently paradoxical position: 'at once an independent colonial autocrat and the metropolitan government's puppet'.[49] This contradiction was heightened both by Somerset's personality and elite family background, and by the context of a profound administrative transition going on within the British empire more broadly. The series of Commissions of Inquiry through the 1820s and 1830s were reducing executive power through the introduction of councils of advice and supreme courts. As we shall see, the decision to fast-track the provision of the former at the Cape came directly out of the libel scandals centred around Edwards, and (as Bathurst put it) Somerset's failings in 'command of temper'.[50] Highly connected aristocrats like Somerset were gradually replaced by men with less elite social status.[51] Yet for all this curb on 'pro-consular despotism' and move away from aristocratic appointments, the governor remained the monarch's embodiment in the colonial realm. As the arguments made in the Cape libel cases demonstrate, such prestige and its corollary of 'wounded majesty'[52] were considered central to concrete questions of state security. As the prosecution put the case against Edwards: 'his crime has therefore almost reached the pinnacle, one step more and the prisoner will contend with the Sovereignty and dare to attack the King on the Throne.'[53] By highlighting the implications of both attacks on

---

[46] Bathurst to Hay, 12 Sept. 1826; Bathurst to Hay, 13 Sept. 1826, both BL, 57/58.
[47] Bathurst to Wilmot Horton, 26 Dec. 1824, Bathurst Papers, SLNSW, A73. The nickname was a common one, given Somerset's known penchant for the turf. It gained an extra resonance with the accusations about corrupt horse dealing. TNA, CO 48/89, D'Escury and Lord Charles Somerset.
[48] Bathurst to Hay, 12 Sept. 1826, BL, 57/58.
[49] Laidlaw, *Colonial Connections*, p. 62.
[50] Bathurst to Somerset, 19 Oct. 1824, BL, 57/65.
[51] Laidlaw, *Colonial Connections*, pp. 47–9.   [52] *RCC*, vol. 17, p. 401.
[53] *RCC*, vol. 17, p. 409.

gubernatorial authority and the remedies sought against this, the Cape libel trials would bare the question of delegated legal authority within imperial sovereignty.[54]

An often-quoted memory of Bathurst alleged that his farewell to colonial governors was 'joy be with you and let us hear as little of you as possible'.[55] This seldom proved to be the case, and Bathurst's relationship with the officials who carried out his directives on the ground was a delicate one. Colonial governors were poised between a number of competing forces. They had extraordinarily wide personal powers, yet they were under the direct command of the secretary of state. They were the obvious target for complaints made on the periphery, which would be transmitted to London to fuel criticism of the Colonial Office in the House of Commons. They were the monarch's personal representative and were chosen with due regard to their social prestige, and yet they needed to be kept on a tight rein. With his high social status and tendency to treat the Cape as a private fiefdom, Somerset exemplified all these contradictory forces more than most.

Bathurst had to make sure his governors obeyed the instructions of the Colonial Office, but he could not issue these instructions, especially in public, in a way that would undermine any sense that their authority or position was not backed up in London. Criticism within the House of Commons and a relentless stream of complaints from interested individuals and lobby groups on the periphery were only increased by the investigations of Commissions of Inquiry. Whatever his own personal views on his governors' mismanagement, Bathurst saw the importance of a united front: 'as you will be attacked upon party principles', he wrote to Somerset (in a letter that was a clear application of the tactics worked out between Lord Granville Somerset and Wilmot Horton) 'you are entitled to party support.'[56]

Bathurst's correspondence with his colonial governors was thus a carefully choreographed dance between issuing strict orders (often unpalatable) to an administrative inferior and showing due deference to a social equal. As Henry Taylor's assessment of Bathurst makes clear, it was a dance at which he excelled.

Analysing Bathurst's correspondence with Somerset over the scandals instigated by William Edwards highlights that this need to keep governors under control without compromising their status necessitated a whole

[54] L. Benton, *A Search for Sovereignty: Law and Geography in European Empires 1400–1900* (Cambridge University Press, 2010), p. 31.
[55] S. Smith Bell, *Colonial Administration of Great Britain* (London: Longman, 1859), p. 460.
[56] Bathurst to Somerset, 19 Oct. 1824. BL 57/65

series of discursive strategies. The aim was to mitigate the frequently unpalatable tone and content required to get the job done. Bathurst excused his reproaches with repeated reference to the claim that he was motivated solely by the need to protect the interests of the person on the receiving end of them. Courteous fictions about errors and miscommunications were deliberately inserted even when both parties clearly knew that the recipient had acted contrary to the secretary of state's wishes and needed to be reprimanded accordingly: 'I cannot believe but there must have been some inaccuracy...', 'I cannot imagine that you would have ...', 'I still flatter myself that you did not....'.[57] We should not see these as mere politeness, however; or rather we should not see this politeness as separate from the operation of politics.

To maintain the facade, even his private correspondence becomes pervaded by a minutely shaded and subtle form of double-speak. Bathurst, for example, knew perfectly well that Somerset had refused to transmit Edwards's and Cooke's memorial on prize slaves to the Treasury, a misjudgement that might easily have proved a potent weapon in the hands of the parliamentary opposition. Even in the safety of his private correspondence, the secretary of state was careful to put this action in more ambiguous terms: 'you appear', he wrote, 'to have refused sending these charges to their Lordships.' For their own purposes, Cooke and Edwards had sent another copy direct, and the secretary of state now seized on this with alacrity: 'I have availed myself of this in my public letter; for if that had not been the case, I should have been under the necessity of at once expressing the King's displeasure at your intercepting representations made by His Majesty's Subjects, properly addressed to that office whose special duty it is to take cognizance of the subject to which those representations related.' Similarly, in the case of arresting a notary who was simply involved in his professional capacity, Bathurst was careful to pretend that Somerset had acted more appropriately than he knew to be the case: 'I say if you did also proceed against him; for, I still flatter myself that you did not include him in the original proceeding & I have taken care so to understand it, when writing on this part of the Subject.'[58] These strategies were not merely ways to smooth relations with a delegated authority, important though that was. Bathurst also used them to signal to a correspondent that he intended to hold to certain fictions in the public domain in order to deflect parliamentary criticism.

What we might be tempted to see simply as tact, then, was in fact integral to Bathurst's system of dual administration:

[57] Bathurst to Somerset, 19 Oct. 1824; 10 Nov. 1825, BL, 57/65.
[58] Bathurst to Somerset, 19 Oct. 1824.

You will receive two public letters from me on the subject of Mr Edward's business and another from me on that which relates to Mr Greig. From all these you will collect that I apprehend that the two cases, as they at present stand, are not satisfactorily explained: and that something more must be known, before either will be in a defensible state. I have reserved for a private letter dealing more openly, lest those doubts which I cannot but entertain of the merits of each case, might, if found expressed in a public dispatch which Parliament might call for, become prejudicial to you, unless they were more entirely removed than I am afraid will turn out to be the Case.[59]

As Bathurst outlined here to Somerset, private and public correspondence were designed to act together: to deal with colonial crises, to protect individual administrators and to deflect the negative attention of public opinion from the actions of the Colonial Office. Managing reputation was key to this process.

If balancing public and private communication with government officials was central to the operation of imperial governance, then so too was the provision of unofficial information from individuals acting in a private capacity. Bathurst would deliberately make appointments with this in mind. Dudley Perceval, son of the assassinated Prime Minister Spencer Perceval, arrived at the Cape in November 1825 to take up the post of secretary to the newly established Council of Advice. Bathurst had arranged for a post for the staunch Tory, and Perceval was keen to reward the investment with detailed updates to both Bathurst and his wife, as well as to James Stephen. His duties were not onerous, nor was he much inconvenienced by his colonial exile, living, as he did, in the largely British-inhabited enclave of Wynberg near the military camp. As he admitted to his brother, 'I go about & dine at two or three English homes, & play at whist or Billiards, & talk nonsense in politics, and take my ride in the afternoon & so forth, much as you would do at a small country town in England.'[60] His letter book also testifies to less unexceptional correspondence, including his relationship with a married woman whose name he was careful to render only in cipher. To this unnamed woman he was far more forthcoming about his dragging sense of ennui: 'my office is a very dull one, and requires little from me but superintendence & perhaps six hours work in a week, my time hangs very heavy on my h[a]nds.'[61]

---

[59] Bathurst to Somerset, 19 Oct. 1824.
[60] Dudley Perceval to Spencer Perceval [brother], 5 April 1826, Dudley Perceval, Letters from the Cape of Good Hope 1825–1828, Library of Parliament, Cape Town, Class a. 916.87, no. 9202
[61] Perceval to unnamed female correspondent, 29 July [1826], Perceval, Letters from the Cape.

'A Daemon behind the Curtain' 81

Perceval's main utility to his party lay not in his desultory administrative duties, but in his unofficial reports on the state of the colony and the personalities with which Bathurst had perforce to deal. Essentially, Perceval's role at the Cape was to listen to gossip and to relay it to London. Perceval considered Somerset to be much maligned, for his enemies had 'artfully combined' misrepresentations and fact. The Dutch colonists had nothing but good to say of him, and they were by far the majority in the colony. Somerset had greatly accommodated them to British rule. They had been refractory in the past, now they were 'excellent subjects', and it was a shame that Somerset should be held accountable to the minority of 'Radicals': 'the spiteful growling of a few discontented ill-disposed English vagabonds, who would howl at St John the Baptist, I dare say, or St John the Evangelist, if he was their Governor.'[62]

For all his Tory sympathies, Perceval clearly saw the weaknesses in Somerset's character. He realised that these made him ill-suited to the circumstances faced by the Colonial Office in London. In writing to Countess Bathurst (a letter that would clearly have been shared with her husband but whose direction created yet another careful layer of privacy around sensitive information) he outlined precisely the same concerns about the governor as the secretary of state and Wilmot Horton would express – his irritable temper, and his outrage that his actions might be subjected to public scrutiny rather than standing on his rank and status. With 'Brougham & Co' actively looking for 'grievances' to 'froth & splutter about', Somerset 'may have involved himself rather too precipitately in measures, which do not fit with the caution that seems to be the order of the day just now'.[63] Perceval summed up the situation exactly when he wrote to James Stephen: 'The only real fault of his government, I apprehend, to have been this. That he seems to have looked upon the Colony as an estate which he was to improve, and it did not matter how.'[64] All seemed in agreement, therefore, that Somerset was a man increasingly out of step with the times.

Somerset returned to London to answer his critics in March 1826, with Major General Sir Richard Bourke to serve as acting governor during his absence. Despite the endless petitions presented by Cape complainants against his administration, despite the opposition forces baying for his political blood at the Cape and in the Houses of Parliament, Somerset escaped the humiliation of impeachment. The opposition case

---

[62] Perceval to Countess Bathurst, 19 Jan. 1826, Perceval, Letters from the Cape.
[63] Perceval to Countess Bathurst, 19 Jan. 1826.
[64] Perceval to James Stephen, 3 March 1826, Perceval, Letters from the Cape.

against him had largely been neutralised when an unexpected change of metropolitan government in 1827 took Somerset off the agenda. The Cape governor (along with other ultra-Tories) resigned from office when George Canning formed a government in the wake of Lord Liverpool's stroke. In an emblematic decision, the Colonial Office chose to confirm Bourke as his replacement, a Whig and known sympathiser to the forces of reform who was charged with implementing the recommendations of the Commission of Eastern Inquiry. Later, in 1831, Bourke replaced a similarly controversial Tory governor in New South Wales, Ralph Darling, and for much the same reasons.

That the parliamentary proceedings against Somerset ultimately collapsed was in large part owing to the successful management of such controversies by the Colonial Office. He was not the only colonial governor that such tactics saved from formal impeachment, if not from vehement public criticism. There were, therefore, definite advantages to be found in Bathurt's dual system of official and unofficial information management. Yet it also presented liabilities. Clandestine information gathering could easily slip into accusations of spying in a political climate that was increasingly hostile to such activities. In the following chapter I begin to trace the theme of espionage through the story of William Edwards. Not only would Edwards face several accusations of being a spy himself, but scandalous claims of espionage would be used in connection with his activities to discredit both the Somerset regime at the Cape and the Bigge Commissions in the Australian colonies.

3 Green-bag-makers and blood-hunters
Information management and espionage

Tracing the tactics by which Colonial Office administrators tried to manage the political fallout of scandals provoked by men like Edwards underlines the impact of ostensibly marginal figures on more mainstream political developments. For the authorities, there were both possibilities and dangers presented by manipulating the different registers of information exchange at their disposal. In many ways they were successful in dealing with their critics, yet the Edwards case also emphasises how such practices, which took place at various levels of secrecy, were compromised by the increasingly damaging political consequences that were presented by accusations of spying. Espionage had seemed (somewhat) acceptable during the threats from revolutionary France in the 1790s. But the tide of public opinion had decisively turned by the time Commissioner Bigge arrived in the Australian colonies on the first of his investigations in 1819. Spies had particular rhetorical power in the highly charged political climate immediately following the Napoleonic Wars. In the midst of the political upheavals I have outlined, dramatic revelations that exposed both the reliance on government spies and the role played by agents provocateurs in anti-government conspiracies significantly undermined the state's position on internal security threats. Being caught using espionage against 'freeborn Britons' was becoming an increasingly serious political liability.

"Spies and Bloodites!!!"

In seeking employment as a clerk with the Commission of Eastern Inquiry shortly after his arrival in Cape Town, Edwards sought to enter a trans-imperial world of law, letters and governance, a world in which an increasing preoccupation with reform saw opportunities opening up for both personal and political ambition. Instead he found employment by setting himself up as a notary, perhaps little anticipating how important a part he would be playing amongst the imperial information networks within a few short months. Edwards was admitted as a notary on

84   Imperial Underworld

23 October 1823, and from November of that year he was employed in a variety of diverse minor legal matters concerning inheritance, business arrangements, drawing up contracts of employment and mediating in interpersonal disputes.[1] On 26 September 1823 he applied for, and was subsequently granted, permission to remain in the colony. The *Hero* was about to depart and needed his paperwork to be cleared before it could do so. Edwards's application described himself as 'having come to this Colony from the Mauritius for the benefit of his health'. As part of the process, two inhabitants of Cape Town had to bind themselves as securities for his good behaviour while the deputy fiscal noted:

I do hereby certify, that the Statement of Memorialist is conformably to truth; and that upon due enquiry made in this Office, nothing has occurred to me that could lead to judge unfavourably respecting Memorialist's Character and Conduct.[2]

Before making his application, Edwards had been anxious to clear up a matter that jeopardised this reputation. On 18 September 1823 he appeared before the notary David Passmore Taylor to complain that George Hunt, master of the brig *Emulous* then lying in Table Bay, had 'caused a report to be circulated tending to impeach his character'.[3] 'Edwards' was not an uncommon name, but in this instance the choice had backfired on Alexander Kaye. Hunt had told several persons (and testimony was provided to confirm that he had done so) that Edwards was in reality a 'laborer or bricklayer one of the people who conspired together to murder the Cabinet Ministers of England in the year 1820'. Hunt had refused to give a source for his information.

About to seek permission to remain in the colony, needing to build up a respectable reputation in order to successfully practice as a notary in Cape Town, William Edwards had been named as George Edwards, government spy and alleged agent provocateur. George Edwards was instrumental in the infamous 'Cato Street conspiracy' of 1820 to murder the Prime Minister, Lord Liverpool, and his cabinet. Exposure of the plot had helped justify the draconian Six Acts that suppressed public assembly and 'seditious' meetings and that significantly retarded the radical press through draconian licensing regulations and the threat of banishment. Five of the Cato Street conspirators were hanged at Newgate on 1 May 1820. Vast crowds were held back at a distance to prevent attempts at

---

[1] Protocol of the notary William Edwards, CA, NCD 27/1, no. 1–105.
[2] William Edwards, Memorial, 26 Sept. 1823, CA, CO 3924/185.
[3] Declaration of William Edwards, 18 Sept. 1823, Notarial Deeds of David Passmore Taylor, CA, NCD 26/1, no. 10.

rescue and to stop the speeches from the scaffold being heard.[4] Five others were transported to New South Wales, where their time at Newcastle overlapped with Edwards's own. As was becoming increasingly the case with government informers, George Edwards was not called as a prosecution witness in order to prevent his being subjected to cross-examination. The defence alleged that George Edwards was an agent provocateur and the chief supplier of weapons and ammunition. He was spirited away by the authorities for his own protection. Ironically, there are reasons to believe (though they are not conclusive) that the real George Edwards was living quietly undiscovered at the Cape by the time that William Edwards was mistaken for him.[5]

William Edwards protested that he 'never did personally know any of the people engaged in the said Conspiracy', that he had never been in Cato Street and did not even know in what part of London it was situated. He got Notary Taylor to put out a version of his 'real' life history, based on his own testimony and that of Isaac Riches, captain of the brig *Hero* on which Edwards had travelled to the Cape. As would become his usual practice, it is an intricate combination of truth and falsehood. In his statement, Edwards claimed that he had left England in June 1818 for Java, having resigned an 'honourable situation' under of the ministers of George III in 1810. None of his family, he hastened to assert, 'were ever bricklayers, mechanics or other Handicraftsmen' (indeed, this slight to his social status seemed to be as wounding to Edwards as the accusations of treason).

In order to prove his case Edwards drew on the testimony from two men who had coincidentally met the real Cato Street spy and maker of 'Plaister of Paris figures', George Edwards. Georg Greig the printer had met George Edwards in 1820, while assisting the landlord of the Hole in the Wall tavern in Baldwin Gardens 'expelling a person in his House' on the grounds of the suspicious company he kept. Greig testified that the conspirator 'was a man of low vulgar appearance, illiterate in his manner & conversation' and that 'he scarcely ever saw two persons more unlike each other, than that man and W. Edwards now present'.[6] James Jury, the

---

[4] Thompson, *Making of the English Working Class*, p. 774.
[5] A 'George Parker', one of George Edwards's known aliases, was listed as a modeller (the same profession as the spy) living in Green Point in 1840. He died there three years later: see R.M. Healey, 'Edwards, George (1787?–1843)', *Oxford Dictionary of National Biography* (Oxford University Press, 2004); online edn, www.oxforddnb.com/view/article/38374 (viewed 10 Jan. 2014); P. Pickering, 'Betrayal and exile: A forgotten Chartist experience', in M. T. Davis and P. Pickering (eds.), *Unrespectable Radicals? Popular Politics in the Age of Reform* (Aldershot, UK: Ashgate, 2008) p. 202.
[6] Declaration of George Greig, 22 Sept. 1823, Notarial Deeds of David Passmore Taylor, CA, NCD 26/1, no. 10.

son of the landlord of the Hole in the Wall, described the real conspirator as 'by trade a bricklayer or mason, a very low, vulgar, illiterate person who frequently spent several successive days drinking and sitting in the Hole in the Wall' and who bore no resemblance to William Edwards of the Cape, whom he had recently met in the Fiscal's Office.

In additional support, Captain Isaac Riches was able to provide a thumbnail sketch of William Edwards's associates in Mauritius. Riches declared before the notary that in Port Louis in May 1823, Philip Krumpholtz, assistant agent general of police, had engaged a passage for William Edwards 'whom he described as a Gentleman being his most particular friend and who wished to proceed to the Cape of Good Hope as he did not in that Island sufficiently recover from the effects of a fever he had long had in Java'. Krumpholtz explained that Edwards had been employed 'in a respectable situation under Judge Christie' during his time on the island, save for a few months when he assisted Colonel Barry, the chief secretary of the government of Mauritius, at Christie's request. Christie had arranged a leaving dinner for Edwards to which Riches was invited as were 'French and English Gentlemen (who were the friends of W. Edwards). Edwards, claimed Riches, was clearly esteemed by Judge Christie, 'living in his House & presiding at one end of his dinner Table'.[7] That Riches's account was not an utter rigmarole paid for by Edwards can be confirmed by the Commissioners of Eastern Inquiry, who provided Bathurst with evidence from both Christie and Krumpholtz that they had had dealings with Edwards in Mauritius.[8]

Edwards further declared that he appointed an advocate to act for him against George Hunt in any future action for 'Slander and Defamation of Character'. In making his statements before the notary, Edwards made sure to emphasise his proper behaviour as a man of honour by asserting he was 'not actuated by any feeling of malice' against George Hunt, nor by any 'pecuniary compensation for the injury to his character as he conceives that no recompense can atone for injured honor and reputation'. Any damages he might gain from a case of defamation against George Hunt would be donated to 'some public Charity after deducting the expenses of Suit'.

There is no evidence that Edwards took the matter any further by bringing a court case against George Hunt, who, in any event, was about to leave the colony.[9] It was probably sufficient for the matter to be heard

---

[7] Declaration of Isaac Riches, 18 September 1823, Notarial Deeds of David Passmore Taylor, CA, NCD 26/1, no. 10.
[8] Bigge, Colebrooke and Blair to Hay, 14 July 1827, *RCC*, vol. 32, p. 199.
[9] Declaration of William Edwards, 18 Sept. 1823, CA, NCD 26/1, no. 10.

before the notary to scotch any rumours that might have prejudiced Edwards's standing in the Cape community. Using notaries in interpersonal disputes of reputation in this way was common. Litigation was usually avoided in these contests, and managing such disputes of honour was part of the routine business of Cape notaries. The point to make here is why William Edwards saw fit to employ a notary to defend his honour in this misidentification in the first place. His going to this trouble and expense is an indication of contemporary attitudes that will prove important at several points in this book. Far from being lauded as heroic undercover agents protecting the public from dangerous acts of terror, government spies were damned as social outcasts as the whole system of state-sponsored espionage came under increasing criticism in the first decades of the nineteenth century.

As historian Paul Pickering argues, the 'whiff of brimstone' that hung around informers and agents provocateurs like George Edwards had deep cultural roots stretching back to Judas himself.[10] Anti-spy paranoia had a particularly rich history in association with concepts of English liberty imagined in opposition to continental despotism. An 1817 pamphlet published in London claimed that espionage was

a system which is of foreign, of *French* origin, for which, as a patriotic nobleman has remarked, our language has not even a name; forcing us to borrow from our enslaved neighbours its appellation, as well as the thing itself under which they groan, and to express the horrible nature of which there is no term sufficiently strong.[11]

Setting aside the selective historical memory of this account, it is true that the British state had a far less well-developed and ad hoc system of domestic surveillance over potential dissenting forces than did continental polities like France (in either its Bourbon or Revolutionary incarnations) or Austria under the Hapsburgs.[12]

In the 1790s crackdown on popular radicalism, extensive use was made of informers. The spy system of Prime Minister William Pitt the Younger largely escaped mainstream parliamentary and popular censure because it was justified as an extension of the war against Jacobin France.[13] But in the aftermath of the defeat of Napoleon, manifestations of popular radicalism were much harder to connect to threats of foreign invasion.

---

[10] Pickering, 'Betrayal and exile', p. 201.   [11] Anon., *Spies and Bloodites!!!*, p. 3.
[12] B. Porter, *Plots and Paranoia: History of Political Espionage in Britain 1790–1988* (London: Routledge, 1989), pp. 9–10.
[13] Porter, *Plots and Paranoia*, p. 41; C. Emsley, 'An aspect of Pitt's "Terror": Prosecutions for sedition during the 1790s', *Social History*, 6:2 (May 1981), 155–84.

88   Imperial Underworld

Informers were paid according to the evidence they produced. The temptation, in modern parlance, to 'sex up' reports was both strong and recognised to be so. It was increasingly widely believed that the authorities were acting to stamp out proper liberties using as their excuse conspiracies that their own informers had engendered. The Cato Street conspiracy of 1820 was the latest in a series of treason trials and uprisings, the revolutionary potential of which has been the subject of considerable historiographical controversy. If the 1817 Committee of Secrecy convened by Parliament in reaction to popular radicalism was convinced that revolution was imminent, much of the evidence that they had for this came from government spies. By the time William Edwards arrived at the Cape and was mistaken for the more notorious George, many would have agreed with the later assessment in the classic account of historian E.P. Thompson: 'If the Cato Street conspirators had achieved their object in the assassination of the Cabinet, the Cabinet would have been slain by conspirators whom their own repressive policies had engendered, and their own spies had armed.'[14]

The full title of the 1817 pamphlet I have quoted, alleging that state-sponsored espionage was in itself a foreign invention, provides an evocative sense of contemporary sentiment:

Spies and Bloodites!!! The Lives and Political History of those arch-fiends Oliver, Reynolds, & Co. Treason-Hatchers, Green-Bag-Makers, Blood-Hunters, Spies, Tempters, and Informers-General to His Majesty's Ministers. Including a complete Account of all their Intrigues, Snares, Plots, Plans, Treasons, and Machinations, in the Metropolis, Manchester, Birmingham, Leeds, and various Parts of the Country, laying open the whole of their Transactions with Government, &c &c.[15]

Spies and Bloodites!!! was part of a wave of popular publishing in this period, testament to what approached mass hysteria about spies by the end of the decade. At the head of its list was the most famous agent provocateur of them all, W.J. Richards, also known as William Oliver and William Jones. He would go down in history under his more common moniker of 'Oliver the Spy'.

Oliver was exposed as a government agent by the Leeds journalist, editor and reform campaigner Edward Baines in the wake of a short-lived armed rising in Pentrich, on the border of Nottinghamshire and Derbyshire.[16] Three leaders would be tried for treason, hanged and posthumously beheaded. Fourteen more were transported to Australia.

[14] Thompson, *Making of the English Working Class*, p. 530.
[15] *Spies and Bloodites!!!* Anonymous pamphlet, John Fairburn, London, 1817.
[16] E. Baines (jnr), *The Life of Edward Baines, Late M. P. for the Borough of Leeds, by his son, Edward Baines* (London: Longman, 1851).

In a series of sensational articles in the *Leeds Mercury* beginning on 14 June 1817, Baines alleged that the unrest had been sparked by the activities of a man known to the protestors as 'London delegate' William Oliver. Baines revealed him to be W.J. Richards, a spy in the employ of Lord Sidmouth's Home Office. The authorities, Baines alleged, had known from Oliver that the rising was imminent, but had let it go ahead in order to further their own political ends. Debate as to Oliver's role and culpability in the rising at Pentrich has raged ever since.[17]

Oliver was by no means the only government agent exposed in this period, as the title of *Spies and Bloodites!!!* suggests. In the same year George Cruikshank published a satirical print [Figure 5] showing three of the most notorious spies of the era in conspiratorial meeting with leading members of the Tory government, a green bag (into which the evidence was packed for the Committee of Secrecy charged with investigating seditious activities) prominently displayed before them. There were three spies featured by Cruikshank along with Lord Sidmouth (home secretary), Lord Castlereagh (foreign secretary) and George Canning (then Cabinet minister). One was Oliver. The others were John Castle, pilloried for his role in the Spa Fields trials (during which the defence dug up sufficient dirt on him to utterly discredit his evidence), and Thomas Reynolds, the Irish informer, who had to be given the post of British consul in Iceland and shipped off to Copenhagen.

Yet in a period that witnessed repeated scandals over government espionage and alleged agents provocateurs, it was Oliver who took on the definite article. As E.P. Thompson puts it, his story 'came to partake almost of the quality of myth' with Oliver as 'the archetype of the Radical Judas'.[18] In part this was clearly because (unlike Castle) the 'blood money' that bought his evidence had led to capital convictions. On the scaffold, William Turner had, claimed Baines, 'exclaimed, in a piteous tone – "This is all Oliver and the government!"'[19] Equally, we must give due credit to Edward Baines, a politician-in-waiting who would become a Whig MP in the wake of the Reform Act. He made brilliant capital out of his exposé, both in the pages of the *Leeds Mercury* (under headlines such as 'Horrible Plot of Spies and Informers to Excite Insurrection'

---

[17] J. L. Hammond and B. Hammond, *The Skilled Labourer* (London: Longman, 1919); A. F. Fremantle, 'The truth about Oliver the Spy', *English Historical Review*, 47 (1932), 601–16; R. J. White, *From Waterloo to Peterloo* (London: Heinemann, 1957), ch. 13; Thompson, *Making of the English Working Class;* J. Stephens, *England's Last Revolution: Pentrich 1817* (Buxton, UK: Moorland, 1977).

[18] Thompson, *Making of the English Working Class*, p. 726.

[19] E. Baines (snr), *History of the Reign of George III, King of the United Kingdom of Great Britain and Ireland* (Leeds, UK: Long, Hurst and Co, 1820), vol. IV, p. 88.

90   Imperial Underworld

Figure 5 George Cruikshank's 1817 satirical print of government ministers arranging rewards for their spies. 'Oliver the Spy' occupies the centre background, seated between Canning and the 'green bag' in which evidence was presented to the Committeeof Secrecy. Amongst the green bag's contents are 'Treasonable papers to be slipped into the pockets of some duped artisans'. In the captions, Canning asks Castlereagh: 'Don't you think my Lord that our friends, Castle & Oliver should be sent to Lisbon or somewhere as Consul Generals, or Envoys?' Castlereagh responds: 'Can't you negotiate for some boroughs.' At the window: 'Oh! Oh I have found out the Conspirators at last, poor starving John is to be ensnared into Criminal acts & then the Projectors & perpetrators are brought forward as principal evidences! This is another Vaughn, Brock & Pelham business, and I suppose they are to be made Consuls too, the high road to Ld Castlereigh's [sic] particular favor – Canning travelled it.'

and 'Exploded Plots, Oliver the Spy'[20]) and in his *History of the Reign of George III* published three years later.[21]

Baines put Oliver and Sidmouth's spy system into a wider reformist agenda, arguing that the 'object' of the Parliamentary Secret Committees of the period was

[20] Also collected in *Spies and Bloodites!!!*, p. 12.
[21] K. McKenzie, *Swindler's Progress: Nobles and Convicts in the Age of Liberty* (University of New South Wales Press, 2009).

to establish the existence of a widely spread conspiracy against the government and constitution [so that] ... many circumstances, in themselves quite insignificant and quite unconnected with each other, are collected together, and by the help of exaggeration, suppression, ingenious combination, and plausible inference, are divested of their true character, and made up into a regular and formidable plot.[22]

In the House of Commons, opposition MPs such as Sir Francis Burdett and Henry Brougham took up the revelations about Oliver to launch extended attacks upon the 'moral character' of the Ministry accompanied by acclamation from the floor.[23] Such was the popular hostility against Oliver that an unfortunate butler was attacked by a violent mob on the streets of London because of his fancied resemblance to the 'arch-fiend'.[24] With the government agent mysteriously vanished, Olivers began appearing everywhere. As a symbol he was far more powerful than he had ever been as an informer; a protean figure who was easily accused of betrayals far removed in time and space from his original activities. We have not heard the last of him in the story of William Edwards.

'A frightful system of espionage': spies at the Cape of Good Hope

The hysteria over Oliver was emblematic of a growing popular attitude to the role of covert information in governance, a shift in public opinion with particular implications for a range of long-established practices. As I have mentioned, the factionalism of colonial administrative politics reached especially paranoid heights during Somerset's second term as governor of the Cape. Upon his return from leave in Britain, Somerset waged a bitter feud against anyone who had been favoured under the interim regime of the acting governor, Sir Rufane Donkin. His sentiments were heartily reciprocated by Donkin, who described Somerset in an insistently non-official letter to Wilmot Horton as

a Man, who to the habit of a Groom, unites the morals of a Swindler, and who, with an array of the worst Qualities I ever saw condensed in any one Human Being, has not the set off of one single redeeming Iota which even approximates to the humblest virtue of the lowest of our species![25]

---

[22] Baines (snr), *History of the Reign of George III*, vol. IV, p. 42.
[23] Reprinted in *Spies and Bloodites!!!*, pp. 22–3.
[24] *Spies and Bloodites!!!*, p. 29.
[25] Sir Rufane Donkin to Wilmot Horton, 20 June 1825 ('private'), Catton Collection, Derbyshire Record Office, D3155/WH2774. Donkin prefaced his invective, of which this is only a sample, by stipulating: 'I am going to take the liberty of addressing this to you personally and not as Under Secretary of State, for I must use some expressions in it, in explanations, which would not do for the Public Eye.'

As the allegations and counter-allegations ground on, one of the most damning made by Donkin was the Somerset regime's use of spies. Making a self-justificatory account of his acting governorship to Undersecretary Robert Wilmot Horton in 1823, Sir Rufane Donkin listed cost-cutting as his first distinction from the Somerset regime. This was predictable, given that Somerset's extravagance was an issue close to the Colonial Office's heart. His second innovation, however, was equally calculated to touch a nerve and to influence public opinion:

> My next departure was, in putting down a system of espionage and tale-bearing about the government house, to which I could not stoop, and which I found operating in the most injurious manner on the society of the colony. I announced at once that I would hear no tales, nor receive any tale-bearers; that if any man had any thing to say of another in office under me, he must bring it forward openly and officially, and that no man should be screened by the hand of power if he did wrong. This determination was very mortifying to many who were disposed to make themselves useful in that way; and their complaints were loud when they found my door shut against them; but I had the satisfaction of seeing the confidence of the inhabitants established, both in regard to one another and myself.[26]

The same accusations featured prominently in Thomas Pringle's account of what he called the 'Cape Reign of Terror' published a decade later:

> A frightful system of espionage pervaded every circle of society, and rendered perilous even the confidence of the domestic hearth.... Informers and false witnesses abounded; and rumours of 'plots' and 'disloyal combinations against the Governor' were assiduously kept afloat, for purposes as obvious as they were mischievous.[27]

Pringle's *Narrative of a Residence in South Africa* paints a vivid picture of a colony paralysed by a regime that ticked every box of 'Old Corruption': 'Mutual confidence was shaken; distrust, apprehension, and gloom everywhere prevailed; and men, according to their several characters and circumstances, were perturbed by angry excitement or prostrated by slavish fear.'[28] The *Reminiscences* published in the 1880s by Louis Meurant (later journalist, editor, publisher and Member of Parliament, but at the time apprenticed to the printer George Greig) presented much the same image: 'A "black-book" was kept at Government-house... in which was entered the names of all who were alleged to be "Liberals", Radicals &c., and those destined for *immediate* destruction were designated by

---

[26] Donkin to Wilmot Horton, 23 June 1823, *RCC*, vol. 16, pp. 82–3.
[27] Pringle, *Narrative*, p. 209.   [28] Pringle, *Narrative*, p. 211.

an X'.[29] In this time of 'partizanship', he remembered, 'great efforts were made by Government spies and others intent upon Government "loaves and fishes", to bring odium on the brave men who were fighting the battle of "Liberty" and the "Freedom of the Press."'[30] Meurant claimed he could have exposed the spies involved in Cape Town but 'for obvious reasons' kept their names out of his published reminiscences, suggesting they were still known to the community some sixty years later.

For Somerset's political enemies, as for their allies in the metropole, spies were a rhetorical weapon in a much broader ideological war over the nature of the British state. We have seen how informal interpersonal information networks were vital to imperial intelligence-gathering even as they were responsible for a strong degree of paranoia being manifest amongst colonial officials. The gossipy letters written by men like Perceval, on the one side of politics, or like Pringle on the other, had an overtly strategic purpose. As I have argued, such correspondents and the information they provided played an important strategic role in party politics. What can more properly be called 'spies' did also undoubtedly exist, though (as we shall see in Chapter 8) informers were more commonly ad hoc and opportunistic members of the wider community than the paid government agents that loomed large in the contemporary imagination.

The increasing political liability presented by espionage in the 1820s meant that such activities are, by definition, difficult to track.[31] Any discussion of such activities needed to be carefully kept beyond the scrutiny of Parliament. Yet there is sufficient archival evidence to suggest that Somerset used regular paid informers who acted covertly to warn the authorities of allegedly seditious activities and to gather discrediting intelligence about both administrative rivals and opponents to the regime. Although there are some hints of this in official sources, as Donkin's account demonstrates, the 'smoking gun' is unsurprisingly to be found

---

[29] Meurant, *Sixty Years Ago*, p. 24.   [30] Meurant, *Sixty Years Ago*, p. 28.
[31] Here the Cape apparently presents a contrast with the situation in India. C. A. Bayly's *Empire and Information: Intelligence Gathering and Social Communication in India 1780–1870* (Cambridge University Press, 1996) argues that British military success in India was fundamentally bound up in their success in taking over and manipulating the long-standing and sophisticated systems of internal espionage and political reporting deployed by previous Indian rulers. What distinguishes this from the Cape discussion, however, is that such activities did not attract the same kind of criticism in England, perhaps because the key targets of Somerset's covert intelligence-gathering at the Cape appear to have been administrative rivals and British settlers. There are, however, very strong similarities in the protests inspired by actions taken against freedom of the press in both Bengal and the Cape, a subject to which I return in Chapter 7.

in the unofficial correspondence, in letters sent to the secretary of state carefully marked as 'Secret and Confidential'.

Pringle's private letters were shot through with the fear that his correspondence was under surveillance. In October 1824 he warned John Fairbairn:

> Even if I had more time I would not write freely on some subjects in a letter going openly through a post office in which I have no confidence and respecting which I have just received a caution from a friend. The *channel* you have at present appears secure enough.[32]

Even a year later he remained cautious. 'I send this through a circuitous route under cover to Mr Paton – which I think a safe and unsuspected channel.'[33] His fears proved only too well founded.[34] Given that the Post Office comprised the earliest and most organised form of British domestic espionage, recognised by statute, Pringle's suspicions no doubt came partly from experience in the metropole. By the early nineteenth century, in fact, the Royal Mail was possibly less effective as a surveillance system precisely because its activities had become well known.[35]

Pringle was right to be concerned about informers. In a letter marked 'Secret and Confidential', Somerset passed on his opinion of Pringle and his allies to the secretary of state:

> It now behoves me to confide to your Lordship the character of persons who, exclusive of the factious party [Edwards and his supporters] alluded to above – are extremely hostile to the welfare of this government & particularly to the Church Establishment.[36]

The Rev. John Philip ('a violent Scotch *Independent* a man of first rate cunning and hypocrisy and indefatigable in his intrigues against the established Church & indeed against the Govt generally') and the Rev. William Wright ('an indiscreet, half crazy Irish Blunderer, steady on nothing but

---

[32] Pringle to Fairbairn, 31 Oct. 1824, *Letters of Thomas Pringle*, p. 130.

[33] George Paton was an Army and general agent domiciled at 16 Strand Street, Cape Town. Pringle to Fairbairn, 22 Oct. 1825, *Letters of Thomas Pringle*, p. 269.

[34] On Somerset's interception of letters between Fairbairn and Pringle, see R Vigne, *Thomas Pringle: South African Pioneer, Poet and Abolitionist* (Woodbridge, Suffolk, UK: James Currey, 2012), pp. 135–6.

[35] In 1711 a much longer practice was regularised with the requirement that warrants be signed by one of the principle secretaries of state before a letter could be opened. A 'Secret Office' dealt with foreign correspondence, a 'Private Office' dealt with domestic letters. As a formal espionage agency, the Post Office had in many ways far more consistency and continuity than the activities of the Home Office. See Porter, *Plots and Paranoia*, pp. 16–17; E. R. Turner, 'The Secrecy of the Post', *English Historical Review*, 33:131 (July, 1918), 320–7.

[36] Somerset to Bathurst, 'Secret and Confidential', 18 July 1824, Bathurst Papers, BL, 57/54.

his secret opposition to the Govt') were determined, with Pringle and Fairbairn, to oppose the government. Somerset based his information on this group squarely on undercover government informers, whose names he would not reveal:

> I should rejoice in an opportunity to expose Philip & Wright but altho' I am aware of all they do by secret Intelligence upon which I can depend, I should if I were to bring their conduct forward disclose the only source of intelligence I can rely upon and which I consider of too much importance to the safety of this Govt to give up.[37]

Somerset pointed out that Greig was producing the *Advertiser* on a press owned by Philip, and that 'my information gives me to understand' that it was really Philip and Fairbairn who were producing the paper. Somerset was concerned that Bathurst use this information circumspectly in public debate:

> Your Lordship will perceive that I have taken the liberty of intruding this detail upon you in the *strictest confidence* – but in the hope that without alluding to it specifically your Lordship may find a means to cause the missionaries from *any* society be restrained from meddling or mingling in local politics.[38]

Whether or not mail was regularly intercepted, it is clear that the practice existed. The same informer was also able to pass information to Somerset about Bishop Burnett's activities in London. In two 1825 letters to Bathurst marked 'Secret', Somerset enclosed copies of letters apparently written by Burnett from London to correspondents at the Cape. Somerset's spy had apparently managed to get hold of the originals in some undisclosed way and copies had been made. Unlike official government copies they lack the usual notation of 'a true copy' or an indication of the scribe's name. From notes made about missing words and torn text it is clear that they were read and copied after the seal on the original had been broken. As Somerset explained:

> I transmit to your Lordship copies of two letters addressed to private Individuals in this place by Bishop Burnet – As I have seen the originals & compared them with letters formerly written by that Individual to me I am able to authenticate the hand writing. Altho' they contain nothing of any material interest they will serve to convey to your Lordship the class of persons by whom I am revil'd. . . . I have obtained a sight of the enclos'd letter thro the same channel that kept me apprized of the plots, intentions & intrigues of Greig, Philip, Fairbairn, Wright,

---

[37] Somerset to Bathurst, 'Secret and Confidential', 18 July 1824, Bathurst Papers, BL, 57/54.
[38] Somerset to Bathurst, 'Secret and Confidential', 18 July 1824.

Pringle &c &c during the troublesome & turbulent times of last year which I always found correct.[39]

The same hand that copied the two letters also later provided a page of background dirt on Burnett. Unsigned, it is simply headed 'Information, which may be relied on', and was transmitted by Somerset to Bathurst in a letter marked 'secret' on 19 July 1825. It is unknown how Somerset's spy got hold of the letters from Burnett without revealing himself. They were dated from Westminster on 31 March and 2 April 1825. They are full of attacks on Somerset, rejoicing that the writer and his cronies are making trouble for the governor in London as much as they can by consorting with his enemies. The letter of 31 March talks of a 'cabinet meeting' of supporters in London and mentions that Burnett thought of asking Sir Rufane Donkin to join him, but thought he should distance himself from the 'government' until he knew better what his strategy should be. They allege the strength of the Beaufort interest in keeping Somerset on at the Cape. The letter of 2 April also indicates that Burnett knew exactly what he was doing in pulling the levers of political manipulation against the Colonial Office: 'I build my hopes of success entirely on their fears and their intense desire to keep Lord Charles's name from coming before the House.'[40]

In keeping with the importance of managing reputation discussed earlier, one of Somerset's techniques was to convey to London as much discrediting information as possible on those who opposed his government. Even to sign the petition for a free press was to expose oneself as an opponent to the regime. One of Cape Town diarist Samuel Hudson's fellow boarders, for example, refused to do so for precisely this reason. Hudson was contemptuous: 'he is at the head of these time serving disgraceful abortions of Englishmen, Caterpillars who are gnawing into the bowels of the constitution and say and do everything their Tyrant wishes them provided it makes anything to their Interest.'[41]

The government had early sought to get information on who had signed. Hudson reported that 'A person was sent from Government House to take the names upon the list but was prevented by the clerks saying it was not allowed another Pill for his Excellency to swallow tho hard to digest.'[42] They may have failed on this occasion, but a copy was duly taken. A suggestively annotated handwritten list of those who signed lies in the Government House archives in Cape Town and bears witness

---

[39] Somerset to Bathurst, 11 July 1825, 'Secret', Bathurst Papers, BL, 57/87.
[40] Enclosure in Somerset to Bathurst, 11 July 182, Bathurst Papers, BL, 57/87.
[41] Hudson, Diary, 24 May 1824.   [42] Hudson, Diary, 20 May 1824.

to Somerset's intelligence resources. It was sent by Somerset to the secretary of state, and almost every name is followed by terse notes in red ink, usually giving information designed to discredit the respectability of those who signed. It was clearly meant to provide ballast to the governor's argument that the commotion for a free press came only from radicals on the margins of society. At the top of the list is James Howell, owner of the bookshop, described as 'an Insolvent' (hardly an unusual failing at the Cape). The informer's attempt to blacken the petitioners' names could be somewhat esoteric: 'Francis, D P – A brokendown man'; 'Hopley, W M – decayed Schoolmaster – notorious drunkard'; 'Dyke, R – Husband of a dressmaker & living by his Wits'; 'Powley, F.G. – Apothecary – notoriously disaffected to Government'. Midway through the list is the name 'Hudson, S.E. – A Bankrupt late Van Buuren & Hudson Uitenhage.'[43]

In this climate, the presence of the commissioners was a double-edged sword. On the one hand, as the prize slave investigation will show, they provided an alternate avenue for both complaint and lobbying. Pringle, however, considered that the population was intimidated against giving such information by pressure from the Somerset administration: 'whoever was discovered to be a complainant to the Commissioners, or supposed to have furnished them voluntarily with any information respecting abuses, was immediately set down as a "marked and ruined man."' According to Pringle's *Narrative*, so strong was this feeling of intimidation that

even the Commissioners themselves... began to be very generally suspected of being either the mere puppets of Earl Bathurst, or the blind dupes of Lord Charles Somerset; an unworthy surmise, arising from the extreme caution which their instructions constrained them to observe in regard to all complaints which related to the personal conduct of the Governor.[44]

With the advantage of hindsight, and having read the commissioners' published reports, in 1835 Pringle could see that the suspicions were 'unworthy'. Writing to Henry Brougham at the time, he was rather less inclined to give the commissioners the benefit of the doubt:

Many persons have an impression that they have a secret leaning to support the Governor at all hazards and are afraid to speak out even to them. I think them honest and honorable men and do not believe this of them. Still I must own there has all along appeared a disposition to shelter and excuse the Governor to a degree scarcely warranted by the necessity incumbent on them of official reserve and the proper respect to constituted authority.[45]

---

[43] Somerset to Bathurst, no. 103, 3 July 1824, Enclosures to Dispatches, CA, GH 28/10.
[44] Pringle, *Narrative*, p. 211.
[45] Pringle to Henry Brougham, 18 Dec. 1824, *Letters of Thomas Pringle*, p. 148.

Contracting 'an itch for political intrigue': spying for Bigge

Edwards had stared down the suggestion that he ranked amongst the most notorious agents provocateurs of the period, but it was not the last time his mysterious antecedents would see accusations of spying attached to his name. When he arrived in Sydney in 1824 on the convict transport *Minerva* under sentence from the Cape, he was immediately linked to John Thomas Bigge's previous activities in New South Wales. Bigge's report had been greeted with outrage by those who supported the emancipist cause. A concerted campaign began to discredit his findings, in which prominent emancipist voices such as William Charles Wentworth were loudest. In 1822 Wentworth had (vainly) challenged Bigge to a duel.[46] Two years later, in his *Statistical, Historical, and Political Description of the Colony of New South Wales*, and in his newly established newspaper the *Australian* (co-edited with fellow Sydney barrister Robert Wardell), Wentworth cast Bigge, in the words of historian John Ritchie, as 'a prejudiced and narrow-minded inquisitor, an official puppet, an accredited spy, and a tool of the exclusives'.[47]

With his uncanny shadowing of Bigge around the outposts of the British empire, these same opposition forces saw in Edwards an opportunity to discredit the commissioner and his unpopular recommendations by attacking *how* his information had been obtained. The *Australian's* attitude to Bigge, the enemy of the emancipists, was unequivocal:

> As a man, the experience we have had of his character, has sunk him beneath our contempt. As a public functionary, we admit that we regard him with unmingled detestation; and, if we had no other reason for this feeling, it would be fully justified by the divisions which he has endeavoured to sow and perpetuate in this community, and by his utter and shameless violation of Lord Bathurst's instructions to him (the most important in our opinion of the whole), which has allusion to the re-admission of the emancipists into the bosom of society.[48]

It is an opinion that proved long-lasting in certain interpretations, as the views of historian J. M. Bennett in 1971 indicate: 'Bigge reported only what he chose, his observations being corrupted by captiousness,

---

[46] Both men were in London at the time. Wentworth (later co-editor of the *Australian* newspaper that would accuse Edwards of being a spy for Bigge) claimed Bigge had misrepresented a statement by William's father, D'Arcy Wentworth. Although William Wentworth was placed under police restraint by Wilmot Horton, Bigge did see some merit in his position. He agreed to expunge the offending passage from his first report and issued an apology in his second. See Ritchie, *Punishment and Profit*, pp. 224–5.

[47] Ritchie, *Punishment and Profit*, pp. 246–7.   [48] *Australian*, 16 Dec. 1824.

sophistry and overwhelming prejudice against Macquarie and his supports on whom he looked with "jaundiced eye".'[49]

Rumours were flying around as soon as Edwards landed back in Sydney as to his previous identity and dealings in the colony. In this murky situation, there was political capital to be made. The *Australian* was keen to represent Edwards as a spy for Bigge, exploiting contemporary questions over the relationship between legitimate and illegitimate information-gathering in its attempt to discredit the commissioner. Later taxed with having 'wilfully misrepresented' the facts, the paper's editors defended themselves by referring to their own system of informants, saying that the statement 'published by us, on the arrival of the *Minerva*, was published on the spur of the moment; the substance of it was collected from what we had a right to consider the most authentic source; from a source, indeed, next to official.'[50]

If the *Australian* was to be believed, Bigge had been the driving force behind Edwards's 'political intrigue'. The newspaper's extensive account of Edwards's travels and activities from New South Wales to Mauritius and the Cape were refracted through the lens of Bigge's own imperial careering:

It appears that during the time Mr. Bigge was executing his Commission of Inquiry here, Lookaye was one of the persons from whom he derived much of that erroneous information contained in his report; and that having contracted an itch for political intrigue, he thought the Cape afforded, during the stay of the Commissioner, a fit scene for this purpose. He accordingly left the Isle of France, carrying off with him, it is said, some valuable MSS belonging to the Chief Justice of that Island, and soon *restored* himself to the Commissioner's recollection.[51]

Ironically, given what we know of the real relationship amongst the commissioners, Edwards and Somerset, the *Australian* considered that the

obnoxious line of conduct the Commissioner pursued towards the Governor General, Lord Charles Somerset, and the representations which he is understood to have forwarded to England against this nobleman, are supposed to have been founded principally on information derived from Lookaye.

---

[49] J. M. Bennett, 'The day of retribution', 91. In 2001, Bennett reiterated these views in his biography of Sir Francis Forbes, 'notwithstanding that it may run counter to a fashionable tide of historical scholarship at the time of writing this, that Bigge was of necessity prejudiced by the terms of his instructions, that he betrayed every principle of judicial independence, and that, on arrival in New South Wales, he allowed his prejudice to expand': *Sir Francis Forbes: First Chief Justice of New South Wales 1823–1837* (Sydney: Federation Press, 2001), p. 51.
[50] *Australian*, 16 Dec. 1824   [51] *Australian*, 25 Nov. 1824.

What was the 'strangest part of the business' was that Bigge denied ever knowing Edwards before he arrived in the Cape and that when the *Minerva* left that colony, it was not 'positively known, though some vague surmises were afloat on the subject', that Edwards had ever previously been in New South Wales.[52]

For its part, the government-orientated *Gazette* was scathing of the *Australian*'s attempts to make use of Edwards:

> much has been put afloat to effect designing purposes. The subject has been too *deeply* entered into, and evidently shews that Edwards would make a good tool to answer certain ends, were not people endowed with the liberty of thinking for themselves.[53]

The *Australian*'s account contains a germ of truth, but one that was carefully grafted onto a conspiratorial interpretation. Edwards and Kaye had indeed shadowed the various Bigge Commissions across their Indian Ocean route, although the parallel journeys had not taken place by design. Nor did they exactly match one another with regards to timing. If there was a connection between Edwards and the Commission, it was constructed by Edwards himself. He not only repeatedly sought employment with Bigge and Colebrooke, claiming that he could be of use to them from his time in Mauritius, but when caught up in the net of the Somerset regime, he also claimed connection with Bigge's time in New South Wales when it suited his purposes. Although all the evidence suggests that Bigge, for his part, kept Edwards at arm's length, the need of the commissioners to solicit information from a broad spectrum of society meant that political opponents could find means to discredit their recommendations by accusations that the sources of that information were tainted.

The *Gazette* insisted that Bigge's alleged use of Edwards made no logical sense: 'Is it at all likely that the King's Commissioner could stoop to elicit information of a newly-arrived prisoner, which it was impossible he should be able to afford?' The *Gazette* also poured scorn upon the *Australian*'s report that Edwards was a 'constant visitor' at Bigge's residence in Sydney and had been 'the closet advisor, the secret informer' that its rival suggested.[54] It outlined in detail timelines that allegedly proved that Edwards and Bigge could not have been acquainted, including that Edwards had been sent straight to Newcastle upon his arrival in Australia and returned to Sydney only seven days after Bigge sailed for Europe.[55]

---

[52] *Australian*, 25 Nov. 1824.   [53] *Sydney Gazette*, 2 Dec. 1824.
[54] *Australian*, 2 Dec. 1824; *Gazette*, 9 Dec. 1824.
[55] It is unclear whether Bigge encountered the convict Alexander Kaye when the commissioner visited Newcastle in January 1820. Certainly Bigge denied any knowledge

Edwards's disputed identity and alleged status as an informer became yet another way for the *Gazette* and the *Australian* to thrash out their differences in the wake of Bigge's Commission of Inquiry. The *Gazette* would later call it 'the first controversial subject on which we had the honor to enter the lists with the *Australian*'.[56] For all that the *Australian* had to concede most of the relevant points of fact in relation to Edwards and Bigge raised by the *Gazette*, the opposition paper's opinion of Bigge and the sources of his information remained unchanged:

> Every one here, or at least every one who was here during the Commissioner's time, is aware that he did not scruple to collect information from the very scum and refuse of the population, that all the w – s, rogues, and vagabonds of the country had free access to him; that some of the heads of departments from whom the most authentic reports might have been collected, were passed by merely because they happened to be friendly to General Macquarie, whilst the underlings attached to their departments were by the joint agency of cajolery and intimidation, invited to make false or highly coloured disclosures; that it was in fact from the foulest sources that the dirt and filth were laboriously scraped together, with which that nauseous production, termed 'The Commissioner's Report' is so plentifully interlarded.[57]

Bennett would criticise Bigge in a similar vein: 'Only part of the evidence was taken on oath; the rest, receiving equal credence, was tattled *in camera* by anyone who had any stories to tell of Macquarie and emancipists in government offices.'[58] In 1826 the dispute was still unfolding and the *Gazette* was still crowing over the manner in which it had discredited the *Australian*'s contention that 'Lookaye was an informer to the Commissioner',[59] for it had become a useful way to discredit any and all attacks on Bigge.[60]

The need to collect accurate information, and to base policy decisions upon official enquiries, was increasingly linked to notions of good governance in the early nineteenth century. The mechanisms by which that knowledge was to be gained were also being subjected to increasing scrutiny in the same period. Like the Colonial Office from which they heralded, the commissioners depended upon both official and unofficial registers of information-gathering, registers that could prove both useful and potentially discrediting. Imperial commissions of enquiry were political enterprises carrying metropolitan power and authority. Their

---

of Kaye prior to his reinvention as Edwards at the Cape. Nor would Edwards have admitted meeting Bigge at a penal settlement. I am grateful to David Andrew Roberts for pointing out the significance of their crossed timelines there.

[56] *Gazette*, 7 May 1828.   [57] *Australian*, 16 Dec. 1824.
[58] Bennett, 'Day of retribution', 92.   [59] *Gazette*, 11 March 1826.
[60] See also *Gazette*, 10 Sept. 1827.

presence upped the ante on pre-existing divisions that linked broadly allied political interests across seemingly disparate and localised concerns. Diverse groups would seek to both harness and contest the opportunities presented by these wide-ranging investigations.[61] It was in this context that a most unlikely whistle-blower could step onto the stage of imperial reform.

[61] Laidlaw, 'Investigating empire', 750.

4 'In return for services rendered'
Liberated Africans or prize(d) slaves?

In 1809, an insignificant French packet ship was intercepted by the English brig *Racehorse* between the enemy ports of St Denis and Port Louis on the islands now known as La Réunion and Mauritius. Proving herself ill-named, *Le Victor* was captured as a prize of war and taken to the Cape of Good Hope. In accordance with the necessary legal procedures, Cape Town's Court of Vice-Admiralty 'pronounced the ship and cargo to be enemy's property at the time of the capture and seizure thereof, and as such, or otherwise, subject and liable to confiscation'. Her 'tackle apparel and furniture, and the goods, wares and merchandizes laden therein' were put up for sale, returning the sum of 16 090 rixdollars to be split between the British Crown and the officers and crew of the *Racehorse*.[1] So far the case of *Le Victor* was entirely routine. There was nothing in the disposal of the ship and her cargo to suggest that the first step had just been taken on a road that would lead to serious charges of corruption in Cape Town's highest circles and political embarrassment for the British imperial government.

On board *Le Victor* were four black passengers: Louisa, a woman of twenty-four or twenty-five; her husband, Jean-Pierre, aged about forty-five; a boy of about sixteen named Denis; and a 'mulatto' man named Jean-Marie, then aged around seventeen years old, who came to be known at the Cape as Jean Ellé.[2] For those who had seized *Le Victor*, the status of this group was simply a matter of cold, hard cash. Both the master and the mate of *Le Victor* told the court that the four were slaves returning to their owners on the Isle de France (Mauritius). *Le Victor*'s master, Claude Guillaume Métairie, described them all as 'domestics'. Louisa and Jean-Pierre

---

Bigge and Colebrooke questioning J. B. Hoffman, *Slaves, Cape of Good Hope: Prize Slaves, BPP*, 1826–1827, xxi (42), p. 129.
[1] *Slaves, Cape of Good Hope: Prize Slaves, BPP*, 1826–1827, xxi (42), p. 39.
[2] Jean Ellé was described as twenty-four to twenty-five years old by the master of *Le Victor*, but later gave his age as 'about seventeen years' at the time: *Prize Slaves*, pp. 38, 127.

were the property of Mr. Josset, a captain of a troop at the Isle of France and a French subject... Denis is the property of Monsieur Dubignon, of the Isle of France, likewise a French subject, and Jean Marie is the property of Monsieur Guerin, likewise a French subject, residing at the Isle of France.[3]

Jean (Marie) Ellé would later claim that he was a free man, insistently describing himself as a 'prisoner of war' and not a slave.[4] Whatever the truth, the commander and crew of the *Racehorse* had every incentive to take the word of Métairie over any claims made by his passengers. According to the British Act abolishing the slave trade from 1807, the officers and crew of a capturing vessel shared in £40 for each adult male slave seized from enemy ships, £30 for each adult female and £10 for each child.[5] Slaves had value as prize cargo. Free passengers did not.

Jean Ellé and his compatriots now found themselves cast into a paradoxical world in which bondage was justified in the name of liberty. They became 'prize slaves'. When Britain had abolished the slave trade throughout its empire just two years previously, it also began a broader attempt to prevent rival nations from engaging in it. Although the legal foundations of these actions would come into dispute, controversy was delayed for around a decade because Britain was at war with most slave-trading European nations.[6] Slaves had hitherto fallen under maritime prize law like any other enemy cargo, to be sold off and their value added to the tally awarded to the enterprising captain and crew who captured them. With the slave trade declared illegal under British law, resale of prize slaves was no longer an option. The seventh article of the 1807 Act decreed that slaves so seized were to be made available first to the army and navy and second to private individuals, to be 'apprenticed' for up to fourteen years.[7] It forbade them from being 'sold, disposed of, treated or dealt with as Slaves', but it did not emancipate them. Instead, in the words of historian Rosanne Marion Adderley, they took on 'a not-slave-but-not-quite-free status under the protection and to a large extent the control of the British authorities'.[8] Known variously as 'prize slaves', 'prize negroes', 'liberated Africans', 'African recaptives'

---

[3] Evidence of Claude Guilliaume Metairie, master, and Pierre Barrant, mate/boatswain of *Le Victor*, 1809, *Prize Slaves*, p. 38.
[4] *Prize Slaves*, p. 7. [5] 47 Geo. III, VIII, 1807.
[6] The other main player, the United States, had also outlawed the Atlantic slave trade in 1807.
[7] 47 Geo. III, VII.
[8] R. M. Adderley, *'New Negroes from Africa': Slave Trade Abolition and Free African Settlement in the Nineteenth-Century Caribbean* (Indiana University Press, 2006) p. 25.

and 'apprentices',[9] between 1810 and 1846 over 116 000 enslaved people captured by the British Navy found themselves entering colonial systems as diverse as the West Indies, Sierra Leone, Mauritius and the Cape Colony.[10]

Once the Vice-Admiralty Court had declared them liable to confiscation, the 1808 Order in Council decreed that prize slaves came under the authority of the local Customs department. The principal officer of that department, the Collector of Customs, therefore had the responsibility of disposing of liberated Africans and supervising their subsequent treatment and relations with their employers. Under these circumstances, individual colonial officials held significant power over how far prize slaves were 'liberated' in any real sense. At the Cape, the Customs Department was the private fiefdom of two men: Charles Blair, Collector of Customs from 1808 to 1826; and William Wilberforce Bird, the comptroller of Customs, whose naming in honour of his more famous relative would prove bleakly ironic.

Viewed from the perspective of human misery, the situation of Jean Ellé was an unlikely catalyst in provoking a scandal over the treatment of liberated Africans at the Cape. For all the suffering they endured as a result of what flowed from abolition's humanitarian intentions – the forced labour, the violent beatings, the children forcibly taken from their parents – the immediate spark for exposing the system's abuses seems an almost obscenely trivial one: the quality of a merchant's dinner. Competition over Jean Ellé's skills in the kitchen led to a violent public argument between Lancelot Cooke, the man who wished to enjoy Ellé's services,

---

[9] Technically the term 'prize slaves' should be distinguished from 'Prize Negroes'. The former were slaves captured from enemy ships before the closure of the trade in 1807 and sold as prizes of war into continued enslavement. After the closure of the trade, captured slaves were classed as 'Prize Negroes' to be 'liberated' in 'apprenticeships'. In fact the investigations into Cooke's complaints suggests that both terms were used at the Cape fairly interchangeably, a slippage in which Christopher Saunders rightly sees significance: see his '"Free, yet slaves": Prize negroes at the Cape revisited', in N. Worden and C. Crais (eds.), *Breaking the Chains* (Johannesburg: Witwatersrand University Press, 1994), p. 100. I am grateful to Patrick Harries for pointing out this distinction.

[10] Saunders, '"Free, yet slaves"', p. 99. More than half were settled in Sierra Leone, and around 40,000 were sent to British Caribbean territories, some directly from captured ships but mostly on indentures from Sierra Leone in the 1840s and 1850s: see J. U. J. Asiegbu, *Slavery and the Politics of Liberation 1797–1861* (London: Longmans, 1969); M. Schuler, *'Alas, Alas Kongo': A Social History of Indentured African Immigration into Jamaica 1841–1865* (Baltimore: Johns Hopkins University Press, 1980); A. J. Barker, *Slavery and Antislavery in Mauritius 1810–1833: The Conflict between Economic Expansion and Humanitarian Reform under British Rule* (London: Macmillan, 1996); Adderley, 'New Negroes'.

and Collector of Customs Charles Blair, the official who wielded the power to distribute them. Cooke's decision to employ a notary named William Edwards to defend his outraged honour would ultimately transform this squabble into a wide-ranging scandal with political, legal and constitutional implications.

The cook, his master, the notary and the governor

After Ellé was declared a prize slave by the Vice-Admiralty Court in 1809 he was apprenticed to a series of masters before coming into the service of one Samuel Murray. In 1817 Murray hired him out to a local merchant house for the substantial income of 35 rixdollars per month.[11] The firm had 'put an advertisement into the Gazette for a good cook',[12] and this was both a skilled and a highly valued position. According to both Ellé and his new employers, all continued well at the firm (bar the odd drunken spree on Ellé's part) for the next six years. Then Samuel Murray died. It was now November 1823, and Ellé's apprenticeship only had some six months to run. He wanted to remain with the firm of Thompson and Cooke, and they wished to retain his services. He was clearly a skilled worker able to support himself through wages, and Lancelot Cooke tried to come to an arrangement on these terms with Blair, the Collector of Customs. This was the moment when things began to go wrong, for as Lady Anne Barnard (wife to the colonial secretary, leading hostess of Cape society and never at a loss for an aphorism to describe it) had commented some twenty years earlier: 'thou shalt not covet thy neighbour's Cook'.[13]

Murray had been Blair's wine merchant, and as such he was someone to whom the Collector of Customs found it expedient to offer favours. But Blair had no such cosy relationship with Launcelot Cooke, and he insisted that Ellé be reassigned to a master of Blair's choosing. He demanded that Cooke deliver Ellé to the Customs House, to be assigned to a Mr H. M. Pigou. Unsurprisingly, Pigou was also a close connection

---

[11] These wages placed Jean Ellé on level with a slave mason, a similarly skilled and respected artisanal position. The more usual hiring-out rate for a slave was 15–20 rixdollars per month plus subsistence and lodging, whereas an unskilled slave labourer would earn 10–12 rixdollars a month. The average monthly wages of free white unskilled workers were 25–30 rixdollars plus subsistence and lodging, and free white artisans could command 40–45 rixdollars: see S. Newton-King, 'The labour market of the Cape Colony', in S. Marks and A. Atmore (eds.), *Economy and Society in Pre-Industrial South Africa* (London: Longman, 1980), pp. 171–207; and Mason, *Social Death and Resurrection*, p. 120.
[12] Testimony of Jean Ellé, *Prize Slaves*, p. 127.
[13] M. Lenta and B. le Cordeur (eds.), *The Cape Diaries of Lady Anne Barnard 1799–1800*, 2 vols. (Cape Town: Van Riebeek Society, 1998–1999), vol. I, p. 71.

of the Customs House cabal, being son-in-law to William Wilberforce Bird. Blair evidently knew of Ellé's skills, for he had frequently eaten Ellé's dinners at Murray's table.[14]

At first Ellé refused to go to Pigou, but he heard that the police were going to arrest him for disobeying orders, and so he handed himself in to the authorities. With Ellé awaiting orders at the Customs House, Cooke tried to persuade Pigou to take another servant – first offering to find him another cook, and second offering to pay him a monthly amount in lieu of Ellé's services – but Pigou rejected the offers in 'considerable indignation'.[15] Cooke then went to the Customs House to try to persuade Blair and confronted both collector and comptroller. A violent argument broke out. Cooke claimed that Blair

in the most violent, loud and insulting manner, holding up his whip of stick in a threatening attitude, said... 'Damn you, sir, don't speak a word, or I'll knock you down. If you had said as much to me as you did to my friend Mr. Pigou, I would have blown your brains out; damn and blast you, I would, you scoundrel.'

As Cooke rode off, Blair called him 'a damned son of a bitch'.[16] Having spent a day in jail for refusing to go to his new master, Ellé was 'put into a cart belonging to Mr. Pigou, and sent to his country estate at Rondebosch'.[17]

Still smarting from Blair's public insults, Cooke approached William Edwards, and together the merchant and his notary explored a variety of responses. Cooke first applied to Deputy Fiscal William Van Ryneveld for redress. Edwards drew up Cooke's written complaint, and according to the usual procedure Van Ryneveld summoned Blair to attend him in his office. While waiting for Blair, Van Ryneveld tried, through intermediaries, to reconcile the two men, but to no avail. Cooke was convinced, as the deputy fiscal later testified, that there was 'a wish on the part of the authorities to screen Mr Blair'. Having failed to bring the parties to a satisfactory resolution, Van Ryneveld felt obliged to take the case before the sitting commissioner of the Court of Justice, but Cooke decided to abandon a criminal prosecution for assault and begin a civil defamation suit against Blair instead.[18]

Then, on the advice of William Edwards, Cooke determined to go over the heads of the local authorities entirely. He abandoned the defamation prosecution as well, and settled upon the remedy of sending a memorial to the Lords Commissioners of His Majesty's Treasury in

---

[14] *Prize Slaves*, p. 127.
[15] Testimony of John Roberts, Customs clerk, *Prize Slaves*, p. 154.
[16] *Prize Slaves*, p. 6.   [17] *Prize Slaves*, p. 127.
[18] Testimony of Van Ryneveld, *Prize Slaves*, p. 168.

London – the office responsible for appointing the Collector of Customs – complaining of Blair's conduct in the assignment of prize slaves.[19] With word of Cooke's intent spreading through the town, other disgruntled merchants saw a way to have their grievances transmitted to the metropolitan authorities, and they provided Cooke and Edwards with chapter and verse on 'many improper acts on the part of the Collector of Customs'.[20] Edwards also took down the testimonies not only of Ellé but of other liberated Africans with personal experience of Blair's corruption and ill-treatment. Even awaiting transportation to the Australian colonies on charges of libelling the governor, Edwards would make sure that these testimonies reached the commissioners.

Cooke sent his memorial to Governor Lord Charles Somerset on 12 January 1824, to be transmitted through the usual official channels. He posted another copy directly to England, a precaution that later paid off. For instead of sending on Cooke's memorial as the petitioners expected, the governor turned it over to the fiscal, Daniel Denyssen, and he brought criminal charges against Cooke and Edwards for defamation of a public servant. Going down this path would prove a serious tactical error on the part of the administration. In March 1824 Cooke and Edwards were acquitted after a month-long trial that only gave more publicity to the initial corruption allegations and that allowed Edwards to launch a broader attack upon the malpractices of the Cape administration. He charged not only that Crown officers had betrayed the ideals of British abolitionism, but that in prosecuting those who sought to expose their corruption they had proved themselves tyrants with no legitimate right to govern free-born Englishmen. Edwards's immediate audience was those who crowded into the Cape Town courtroom. Because the case was reported by a newly established Cape press, he also attracted enthusiastic supporters in both the colony and metropole, in particular those seeking evidence to attack the Tory-backed Somerset regime.

Concern over issues raised by slavery and suppression of the slave trade had loomed large in the parliamentary debates that led to the appointment of the Commission of Eastern Inquiry in the first place.[21] The decision to put Edwards and Cooke on trial only garnered negative publicity for a sensitive subject – the treatment of liberated Africans – already marked down for investigation. Once the trial was under way, Edwards soon came to dominate proceedings and set the terms of the contest that followed. By manipulating the emotionally charged subject of abolition, Edwards turned what had been an interpersonal dispute

---

[19] *Prize Slaves*, p. 6.   [20] *RCC*, vol. 17, p. 194.
[21] Laidlaw, 'Investigating empire', 753–4.

over injured personal reputation into a broader debate about national honour and imperial loyalty. How he did so is the subject of the following chapter. In order to understand how these debates unfolded, however, we first need to understand the prize slave system itself.

The remainder of this chapter puts that system in its broader colonial and imperial context and then explores it from the perspectives both of the prize slaves themselves and of those who sought to profit from their 'liberation'. Although the scandal of Jean Ellé pushed the issue up the agenda and dominated the structure and content of their final report, the prize slave system had already been flagged for the attention of John Thomas Bigge and William Colebrooke's Commission of Eastern Inquiry.[22] Similar investigations were made in the West Indies in 1827 and 1828, with direct interventions by the colonial authorities against slave-holder attempts to erode the freedom of liberated Africans in Trinidad and the Bahamas.[23] The British government was well aware that it faced criticism that the suppression of the slave trade had degenerated into an exercise in hypocrisy and a scheme to seize slaves bound for the colonies of rival powers in order to misuse them in British ones.[24] Furthermore, they recognised that most liberated Africans were being integrated into slave-labour plantation economies, where potential masters looked towards the new arrivals to supplement their bonded labour practices.

The result, in the Colonial Office, was 'a mixture of genuine concern and political sensitivity on the part of various civil servants'.[25] The rules that structured the prize slave system were designed to stop perceived abuses from both sides: masters were to be prevented from treating liberated Africans like chattel slaves; prize slaves were to be prevented from exercising unlicensed freedom. The result was 'a regulatory field'[26] through which both sides manoeuvred, but one in which the odds were heavily stacked against the latter. Exploring the quotidian struggles between prize slaves and those who sought to profit from them allows us to navigate this regulatory field and to track how what ended up in the sphere of public opinion (in the domain of the courts, the press and Parliament) began in the intimate space of master–servant relations.

---

[22] Bathurst to Somerset, 14 July 1823, Bathurst Papers, BL, 57/66. Laidlaw, 'Investigating empire'.
[23] Adderley, *New Negroes*, p. 16.
[24] On criticisms of the intention to 'achieve world supremacy under the cover of universal philanthropy', see C. L. Brown, *Moral Capital: Foundations of British Abolitionism* (University of North Carolina Press, 2006), pp. 11–12.
[25] Adderley, *New Negroes*, p. 15.
[26] L. Benton, 'Abolition and imperial law 1790–1820', *Journal of Imperial and Commonwealth History*, 39:3 (Sept. 2011), 356.

The prize slave system in imperial context

Historians estimate that between about 2000 and 3000 prize slaves entered the Cape Colony between 1808 and 1816.[27] Although most were seized on the high seas as prizes of war, others were 'liberated' into apprenticeships after being confiscated from those attempting to land slaves in the colony itself. By definition, the clandestine activities of illegal slave traders make the exact figures hard to pin down. In the context of the Cape labour market, prize slaves represented small numbers when compared with those of chattel slaves proper or with the indigenous Khoekhoen.[28] Yet the liminal position of prize slaves in particular throws several of the paradoxes of imperial liberty into especially sharp relief.

The abolition of the slave trade quickly became an emblem of British virtue, more especially in the context of war with the French, who reopened the trade in 1802. Slaves rescued from foreign ships were held up as a symbol of national honour, a sign that right was on Britain's side, and a powerful justification of divinely ordained victory over her rivals. The apprenticeships that followed the slaves' rescue were intended to bring forth a suitably devout and industrious class of working people from the ranks of the liberated Africans. In practice, the system by which prize slaves were assigned and controlled at the Cape (and elsewhere) opened up rampant opportunities for personal gain. Critics like Edwards pointed out that the honourable intentions of an abolitionist nation had been ruthlessly perverted by the corrupt behaviour of dishonourable officials.

The prize slave system at the Cape also unfolded within a set of broader imperial developments. British naval superiority in 1807 made actions to suppress the slave trade increasingly feasible, with the rules of war providing a convenient legal framework to justify abolitionist activities. There was, as the legal historian J. P. van Niekerk puts it, 'a seemingly natural connection between the abolition of the slave trade specifically (as

---

[27] Until recently, prize slaves at the Cape have received relatively little attention from historians, with the long-standing work of Christopher Saunders a notable exception. Saunders was first inspired to investigate the topic in the mid-1970s after attempts were made by the apartheid regime to forcibly remove black Africans from the Western Cape on the grounds that they (unlike those of mixed descent classified as 'Coloured') were recent arrivals to the region: see his 'Liberated Africans in Cape Colony in the first half of the nineteenth century', *International Journal of African Historical Studies*, 18:2 (1985), 223–39 and 'Free, yet slaves', pp. 99–115.

[28] R. Elphick and H. Giliomee's calculations of the Cape Colony population in 1820 are 42 975 whites, 31 779 slaves, 1932 free blacks and 25 975 Khoi: 'The origins and entrenchment of European dominance at the Cape 1652–c. 1840', in R. Elphick and H. Giliomee (eds), *The Shaping of South African Society 1652–1840*, 2nd edn (Cape Town: Maskew Miller Longman, 1989), p. 524.

opposed to enemies' colonial trade generally) and the rules of maritime warfare' that upheld the rights of search and detention.[29] The end of the Napoleonic Wars, however, shifted the legal landscape. An 1817 decision in the British courts ruled against unilateral action being taken against slave trading in time of peace.[30] The result was a new strategy of bilateral treaties between Britain and other nations, leading to the establishment from 1819 of Mixed Commissions to adjudicate slave ship captures.[31] These 'international courts of arbitration'[32] have become the focus of widespread interest by scholars of international and human rights law.[33]

During the Napoleonic Wars the Royal Navy squadron stationed at the Cape was more concerned with protecting the all-important sea route to India than with capturing slave ships. Those prize slaves whom they did seize were usually a by-product of more general action taken against enemy trade, as in the case of *Le Victor*. Far more significant inroads against the slave trade would be made in targeted and deliberate actions from the Cape during a second, postwar phase of anti-slaving activity in the 1830s and 1840s.[34]

The Cape labour market of the early 1820s, including the prize slave system, needs to be considered within the context of an expanding economy. British concerns with a severe trade deficit in its new colony prompted a search for a profitable export commodity, and, after several false starts, wine proved to be the solution. In 1813, upon the urgings of the Cape governor, Sir John Cradock, the duty on Cape wines imported into Britain was reduced to a third of its previous level. As

---

[29] J. P. van Niekerk, 'British, Portuguese, and American judges in Adderley Street: The international legal background to and some judicial aspects of the Cape Town Mixed Commissions for the suppression of the transatlantic slave trade in the nineteenth century', 3 parts, *Comparative and International Law Journal of Southern Africa*, 37 (2004), part 1, 7.

[30] The crucial decision involved the *Louis*, a French merchant ship captured in 1816 and condemned as a prize by the Vice Admiralty Court in Freetown, Sierra Leone, on the grounds that it was engaged in illegal slave trading: see van Niekerk, 'British, Portuguese, and American judges', 11–15.

[31] By the end of 1820 there were six mixed commissions in existence – an Anglo–Portuguese commission at Rio de Janeiro, an Anglo–Spanish commission at Havana, and three commissions (Anglo–Spanish, Anglo–Portuguese and Anglo–Dutch) at Freetown, Sierra Leone: see Adderley, *New Negroes*, p. 45.

[32] P. Harries, '"The hobgoblins of the Middle Passage": The Cape and the Trans-Atlantic slave trade', in U. Schmieder and K. Füllberg-Stolberg (eds.), *The End of Slavery in Africa and the Americas: A Comparative Approach* (Münster: LIT Verlag, 2011), p. 30. See also Patrick Harries, 'Negotiating abolition: Cape Town and the trans-Atlantic slave trade', *Slavery and Abolition*, 34:4 (2013), 579–97.

[33] van Niekerk, 'British, Portuguese, and American judges'; Harries, 'Hobgoblins'. Lauren Benton takes issue with the interpretation of mixed commissions as early human rights law or positivism in international law: 'Abolition and imperial law', 355–74.

[34] Harries, 'Hobgoblins'.

we have seen, this was a significant source of the British administration (and Somerset's) Cape Dutch support. By 1821 wine exports had risen to almost 63 per cent of all colonial exports, and by 1822 made up 10.4 per cent of all wine consumed in Britain.[35] Yet the financial advantage brought by the wine boom was largely monopolised by a small group of wealthy, intermarried families in the south-western Cape – the same families who dominated the key appointments in Governor Somerset's Anglo-Dutch administrative alliance.[36] Although the wine industry may have been dominated by a small oligarchy, slave ownership itself was not the prerogative of an elite, but common across all social levels. Between 1750 and emancipation in 1834 around half the adult male settlers in the colony owned slaves. Slave-labour usage was particularly high in Cape Town and the western districts of the colony, with 84 per cent of all slaves in those areas, whereas dependence on indigenous sources of labour was stronger towards the frontier.[37] Any restrictions on importing slaves therefore would have widespread impact across the economy.[38]

As historian Wayne Dooling points out, it was 'one of the great ironies of British rule at the Cape' that its support of a wine industry dependent on slave labour coincided with efforts to initiate a free labour market and ameliorate the situation of those in bondage.[39] Slave trading at the Cape greatly increased during the early nineteenth century, with more slaves imported between 1803 and 1808 (just under 4300) than in any equivalent period during VOC rule.[40] This was despite the fact that rising abolitionist sentiment at home inspired the metropolitan government to restrict slave trading in the colonies they had seized from the French and Dutch in this period. Correspondence between the Cape governor and the Colonial Office in the 1790s not only reveals the sensitivity of the issue to metropolitan audiences, but in the secretary of state's instruction to keep 'the Negro-subject' out of public despatches and avoid 'the ordeal . . . of Parliament', it demonstrates the same problems

---

[35] Dooling, *Slavery, Emancipation and Colonial Rule*, p. 81; M. Rayner, 'Wine and slaves: The failure of an export economy and the ending of slavery in the Cape Colony, South Africa 1806–1834', unpublished PhD dissertation, Duke University (1986), pp. 80–1; W. M. Freund, 'The Cape under the transitional governments 1795–1814', in R. Elphick and H. Giliomee (eds.), *The Shaping of South African Society 1652–1840*, 2nd edn. (Cape Town: Maskew Miller Longman, 1989), p. 329.
[36] Rayner, 'Wine and slaves', pp. 95–7.
[37] Mason, *Social Death and Resurrection*, pp. 17–18.
[38] Newton-King, 'The labour market of the Cape Colony'.
[39] Dooling, *Slavery, Emancipation and Colonial Rule*, p. 82.
[40] M. C. Reidy, 'The admission of slaves and "prize slaves" into the Cape Colony 1797–1818', unpublished MA thesis, University of Cape Town (1997), p. 6.

for the Colonial Office that we saw Bathurst dealing with in the previous chapter.[41]

Between 1808 (when the British closed the slave trade) and the mid-1820s (when they were investigating the charges of corruption brought by Edwards and Cooke) the price of slaves doubled at the Cape.[42] Similar tensions between economic growth and labour shortage were playing out contemporaneously in Ellé's home, Mauritius, where a sugar boom followed that colony's incorporation into British trade networks. In both Mauritius and the Cape, British officials were caught between instructions from London and their desire to placate a collaborating class of local planters. In these circumstances opportunities for personal gain abounded. In 1826, the same year that the investigations into prize slave corruption at the Cape were published in the Commons, abolitionist MP Thomas Fowell Buxton publicly accused former Mauritius Governor Robert T. Farquhar of having colluded in the illegal slave trade. That scandal was heightened by the prominent position that Farquhar had recently secured for himself in the abolitionist movement – as vice-president of the African Institution – upon his return to Britain. What had seemed an astute strategic choice on Farquhar's part now looked like rank hypocrisy and a potential disaster for his public reputation. Controversy over the place of Farquhar and the British administration in the slave-trading system of the Mascarenes Islands raged on in public debate until his unexpected death in 1830.[43]

When Edwards arrived at the Cape from Mauritius in 1823, the illegal slave trade in the south-west Indian Ocean was already notorious, and suspicions that British officials were complicit in it were increasingly widely held. The subject was known to be marked for investigation by the Commission of Eastern Inquiry. Edwards had sought to exploit this in his campaign to find work as a clerk with the commissioners, demonstrating his potential utility to them in their enquiries in Mauritius (where 'I know there is an agreement among the people not to tell you of the slave trading of that place'). He provided the commissioners with information and

---

[41] Dundas to Macartney, 26 Jan. 1798, and Macartney to Dundas, 7 May 1798, quoted in Reidy, 'Admission of slaves', pp. 43–4.

[42] See R. Shell, *Children of Bondage: A Social History of the Slave Society at the Cape of Good Hope 1652–1838* (Johannesburg: Witwatersrand University Press, 1994), pp. 122–3.

[43] The question of their degree of culpability continues to occupy scholars. A. J. Barker, 'Distorting the record of slavery and abolition: The British anti-slavery movement and Mauritius 1826–1837', *Slavery and Abolition*, 14:3 (1993), 185–207; Barker, *Slavery and Antislavery*. For a survey of the scholarly views taken on Farquhar and the British colonial regime in Mauritius, see R. B. Allen, 'Licentious and unbridled proceedings: The illegal slave trade to Mauritius and the Seychelles during the early nineteenth century', *Journal of African History*, 42 (2001), 91–116.

transcriptions of supporting documentations that he claimed could prove the corrupt practices of several individuals 'both high in the confidence of Govr Farquhar, & notorious slave dealers'.[44]

Although it clearly got him nowhere with the commissioners, the information that Edwards provided was in fact accurate. Those he named – Charles Telfair (Farquhar's private secretary) and Major Waugh – had already been the focus of 1818 allegations made to Bathurst by the acting governor whilst Farquhar was home on leave. In circumstances reminiscent of the Customs House cabal at the Cape, Telfair was registrar of the island colony's Vice-Admiralty Court, which adjudicated the cases of alleged illegal slave trading, and Waugh served as his deputy. Allegations of atrocities at Telfair's 'Belle Ombre' estate, of whose management Edwards promised to give details to the commissioners, would later be the centrepiece of the attacks on Farquhar in the *Anti-Slavery Reporter*.[45]

Stamping out the slave trade on the island was so difficult that Farquhar, from motives that continue to inspire debate, tried instead to stop the supply at the source through diplomatic negotiation with regional African and Indian Ocean leaders. Even the most committed abolitionist official faced the challenge of insufficient resources against a trade conducted close to the source of slaves and run by men with extensive local knowledge and experience. Many officials were openly sympathetic to planter interests and, like Telfair, were profiting directly from the sugar boom with their own slave-run plantations. The planters obstructed abolitionist efforts at every turn, from refusing to submit registers listing their bonded labour to using the cover of epidemics to replace the names of dead slaves with those of illegally captured or acquired ones. The documents that Edwards provided to the Commissions at the Cape included suspiciously convenient claims that 'Belle Ombre' had suffered no loss of life at all during recent outbreaks of smallpox and measles.[46] The Commission of Eastern Inquiry's final report of 1828 testified:

nothing but a general disposition in the inhabitants in favour of the slave trade, and the negligence or connivance of the civil authorities in the districts, and the great inefficiency, if not culpability in the police department, could have enabled bands of negroes to be landed and carried through so small an island and disposed of without detection.[47]

---

[44] Edwards to Commissioners, 2 Oct. 1823, TNA, CO 414/9.
[45] Barker, *Slavery and Antislavery*, pp. 26–7; 'Distorting the record', 198.
[46] Edwards to Commissioners, 2 Oct. 1823.
[47] *Report of the Commissioners of Inquiry upon the Slave Trade at Mauritius, BPP*, 1829 (292) Mauritius, pp. 14–15; Allen, 'Licentious and unbridled proceedings', 106.

The Cape's geographical location made an illegal slave trade far harder to sustain than was the case in the Mascarenes, but it nonetheless continued after 1808. When illegal slave traders were caught, their human cargo were designated Prize Negroes, to be apprenticed and eventually liberated – at least in theory. In practice, many illegally traded slaves remained clandestinely in bondage.[48]

Whatever the mode of their 'liberation', once they landed at the Cape, responsibility for distributing prize slaves lay with the Customs department. In a detailed account of the colony titled *State of the Cape of Good Hope*, published anonymously by 'A Civil Servant of the Colony' in 1823, the author described the Collector and Comptroller of Customs as 'laborious offices', the incumbents of which were not only hard working but scrupulously honest: 'There are no fees of any description received for their own use by the principal or inferior officers of customs; no candle-ends nor cheese-parings – all goes to the colonial government.' As *State of the Cape* went on to explain, the lesser officers of the Custom department were colonial appointments 'and removable by the Cape government'. The Collector and Comptroller, however, were both Treasury appointments, and thus directly accountable to London.[49] This dedicated, hard-working picture of the Collector and Comptroller in *State of the Cape* is unsurprising, given that the anonymous author was William Wilberforce Bird himself.[50] Despite the redirection of customs fees to the colonial government, the two officials still found numerous ways to profit from their office.

In theory, the need to prepare captured slaves for the burdens of freedom by apprenticing them for up to fourteen years was discretionary, as was the length of their indenture. This, at least in the opinion of Commissioners Bigge and Colebrooke's investigation, was the meaning of the sixth clause of the Order in Council of 16 March 1808. The commissioners considered that it justified remitting an apprenticeship when the prize slave had proved himself or herself worthy of independence. This was, however, an interpretation rather than an exact reading of the sixth clause, which spoke of appointing a new master when 'any such apprentice Negro, male or female, shall be thrown out of service or employment before he or she has acquired knowledge enough to gain his or her own support', but did not stipulate what should happen if such knowledge

---

[48] A. M. Rugarli, 'Eyes on the prize: The story of the prize slave present', *Quarterly Bulletin of the South African Library*, 62:4 (2008), 161–72.
[49] Anon., *State of the Cape of Good Hope in 1822*, facs. edn. (Cape Town: Struik, 1966), pp. 135–6.
[50] The authorship was an open secret in the colony, despite the comptroller's vehement denials: e.g., Hudson, Diary, 24 May 1824, Hudson Papers, CA, A602, vol. 3.

116   Imperial Underworld

had been acquired.[51] Blair chose to interpret it differently, claiming he had no right to remit such apprenticeships. In practice, therefore, those fourteen years translated into a de facto commodity – a source of free labour in a colony suffering an acute labour shortage brought on by the closure of the slave trade and a boom in the wine economy. The right to distribute this highly prized commodity was in turn a valuable source of power and patronage to those who held it. Contemplating the situation into which the provisions of the Anti-Slavery Act had placed them, it is abundantly clear that Blair and Wilberforce Bird asked themselves not what they could do for liberated Africans but what liberated Africans could do for them.

That men and women captured like Jean Ellé were so often called 'prize slaves', argues historian Christopher Saunders, 'was not so much a reflection of their slave status before "liberation" as of their status afterwards'.[52] In practice, their day-by-day experience differed little from those of slaves. As several witnesses testified to the Commissioners of Inquiry, Prize Negroes and slaves were on 'exactly the same footing, as to treatment'.[53] Newspaper notices about absconding apprentices, for example, were almost indistinguishable from those for runaway slaves.[54]

Yet for all the attempts of Cape masters to make them so, liberated Africans were *not* slaves, and both the imperial and local governments issued a series of regulations designed to prevent their being treated as such. The duration of their indenture and the date of their freedom was (again in theory) carefully documented and publicised; they could not be bought or sold; their children were free (unless born to a liberated African father and a chattel slave mother); their indentures could not be sold or transferred directly from one master to another; and they could not be flogged directly by their masters, but had to be sent to the authorities to be punished. In order for the employers to treat prize slaves as chattels, ways had to be found to circumvent these rules. The ambiguity inherent in the status of prize slaves therefore lay at the centre of a series of quotidian struggles involving the officials responsible for distributing prize slaves, the prize slaves' masters, and of course the liberated Africans themselves.

The boundaries of liberty: prize slave complainants

A significant number of prize slaves approached the Commissioners of Eastern Inquiry with complaints, shedding light on the large variety of

---

[51] *Prize Slaves*, p. 43.   [52] Saunders, 'Free yet slaves', p. 100.
[53] Testimonies of Thwaits and Lusebrink, *Prize Slaves*, pp. 131, 150.
[54] *Cape Town Gazette and African Advertiser*, 22 March 1823; 22 May 1824.

'In return for services rendered' 117

ways in which their liberty was eroded. These included inaccurate record keeping, as in the case of a mother and daughter named Marianna and Sarah. The two women found themselves in legal limbo after fourteen years of being told they were detained as prize slaves. All prize slaves were supposed to be registered and official notice of their freedom published, yet no record could be found of their original indenture or of their release. Without paperwork, the women were vulnerable. They could not rent lodgings without proof of freedom, and during the investigations Marianna ended up in jail for being out at night without a pass.[55]

Although the case of Marianna and Sarah underscores the persistent gaps in record keeping in the colonies, the growing anti-slavery lobby in the House of Commons prompted increasing efforts in this period to exert official control over bonded labour systems. Amelioration initiatives were designed to ease the transition to the free labour market and interpose a benevolent state between masters and their remaining slaves. In March 1823 Somerset issued a proclamation in this spirit directed at chattel slavery at the Cape. Its provisions included the right to legal Christian marriage with their masters' consent; a prohibition from selling children under ten years old away from their mothers if those mothers were Christians; accepting the testimony of Christian slaves under oath; and limiting hours of work and degrees of punishment. It remained in place until 1826 when Ordinance 19 significantly widened the rights of slaves, extending the privileges to non-Christians (a significant proportion, particularly in Cape Town, were Muslim). Most important, Ordinance 19 gave slaves the right to purchase their freedom, with or without their masters' consent, and created the office of the Guardian (later Protector) of Slaves, to which slaves – and Prize Negroes[56] – could bring complaints. Somerset's proclamation of March 1823 has been much discussed by Cape historians, particularly because it played a role in the colony's most significant slave rebellion.[57] By contrast, a second proclamation issued two months later relating to Prize Negroes has received almost no attention.

Like its counterpart for chattel slaves, the proclamation of 23 May 1823 also endorsed marriage rights:

---

[55] Case of Marianna and Saartje [Sarah], Commission of Inquiry: Prize Negroes and Free Blacks, TNA, 414/6, D.21
[56] Rugarli tracks one such complaint in 'Eyes on the prize'.
[57] In 1825, a mistaken belief that the proclamation had freed them allegedly inspired a group of slaves and indigenous bonded labourers to a small but violent uprising against their masters.

no Master or Mistress with whom the female Negroes shall enter into contract of service, shall throw any unjustifiable impediment in the way of such female Negro entering into the state of Wedlock, if circumstances shall admit thereof, on pain of forfeiting his claim to the remaining term of such Female's service.[58]

No explicit mention was made of religion. At least one prize slave woman enforced her right to marriage against her master's wishes on the basis of the terms of the proclamation.[59]

The main thrust of the proclamation, however, concerned the question of children born to prize slave mothers. Somerset declared that all children born to prize slave women during their apprenticeships and aged between five and eighteen years old, should be placed 'under the charge and care of the Masters or Mistresses to whom the Mother was last engaged: excepting in such cases, wherein the Mother can shew just cause of objection to such Master or Mistress'. Under threat of paying a fine of up to 100 rixdollars, the masters and mistresses were required to send the children to the Free School (should one be readily available) for at least three hours a week and to church on Sundays.

The motivation, as stated by the proclamation, was that 'provision should be made for the support, protection, and religious instruction of such Children'. Equally important, however, was compensation for their masters and mistresses who 'have incurred considerable expense and loss of labour, in those instances in which female Apprentices have been in a state of pregnancy, and during the infancy of the Children born to them'. Direct allusion was also made to the state's forcible control of Khoekhoen children, referring to

> the Laws of this Settlement, relative to the free Hottentot population, promulgated on the 22nd April 1812 and 18th July 1819, [which] declare it to be the duty of the Local Authorities to cause all Hottentot Children, deprived of their Mothers, to be immediately indentured to humane Masters and Mistresses [until the age of eighteen].

Indeed the 'Hottentot' model was so closely followed that the same printed indenture forms were used, reference to the date of the Proclamation of 1819 simply being scratched out and 23 May 1823 substituted instead. Thus 'as far as the case admits, in conformity with Laws so wisely established for the support and protection of free unprotected native Children', the same arrangement should be made for children of prize slave mothers 'born during the period of servitude'.[60]

[58] *Cape Town Gazette and African Advertiser*, 23 May 1823.
[59] Truter to Brink, acting colonial secretary, 9 July 1824, no. 45, CA, CO 214.
[60] Based on copy of proclamation filed in the Commission of Inquiry's case of Saartje.

Although the proclamation emphasised that masters and mistresses had to care for prize slaves' children of all ages, in practice the system meant that children could be taken from their parents from as young as six years of age (in contrast to those of chattel slaves, who retained their children until the age of ten). From six to eighteen, these children could be sent out to work and various pressures could be exerted upon their ostensibly free parents by the masters who controlled these children's lives.

The testimony before the Commissioners of Samboo, one of Collector of Customs Charles Blair's own prize slaves, underlines this point. He was uncertain about how long he had been apprenticed – all he knew was that he was bound to serve Blair for fourteen years. In a poignant reminder of who had access to official record keeping and who did not, he begged that the commissioners would investigate for him: 'I further wish, that the Commissioners would find out how long I have to serve, as I do not know'. He gave a guarded account of his situation under Blair, complaining only that Blair had apprenticed out all his children. Samboo and his wife Rosina (who lived apart from him) had five living children, but only the youngest lived with their mother. He specifically requested that one of his children be returned to Rosina: 'I have no complaints to make, except that my children are all apprenticed out, and I wish the one which is with Mr. Moore, a baker at Wynberg, should be returned to his mother; it is only six years old.'[61]

Children were a significant pressure point that could be used to blur the lines between chattel slaves and supposedly liberated Africans. The case of a former prize slave named Saartje, who came with her husband ('Assam a Chinese') to complain to the Commissioners of Eastern Inquiry in late 1824, graphically underlined how masters could continue to coerce labour from parents by holding apprenticeships over their children.[62]

No record was made of any outcome from these cases. Nor do we know whether Marianna and Sarah were able to resolve their bureaucratic impasse. Was Rosina and Samboo's six-year-old child retained by the Wynberg baker? Were Saartje and Assam able to extricate their children from the clutches of the couple who had, Saartje claimed, illegally held the mother as a Prize Negro (like Jean Ellé, Saartje also insistently described herself as a 'prisoner of war')? The lack of any kind of resolution in the archive is eloquent testimony to a disjuncture between the

---

[61] Evidence of Samboo, *Prize Slaves*, p. 169.
[62] Commission of Inquiry: Prize Negroes and Free Blacks, TNA, CO 414/6, D18.

needs of the Commissions of Eastern Inquiry and the hopes of those prize slaves who came to testify before them.[63]

In such a situation, prize slaves evidently saw in the presence of the Commission of Eastern Inquiry an alternative route for redress, one through which they might bypass local authorities and appeal directly to a metropolitan power whose views on slavery were no secret to people in bondage at the Cape. But the 'job of a commissioner was to *inquire* and not to *determine*'.[64] Commissioners Bigge and Colebrooke were investigating the situation of prize slaves in order to make general recommendations about British policy. They were not at the Cape to provide remedies for individuals seeking redress from their bondage, though their investigations *would* lead to the establishment in 1826 of the office of guardian (later protector) of slaves, an office that was specifically authorised to make judgements on the basis of such complaints. Individual cases of *official* misconduct, however, had far more serious implications, for they threatened to undercut the dictates of imperial policy and the reputation of an abolitionist nation. In so far as the commissioners' investigations passed judgement on particular accusations, therefore, their focus rested on the accusations of corruption made by Cooke with the assistance of Edwards.[65]

The boundaries of liberty: patronage and corruption

Ranged against prize slaves in the battle over defining their 'liberation' were not only their masters, but also the colonial officials delegated by the imperial state to protect their interests. As the investigations prompted by Cooke and Edwards revealed, however, these officials were often far more concerned with profiting from the system they controlled than with protecting the rights of those placed under their charge. Scholars have long recognised (as did contemporaries) that corruption ran rampant through the prize slave system at the Cape. They have paid less attention to unpacking the wider implications that flow from studying *how* this

---

[63] From 1826 the office of guardian (later protector) of slaves was specifically authorised to make recommendations on slave complaints. For all the limitations identified by historians it forms a contrast to the investigations of the commissioners.

[64] Ritchie, *Punishment and Profit*, pp. 99–100.

[65] For their parliamentary report into the complaints sparked by Cooke's memorial, Bigge and Colebrooke published the testimony of over forty witnesses between 7 May and 21 July 1825. These included both prize slaves and former prize slaves, those to whom they were assigned and others connected with the specific allegations against Blair and Wilberforce Bird. As part of their general investigations into circumstances at the Cape they also heard complaints from prize slaves filed within a volume titled 'Prize negroes and free blacks', TNA, CO 414/6.

corruption was managed in practice. The first strategy by which Blair, Wilberforce Bird and their allies exacted personal benefit from the prize slave system was a web of patronage that wove lines of reciprocity and debt (both financial and obligational) vertically through Cape society from the highest official level right down to the ranks of former chattel slaves. In the context of debates over 'Old Corruption', patronage networks were increasingly attracting negative attention. But they were nevertheless more easily excused than the second key strategy adopted by officials in the Customs Department, one that transformed supposedly liberated Africans into alienable property. Both mechanisms, however, relied upon unstated 'gentlemanly' agreements and reciprocal favours and were structured by both gender and social status. Most (though not all) involved elite men and those with immediate obligation to them. Tracing these methods underlines how clientage relationships formed part of the quotidian operation of imperial power. The criticism they attracted should be seen as part of a broader breakdown in consensus over appropriate official conduct and a wider transition in imperial politics and governance explored in the previous chapters of this book.

In theory, the length of apprenticeship was discretionary and dependent upon whether a prize slave could support himself or herself. Yet at the Cape, Blair and Wilberforce Bird routinely apprenticed prize slaves for the maximum allowable period. Liberated Africans' apprenticeships therefore represented fourteen years of enforced labour without even the purchase price of a slave being required, making them a valuable commodity in a straitened labour market.

Cape masters did all they could to take advantage of this virtually free labour source. In the course of his investigations for Cooke, Edwards collected correspondence from masters seeking to persuade Blair that they should be assigned incoming labour. J. B. Hoffman, who would later be indicted for copying Cooke's Memorial to the Lords Commissioners of the Treasury, had tried to influence Blair to assign him apprentices by invoking the principles of British humanitarianism: he proposed doing his bit towards ending slavery at the Cape by manumitting his female chattel slaves in return for being apprenticed Prize Negroes. (It would of course do Hoffman no harm to exchange 'children of the female sex' for the much more profitable free labour of adult men.) Hoffman got nowhere, however, and the prize slaves were distributed elsewhere – no doubt to the benefit of the customs officials. Called to give evidence to the commissioners, Hoffman had ample opportunity for revenge. Asked whether he knew of instances in which Blair and Wilberforce Bird had 'distributed Prize Negroes in return for services rendered to them, or in payment of debts due to them', Hoffman named names, detailing farm produce that was paid, horses that were stabled, accounts that were settled and debts cancelled, all in return for the assignment of prize slaves.[66]

Liberated Africans themselves were of course also in a position to expose the system. William Cousins, who had been fourteen years a prize slave in the service of Charles Blair himself, provided detailed testimony for Edwards, not only about how badly Blair treated his apprentices, but also how he had exchanged the distribution of liberated Africans for 'presents' of barley, veal, fruit and game, and forage for his livestock. From Cousins's testimony and from the later investigations of the commissioners, it became clear that this was all done informally, thus leaving no incriminating trace in official records.[67]

On the basis of such tip-offs, the investigations of the commissioners uncovered how Blair used his control over the distribution of prize slaves to grant labour to his friends, relatives and creditors in lieu of payment of his own obligations. He also assigned a considerable number of prize slaves to himself (fifty-four were discovered in the subsequent enquiry, although there were probably more) and to William Wilberforce Bird (who took twenty-three). Blair, alleged Cooke in his memorial to the Treasury, 'acquired consequence and credit by disposing of so many Slaves of the most unfortunate order'.[68]

Prize slaves were not just a labour commodity, but could also be used as a source of real income in ways other than by apprenticeship. They were frequently hired out by their masters to others in exactly the same way as chattel slaves.[69] The commissioners pointed out that

the instances are numerous and of daily occurrence, in which Prize Negroes, who are perfectly competent to support themselves, are reapprenticed by the Collector and Comptroller, and become a source of profit in the hands of poor masters, who derive considerable profit, if not their principal subsistence, from hiring out the Negroes to other persons.[70]

This practice of hiring out, claimed the commissioners, 'is invariably accompanied by a great rise in the price of labour in Cape Town, to industrious individuals who have not been fortunate enough to share in the same indulgence'.[71]

---

[66] Testimony of J. B. Hoffmann, *Prize Slaves*, pp. 34–5, 129.
[67] Testimony of William Cousins, *Prize Slaves*, p. 32.
[68] Memorial of Cooke, *Prize Slaves*, p. 48.
[69] For a discussion of the role of hiring out in the urban economy see A. Bank, *The Decline of Urban Slavery at the Cape 1806–1843* (Rondebosch: Centre for African Studies, 1991).
[70] *Prize Slaves*, p. 14.   [71] *Prize Slaves*, p. 106.

When Jean Ellé was apprenticed to Samuel Murray he was one of no fewer than twenty-two prize slaves assigned to the Collector's wine supplier. Many of these apprentices, including Ellé, were then hired out by Murray to masters around Cape Town, thus providing Murray with his main source of income.[72] W. J. Birkwood, whose job it was to complete the indentures of prize slaves for Customs House, knew of 'no other reason' for Murray receiving so many prize slaves but for him being 'extremely intimate with Mr. Blair'.[73] No less a person than Murray's brother testified that 'he always considered it to be an act of friendship in Mr. Blair to assign so many Prize Negroes to him'.[74]

Although they could find little direct evidence that Blair had used the assignment of prize slaves to cancel his debts, the commissioners remained in no doubt that his creditors had benefitted from preferential treatment and had returned the favour by granting more than usual leniency in demanding payment.[75] The assignment of liberated Africans at the Cape was built into already established practices of extending lengthy credit to high-status individuals, especially officials with significant powers of patronage.[76] Many of those giving evidence before the commissioners were closely questioned as to whether they had given Blair long-term credit in exchange for being assigned prize slaves, and it became clear that he was living beyond his means and owed money all over the city.[77]

Charles Dixon was one such creditor who benefitted from Blair's ability to dice with the lives of liberated Africans, and Blair's transactions with him came closest to finally tripping up the Collector of Customs. Dixon (who placed repeated notices advertising prize slave runaways in the *Cape Town Gazette*[78]) had lived at the Cape since 1806 and established his livery stables in 1809. He first received prize slaves in 1812, and it was reported in the town that 'he could not have succeeded in his business, if it had not been for the Prize Negroes that the Collector had given him'.[79] When Blair left for England in 1820, he still had an unpaid debt of 1441 rixdollars with Dixon, a sum he promised to pay upon his return to the Cape. As Dixon delicately put it, 'I did not like to press him for the payment of his bill when he was going home in a hurry, especially as he had been a good friend to me, and had given me the Prize Negroes.'[80] After Edwards began to make inquiries, Dixon got anxious and started

---

[72] *Prize Slaves*, p. 12.   [73] Testimony of W. J. Birkwood, *Prize Slaves*, p. 146.
[74] Testimony of John Murray, *Prize Slaves*, p. 143.   [75] *Prize Slaves*, p. 19.
[76] Testimony of W. Heyward, *Prize Slaves*, p. 172.
[77] Testimony of Christina Maria Lusebrink, *Prize Slaves*, p. 151.
[78] *Cape Town Gazette*, 22 March 1823; 20 Sept. 1823; 12 April 1824.
[79] *Prize Slaves*, p. 104.   [80] Testimony of Dixon, *Prize Slaves*, p. 140.

tampering with the records of his dealings with Blair, as his accountant John Warden testified before the commissioners. Dixon admitted to the commissioners that he had manipulated the records once he received a belated promissory note from Blair:

> I requested him to antedate it that I might make it appear in my book that the account had been settled long ago, being apprehensive, as I said, that Mr. Edwards would give trouble, as he had been making inquiries about Prize Negroes.[81]

The second strategy that Blair and Wilberforce Bird used to profit from the prize slave system involved turning liberated Africans into alienable property. This was potentially more risky for an official than invoking patronage networks, for it was directly contrary to the provisions of the Abolition Act. The solution was once more to keep arrangements informal and outside official scrutiny. When Blair's estate 'Stellenberg' was sold in 1819, it was commonly believed that the apprenticeships of the prize slaves working there would be transferred with it, with significant implications for the price.

Wilberforce Bird, it was claimed, used similar tactics to push up the value of his own landed property, 'Groene Rivier'.[82] Officially this was illegal, but Captain William Hollett, who had unsuccessfully bid for Blair's estate at public auction (he offered 110 000 guilders when the asking price was set at 120 000) gave testimony of the gentlemen's agreement by which this was done. Not only did several persons tell him that he could be assured that the labour (as he remembered it, six men, two women and two children) would stay with the estate, but 'when Mr. Blair offered the estate to me after the sale, he said that he would pledge his word and honour that the Prize Negroes should not be removed after the expiration of their term.'[83] Their bonded labour, Hollett calculated, would add at least 20 per cent to the value of the estate.

The evidence presented of such transactions was often contradictory, suggesting that such discussions were coded and set about with caveats as they were well known to be illegal. Assertions of 'word and honour' had to take the place of legal documents. Hollett, for example, claimed he had been told by several people, including Blair's agent in the sale, that he could expect the estate of Stellenberg to be sold with the continuance of those prize slaves working on it, at a minimum up to the end of their

---

[81] Testimony of Dixon, *Prize Slaves*, p. 172.   [82] *Prize Slaves*, p. 15.
[83] Testimony of William Hollett, *Prize Slaves*, p. 135. One of the 'several persons' was Charles Dixon, whose transactions with Blair were a key line of enquiry in the corruption investigations. Dixon, however, denied this: *Prize Slaves*, p. 141.

indenture. It was, indeed, upon this expectation that he had bid the price he did. Meeting Blair by chance afterwards, he first testified that Blair seemed 'surprised' at his assumption and asked 'how I could have formed such an idea, for he said that they could not be regularly sold or assigned at the sale'. And yet he also testified that during this conversation Blair had said that

> he was sorry that I had not purchased the estate, and that it was worth a great deal more than I had bid for it; he asked me if I was aware of the Negroes that were upon the estate, and their value; I answered that I was, and that if I had not been aware of it, I should not have bid the sum that I did.[84]

The man who successfully bought 'Stellenberg' took over the indentures of 'ten boys and a girl' and still retained them at the time of his questioning by the commissioners in 1825. Although he claimed not to have been influenced by the prospect of their labour in making the purchase, he admitted that 'several people told me that the Prize Negroes would make a great deal of difference in the value of the estate'.[85]

Blair himself never denied that the transfer had been made, although he put a very different gloss on it. All these arrangements, he claimed, were for the benefit of the labour rather than to enhance the value of his own property. He claimed he had

> left certain Prize Negroes on the Stellenberg estate, on which they had been employed for some years, on which their wives and children lived, and to which place they were much attached; Mr Blair was then about to go to England, and to sell his estate, and had no occasion for their labour.[86]

After his arrest for criminal libel, Edwards argued from jail that such practices were clearly evidence that Blair, the 'great Prize Negro Merchant', was 'trafficking and trading in Prize Negroes', and that this represented evidence of 'a worse corruption than that pointed at in my memorial'.[87]

Yet another example of how prize slaves were treated as real property came from the testimony of James Onslow Williams, employed by the Customs House since 1815. It also underlines how patronage networks extended far beyond the immediate colonial community, binding emigrants into links of reciprocity that stretched back to their previous lives. Together with Francis Dashwood, Williams was granted a twenty-one-year lease on a property in the colony's south-west in 1810. The yearly

---

[84] Testimony of William Hollett, *Prize Slaves*, p. 136.
[85] Testimony of John Amber, *Prize Slaves*, p. 138.
[86] Letter of Wilberforce Bird and Blair, *Prize Slaves*, p. 108.
[87] Letters from Court of Justice, CA, CO 214, no. 31, 1824.

rent was 800 rixdollars, with the property held on condition of Dashwood and Williams erecting a house and farm buildings and 'promoting the breed of Spanish sheep'. Dashwood advanced the capital necessary for the buildings and for purchasing the stock, but the venture clearly did not prosper. Five years later, Williams gave up the farm to Dashwood, to whom he was now in debt to the tune of 10 000 rixdollars.

Up to that point, Williams had received sixteen prize slaves, all of whom were employed on the estate. When he left the venture, Dashwood wanted their indentures signed over, but Williams 'declined for a long time, and refused on the ground of my not having any right to dispose of the services of Prize Negroes that had been indentured to me'. Dashwood pressured him by saying that Blair would allow it, and, being in financial embarrassment at the time, Williams assented, writing a letter to Blair confirming that the indentures of the prize slaves had been transferred to his former partner. Blair, claimed Williams, had reprimanded him about it: 'In the name of fortune what could have induced me to write him the letter he had received, requesting his permission to assign over the services of so many Prize Negroes to Mr Dashwood'. Blair denied that he had ever told Dashwood that this procedure was authorised. But the Collector and Williams had long-standing family connections in Dorset ('his father and mine were very intimate') and the bonds of reciprocity were strong. Blair proceeded to honour the agreement ('As you had written such a letter to me, I could not do otherwise than assign over the Negroes to Mr. Dashwood'). But he was careful to keep the arrangement informal, rather than altering the indenture papers. It appeared abundantly clear that by means of the arrangement Williams was writing off his debt to Dashwood, although the farm did not remain in operation for more than one year. Such informal arrangements allowed prize slaves to become de facto commodities, but they could not be official ones, which had the added advantage that they escaped sequestration when a master went bankrupt.[88]

As Cooke and Edwards were brought before the court, the diarist Samuel Hudson repeated what was clearly common gossip in the town. The 'transactions' of Blair, he claimed, were 'notorious and in the possession of every one who cares to listen to them'. As he continued:

I am pretty certain the assertion is true that the prize slaves have paid his debts tho it may be difficult to prove.... I have heard repeatedly that he has cancelled considerable debts by this means and from those who actually had experienced it

---

[88] Testimony of J. O. Williams, *Prize Slaves*, pp. 149–50.

'In return for services rendered' 127

I make no doubt from a thousand circumstances that he is guilty Wilberforce Bird more so and Pigou a brother and colleague in providing the nefarious business.

Hudson also anticipated that, with the source of patronage removed, it might be easier to get people to talk 'as there is no more expectations in future it may make some of them fearless and induce them to speak the truth otherwise Interest might keep their secret'.[89] His predictions were both proved right. People did begin to talk, but Blair and Wilberforce Bird had employed unstated obligations to excellent effect. The informal nature of all these arrangements made them almost impossible to pin down with real evidence.

Faced with the testimony assembled by the investigations of the commissioners, Blair and Wilberforce Bird vehemently protested their innocence. They would have no trouble in countering the charges of 'neglect or corruption in the discharge of our duty', they argued, because they were clearly

so confused and improbable, so weak in attempted proof, so abundant in spite and malice, so defective in the display of those honest, conscientious and honorable motives which ought to actuate individuals in their attacks upon public servants.

Blair claimed it was simply his duty to 'apprentice Prize Negroes to good and humane masters', and this was precisely what he had done. In seeking such masters, it could not be expected that he should pass over every connection of his own:

Do his accusers mean to argue, that in the discharge of his duty of distribution, he was to pass by all with whom he might happen to be connected socially, or even interestedly, and seek out other persons unknown or unfriendly?[90]

In his defence, Blair gets to the heart of the matter: should an official administer advantages impartially or should a distinction be made between the 'unknown or unfriendly' and those who could offer him some benefit? This was part of the much broader discussion raised in the previous chapters over 'Old Corruption': the idea of public office as private property and the untrammelled operation of patronage and governance by personal network.[91] An increasing climate of hostility towards corruption and the need to reduce expenditure stimulated metropolitan interference in the near absolute power of colonial governors in the 1820s.[92] Reformist Tories emphasised the importance of governing frugally and

---

[89] Hudson, Diary, 16 Feb. 1824.
[90] Letter of Blair and Wilberforce Bird, 21 June 1825, *Prize Slaves*, p. 107, 109.
[91] Harling, *The Waning of 'Old Corruption'*; J. M. Bourne, *Patronage and Society in Nineteenth-Century England* (London: Edward Arnold, 1986).
[92] Laidlaw, *Colonial Connections 1815–1845*, pp. 51–2.

5 'The dishonorable Court of Gothamites'
Corrupting abolition

Charles Blair was widely recognised by both bond and free as a man of hot temper. William Cousins, a prize slave assigned to the Collector of Customs, testified that Blair 'whips and flogs all the Prize Negroes in his service in a most cruel manner', and that he had shot a prize slave named Jack in the hand as punishment for an attempted escape.[1] So when Blair and merchant Lancelot Cooke got into an argument over the assignment of Jean Ellé, it was perhaps predictable that Blair would lose his temper. Blair might also have expected that his use of intemperate language and violent threats would have consequences. Managing the parameters of such public altercations provided routine business for local notaries like William Edwards.

What Blair clearly did not anticipate was that the insulted Cooke, advised by Edwards, would abandon the conventional social and legal remedies laid down for public insults in favour of a complaint to the Treasury in London. In going over the head of local authorities and involving the institutions of the imperial government, Edwards took the first step in transforming a dispute between two men into a much broader debate over national character.

Edwards's memorial to the Lords Commissioners of His Majesty's Treasury linked the particular offence against Jean Ellé and Lancelot Cooke to the general principles underpinning the abolition of the slave trade with devastating clarity:

The English Senate intended to have been the friend and protector of the wretched Negro; but in this case it has been the greatest misfortune. Here is a man well able to earn thirty-five rixdollars per month as a cook, who, on pretence of being taught a business, is bound, by the ruthless cupidity of His Majesty's

---

Diarist Samuel Hudson's assessment of the Somerset administration and its allies. Diary, 4 May 1824, Hudson Papers, CA, A602, vol. 3.

[1] Testimony of William Cousins, *Slaves, Cape of Good Hope: Prize Slaves*, BPP, 1826–1827, xxi (42), p. 32.

servants, to serve the most valuable part of his life in the favours of the Collector of Customs at Cape Town.... Your Lordships will feel how inconsistent is such conduct with the philanthropy that abolished Slave-dealing.[2]

Through the violence of his language, the unfairness of his conduct in separating master from servant and the 'violation of every principle of humanity towards the poor man', Collector of Customs Charles Blair had betrayed the trust placed in him by the king, a position 'in which equanimity of temper, humanity, disinterestedness and benevolence of heart, ought to shine in a superlative degree' – all this 'merely to supply Mr Bird's son-in-law with a cook'. Personal honour and civic duty went hand in hand in the complaint. Cooke claimed:

> he owes it to his own rank in society, to call from Your Lordships for justice on Mr. Blair, who has thus trampled on all the decencies of life; and he does this more confidently, knowing that You are most able and most willing to screen gentlemen from the insolence of office.[3]

In this chapter I track the theme of honour through three registers in order to demonstrate the broader implications of both the prize slave scandal and of how Edwards manipulated it for local and metropolitan audiences. In the first place, the entire controversy arose from an interpersonal dispute in which one party publicly insulted another. What was it about Cooke's actions in seeking to retain the services of Ellé that provoked such offence and such a violent response from Blair? In return, why was Cooke so determined to take the matter further, and what light does the altercation throw on masculine honour, paternalism and ideas about the master–servant relationship? In the second section, I discuss how Edwards's and Cooke's trial for criminal libel highlights the slippery legal distinction between actions taken from a desire to defend oneself against personal insult and actions taken from a desire to expose official corruption for the public good. This was a key question upon which the specific action turned, but William Edwards's grandstanding through the proceedings also gave attention to wider issues regarding the relationship between personal reputation and the state. In the final section of this chapter I place the question of honour in a national framework, demonstrating how both Dutch and British colonial officials employed the rhetoric of abolition to defend themselves against charges of corruption and disloyalty. It was similarly important to Edwards and his allies in their attempt to extricate themselves from the persecution of the Somerset regime.

---

[2] Memorial of Cooke, *Prize Slaves*, p. 7.   [3] Memorial of Cooke, *Prize Slaves*, pp. 7–8.

Mr Blair's bad language: honour and paternalism in master–servant relations

The first area in which the prize slave scandal raised issues of liberty and honour relates to the increasingly vexed position of the master–servant relationship within the 1820s amelioration policies of the imperial state.

Blair guarded his right to control the distribution of prize slaves extremely jealously. One Cape Town merchant, who had earlier found himself at odds with the Collector over this issue, was not only quick to obey his commands but also anxious to apologise to Blair for actions that 'might have given him offence'.[4] Nevertheless, a wide cross section of Cape society was shocked at Blair's lack of self-control. Diarist Samuel Hudson, having read 'the different documents respecting Blair Cook and Edwards', was immediately struck by the importance of this aspect of the case:

[I] must confess Blairs conduct and language is most scandalous as a Man and a Servant of his Majesty – it must strike the Lords of the Treasury with astonishment when they peruse the damning proof of this mans rascally proceedings.[5]

Some thought that Cooke, to defend his honour as a gentleman, should have challenged Blair to a duel.[6] Social status and ideas of masculinity were foundational to how onlookers, both sympathetic and opposed, viewed the affair. Governor Somerset was utterly convinced of Blair's innocence, as he wrote in private to Commissioner Bigge:

the whole of the rumours inimical to Mr Blair are calumnies & without foundation – indeed I never thought otherwise. Mr Blair was born a Gentleman & I am slow to believe that any *Gentleman* would readily compromise his honour, more particularly when he is acting for the Justice of where a sense of Duty is the innate feelings of rectitude.[7]

Ironically, it was upon precisely these kinds of assumptions about position (basing financial arrangements with 'gentlemen' on trust rather than putting them in writing) that had allowed the corruption in the prize slave system to flourish. Edwards, by contrast, was entirely dismissive of the suggestion that anyone who spoke in public as Blair had done could lay claim to gentlemanly status. Referring to Blair's supporters, he wrote:

[4] Testimony of John Deane, *Prize Slaves*, p. 165.
[5] Hudson, Diary, 3 March 1824, Hudson Papers, CA, A602, vol. 3.
[6] Hudson, Diary, 11 March 1824.
[7] Somerset to Bigge, 2 April 1824, Bigge–Somerset correspondence 1823–1826, Rhodes House, University of Oxford, MSS Afr s. 24 (original emphasis).

They could not suppose I should believe all they said of this true gentility or else they thought I was unable to read the records of the numerous charges and the convictions against him before the Court.... Surely they must have thought I had been born and bred in Billingsgate to call that Man a Gentleman who uses the expression he did to Mr Cooke. What true, what real Gentleman ever phrased even a dog 'a damn son of a Bitch'.[8]

The language of mutual respect was central to structuring relations between elite men. In the Cape context, a slave society and a society dominated by a strong military presence combined to reinforce an honour culture amongst both Dutch and British.[9] For a colonial official to offer such language to a respectable city merchant was a serious matter. When summoned before the deputy fiscal during the original attempt at a reconciliation, Blair expressed himself outraged at Cooke's conduct. Charged with the accusations of Cooke, he answered that 'if the expressions imputed to him were true, he had uttered them in the heat of passion, but that Mr. Cooke's conduct had greatly irritated him'.[10] As we saw in the previous chapter, the spark that ignited the dispute was that Cooke had suggested paying off H. M. Pigou in order to retain Ellé's services. Both the memorial and the commissioners' report pointed out this aspect of the case. As Cooke put it,

if Your Lordships would afford Your protection against the future oppressions of the officers of Customs, several cases should appear before You of Mr. Blair's privity to such contracts as that offered to Mr. Pigou, at which he expressed such indignation; to contract even more corrupt.[11]

The commissioners similarly recognised that

Mr Blair might have pleaded in extenuation of his violence the offensive offer that had been made by Mr. Cooke to Mr. Pigou, and which implied a corrupt

---

[8] Letters from Court of Justice 1824, CA, CO 214, no. 31.
[9] J. E. Mason, 'Hendrik Albertus and his ex-slave Mey: A drama in three acts', *Journal of African History*, 31 (1990), 423–45; W. Dooling, 'The good opinion of others': Law, slavery and community in the Cape Colony c. 1760–1840', in N. Worden and C. Crais (eds.), *Breaking the Chains: Slavery and its Legacy in the Nineteenth-Century Cape Colony* (Johannesburg: Witwatersrand University Press, 1994); R. Ross, *Status and Respectability in the Cape Colony 1750–1870*: K. McKenzie, *Scandal in the Colonies: Sydney and Cape Town, 1820s–1850s* (Melbourne University Press, 2004); Dooling, *Slavery, Slavery, Emancipation and Colonial Rule*; N. Worden, 'Artisan conflicts in a colonial context: The Cape Town blacksmith strike of 1752', *Labour History* 46:2 (May 2005), pp. 155–84; N. Worden, 'Demanding satisfaction: Violence, masculinity and honour in late eighteenth-century Cape Town', *Kronos*, 35 (2009), 32–47; R. L. Watson, *Slave Emancipation and Racial Attitudes in Nineteenth-Century South Africa* (Cambridge University Press, 2012).
[10] Testimony of W. C. van Ryneveld, Deputy Fiscal, *Prize Slaves*, p. 168.
[11] Memorial of Cooke, *Prize Slaves*, p. 7.

connivance, in the payment to him of a pecuniary indemnity for the services of a Prize Negro.[12]

The immediate cause of the violent response therefore was that Blair had been backed into a corner. Cooke had publicly, and before witnesses, demanded access to the unstated system of kickbacks and illegal transfers that had been taking place in private.

Beyond the implication of corruption, however, there also echoed deeper resonances in the case for the way honour and status were conceived within the Cape slave society. Interfering between a man of status and his personal servant, or offering a man of status money in lieu of that servant, was a potential source of deep offence. The commissioners showed themselves well aware of the degree to which the insults offered undermined a master's right to respect in their report. The resentment came first from the 'personal affront and insult' that Cooke had suffered from Blair when he tried to give an explanation as to 'an apparent inattention to the Collector's orders'. In the second place, offence lay in what was cast as officious meddling – in the removal of Ellé from a service 'in which he was happy and contented' to that of Mr Pigou, 'a near connexion of the Comptroller of Customs, for whose service he had manifested the greatest aversion, and at a period when he was perfectly competent to provide for his own support'.[13] Ellé told Edwards that he was 'uncomfortable and miserable in the employ of Mr. Pigou', and that even though Mrs Pigou had promised to pay him wages after the expiration of his apprenticeship, he intended to return to the firm of Cooke and Thompson as soon as he could. These emotions, it was clear in the testimony Ellé gave before the commissioners, were rooted in the coercion he had suffered.[14] Bigge and Colebrooke concurred, remarking on

> the superior advantages of a service, in which the relation of the master and servant is founded upon the basis of reciprocal attachment and of one wherein it is supported only by coercion and countracted by a strong sense of hardship and injustice.[15]

Both Cooke and Edwards emphasised the personal bond between master and servant, Edwards constructing an imagined dialogue between Cooke and Ellé in the trope of paternalist melodrama:

'Oh! Master save me from Mr Blair save me from the disgrace of a Gaol; save my aged Shoulders from the Lash. Remember my dear Master I have long served you faithfully and I never deserved that you should desert me; but I will obey you

---

[12] *Prize Slaves*, p. 24.   [13] *Prize Slaves*, p. 13.
[14] Testimony of Ellé, *Prize Slaves*, pp. 30, 128.   [15] *Prize Slaves*, p. 13.

Master; I will force myself away from you; I will go to this unfeeling monster, I shall be again free in the first of March then I will return and die in your service; I am now torn from you to live with strangers; torn from my wife and my children; You have been a good Master to me I shall never forget your Kindness in Excilement.' Jean Ellé delightful pattern of grateful fidelity. Glorious Mr Cooke Benevolent example of humanity!'[16]

The entire investigation – of the prize slave system in general and of the Ellé case in particular – was shot through with this language of paternalism. It grounded the discussions of British policy towards liberated Africans as well as the justifications given by individual masters and officials for their actions with regard to them. The fate of William Cousins, previously quoted complaining of ill-treatment by Blair, is a case in point. After the end of his apprenticeship, Cousins had applied at the Customs House to be employed by a local merchant firm, but his new employer testified that Blair had 'assailed the said William Cousins with the most violent threatening and abusive language, and swore he would never give him a certificate to enable him to procure employment'. Blair, it was clear, wished to pressure Cousins back into his own service, but Cousins refused and remained (albeit without the necessary certificate that his apprenticeship had come to an end) with his new employers.[17] Edwards was eager to present this action in a heroic light, claiming that any attempt to misrepresent it (as he claimed the fiscal had in his indictment)

> was a libel on the whole race of Negroes (for whom the King & British Senate have evinced so anxious a solicitude) in saying that the unfortunate Will. Cousins would not, and had not resolution to, resist the oppression; but would have returned to his tyrannical Master.[18]

Blair similarly invoked arguments based upon paternalism, although unsurprisingly with the opposite conclusion. He denied any cruelty towards Cousins or indeed towards his other prize slaves. To add insult to injury, he alleged that Cousins had been 'landed from the ship in a dying state, rejected as an apprentice by every one, and received and nurtured by Mr. Blair from humane motives, as though he was an individual of his own family'.[19]

In a dispute between Blair and another Cape Town merchant, William Corbitt, over the assignment of a prize slave child known as Malamo (the name he gave in his own testimony) as well as Jack and John, both sides

---

[16] Memorial of Cooke, *Prize Slaves*, p. 7; Letter of William Edwards, CA, CO 214, no. 31, 1824.
[17] Testimony of Thwaits, *Prize Slaves*, p. 31.   [18] CA, CO 214, no. 31, 1824.
[19] Letter of Blair and Bird, *Prize Slaves*, p. 109.

Dutch-speaking slave- owners of the period referring to their slaves as their *volk* (people).[27]

Yet these same analyses suggest there existed a fundamental distinction between colonial officials and Cape slave owners.[28] For the official, argues Mason, the 'fundamental social relationship was the one that existed between the subject and sovereign or the sovereign's representatives, not the relationship between slave and slave owner'.[29] This was not to say, as Mason continues, that British officials sought to undermine master–slave hierarchies, but by subordinating the master–slave relationship to that between the slave and the colonial state, this was precisely the effect.

In investigating the prize slave system, the commissioners clearly articulated the idea that colonial officials should stand outside, and indeed above, the paternalistic bond. Answering the question as to why he had seen fit to assign prize slaves to himself as an individual, Wilberforce Bird claimed legal precedent in an Elizabethan apprenticeship law that 'not only allows, but encourages a parent to indenture to himself his own son'.[30] The commissioners reported to Parliament that 'he has considered himself and the Collector to stand in the same relation, or in that of guardian, towards the Prize Negroes.' But they had no sympathy with the analogy between the 'framers of the Act of Elizabeth and of the Order in Council' regarding prize slaves:

> The object of the latter is to provide protection for those persons by the selection of good and humane masters; and we do not think that this object is attained, while it certainly may be risked, by the combination in one and the same person of the interest of a master and the duty of protector.[31]

Nevertheless, the testimony in the prize slave debates offers us a rather different gloss on the existing scholarly literature regarding the status of the master–servant relationship within a reforming imperial state. Almost all those who testified in the investigations were British, which is perhaps unsurprising given that Blair tended to favour his own personal connections in assignment. The liminal position of prize slaves between bondage and freedom highlights the question of where British (as opposed to Cape Dutch) colonists stood with regard to this evolving relationship. The extremely strong flavour of paternalism voiced by all involved – from

---

[27] Mason, *Social Death*, p. 71. This collective term for 'their' labourers continued in use by white farmers of the region well into the twentieth and indeed twenty-first centuries.
[28] The approach is exemplified in John Mason's now classic analysis of the worldviews of the slave, the slave-holder, and the British official hearing the case of complaint brought before the office of the slave protector: 'Hendrik Albertus and his ex-slave Mey'.
[29] Mason, *Social Death*, p. 56.   [30] Bird to the Commissioners, *Prize Slaves*, p. 110.
[31] *Prize Slaves*, p. 15.

Edwards to Blair himself – is important precisely because it was clearly in part opportunistic. Paternalism was evidently seen by British settlers as the 'right tone' to strike when dealing with government investigators and with metropolitan audiences more generally. On the one hand, like their Dutch counterparts, British masters of prize slaves showed little sense that a slave, or even an apprentice, might be an independent agent in relation to the state. Instead, they placed a great deal of emphasis on a paternalistic master–servant relationship, and resentment against the interference of officials. On the other hand, as I explore in more detail presently, Edwards put forward an alternative view of a paternalistic abolitionist state that had been betrayed by its corrupt and self-serving administrators.

Personal interest or public good: defining criminal libel

If Blair's insulting language opens one route into our understandings of honour in the Cape slave society, then Cooke's and Edwards's trial for criminal libel raised another, more legalistic, set of questions. In defining criminal libel, what was the relationship between personal interest and the public good?

The trial began on 16 February 1824 and lasted a month. The basis of the indictment was the memorial to the Lords of the Treasury that was libellous because it accused Blair of malpractice and accepting bribes. Making such serious accusations against a public official constituted a breach of the peace,[32] rendering the trial a criminal rather than a civil prosecution. Blair, in the words of the court, had allegedly 'made donations of these people [prize slaves] to satisfy the claims of several of his creditors'.[33] More generally, the memorial declared him guilty of

Premeditated and wilful neglect in the execution of the duty of the office of the Collector of Customs, to protect the Prize Negroes entrusted to him by His Majesty's Government, by sacrificing their interests and prosperity to unmerciful covetousness, and apprenticing them to his particular favourites at the expense of their own comfort and happiness.[34]

---

[32] Under English common law, where criminal libel was much more commonly used than at the Cape, this definition of 'breach of the peace' took several forms. It might be direct (as in inciting those insulted to violence) or it might be indirect by bringing established institutions or prominent persons 'into contempt, or hatred, or ridicule' so that the public's mind might be 'unsettled' and social order thereby threatened: see W. H. Wickwar, *The Struggle for the Freedom of the Press 1819–1832* (London: Allen & Unwin, 1928), pp. 20–1.

[33] RCC, vol. 17, p. 178. [34] Record of the trial, *Prize Slaves*, p. 75.

Cooke was charged with having written and signed the memorial, Edwards with having drawn it up and forwarding it to the governor, and the clerk Jan Bernard Hoffman with having copied it. Edwards mocked the prosecution by asking why they had not bothered to put on trial the papermaker or the goose that provided the quill with which the memorial had been written.[35] Hoffman's involvement, however, was soon over. He denied all knowledge of the transaction. Witnesses were called as to the similarity of his handwriting with that of the memorial, but the evidence against him was slim, and soon dismissed. He was pronounced acquitted.[36]

The main focus of the debate would be on bigger prey: Cooke and, increasingly, Edwards. Both began their case by putting forward exceptions to the legality of the whole proceedings. Edwards also used the opportunity of the trial for an extended attack upon the regime itself, a course of action he would follow increasingly as the trial, and the debate inspired by it, unfolded. Rather than perform their duty to stamp out official corruption, Edwards argued, the colony's judicial officers had arrested those seeking to expose it to the legitimate authorities. Edwards protested against the conduct of the fiscal in such vehement terms, and despite repeated warnings by the judges to desist, that he was charged with contempt of court and spent a month in prison in consequence.

The elite of Cape Town usually brought defamation actions in defence of their personal honour only as a last resort. There existed a whole series of less costly mechanisms to manage conflict resolution. Avoiding a court action was not necessarily about avoiding publicity. Non-legal methods of redress could involve declarations of apology and character endorsement that could be made public by the parties who considered themselves insulted. Notaries like Edwards were routinely employed to gain letters of apology and redress from those who had proffered insults. The Cape was nevertheless a highly litigious society, with actions for defamation common.[37] These, however, were civil actions. If the offended party's complaints were upheld, Roman–Dutch law usually imposed two remedies to compensate the injured party. A defamer would need to make *amende honorable*, which constituted his public apology (both parties in

---

[35] *RCC*, vol. 17, p. 186.   [36] *RCC*, vol. 17, pp. 183, 187–8.
[37] N. J. J. Olivier, 'Laster', in G. G. Visagie, L. F. van Huyssteen, C. R. de Beer, N. J. J. Olivier, W. du Plessis, J. Th. de Smidt and H. C. Gall (eds.), *Die Siviele Appèlhof en die Raad van Justisie, Hofstukke en Uitsprake wat Betrekking het of Siviele Sake, 1806–1827: 'n Evaluering van Capita Selecta uit Bepaalde Gebiede van die Reg aan die Kaap* (Die Kaapse Regspraak-Projek, final research report. University of the Western Cape, Potchestroomse Universiteit vir Christelike Hoër Onderwys, Leiden University, 1992).

such actions were usually male[38]) and *amende profitable*, by paying a sum of money to a charity of the victim's choice.[39] Direct monetary compensation to the person defamed (the usual remedy in English civil actions) was not the practice at the Cape. Instead a man's honour was restored by his insistence that the offending party distribute public largesse in his name to a worthy cause.

The case against Cooke and Edwards, however, was highly unusual in being a criminal and not a civil action. Actions for *criminal* defamation were extremely rare at the Cape, and indeed in Roman–Dutch law more generally.[40] In outlining the system to Bathurst, the commissioners explained that

Verbal injury or defamation . . . is not made the subject of criminal inquiry except in cases where the highest authority or members of Government are defamed, or where the defamatory words have been spoken in public or are accompanied by acts of violence.[41]

Both kinds of cases were frequent under English law, a key difference between them being that a criminal action had to include a tendency to cause a breach of the peace. Under English law, historian W. Hardy Wickwar summarises, criminal libels were 'distinguished as *defamatory, obscene, blasphemous,* or *seditious* libels, according as they treated of personal, sexual, religious, or political matters'.[42]

A key element of the Cooke and Edwards case became the question of whether the memorial should be regarded in law as a vehicle of personal revenge for a private insult, or whether it should be seen as a legitimate mode of public complaint against an allegedly corrupt official. What made the Blair/Cooke altercation particularly distinctive was the way an overtly interpersonal dispute between two men of status had been converted into and overlapped with a public complaint about official misconduct: the two were deeply entangled in one another from the start.

---

[38] On the gender dimensions of defamation actions at the Cape in the early nineteenth century see my *Scandal in the Colonies*. Because female honour was defined primarily in terms of sexual virtue, it was more usually defended through actions of breach or promise of marriage or seduction than it was the subject of actions of defamation.

[39] Commenting on the role of truth in civil prosecutions for defamation at the Cape, the Commissioners of Inquiry noted that 'if the truth of the libel be established the act of recantation is excused, but the defendant remains still liable to the pecuniary fine or "profitable amends"': Report of the Commissioners of Inquiry upon criminal law and jurisprudence, *RCC*, vol. 33, p. 21.

[40] B. Ranchod, *Foundations of the South African Law of Defamation* (Leiden University Press, 1972).

[41] Report of the Commissioners of Inquiry upon criminal law and jurisprudence, *RCC*, vol. 33, p. 19.

[42] Wickwar, *Struggle for Freedom of the Press*, p. 19.

Cooke's memorial laid out both the circumstances of the insult to himself and the broader picture of the prize slave system. Facing criticism from London for arresting the complainants in the first place, the Somerset administration argued that the fiscal

> saw reason for concluding that his [Cooke's] object in writing and sending it was dictated rather by a spirit of revenge for the insult offered to him by Mr Blair, and the loss of a servant, than by a desire to procure a reform of any abuses in the system of distributing the Prize Negroes.[43]

This slippage between private dispute and public complaint also became a central theme in the investigations of the Commissioners of Inquiry that followed.

Although both prosecution and defence sought to call witnesses as to the truth or falsehood of the charges in the memorial itself, the judges would not allow this. In the 1825 investigation over the conduct of the trial, Somerset submitted an opinion written by Chief Justice Truter on 17 March 1824 justifying this decision. As Truter explained, 'in cases of *criminal* prosecution for libel, the offence is the same whether the matter be true or false, so that the defendant is not allowed to *allege* the truth of it by way of justification.'[44] As the following chapter will demonstrate, there were important differences being argued between the Roman–Dutch and English law of defamation in this period. The irrelevance of truth in charges of *criminal* libel was, however, a key point of agreement between them. Rather than the truth or falsehood of the accusations, therefore, the two key points argued in the case were these: first, whether the memorial constituted publication (which was necessary to prove defamation); and second, whether the memorial had been motivated by personal insult (in which case it was defamatory) or by a desire to protect the public good by exposing official corruption (in which case the charges could not be sustained).

In making his defence, Cooke proclaimed himself 'Impelled by a sense of duty towards the public, and to several unfortunate subjects, whom I saw the silent victims of arbitrary power'. He had

> become myself the object of violence and insult, because I presumed in the mildest manner to advocate one of these, who had faithfully served me for several years, to whom I felt a reciprocal attachment, and hearing at the same time from various channels, of similar and worse practices in the disposal of Negroes, I thought it a duty to them as well as to society in general, to represent such cases, of which I had proofs in support of my assertions, through the proper official channel.[45]

[43] *Prize Slaves*, p. 22.   [44] Opinion of Truter, 17 March 1824, *Prize Slaves*, p. 123.
[45] Records of the trial, *Prize Slaves*, p. 55.

His memorial, he continued, contained charges solely respecting Blair's 'public situation', not his 'private character', and that it was 'not published, [and] no publicity whatever was given to it here'. The copy given to the governor was 'the proper channel of official intercourse' with the home government. In essence Cooke's argument was that without publication in a legal sense, there was no criminal case.[46]

Edwards mounted an analogous defence, quoting Blackstone and Justinian upon the 'duty of every good subject to inform His Majesty of the mal-practices of his servants'.[47] As James Stephen, then legal advisor to the Colonial Office, later explained it, the argument

insisted, that a communication made to Government as to the misconduct of one of its own officers, was a privileged communication, for which no man could be lawfully required to answer in a poenal [criminal] action in a court of justice.[48]

Fiscal Daniel Denyssen countered these defences in court by arguing that the 'writing originates in bad faith'. The memorial, he argued, was personal revenge for injured honour rather than a disinterested desire to serve the public. Even if the facts complained against Blair were true, then Cooke was 'one of the principal accomplices'. Using the claims that Ellé had always made to being a prisoner of war, the fiscal argued that it was Cooke who had kept a supposedly free man in apprenticeship for many years, 'notwithstanding he maintains that that person, from the very beginning, felt himself aggrieved at the injustice he suffered'. The root and branch of the charges within the memorial were the 'personal interest' of Cooke, rather than the 'public good'; it was the insult he had been offered that was the driving force behind the memorial, and the main thrust of the charges within it.

In making this argument, Denyssen made much of the fact that the memorial had originated in a personal altercation, against which Cooke had originally made a civil claim to the deputy fiscal. Using the established language of honour, Denyssen claimed that Cooke had written to the deputy fiscal describing 'the object of the Memorial in these words, *to procure me satisfaction*'.[49] Denyssen was, he argued, in no wise wishing to deprive anyone from 'bringing to light the misconduct of government servants, if such actually exist, providing it is preferred in a proper and lawful manner'. But he presented Cooke as a man who would

---

[46] James Stephen to Robert Wilmot Horton, 12 Aug. 1824, TNA, CO 48/95.
[47] *RCC*, vol. 17, p. 183.
[48] James Stephen to Robert Wilmot Horton, 12 Aug. 1824.
[49] Records of the trial, *Prize Slaves*, pp. 55–6 (original emphasis). The original letter containing the phrase is also reproduced, p. 59.

under the cloak of complaining of what has happened to him personally, attack the government servants with a number of complaints unconnected with his case, in a manner affording him a chance of escaping the investigation of such accusations.[50]

The heart of Advocate Hendrik Cloete's defence of Cooke was that the memorial constituted an official complaint addressed to the proper authorities and could not be held criminal. Although he was careful to indicate that the charges of Blair's corruption could still be proven to be true, what was at issue was whether by composing and signing the memorial Cooke had acted contrary to the law. The defence denied the prosecution's allegations that the memorial was 'calculated to produce disorder' (another necessary element of criminal libel) because it complained of personal insults given to Cooke by the Collector of Customs and therefore contained 'marks of bad faith and irrelevant matter'. If this were true, then Cooke should have been prosecuted for the complaint he previously laid before the deputy fiscal about the personal insult, not the memorial he had drawn up about the official system.[51] This earlier complaint might have been deemed an action that would 'tend to disturb the peace, and the respect due to persons high in office'. Instead, the fiscal had moved against Cooke on the basis of the memorial, a document that was 'not a private writing, but an official instrument' addressed, as was appropriate, to the Lords Commissioners of the Treasury. This, then, was the basis for the defence:

The English laws on this head agree so perfectly with the Roman and Dutch laws that either may be referred to. These unanimously enact, that it is not lawful for any man to utter, write, or publish anything with the intention to injure another's character; doing this renders him liable to a civil action for defamation; and if accompanied by any act disturbing the peace, also to a criminal action.

An exception, however, was to be found when 'any person or magistrate is formally charged with acts in which the public is interested, and which call for an inquiry, in order that the offenders may be brought to justice'.[52]

---

[50] Records of the trial, *Prize Slaves*, p. 60.
[51] The earlier complaint was first taken to the deputy fiscal 'where it lay dormant in his office from 26 November until the 12 January': *RCC*, vol. 17, p. 196. The deputy fiscal later excused his delay in putting the case before the sitting commissioners on the basis a backlog of cases and because 'this of Mr. Cooke not appearing to me to require any immediate haste'. It was clear that the broader implications only gradually dawned on van Ryneveld. When Cooke decided to approach the Treasury instead, 'I considered the case to be of so much importance, that I requested him to give me a notice in writing of his wish to withdraw the prosecution': W. C. van Ryneveld to the Commissioners, 8 June 1825, *Prize Slaves*, p. 168.
[52] *RCC*, vol. 17, pp. 197–8.

Advocate Cloete cited the Roman and the Dutch legal authorities of Voet, Grotius and Groenewege to establish that Cooke had acted just as he ought in a matter that gravely concerned the public, the government, and the administration of justice. He then went on to refer to Blackstone, and to Holt's *Law of Libel*, on the right of a subject to petition the proper authorities for redress of grievance, although claiming that having proved the case in the Roman and Dutch law, 'it will scarcely be necessary to refer to the laws of England, laws which, more than any others, have secured the liberty of the subject'. He further referred to examples in both British and Cape history, including the impeachment proceedings against Warren Hastings (1788–1795) and Lord Melville (1805–1806), the 1705 complaints against Governor Willem Adrian van der Stel, and the 1780 'Patriot' deputation of complaint to the directors of the Dutch East India Company.[53]

In pleading Edwards's case, Advocate Christoffel Brand spent significant time trying to get his client discharged from confinement for contempt, arguing that his unjust treatment by the fiscal leading up the trial had made his client's attitude in court 'altogether pardonable'.[54] 'The appellant, an English burgher,[55] avails himself of his right in petitioning the King and Parliament; the Memorial is sent in by him in a legal manner to the competent authority' and yet he finds himself 'criminally prosecuted for that very petition', a prosecution that, according to Blackstone, was 'illegal in itself'. At every step Edwards had been ruthlessly treated, and the court should consider 'the odiousness and difficulties to which the appellant has been exposed by this action'.[56]

For his part the fiscal denied any such persecution, reiterating that it was his 'public duty', not personal animosity, to bring a prosecution when the memorial was handed over to him. Furthermore, Edwards had been rightly condemned for 'contempt of the judicial authority'. Personal honour, the fiscal was careful to maintain, had never been his motivation. Citing Blackstone, Denyssen claimed for the protection of the court, 'judicial dignity' must be protected to maintain 'judicial authority'.[57]

---

[53] *RCC*, vol. 17, pp. 198–9; *Prize Slaves*, pp. 72–3. Cloete was well placed to cross such jurisdictional boundaries. He had taken a doctorate in law in Holland in 1811, after study at Utrecht and Leiden. Dodging the draft that the French imposed on the Dutch in the Napoleonic Wars, he made his way clandestinely to Britain, where he studied at Lincoln's Inn: see *Dictionary of South African Biography*, vol. I, pp. 171–2.

[54] *RCC*, vol. 17, p. 202.

[55] A revealing choice of words on the part of Brand. The status of *burgerschap* conveyed particular rights upon an individual during the VOC period: see Baartman, 'Fighting for the spoils'.

[56] Records of the trial, *Prize Slaves*, p. 92.

[57] Records of the trial, *Prize Slaves*, p. 93.

146   Imperial Underworld

The commissioners' later report on the prize slave system was similarly cognisant of the slippage between private insult and public complaint that marked both the original memorial and the progress of the criminal libel trial itself. They rejected the fiscal's argument that Cooke's decision to abandon his civil case in favour of the memorial to the Treasury reflected

> a desire of revenging himself for a personal insult received from Mr Blair, by exposing and denouncing in vehement language acts of corruption and oppressive conduct, rather than to the more laudable and disinterested motive that he professed, of affording impartial information to the Lords Commissioners of the Treasury of abuse of authority committed by one of their officers.[58]

Yet, the commissioners pointed out, the right of Cooke to complain to the Lords Commissioners of the Treasury 'was generally believed', and even if it were true, as the fiscal asserted and indeed as they concurred, that he had done so from motives of personal insult, the criminal prosecution was unwise. The prosecution for writing the memorial could only 'have the effect of giving publicity to the imputations that it conveyed, without affording the means of establishing their truth or falsehood'. Although Blair had himself called for a full inquiry, the entire community now believed him to be guilty.[59] It was clear from the witnesses that the prosecutor had wished to call (disallowed by the court), and from Mr Blair's own co-operation in the case, that the fiscal felt he could disprove the charges against Blair. But the commissioners were doubtful of this, considering the number and strength of the allegations and the witnesses that the defendants were able to bring.

Drawing on a detailed report from James Stephen, the secretary of state made these failings on the part of the regime abundantly clear when writing to Somerset about the affair: the administration had intercepted Cooke's complaint, properly addressed to the appropriate office in London, and converted it into a public libel. To make matters worse, they had then arrested and charged not only the complainant but a notary and a scribe who had been merely acting as agents in their professional capacity. Stephen acknowledged that personal revenge and public duty were deeply bound together in the memorial, but asserted that this was not the key point at issue. What was important was 'the maintenance of the general principle of the right of petitioning, and not the merits of any individual case ... and I cannot but think that, in the persons of Cooke and Edwards, that principle has been violated'.[60] Based on Stephen's report, Bathurst's official response to Somerset was severe. There was no

[58] *Prize Slaves*, p. 24.   [59] *Prize Slaves*, p. 25.
[60] James Stephen to Robert Wilmot Horton, 12 Aug. 1824.

evidence that the accusations had been published in the colony. If communicating the contents of the memorial to Blair constituted publication, then it was actually Somerset himself who was guilty of publishing the memorial, rather than the accused.[61]

Loyalty and national honour

As Bathurst, Stephen and Commissioners Bigge and Colebrooke all recognised, a case designed to silence miscreant voices had turned into what we might call a public relations disaster for Somerset's administration. Edwards proved himself extremely adept at linking corrupt behaviour in the cause of abolition with general accusations of tyranny and disloyalty. As a result, his libel trials became both a *cause célèbre* and the most popular entertainment in town. 'Long prior to the opening of the Court', wrote the *Advertiser*,

> every avenue was crowded; and an expression of the deepest interest visible in every countenance. On the Court being opened, the rush was tremendous. In a few moments every place, affording the least chance of hearing, was occupied.[62]

Somerset complained privately in a letter to Commissioner Bigge that an 'immense Crowd attends the Sitting every day', and that when the doors were open his enemies 'burst in at the Head of the Mob daily & remain there during the whole sitting paying the attentions of H. of Common reporters'.[63]

The tumult in the courtroom was bad enough, but for those unable to squeeze inside, as much of the proceedings as could be hastily scribbled down were duly transcribed and printed, both in the *Advertiser* and in pamphlet form, by printer George Greig, together with an 'appendix of papers illustrative of the case'.[64]

That assiduous diarist, Samuel Hudson, wrote similarly in the midst of the excitement:

> The Newspaper had given us the particulars of the Trial of Edwards Hoffman and Cooke, which news astonished the Cape people that any man could dare to use such bold language to their Dragon [the Fiscal], tomorrow the case comes on again and there are placards pasted up at the Corners of the Streets truly expressive of the Indignation of the generality of the people which the Officers are busy in tearing down.

---

[61] Bathurst to Somerset, 28 Sept. 1824, *RCC*, vol. 18, p. 323.
[62] *South African Commercial Advertiser*, 3 March 1824.
[63] Somerset to Bigge, undated [1824], Bigge–Somerset correspondence, Rhodes House, University of Oxford, MSS Afr, series 24.
[64] *RCC*, vol. 17, p. 177.

He also gleefully quoted a placard that he had seen in the town deriding the 'rascally Fiscal':

Each Dog we know must have his day
but when the farce is ended
Dog Dan must be *suspended*.[65]

The trial was causing a great 'stir', and Hudson predicted it would 'not terminate without a more serious consequence than the imprisonment of Edwards'. There were rumours that Cooke might back out and leave Edwards in the lurch, for it was 'Edwards, the champion' (as Hudson called him) whom the authorities clearly regarded as the wellspring of the case against them. Indeed Hudson saw Edwards as the hero of a new model of politics: 'Edwards will attack them with his own weapons and conquer them by good sense and sound Law precedings.'[66]

Edwards made a sensation in court by turning the prize slave libel trial into a general attack upon the actions of a despotic administration. On being asked whether he had any excuse to offer for having drawn up the prize slave memorial, he replied: 'I justify it – I glory in it. It is the duty of every good subject to inform His Majesty of the mal-practices of his servants. I have ever done it, and ever will.' The criminal charges against him were part of a 'system of persecution' for doing what Denyssen 'had not courage to attempt'.[67]

Given how unpopular the fiscal was amongst the wider community, Edwards's attacks were stirring stuff. Cranking the rhetorical wheel with a heavy hand, he insisted that his legal standing rendered him undaunted before the threat of corrupt authority:

I am, at the very, very least, his equal – taking his gown, his influence, his office, and his authority into the bargain; he would have known there was something in the free, honest, unbending spirit of an English lawyer, not to be insulted with impunity; he would have known it would take more grates, bars, and oppressions than he can possess, to tame a soul reared in the lap of liberty; he would have known that he may manacle my hands, he may shackle my feet, and he may cast my person into a cell; but I can tell him my soul bids defiance to every Fiscal; it will soar above him, it will hover over him, it will pounce upon him when and where he least dreams.[68]

Louis Meurant provided an account of the reaction to this speech in his memoirs:

[65] Hudson, Diary, 25 & 27 Feb. 1824.
[66] Hudson, Diary, 24 Feb., 11 March, 30 April 1824.
[67] *RCC*, vol. 17, pp. 183, 184.   [68] *RCC*, vol. 17, p. 185.

The writer was in the court and perfectly remembers this peroration and the effect it had upon the listeners. Mr Edwards was a tall handsome man (an Irishman the writer heard)... There was an irrepressible burst of applause (not, however, reported), and the words have ever since been deeply impressed on the writer's memory. Often and often has he thought of them.[69]

Against the repeated objections of the Fiscal to these personal attacks, Edwards declared himself 'an undaunted patriot' who 'knew better than to assail a snake in its own hiding place. It was nothing encouraging to him to be told by the same breath that sent him to prison for exposing the Fiscal's falsehood, that he might prosecute him for it.'[70]

Cooke and Edwards were acquitted of the libel charges on 26 March 1824, after an appeal to the full court. In their report upon the events, the Commissioners of Eastern Inquiry would later declare themselves unsurprised. As they explained, 'denunciation to the magistracy, of abuses that the interest of the state requires to be revealed' was 'a well known exception in the Roman law' to the charge of libel.[71] For his part, Somerset found the decision 'inexplicable', the judgement so arbitrary that he likened the court process to a lottery. Nonetheless he was relieved to report to Bigge (then absent from Cape Town) that 'The Turbulence here has for the moment subsided.'[72] It would prove to be the briefest cessation of hostilities.

By tapping into a wider rhetoric of civil virtue, Edwards and Cooke had prevailed in the messy debate between personal vengeance and public duty. Their acquittal, however, had implications beyond the individual humiliation of those who had mounted the case for the prosecution. The government's defeat was rendered all the more embarrassing by the political sensitivity of the issue at hand – the consequences of abolishing the slave trade. It was this that allowed the case to speak not only to personal status, or even to official rectitude, but also widened the parameters to the third iteration through which honour played out in the affair: the question of national reputation.

Bringing the charges in the first place had proved a serious miscalculation on the part of Somerset's administration. No less close and personal an ally than the governor's own nephew, Tory MP Lord Granville Somerset, recognised that fact. As we saw in Chapter 2, in the wake of the Edwards trials, Lord Granville Somerset worked closely with Under-Secretary of State Robert Wilmot Horton to devise a strategy of damage

---

[69] Meurant, *Sixty Years Ago*, p. 41. Ironically Meurant wrote that Edwards reminded him of a young William Porter, the Irish attorney general who would supplant Denyssen under the new Cape legal system in 1828.
[70] *RCC*, vol. 17, p. 187.   [71] *Prize Slaves*, p. 25
[72] Somerset to Bigge, 2 April 1824, Bigge–Somerset correspondence.

control in relation to ongoing parliamentary debates over the conduct of Cape politics. Writing privately to Wilmot Horton in December 1824, Lord Granville Somerset saw clearly that although the memorial was 'evidently an attempt to revenge by pretended publick spirit', Cooke 'very wisely enlists in his service the cause of the Negro Slaves'. It was extremely unwise for Somerset to have drawn the fire of the Whig and Radical opposition by sanctioning a Crown prosecution for libel before he had even investigated whether the charges were true. Lord Granville Somerset feared 'the holy fervour of the Saints' on 'a Slave case' being marshalled against his uncle in Parliament.[73]

Bathurst had already warned the governor that the prize slave situation was a problematic issue and one to be handled with delicacy. The secretary of state feared that the powerful anti-slavery lobby in Britain had the system in its sights, that it was contemplating sending their own fact-finding mission and that the information uncovered would be a gift to the opposition in Parliament. He wrote to Somerset in July 1823, warning of the rumours current in London:

I think it my duty to inform your Lordship that a notion is entertained by some persons in this country that there have existed certain malpractices in the system of apprenticing slaves at the Cape of Good Hope, and I think it highly probable that a person of some reputation may visit the colony for the purpose principally of collecting information on the subject in question, which might, therefore, eventually come under the notice of parliament, or in some shape or other before the public.

Having thus given you this information as I received it, you will of course be best able to appreciate its value, as well as the necessity of arming me with the means to repel any sudden attack for which I am not as present prepared.[74]

It was a highly ironic description of exactly what occurred six months later, although the whistle-blowers would prove to be self-interested colonial merchants rather than a delegation of metropolitan humanitarians.

Somerset was already well aware that a commitment to the ideals of abolition was becoming an increasingly important public virtue in the metropole. Indeed, his amelioration proclamations of 1823 were largely an attempt to see off wider reforms. Shortly after Bigge's arrival, in September 1823, the commissioner sent a confidential summary to Wilmot Horton of the key issues needing his attention, noting that

---

[73] Granville Somerset to Wilmot Horton, 5 Dec. 1824, Catton Collection, Derbyshire Record Office, D3155/WH 2876.

[74] Bathurst to Somerset, 14 July 1823, Bathurst Papers, BL, 57/66. Bathurst recommended that Somerset send him full documentation of the apprenticeship of prize slaves at the Cape in order to ward off such attacks.

we have reason to apprehend that the observance of the regulations presented by the Order in Council has been very lax & insufficient. The Prize Negroes have been treated in every respect in the same manner as Slaves, & are in many Instances a source of Profit to their Masters.[75]

The accusations against Blair were therefore a political liability both for the official in particular and for the regime in general. Writing to Bigge, Somerset was concerned to exonerate the Customs Department.[76] He assembled his own committee of enquiry in March 1824 to investigate the charges against Blair, but it was too little too late. Cooke refused to testify to it on the grounds that he was concurrently defending himself against a libel action on the same topic.[77]

Of all the players Edwards was perhaps the most alive to the political and moral traction that could be gained from accusations about misappropriating prize slaves. It was precisely because of the emotive national resonances of abolishing the slave trade that mistreatment of Prize Negroes and exploitation of their situation could prove a powerful weapon against political opponents.

The libel action, then, had proved itself a political liability not only by exposing Blair's corrupt practices in relation to prize slaves, but also by highlighting the more questionable practices of the local government in arresting those seeking to complain to the metropolitan authorities. As the wording of the memorial made clear, critics of the regime could argue that British honour in abolishing the slave trade was being violated by officials who had perverted the cause of justice for their own corrupt ends. Edwards developed this idea at length in a letter he wrote to the Commissioners of the Court of Justice during his imprisonment for contempt of court. Ostensibly it was a request to prosecute the fiscal for Denyssen's persecution of him, but he also spent considerable time recapitulating the case of Blair and Cooke and providing further evidence as to the truth of the allegations, evidence that witnesses had been prevented from giving in court. At some 18 000 words and 88 pages of manuscript, however, it goes far beyond the immediate stated purposes. Part confessional, part manifesto, part diatribe, it is rambling and occasionally incoherent – but nonetheless a startling illumination of the pressure points that could be usefully manipulated in the political context of the day.

Much of Edwards's letter is an extended attack on the actions and character of Daniel Denyssen, but it is shot through with wider concerns over an unholy alliance of corrupt British officials and Dutch notables

---

[75] Bigge to Wilmot Horton, 25 Sept. 1823, Catton Collection, D3155, no. 53.
[76] Somerset to Bigge, 5 March 1824, Bigge–Somerset correspondence.
[77] Letter of Cooke, *Prize Slaves*, p. 53.

operating at the Cape. As such it spoke to the continued dominance of Cape Dutch interests in the administration and legal system of the colony, an alliance under increasing criticism from more recently arrived British settlers and one set to be unpicked by the investigations of the Commission of Eastern Inquiry. Edwards placed this in squarely national terms. In attacking (as he put it in a letter to Somerset) 'the omnipotent Fiscals presuming to punish the People of England, for endeavouring to exercise their most undoubted rights', Edwards entered into an extended discussion contrasting his own loyalty to the British state with that of Denyssen. Denyssen had held office under the interregnum of the Batavian Republic and was as a consequence, in Edwards's view,

Suckled by the bosom of Rebellion – who had Sworn truly to Serve a revolutionary Horde:– and who retired from a Seat on its revolutionary Tribunal in this Colony, when the conquering arms of my brave Countrymen Subdued it:– because he would not serve any legitimate Prince.

By contrast, for having exposed the corrupt trade in prize slaves, Edwards trumpeted:

I glory in having done my duty. I am proud to be the humble hand to open the eyes of a beneficent Monarch. I owe it to his Majesty not to leave him ignorant of the abuse of his officers. I will have the glory to be a broom in the hands of Royalty which shall cleanse this Augean Stable and bury every pander in his own filth!

The fiscal's claim that Blair would be exposed to the 'hatred and contempt' of the Lords of the Treasury was, claimed Edwards, an insult to British governance since he supposed that august body to be 'renegadoes of Amsterdam and not Nobles and Gentlemen of England'.[78]

Denyssen was equally eager to defend himself directly against such charges, considering that his reputation as a loyal British official was being muddied both in the eyes of the Colonial Office and in discussions in Parliament. In February 1824 he wrote a long defence of his 'name and character' to Robert Wilmot Horton.[79] According to historian James

---

[78] Edwards to Somerset, 3 Feb. 1824, CA, CO 214, no. 31, 1824.
[79] Somerset was highly critical of this move, which he considered a tactical error on the parliamentary battlefield. He confided confidentially to Bigge that 'I objected highly to this mode in the first place a Letter of Explanation or Defence from the Fiscal wd by no means be so effective in Mr Wilmot's hands in his place in the Commons as a copy of the sentence of this legal court here condemning the accuser & culminator to publishment & in the next place it would be a tacit avowal that our laws were not competent to our protection – a most mischievous idea': Somerset to Bigge, undated, 1824, Bigge–Somerset correspondence.

Sturgis, Wilmot Horton was the 'chief protagonist of Anglicisation within the Colonial Office'.[80] Denyssen's letter suggests he may have agreed. It began with a vehement assertion of his British loyalty: that he had not 'sworn allegiance to any still subsisting government excepting that of His Majesty'; that in the years he had served as fiscal he had been 'blessed with a family of six children, all British born subjects'; and that he had 'constantly experienced His Excellency the Governor's implicit reliance in the integrity of my official conduct'. In all these circumstances, wrote Denyssen, 'I would be at a loss to guess what better pledge for my true and faithful allegiance to His Majesty could be offered.'[81]

Edwards, conversely, neatly linked a betrayal of British reformist ideals to the 'revolutionaries' and 'renegadoes' exemplified by the Cape Dutch. In fact, as Blair and his cronies demonstrated, British officials were more than willing to partake in the opportunities abolition opened up. They also drew on a tradition of using public office for personal enrichment that may have been increasingly out of favour in Britain but which remained a strong legacy of the VOC at the Cape.[82] Wartime expediency had forged a powerful bond between the imperial state and a class of local collaborators, but this was under increasing strain by the 1820s. In picking at the sore of this cosy alliance, Edwards tapped into yet another powerful vein of sentiment in both the Cape and London.

Edwards insisted that he had exposed 'how great a curse the abolition act has been rendered to the unfortunate persons for whose happiness it was intended'. As a 'Patriot' (a word he uses more than once to refer to himself), Edwards exclaimed that

> I have lived long enough to know that my life is only valuable in as much as it serves my fellow Creatures and if I should ever be martyred in the perseverance to destroy effectually the slavery my loved country has abolished it will be a pious consolation to my soul to know how greatly I have served and saved an unhappy an oppressed, an injured, a patient, a forbearing race of the creatures of the Almighty.

---

[80] J. Sturgis, 'Anglicisation at the Cape of Good Hope in the early nineteenth century', *Journal of Imperial and Commonwealth History*, 11 (1982), 25.
[81] Denyssen to Robert Wilmot Horton, 29 Feb. 1824, TNA, CO 48/95. This letter underscores the extent of the reversal that Denyssen underwent in the aftermath of the new British legal regime. In 1835 he addressed the Maatschappij ter Uitbreiding van Beschaving en Letterkunde on the importance of recognising the singularity of Cape Dutch culture, identity and history, and he would become a central figure in the establishment of an ethnically conscious intelligentsia: *DSAB*, vol. III, pp. 207–8.
[82] On some extraordinary instances of outright theft from government coffers in this period, see Dooling, *Slavery, Emancipation and Colonial Rule*, pp. 74–5.

Edwards seems to have been aware of the rumours that he was not acting from his own motives, for he complained in his letter to the Court of Justice that such accusations robbed him 'of the honor of my patriotism and public Spirit'.[91] Although recognising that Edwards and others made common cause with Somerset's critics in both the colony and Britain, it would be wrong to argue that he was simply a puppet being manipulated by others. As always with Edwards, there is likely to be a variety of both self-interested and idealistic reasons behind his invocation of abolitionist sentiment.

Edwards would surely have recognised the importance of emphasising his commitment to abolition in an attempt to enlist the support of powerful interests in the mother country in general and the House of Commons in particular. Although we can only speculate about the purpose for which Edwards intended his letter, it is highly likely that he planned its publication (perhaps by his friend and ally George Greig) in order to galvanise local and, especially, metropolitan political allies. Similar accounts of incarceration at the Cape by Edwards's friends and allies John Carnall and Bishop Burnett would indeed appear in print and garner substantial parliamentary and press attention. Taken up by Radical and Whig MPs they would provoke heated debate in the Commons about the possible impeachment of Somerset. All show distinct similarities of genre. As James Epstein points out in his analysis of 'radical underworld' member P. F. McCallum's time in jail in Trinidad, such accounts allowed 'histrionic re-enactment of the well-worn theme of the free-born British subject who confronts the unlawful powers of government, anticipating, indeed welcoming, his role as martyr in the cause of liberty'.[92]

In her studies of British identity in the Atlantic world and beyond, Kathleen Wilson has emphasised the importance of theatre – both literal and figurative – to the emergent governmentality of imperial society.[93] Theatre socialised 'British people into *recognising* difference, especially the historical difference and distinctiveness of the English nation'. It formed part of what she calls the 'national performative'. This was a

---

[91] Edwards to Somerset, 3 Feb. 1824, CA, CO 214, no. 31, 1824.
[92] J. Epstein, 'The radical underworld goes colonial: P. F. McCallum's *Travels in Trinidad*', in M. T. Davis and P. Pickering (eds.), *Unrespectable Radicals? Popular Politics in the Age of Reform* (Burlington: Ashgate, 2008), p. 153; and *Scandal of Colonial Rule: Power and Subversion in the British Atlantic during the Age of Revolution* (Cambridge University Press, 2012).
[93] K. Wilson, *The Island Race: Englishness, Empire and Gender in the Eighteenth Century* (London: Routledge, 2003); and 'Rowe's *Fair Penitent* as global history: Or, a diversionary voyage to New South Wales', *Eighteenth-Century Studies*, 41:2 (2008), 231–51. On the theatricality of Georgian society as a whole, see G. Russell, *The Theatres of War: Performance, Politics and Society 1793–1815* (Oxford: Clarendon Press, 1995).

process that both asserted national difference in order to establish and stabilise colonial structures of rule and witnessed a sustained attack on these categories by those deemed subject to them.[94] It took place not only within the theatre itself, but also in other performance spaces that exercised power more literally, such as the courtrooms. Edwards had been drawn into Cape politics through his routine work as a notary. James Stephen, Lord Bathurst and the Crown Commissioners all agreed that for the Cape authorities to arrest a man acting in his professional capacity for alleged criminal libel committed by his client was legally absurd. Once he was embroiled in conflict with the Somerset regime, however, it was worth making as much noise as possible. Edwards needed to put on a performance that would appeal to certain powerful beliefs about the proper conduct of both the self and the nation.

This is not to make a simplistic accusation of insincerity against him. All the evidence suggests that Edwards was genuinely outraged by the situation of prize slaves at the Cape. It was he who urged Cooke to widen the issue from a personal insult to a complaint against the system by means of a memorial to the Treasury. Even after he was sentenced to transportation from the Cape to New South Wales, he was making the effort to ensure that Bigge and Colebrooke had all the testimony he had collected from prize slaves about their mistreatment.[95] We should also not be too quick to dismiss the melodramatic anecdotes of his month in jail as mere cynical calculation. Nor should we discount the possibility that casting himself in the role of hero and patriot was not a genuine belief. For all that he was ultimately acquitted, Edwards's dubious arrest, along with his month in jail for vehemently protesting against it in court, understandably increased his resentment of the Somerset regime. That, and the adulation he had inspired in the wider community, may have influenced a transformation into imperial reformer, albeit an unconventional one. The sentiments he expressed about abolition had deep cultural resonance by this period, which is precisely why they were so useful. The role that Edwards enacted through his court appearances and his correspondence was thus part of Wilson's 'national performative', one that asserted a particular vision of Britishness at the Cape. But it should also be read as a calculated strategy that would place Edwards' individual travails before the right audience.

Whether the secretary of state was motivated to intervene in Edwards's case by any sense that he was a 'patriot' defending British liberties is unlikely. Bathurst was, however, fully alive to the political capital that Edwards's travails would have for the Whig and Radical opposition. In

[94] Wilson, 'Row's *Fair Penitent*', 232–3. [95] *Prize Slaves*, p. 14.

playing to the multi-tiered audience that constituted British public opinion, Edwards had the perfect issue to hand, and he made consummate use of it in his rhetoric. Not only did the case of prize slaves involve what was by any set of standards a breathtaking degree of hypocrisy, but it also set Edwards's own feet firmly on the unassailable ground of national virtue. Furthermore, his attack on the Somerset regime absolved the British empire of violating its own code of liberty by neatly displacing responsibility onto corrupt officials who had made common cause with the 'revolutionary Horde' of the Cape Dutch.

Christopher Leslie Brown suggests that the growing adherence to the cause of abolitionism in Britain can be traced to the 'moral capital' that the movement came to acquire in the context of imperial crisis over the American Revolution.[96] In the scandal over prize slaves at the Cape of Good Hope, we can see an analogous moment of anxiety over whether the right kind of Empire, run by the right kind of people, was in play, or whether it had been corrupted. At precisely the moment that the Commission of Eastern Inquiry was making an investigation into the nature of Cape colonial governance in general, the prize slave scandal threatened to expose British liberty as a mask of hypocrisy behind which self-interest and tyranny could flourish.[97] This was its rhetorical power, and once the genie was out of the bottle, the limitations and terms of the debate would prove extremely hard to control.

---

[96] Brown, *Moral Capital*, pp. 457–8.

[97] In this regard it is worth noting that although Pringle was secretary of the Anti-Slavery Society by the time he wrote his account of these events, nowhere does he mention in his *Narrative* that the Edwards trial arose from a scandal over the administration's treatment of prize slaves. What Edwards and Cooke's accusations had revealed about the corrupt manipulation of the slave trade's abolition would clearly have sat uneasily with Pringle's account of the triumph of British liberty written on the eve of slave emancipation a decade later.

6 'Under the cloak of liberty'
Seditious libel, state security and the rights of 'free-born Englishmen'

In the prize slave libel trials, Edwards had used the courts as a political theatre, exposing government corruption, defending national honour for the greater good of British abolition and casting himself in the part of 'undaunted patriot'. Not only had the charges of criminal libel been disproved, but it was also widely acknowledged that Edwards had humiliated his opponents. Only a month after his acquittal, Edwards faced criminal charges once more, this time for sending two libellous letters to Governor Somerset. The prospect of his enacting a similar performance, and with the governor now his target, prompted the authorities to close down South Africa's first independent newspaper. It was the opening gambit in a battle that would bring victory for freedom of the press five years later with Ordinance 60 of 1829.[1]

As the catalyst of this foundational moment in the annals of Cape liberalism, Edwards is apparently confirmed in the heroic role he claimed for himself at the time. Yet we have already witnessed the anxiety being expressed amongst anti-Somerset activists as events unfolded. This disquiet was aired even before Edwards was discredited as escaped convict Alexander Kaye. Men like Pringle and Fairbairn were voicing private doubts about the notary's motives, for all that they saw in his case a useful public rallying point against the Tory administration. The reasons behind this gathering uncertainty are crystallized when we consider the documents that prompted his second arrest. The two letters were sent in quick succession to Somerset in April of 1824, around a month after his acquittal of libel in the prize slave affair. If Cooke's memorial to the

---

Daniel Denyssen in *Fiscal v. Edwards*, RCC, vol. 17, p. 390.

[1] The ordinance did retain limitations in that it required affidavits to be presented to the secretary of government giving the names of editors, publishers, printers and proprietors. Sureties were required against publishing libellous articles. A conviction for libel would deprive the culprit of his position at the paper, and a second offence would lead to banishment from the colony. See Botha, *John Fairbairn in South Africa*. In relation to the arguments advanced in the next chapter it should be noted that this was judicial rather than extra-judicial banishment.

Treasury could be relatively easily cast in the mould of legitimate protest (a contributing factor in the acquittal), Edwards's letters to Somerset are far more murky.

Of all the difficulties in telling Edwards's story, the most challenging is the near impossibility of interpreting his reasoning and motives. These were as baffling to contemporaries at the time as they have proved problematic to historians since. Edwards may not have anticipated the draconian response to his involvement as a notary in the prize slave corruption allegations. Having become the target of the administration's punitive justice, there were strategic benefits to be found in then casting his role in the language of imperial reform and in situating his own troubles within a wider political struggle. Not only is it plausible to assume that these choices dovetailed with genuinely held and increasingly common beliefs about liberty and abolition, they were also the surest route to gaining powerful allies beyond the shores of the Cape. Yet Edwards's next move in his cat-and-mouse game with the Cape authorities is both less easy to categorise and more difficult to explain.

Edwards re-enters the 'labyrinth of injustice'

Edwards and Cooke were acquitted of the criminal libel charges on 26 March 1824. Cooke departed the colony for England some three weeks later, but Edwards was not done in his dealings with the regime. His intentions were apparently to depart the colony and put his case before Parliament. Two letters sent to Somerset, one on 22 April and the second four days later, would put paid to these plans. In the first, Edwards asserted that his original resolution had been to 'waive all further correspondence with your Excellency on my own grievances, until we met on more equal terms before the Parliament of our Country', but that he now felt compelled to protest his treatment once more. In discussing these letters, historians have generally focussed upon the opening paragraphs, where Edwards expressed resentment at having been dubbed a 'Radical' by the administration.[2] Yet these were by no means straightforward ideological manifestoes. If we parse them carefully, we see Edwards claiming that the immediate motivation arose from a private brawl, an incident quite unconnected with the Cooke affair.

Edwards had been fined 300 rixdollars following a charge of 'house molestation' brought by Pieter Auret, the fiscal's clerk. 'When I sat down', explained Edwards in his first letter to Somerset, 'my only intention was

---

[2] Edwards to Somerset, 22 April 1824, *RCC*, vol. 17, p. 268. See Cory, *Rise of South Africa*, p. 264.

to complain that I am prevented from leaving the Colony by an excessive fine, levied on myself and my friend Mr. Richardson for telling a cheat of his roguery.'[3] In the second letter Edwards explained that he was taking depositions for an impeachment action against Somerset before the House of Commons, specifically concerning an 'illegal Sentence and interference of the Court of Appeal'.[4]

These may indeed have been the original purposes he claimed them to be, but so many and so various are the complaints, allegations and threats of vengeance ('the incoherent attacks',[5] as Somerset described them to Bathurst) in these two letters that it is difficult to disentangle them. At one point, even Edwards himself appears to recognise this: 'I am sorry to find that lost in the maze, the labyrinth of injustice, incongruity, and inconsistency, which surrounds me, I have wandered from my subject.'[6] Steeped in the minutiae of interpersonal vexations yet wrapped up in the language of political virtue, the rambling accusations are typical of their author.

In later justifying the judicial action brought against Edwards on the basis of these letters, Somerset went through them point by point, providing detailed refutations in the margins for the attention of the secretary of state.[7] Yet the complex details of the specific allegations contained in the letters are perhaps less significant than the way in which Edwards characteristically linked interpersonal conflicts with contemporary political questions. In the first letter, Edwards complained that members of the administration had 'branded' him with 'the odious and hateful appellation of a "Radical"'. He began the correspondence by asserting 'my loyalty to our Monarch, and affection to his Ministers'. Once underway, Edwards's targets proved wildly diverse. They ranged from Peter Auret, the fiscal's clerk ('a fellow of no education, family, or connection, the son of an unwashed Artificer married to the Daughter of a menial of the Court by a Bastard Hottentot'[8]) to Fiscal Denyssen, William

---

[3] Somerset described the incident as 'a violent and unprovoked assault upon a respectable person'. Edwards represented it as righteous anger framed in both class and ethnic terms: 'we (being Englishmen) who only told the truth, are put to an expence of near Six Hundred Rds. by a Dutchman, once a humble clerk in a Law Office': *RCC*, vol. 17, pp. 269–71. James Richardson, formerly of Ceylon, ran a fishing business in Cape Town. Edwards may have come to know Richardson through his business as a notary for he completed the arrangements of seven indentured Irish labourers between Richardson and John Ingram, the labour speculator who appears in a later chapter: see Protocol of the Notary William Edwards No. 1–105, CA, NCD 27/1.

[4] Edwards to Somerset, 26 April 1824, *RCC*, vol. 17, p. 276.
[5] Somerset to Bathurst, 21 May 1824, *RCC*, vol. 17, p. 350.
[6] Edwards to Somerset, 22 April 1824, *RCC*, vol. 17, p. 270.
[7] Copies of the annotated letters are to be found in *RCC*, vol. 17, pp. 268–71, 276–7.
[8] *RCC*, vol. 17, p. 270.

Wilberforce Bird and the governor himself. A repeated complaint behind the numerous separate cases referred to in the letters is Somerset's personal and illegal interference in the processes of the law. Although not stated directly in these terms, the common theme behind such implications relates to the improper use of executive power in judicial processes, a persistent *leitmotif* in the 1820s constitutional discussions over both the Cape and New South Wales.

As a consequence of the letters, Edwards was arrested on 28 April and charged with libel. Within a month of his previous acquittal, he found himself in jail once more. The traditional accounts of Edwards's story that I discussed in the Introduction have generally dismissed the allegations contained in the letters as unfounded, and have left explanations there. Depending on the writer's attitude to Somerset, the implication is that they were prompted either by an irrational malignancy or by a general sense of justified resentment against the regime. If it is plausible to assume that Edwards might not have anticipated being arrested for drawing up Cooke's memorial, by this point he had ample experience of the Somerset administration's response to such insults. What are we to make of this seemingly unwise decision by an escaped convict, newly acquitted of criminal libel, to stick his head above the parapet yet again?

A variety of intertwined motivations probably lay behind it. There is the possibility of a grudge against the Beaufort family dating back to Alexander Kaye's time in England. More definitely, as William Edwards he certainly had reason to resent the treatment he had suffered in the prize slave libel trials. There is also the undoubted rashness of his temperament. Abandoning his legal studies in favour of banking, practicing law without a license, making the choice to mutiny en route to New South Wales, successfully escaping sentence as a convict: these all give us some clues (albeit opaque ones) as to his character. Sometimes such risks paid off, at other times they did not. We can also make some suppositions about less pleasant aspects of his personality. We are reminded not only of the family accounts of Alexander Kaye (specifically the 'disgust & abhorrence' expressed by his sister Mary[9]) but also of the alleged assault charge in Chester that never came to trial, and the disputes he appears to have been involved in at the Cape, again including allegations of assault. Certainly his entire colonial career was marked by an apparent inability to refrain from injudicious personal attacks on any figure in authority.

In judging why Edwards sent these letters to Somerset, we might also speculate that his head had been turned by the prize slave trials in which

---

[9] Mary Kaye to Thomas Shuttleworth, 17 Feb. 1816, Records of the Chancery Court, Palatinate of Lancaster, TNA, PL 14/84.

he had triumphed against the authorities, a triumph that had witnessed his reincarnation as 'Edwards, the champion', the hero who was willing to speak the truth to power. Commissioner Bigge would later describe Edwards's position in Cape Town at the time like this:

> from intelligence in the transaction of Business and from the popularity that he had acquired amongst a certain Class of the population by successfully conducting a defence against a Government Prosecution, he obtained a large share of Business.[10]

Earlier in this book I quoted Edwards as apparently boasting around this time of his ability to provoke 'agitation' across the British imperial world.[11] Rather than the inspiration for 'bombastic nonsense' claimed by Somerset, Edwards's time in jail may genuinely have proved the transformative experience the notary claimed it had been. Edwards was undoubtedly addicted to self-aggrandisement, but this does not preclude his possessing a genuine sense of outrage at the indisputable excesses of the regime.

Ultimately it is impossible to disentangle exactly the reasons that prompted Edwards to send these letters. The admissions of distraction he made in the first letter ('I have wandered from my subject') suggest he may not even have known himself. Whether or not Edwards genuinely harboured delusions of revolutionary grandeur, these alleged proclivities were made much of by the authorities in court during his second libel trial. As a criminal case, it was necessary to prove the libel's tendency to provoke a breach of the peace. The fiscal, observing Edwards's demeanour in court, argued that he showed a 'laughing countenance' and 'seemed to await the approbation of the Public to whom he turned round' in giving his performance. He may have denied writing the letters, but his denials came 'with such a countenance, as plainly said to anyone who paid the smallest attention, "I am the man that dare do such things, follow my example and you shall find in me a head and a Leader that will undertake anything."'[12] The motivation behind the letters remains obscure, but we are on much more certain ground when we track their consequences and their broader implications for imperial politics and reform.

---

[10] Bigge to Brisbane, 24 Sept. 1824 (enclosure in Darling to Murray, 23 Nov. 1829, *HRA*, 1:15, p. 268.
[11] Testimony of Daniel Shee, Council of Justice, CA, CJ 3352. It should be pointed out that Shee, who also appears in Chapter 7, was regarded by many as an unreliable witness.
[12] *RCC*, vol. 17, p. 408.

Of libel and liberty

In acting against Edwards's insults to Somerset, the Cape authorities set off a series of vexed debates over imperial policy, debates that touched on issues far beyond the borders of the colony itself. Over the next two chapters, I turn to what is the best-remembered episode in Edwards's career: his trial for libelling Somerset and the actions taken by the administration to suppress *The South African Commercial Advertiser* before the paper could report these court proceedings. In doing so, however, I want to take our understanding of these events in two directions hitherto ignored by historians. In this chapter, I return to the problem we encountered in the prize slave trial – of whether complaints against high-ranking officials should be defined as libel. This was an issue upon which Cape Dutch and English practice differed, and although Roman–Dutch law was still ostensibly in operation at the Cape in 1824, the situation on the ground was rather more fluid than a strict application of the law of conquest might suggest.[13] In the following chapter, I explore how Somerset's attempt to use established Cape Dutch practices of executive banishment against his English settler critics raised vexed issues of sovereignty and constitutional law. In both cases, a fundamental question turned on the extent to which British settlers carried what they considered their traditional 'rights' into the colonies. The confusion between English and Dutch law highlighted by these cases and their aftermath reveal constitutional debates that underscore the deep contingency of conquest law at a highly unstable legal and political moment. The political disputes inspired by these actions demonstrate that conflicts between common and civil law traditions need to be more clearly recognised as instrumental to the strengthened implementation of British imperial legal hierarchies in colonial localities in this period.

Both chapters place the relationship between Dutch and British colonial governance at the Cape in the wider context of a 'legal ferment', to use historian Lisa Ford's term, taking place across the British Empire in the 1820s and 1830s.[14] Scholars have long recognised that colonial societies are particularly fruitful environments in which to understand the fractured authority of 'plural legal orders'.[15] The 'jurisdictional jockeying'[16] that ensued within the context of imperial expansion and

---

[13] The Cape remained under Roman–Dutch law rather than the French-influenced civil code introduced in the Netherlands proper during the Napoleonic period.
[14] Ford, *Settler Sovereignty*, p. 4.
[15] L. Benton, *Law and Colonial Cultures: Legal Regimes in World History 1400–1900* (Cambridge University Press, 2002), pp. 9–10.
[16] Benton, *Law and Colonial Cultures*, p. 3.

'Under the cloak of liberty' 165

reform outlined in Chapter 1 was fundamental to the process by which colonial orders both imposed legal systems on new territories and established the position of particular actors under the law.[17] Existing work pursuing these themes tends to focus on understanding the contested process through which marginalised groups (indigenous people, slaves and convicts) were brought under the dominant powers' legal regime. We need to add an extra layer of complexity to this story. Increasing numbers of Britons in this period were emigrating to colonies where they found themselves subject to foreign laws. What would the jurisdictional consequences of this process be? Scandals over gubernatorial excess orchestrated by men like Edwards underscore how assertions of supposedly inherent British rights were undercut by exerting colonial authority through alien judicial systems. In turn, the resulting protests may have tipped the balance in favour of a more robust assertion of British legal regimes over colonies of conquest.

In July 1825 Sir Richard Plasket, newly appointed secretary to government at the Cape of Good Hope, wrote promising to 'use every exertion in my power' to give advance warning to the Colonial Office of matters 'which are likely to become subjects of discussion in Parliament'. Plasket was well aware that he was joining a scandal-plagued administration that was proving itself a gift to opposition Whigs and Radicals. In outlining to Under-Secretary of State Robert Wilmot Horton the immediate problems he had identified upon arrival in the colony, it was the law that loomed largest in Plasket's mind as a threat to 'tranquillity':

The only fear I have of our getting into Scrapes here, is through our Judicial Proceedings, the Law itself is so uncongenial to British feelings, the Composition of the Courts is so irregular and so inefficient, and the practices under them is so mismanaged that I see no end to grievances when a *clever fellow* comes under their lash, so long as the present system exists. An English Chief Justice of high character and a more efficient lot of Judges and law officers is absolutely necessary to keep this Colony in a state of tranquillity.[18]

Plasket's report underlines contemporary recognition of what the prize slave libel trials have already taught us: that judicial proceedings taken to neutralise troublemakers could backfire. The legal 'scrapes' that Plasket referred to in his letter were the three criminal libel trials that had taken

---

[17] On this broader question see L. Benton and R. Ross, 'Empires and legal pluralism: Jurisdiction, sovereignty, and political imagination in the early modern world', in L. Benton and R. Ross (eds.), *Legal Pluralism and Empires 1500–1850* (New York University Press, 2013).
[18] Richard Plasket to Wilmot Horton, 20 July 1825, *RCC*, vol. 22, pp. 287–8 (original emphasis).

place over the previous year: the prize slave libel trial of February 1824, Edwards's trial for libelling Somerset in May 1824 and the July 1824 trial of 1820 settler Bishop Burnett, who had been arrested for libels against the Cape judiciary.[19] Cape historians have recognised how these trials highlight the administrative system's failings in the years immediately prior to the new Charter of Justice. Yet the full significance of these cases has yet to be recognised by either historians or legal scholars. They were actions for criminal libel, yet their legal foundations as such have been assumed rather than analysed. Furthermore, both the constitutional discussions they prompted and the broader imperial context in which they took place have been ignored.

In the past two decades a rich literature has developed concerning honour and its defence in the eighteenth- and nineteenth-century Cape.[20] Yet, although much has been written on how honour operates in everyday social interaction, we have yet to explore how the implications of defamation might be tracked through the formal political and constitutional realms. Seditious libel actions like those against Edwards offer us precisely such a possibility in the way they police the interface between freedom of expression and state security. These cases unfolded at the Cape in the midst of the Commission of Eastern Inquiry's investigations, a context that highlighted the problems presented by subjecting British settlers to foreign laws in British colonies. In the conflicts that arose at the Cape between English common and European civil law practices we can see a new way of considering sovereignty debates and the shift towards a more hierarchical legal framework in British imperialism in the early decades of the nineteenth century. The trials therefore need to be understood as part of a wider crisis in legal pluralism.

In accordance with the law of conquest, 'the Laws and Institutions that subsisted under the ancient Government' remained in force at the Cape, and governors received their instructions to this effect.[21] This doctrine underpinned two influential 1774 judgements by Lord Chief

---

[19] Unlike English law, Roman–Dutch law makes no distinction between libel (written) and slander (verbal) defamation. In spite of this, 'libel' was the term most commonly used by all those involved in the 1824 trials, whether English or Cape Dutch. Nic Olivier points out that the attempt to find commonality between English and Roman–Dutch law in this period led jurists to act as if defamation and libel (or slander) were the same thing; 'Laster', p. 32.

[20] See the citations of the previous chapter, footnote 10.

[21] Instructions to the Earl of Caledon, *RCC*, vol. 6, p. 9; E. Fagan, 'Roman-Dutch law in its South African historical context', in R. Zimmermann and D. Visser (eds.), *Southern Cross: Civil Law and Common Law in South Africa* (Oxford: Clarendon, 1996); R. W. Kostal, *A Jurisprudence of Power: Victorian Empire and the Rule of Law* (Oxford University Press, 2005), pp. 2–3; Epstein, *Scandal of Colonial Rule*, pp. 122–3.

Justice Mansfield, both of which featured in the constitutional discussions provoked not only by the Cape libel trials but more particularly by Somerset's actions against the press.[22] This late eighteenth-century trend in legal thinking, however, failed to resolve the profound ambiguities inherent in colonial sovereignty.[23] Such issues, and the associated problem of how far claims of traditional liberties had traction for British subjects in colonial territories, remained anything but clear.[24] By this period, questions raised by the definition of the British subject, and debates over the rights held by those so defined, over the rights of unfree labourers such as slaves and convicts, and over the place of indigenous people under the law, were all becoming increasingly problematic.[25]

'Tending to vilify the High Authority and Dignity of His Excellency'

On 4 May 1824, the trial of Edwards began 'on a Charge of Composing, Writing and Publishing a Libel against His Excellency the Governor, as well in this His Capacity, as in that of Judge of Appeal'.[26] As we saw in the prize slave dispute, criminal libel rested upon the perceived

---

[22] *Campbell v. Hall* concerned Grenada (conquered from the French in 1763) whereas *Fabrigas v. Mostyn* involved Minorca (ceded to the British by the Spanish in 1713).

[23] J. M. Ward, *Colonial Self-Government: The British Experience 1759–1856* (London: Macmillan, 1976); P. J. Marshall, 'Britain and the world in the eighteenth century: The turning outwards of Britain', *Transactions of the Royal Historical Society*, 11 (2001), 1–15; Ford, *Settler Sovereignty*.

[24] Despite its later evocation by eighteenth- and nineteenth-century propagandists of settler rights (as well as by historians) recent discussions of the seventeenth-century origins of these debates have argued for a more constrained interpretation of the degree to which these foundational decisions accepted any extension of English liberties into colonial settings: see D. Huselbosch, 'The ancient constitution and the expanding empire: Sir Edward Coke's British jurisprudence', *Law and History Review*, 21 (2003); *Constituting Empire: New York and the Transformation of Constitutionalism in the Atlantic World 1664–1830* (University of North Carolina Press, 2005), esp. pp. 20–8; and C. Tomlins, *Freedom Bound: Law, Labor, and Civic Identity in Colonizing English America 1580–1865* (Cambridge University Press, 2010), pp 82–92.

[25] For a survey of some of the latest scholarship on issues of law and colonialism see Z. Laidlaw, 'Breaking Britannia's bounds? Law, settlers and space in Britain's imperial historiography', *Historical Journal*, 55:3 (2012), 807–30.

[26] Wanting to focus on the problem of the relationship between Dutch and British law, I have spared the reader the intricacies of a blow-by-blow account of the different phases of Edwards's trial for libelling Somerset or the extensive arguments mounted within it. Detailed transcripts are to be found in *RCC*, vol. 17, pp. 373–452. In brief, after three days debating the exceptions that Edwards presented to the case, the trial proper began on 7 May. Edwards was offered the opportunity of choosing an advocate in his defence but chose to represent himself. He was found guilty on 11 May and immediately appealed his conviction. Now represented by Advocate Christoffel Brand, the appeal was held on 28 May, and the guilty verdict upheld.

relationship between political order (it was necessary to prove a breach of the peace) and the personal reputation of public officials. In this instance, the stakes were raised by the governor's position as the embodiment of the sovereign. The Act of Accusation made before Edwards at the commencement of the trial underlined this. It included that the libels were

> tending to vilify the High Authority and Dignity of His Excellency the Governor as well in His Function as representing His Majesty the King, as in that of Judge of the High Court of Judicature within this Colony, and likewise atrociously to calumniate and defame His Excellency the Governor as well personally as in both His above mentioned Functions.[27]

In bringing this case against Edwards, Somerset's actions were out of step with political practice in Britain, where the pitfalls of bringing cases of criminal libel had become increasingly evident. In the absence of press censorship, charges of seditious libel had been a key strategy against English dissidents in the late eighteenth and early nineteenth centuries, and the judicial system was used to harass them as far as possible even if a trial did not eventuate. Yet libel trials remained a gamble and could ironically provide a useful venue for the defendant's ideology to be expressed. After Fox's Libel Act of 1792 it was up to the jury rather than the judge to decide on whether the printed matter in question had a tendency to provoke a breach of the peace, making the case potentially more vulnerable to shifting public opinion. As historian Philip Harling argues, ultimately 'the uncertainty of language doomed the crown lawyers to failure, because they had too much difficulty convincing juries that what they called libels were indeed libellous'.[28]

The notorious Six Acts, passed by the British Parliament in 1819 with the intent of cracking down on popular radicalism, included both the Blasphemous and Seditious Libels Act, and the Publications Act. But it was the latter, which imposed taxes on publications to make them less profitable, that soon proved decisive in the state's battle against dissent. The harsh penalties for criminal libel laid down in the former act were largely a dead letter because courts refused to impose them. Under pressure from the Whigs, the Blasphemous and Seditious Libels Act specified 'banishment' rather than 'transportation' for a second offence, the term of years to be ordered by the court. Parliamentary debates on the act discussed the relative punishments of transportation and banishment at

[27] *RCC*, vol. 17, pp. 373–4.
[28] P. Harling, 'The law of libel and the limits of repression 1790–1832', *Historical Journal*, 44:1 (March 2001), 111; I. Loveland, *Political Libels: A Comparative Study* (Oxford University Press, 2000).

'Under the cloak of liberty' 169

some length. A person sentenced to banishment and found to be at large within Britain or its colonies within forty days of the sentence, or before the term of banishment had expired, could then be transported.[29] Anyone without the financial resources to support themselves in foreign territory during the period of banishment was thus effectively subject to transportation. The reluctance of the court to impose such sentences on second-time offenders, however, made the debate over these distinct varieties of punishment largely redundant. Seeking to explain why the provision made it onto the statute books when it was clear that judges would refuse to exercise their discretion by enforcing it, historian W. Hardy Wickwar argues that the Blasphemous and Seditious Libels Act should be seen in political rather than legal terms. Unlike the Publications Act, it was always intended to operate more as a deterrent than a punishment.[30] In the following chapter we will find Bathurst making analogous arguments about the "salutary effect" of threatening an "Instrument of Authority" without exercising it.[31] By the time of the Cape libel trials in the 1820s there had been a dramatic decline in the use of seditious libel prosecutions in English law. Setting aside the question of punishment, they were now considered 'politically crude and maladroit' for the way in which they provided critics of authority with opportunities for greater publicity.[32] These concerns, already demonstrated in the prize slave libel trials, would return in the course of Edwards's trial for libelling the governor.

As he had done previously, Edwards used the court as a vehicle to pour down as much scorn on the administration as possible, this time with the governor as his target, claiming in his defence that the alleged libels were no more than the truth. It perhaps bears repeating that truth as a justification against charges of defamation is one key difference between the English and the Roman–Dutch systems. Unlike English law, under modern Roman–Dutch law truth must in addition be proven to have been published for the public benefit. Yet Cape courts at this time showed a

---

[29] The distinctions between transportation and banishment are discussed at greater length in the next chapter.
[30] W. H. Wickwar, *Struggle for the Freedom of the Press 1819–1832*, pp. 138–9, 154–5; House of Commons Debates, 21 December 1819, vol. 41 cc. 1414–45.
[31] Bathurst to Somerset, 19 Oct. 1824, Bathurst Papers, BL 57/65.
[32] K. Smith, 'Securing the state, the institutions of government, and maintaining public order', in W. Cornish et al. (eds.), *The Oxford History of the Laws of England* (Oxford University Press, 2010), vol. XIII, p. 336. On the implications of this shift in metropolitan thinking on the colonies of Upper Canada and New South Wales, see B. Wright, 'Libel and the colonial administration of justice in Upper Canada and New South Wales c. 1825–1830', in H. Foster et al. (eds.), *The Grand Experiment: Law and Legal Culture in British Settler Societies* (University of British Columbia Press, 2008).

great degree of confusion over the question of truth in cases of defamation, possibly as a result of the growing influence of English law.[33] As we saw in the last chapter, however, this distinction is of far less relevance in cases involving criminal charges. In the English law of criminal libel, truth was not a defence. Similarly, in the Cape criminal libel cases under discussion, Bigge reported that 'evidence tending to establish the truth of the allegations was rejected'.[34] In civil defamation cases at the Cape, truth could excuse a defendant from being made to utter a public recantation (*amende honorable*) but not from the pecuniary fine (*amende profitable*) that was paid to a nominated charitable institution.[35]

In the first stages of the trial for libelling Somerset, Edwards conducted his own defence. Perhaps placing political grandstanding above legal niceties, he showed himself blatantly unconcerned by truth's dubious status as a justification for criminal libel. First, he explicitly denied writing the letters. Second, he argued that, even if he had written the letters, he had not published them as they were private letters to the governor. Third, he argued that even if he had written and published the letters, they were not libels as the contents were true. And finally, Edwards argued that even if the contents were not true, Somerset's reputation was so low that making such accusations could not constitute a libel.[36] None of this was pleasing to the authorities. Edwards's accusations seemed to confirm that they had taken the right decision in pre-emptively muzzling the Cape press from reporting the case. Despite the Council of Justice's warnings against 'personal reflections which could probably aggravate his Case', Edwards continued to refer back to the contents of the letters, asserting their truth and denying therefore that they were libellous. The fiscal tried repeatedly to silence the prisoner on the grounds of state security, arguing that the matters he raised did not belong to his defence but 'can have no other tendency than to create disaffection towards Government'.[37]

Edwards submitted a list of fourteen witnesses, including the governor himself, whom he clearly intended to subject to examination before the court. Most of those named can be connected to the specific allegations made in the letters. Others were clearly intended to cause the government acute embarrassment by humiliating Somerset as far as possible. The first object of the fiscal therefore was to prevent such insults. He must 'respectfully... insist from the Court, that it may be rejected as bearing the most contemptible Marks of Calumny and Malice of the Prisoner, and

---

[33] Olivier, 'Laster', p. 33.   [34] *RCC*, vol. 33, p. 20.
[35] *RCC*, vol. 32, p. 21; Olivier, 'Laster', p. 33.
[36] My thanks to Peter Burbidge for his expertise in analysing this testimony.
[37] *RCC*, vol. 17, pp. 382, 384.

that the Investigation may be declared closed'. The prisoner's purpose in calling his witnesses, claimed the fiscal, was to expose them to the 'ridicule and derision of the Prisoner and his party' and to 'destroy all feelings of respect and reverence for the existing Government, to Stir up the Inhabitants against Government, and to induce them to follow the prisoner's example'. The court must take action, because the threat was not only personal but also overtly political:

> it is time Your Worships that we stop him in his purpose before the Government be deprived of all its power and energy, and under the Cloak of Liberty to speak and write, all confidence in, and Goodwill towards Government destroyed, all the bonds of unanimity torn asunder and disaffection and Confusion established in the place of Good Order and Tranquility.[38]

Amongst the witnesses whom Edwards wished to call was listed 'A Manumitted female Slave of Mr. van der Riet, a *Concubine* living with Lord Charles Henry Somerset'.[39] Edwards alleged that Somerset had secured her emancipation by offering her master prize slaves in exchange. The authorities did all they could to avoid a description of this witness being entered into the record. The fiscal argued that Edwards's inclusion of her in the list demonstrated that his calling of witnesses was '*Animi injuriandi*', the 'clearest and evident proof of the wanton and humiliating purpose of the prisoner'.[40] For his part, Edwards did everything he could to describe her as fully as possible (even if he was forbidden from calling her as a witness):

> The witness on my List no. 12 is a manumitted female Slave of Mr. van der Riet the Concubine of Lord Charles Somerset, now living with him whose name I was not able to ascertain, and I would have proved how many prize Negroes were given for her manumission.[41]

---

[38] *RCC*, vol. 17, pp. 388, 390.   [39] *RCC*, vol. 17, p. 376.
[40] *RCC*, vol. 17, p. 390.
[41] *RCC*, vol. 17, p. 392. When the *Times* got hold of the information, it published as much salacious detail as possible (5 Oct. 1824). Citing as pressing issues the political capital that opponents could make of such charges and the publicity to be gained from their appearance in the London press, Commissioners Bigge and Colebrooke sent their own investigation into the matter in order to arm Bathurst against Somerset's critics. Although admitting that the slave, Carolina, was indeed Somerset's mistress, they exonerated him from the charge of misusing prize slaves to secure her emancipation and provided supporting documents as to the circumstances of Carolina's emancipation to prove it. It was Carolina's mother, Regina, who had paid her manumission. Where Regina might have got the 4000 rixdollars required was not mentioned, although the commissioners carefully noted that the transaction took place after the death of Somerset's first wife, Lady Elizabeth Courtenay, and before his departure from the colony on home leave – which certainly implies that the governor was involved. They were also keen to point out that Carolina's relationship with Somerset had not continued after his

There was no possibility, continued the fiscal, for these witnesses to shed light on the question of whether or not Edwards had written the letters, and this would be the only legitimate reason for them to be called. Truth was not at issue:

> The only question here is, Are the Two Letters Libellous? the answer to this question does not depend in this Case on the Enquiry into the truth or untruth of what the prisoner has written therein against His Excellency the Governor, but on the mode in which he has composed them and the person to whom he addressed them.

Any discussion of the subject of the letters, he concluded, would have a 'highly offensive and seditious tendency'.[42] In answer, Edwards referred obliquely to (a version of) his past:

> Any man who is accused of having committed a breach of the Law ought to endeavour to clear himself and need not to be ashamed of it, but the more shame it is for Lord Charles, as shall be proved by calling the Witnesses. When I was here six years ago and on more important business, I then had already marked this Colony for my prey.[43]

Going through the list of his witnesses, Edwards layered insult upon insult upon the Governor. The fiscal repeatedly called upon the court to restrain the prisoner in his

> improper observations, as such can have no other tendency than to stir up the minds of the disaffected against Government, and that as long as the reins of Government are in the hands of His Excellency, it is but the duty of everyone to protect him.[44]

Denyssen succeeded in his key aim, for the court ruled against allowing Edwards to call any of his witnesses, but he had signally failed in keeping the contents of the letters out of the discussion.

In mounting the case for the prosecution, the fiscal made much of the security ramifications of Edwards's insults to Governor Somerset. The thrust of his argument was loyalty and sedition; the colonists had ever proved themselves 'worthy of the protection they enjoy from the Mother Country':

> shall then a stranger who till a few months since has lived far from our shores poison the minds of the well-thinking Colonists by stirring them up against the

---

second marriage. Bigge and Colebrooke to Bathurst, 14 Feb. 1825, Bathurst Papers, BL, 57/87.
[42] *RCC*, vol. 17, p. 391.
[43] *RCC*, vol. 17, pp. 391–2. It was in fact five years since the *Atlas*, carrying Alexander Kaye, had stopped briefly at the Cape en route to New South Wales.
[44] *RCC*, vol. 17, p. 393.

Government, and the existing Order of things, especially against Him who is at the Head and who is charged with the execution of the Laws of the Sovereignty?[45]

In all his activities in the colony, Edwards's

sole plan has appeared to me to be to overturn the present order of things, who has at least made preparations to substitute a new one in its place, to hold up the Governor to public hate and aversion, to make the Laws of the Land the object of disrespect and violation, and to make the public confidence in the Officers of Government appear as a tissue of partiality and oppression.[46]

Citing as authorities the Roman law, Grotius, Blackstone and Holt, the fiscal argued that the crime had been 'consummated' by the letters being sent. As Holt demonstrated,

the sending of such Letter (an abusive Letter filled with provoking Language to another) without other publication is clearly an offence of a public nature, and punishable as such, in as much as it tends to create ill blood and causes a disturbance of the public peace.[47]

Turning to the question of what the nature of this punishment should be, the fiscal asserted the doctrine of Roman law that 'the crime increases in proportion to the high rank and situation of the person against whom the abuse is levelled'. The governor was not 'raised above the Laws' but he was the monarch's embodiment in the colonial realm. Such prestige, and its corollary of 'wounded majesty', was considered central to concrete questions of state security. As the prosecution put the case against Edwards: 'his crime has therefore almost reached the pinnacle, one step more and the prisoner will contend with the Sovereignty and dare to attack the King on the Throne.'[48]

Furthermore the crime was exacerbated by the continued insults heaped on the governor in the arguments offered in court over the list of witnesses:

He has endeavoured by his seditious discourse in the hearing of the public to form a party, and where will it end, if the weak and the credulous among the public are not deterred from following the same steps by the exemplary punishment of the prisoner?[49]

Edwards had proved himself a repeated troublemaker in the colony, 'he allows nothing to impede him in his mad course. There must therefore once be an end to such gross and indecent irregularities.'[50] The fiscal reminded the court that 'the punishment of the crime of injury is

---

[45] *RCC*, vol. 17, p. 396. [46] *RCC*, vol. 17, p. 396. [47] *RCC*, vol. 17, p. 406.
[48] *RCC*, vol. 17, pp. 401, 408–9. [49] *RCC*, vol. 17, p. 409.
[50] *RCC*, vol. 17, p. 410.

discretionary', and that within the Roman law the highest degree thereof was death. Edwards, claimed the prosecution, had 'by his conduct rendered himself unworthy and totally incapable either to act as Notary, to remain in this Colony, or to have the liberty of renewing his evil course in another country'. He should be found guilty of the crime of libel, 'aggravated by the incorrigibleness of his conduct'. He should be dismissed as a notary public and 'condemned to be transported to New South Wales or to some other Island beyond the Seas in the possession of His Majesty for the term of seven years'.[51] As was the usual practice, the fiscal called for Edwards to be confined to Robben Island until such time as this could be arranged.[52]

'The positive rules of law': legal pluralism at the Cape

Although historians have largely ignored the role of libel law in Cape politics, legal scholars have paid a great deal of attention to the differences that exist between the Roman–Dutch and the English legal systems with regard to defamation. In the twentieth century, this area of the law would become one of the most hotly debated areas for jurists battling their relative influence in South African delict (tort, in common law parlance).[53] Such influence waxed and waned according to political context. English law was at its zenith in the half-century from 1860 to 1910, whereas an emphasis on the civilian basis of law can be linked to the rise of Afrikaans-medium law faculties in the twentieth century and their dominance during the apartheid era.[54]

Yet legal scholars, even where they have accorded the developments of the nineteenth century a due measure of attention in understanding the relationship between civil and common law, almost entirely ignore the period before the Charter of Justice that came into effect from 1828.[55]

---

[51] On the long-standing association of islands with practices of forcible exile, see Benton, *A Search for Sovereignty*.

[52] *RCC*, vol. 17, p. 410.

[53] L. W. Athulathmudali, 'The law of defamation in Ceylon: A study in the interaction of English and Roman-Dutch Law', *International and Comparative Law Quarterly*, 13:4 (Oct. 1964), 1368–1406; Ranchod, *Foundations of the South African Law of Defamation*; Reinhard Zimmermann and Daniel Visser (eds.), *Southern Cross: Civil Law and Common Law in South Africa* (Oxford: Clarendon, 1996), esp. chapters by E. Fagan and H. J. Erasmus.

[54] Zimmermann and Visser, *Southern Cross*, pp. 23–4.

[55] An exception, though restricted to civil rather than criminal defamation, is Olivier, 'Laster', which emphasises the internal evolution of Cape defamation law in this period. Olivier's analysis of civil cases (p. 32) confirms the extremely wide range of legal sources drawn on by jurists in this period and the attempt to find common ground between English and Roman–Dutch law.

'Under the cloak of liberty' 175

The 1824 libel trials predate the formal adoption of English legal practices by the Cape courts, and Roman–Dutch law was ostensibly still in operation. The situation on the ground, however, was far more fluid. With the commissioners making their investigations into the colony's legal system at the very moment the libel trials were proceeding, it was common knowledge that a new judiciary was only a matter of time. Many expected that reforms would go much further than they did in replacing the existing judicial system.[56] As former chief justice of Trinidad, Bigge was known to have recommended the gradual introduction of English law to that former Spanish colony.[57] Defamation trials in this period (whether civil or criminal) reveal that all those involved were eager to hedge their bets. Both prosecution and defence drew on multiple authorities, from Grotius and Voet to Blackstone and Holt, and as far as possible sought to find agreement between them.

In his report on the Courts of Justice, Bigge noted with approval of the Cape Dutch legal fraternity that

we have not been insensible to those involuntary testimonies of respect that are paid by the Judges themselves, the Advocates, and the Agents, to the superiority of English Law and authority, by the frequent quotations which they are in the habit of making from the great Expounder of our System [Blackstone]; and even by the most minute references to Writers of much less authority and credit.[58]

Others held a more jaundiced view. As William Edwards complained, the fiscal 'has made quotations from the Roman, English and Dutch law, and springs so from one to the other that I really do not know where to meet him'.[59] For his part, Bishop Burnett protested that 'I am well aware that it has long been the practice at the Cape to try the colonists

---

[56] Although certain areas of what would become South African law would be almost entirely transformed by English common law, one area that remained largely untouched was that of marriage and inheritance. Roman–Dutch law accorded far greater rights to women than did English common law in this period. Frequent complaints made by British men who had married at the Cape and found themselves subject to Roman–Dutch law led to a Commission of Inquiry into the matter in the 1860s: Governor and Legislative Council, Cape of Good Hope, *Report of the Law of Inheritance Commission for the Western Districts*, G 15–65 (Cape Town, 1866). The Commission dismissed their concerns, claiming that it was possible to avoid the provisions of Roman–Dutch law by drawing up an antenuptial contract. What is significant for the purposes of this argument is the continued belief articulated by complainants that, as British settlers, their marriages (regardless of where they had taken place) should be subject to English law.
[57] He would also have been entirely familiar with the problems of exercising Spanish law in a British colony, problems that had been popularised by the Luisa Calderon scandal that is discussed in the following chapter.
[58] Report of Bigge to Bathurst upon the Courts of Justice, 6 Sept. 1826, *RCC*, vol. 28, p. 14.
[59] *RCC*, vol. 17, p. 420.

by Roman, Dutch or English laws indiscriminately; adapting this caprice to the relative severity with which they may be applied to the respective cases.'[60] He argued that

> a British-born subject carries his constitution about him in every part of His Majesty's dominions as his indefeasible birth-right, and that in cases affecting his life, his liberty, or his fair fame, he is entitled to be adjudged by the laws of his own country.[61]

Legal actors in this drama manifestly failed to obey the lines that supposedly separated one system from another. They appealed to multiple authorities, and often drew on folk beliefs and a vernacular sense of their rights and privileges that bore little resemblance to their actual position under the law. Such popular attitudes exasperated lawyers like James Stephen: 'Nothing can be more loose and inaccurate than the views which are taken ... by persons who rely upon their natural sagacity, rather than upon an acquaintance with the positive rules of law.'[62]

Yet, the legal status of Britons in British colonies with foreign legal systems was, as I argue, by no means clear even to the most expert. Furthermore, the heightened political context in Britain could give rhetorical power to organic ideas about the 'rights of freeborn Englishmen' regardless of whether they carried genuine legal weight. If social historians of the Cape have largely ignored the political and constitutional problems posed by defamation law, then legal scholars of defamation in South Africa have confined their attention to discussing the writings of jurists. Yet this was a world steeped in popular conceptions of the law. In broadsheets posted on the streets of Cape Town, in newspaper reports across colonies and in the metropole, and in parliamentary debate, the broader community view of the law (frequently at odds with that of the experts) was freely expressed and could have real impact on constitutional change.

In 1822 Somerset had issued a proclamation that English would gradually replace Dutch over the next four years as the official and judicial language of the Cape. Both of the key advocates in the Edwards case, Hendrik Cloete and Christoffel Brand, had strong English-language skills, having

---

[60] Records of the Court of Justice, CA, CJ 632; *BPP*, 1826 (431), *Mr. Bishop Burnett, Cape of Good Hope*, p. 24.
[61] *Mr. Bishop Burnett, Cape of Good Hope*, p. 26.
[62] James Stephen, annotated commentary on amendments to the New South Wales Act of 1823, Offices: House of Commons, Admiralty, Crown Agents, King's Agent, Commander in Chief, Board of Trade, East India Company, Foreign, Home and Law Officers, TNA, CO 201/195.

studied at Lincoln's Inn and Edinburgh University, respectively.[63] Several key members of the Cape judiciary, notably Fiscal Daniel Denyssen and Chief Justice Johannes Truter, were bilingual; others, however, were not, and neither were the Britons being prosecuted.[64] The libel trials, therefore, took place in both Dutch and English. Proceedings were frequently held up as translators struggled to ensure that the key protagonists could understand and respond to one another. This Babel of voices became a central factor in Edwards's conviction and transportation. The Commissioners of the Court of Justice, listening to this testimony in translation, claimed that Edwards had confessed to writing the letters, and (together with some very shaky physical evidence in the form of handwriting analysis) they accordingly pronounced him guilty of criminal libel.

The argument that the letters – whoever had written them – were *not* libellous in law had thus been translated into a confession. This occasioned much anxious discussion amongst the British spectators. As Bigge and Colebrooke reported to Secretary of State Lord Bathurst, there was considerable 'alarm' amongst 'the English inhabitants' of the colony at 'the adoption of a principle by the Court of Justice that seemed to impart to a hypothetical argument the force and effect of a judicial confession and acknowledgement of guilt'. Those native English speakers listening to the trial claimed that Edwards's supposed confessions were 'invariably hypothetical'. In outlining their 'doubts' as to the 'legality of Edwards's conviction' and 'the points that are likely to attract notice and excite surprise in England', Bigge and Colebrooke concluded that 'the evidence upon which he was convicted was in its nature presumptive, and that it did not constitute that legal and conclusive proof

---

[63] Christoffel Joseph Brand, who was named for his godfather, the English botanist Sir Joseph Banks, spent most of 1820 studying for a master's degree at Edinburgh, specifically to improve his English-language skills preparatory to returning to the Cape bar. He had previously obtained two doctor's degrees, one in literature and one in law, at the University of Leiden. His doctorate in law, *Dissertatio politico-juridica de jure coloniarum*, came down heavily on the right of colonies to legislate their own affairs independently of the mother country. It worried the classically literate Cape colonial secretary, Colonel Christopher Bird, until he was reminded that few at the Cape possessed the linguistic ability to read its allegedly seditious arguments: *Dictionary of South African Biography*, vol. II, pp. 78–84.

[64] Edwards sneered at the fiscal's English during the course of his trials, but the numerous manuscripts that survive in their own handwriting suggest that both Truter and Denyssen had a high level of proficiency in that language. Truter retired, and Denyssen resumed private practice as an advocate after the new judicial system was introduced at the Cape. Denyssen later became an outspoken critic of anglicisation, and his decision to leave colonial service is likely to have been politically rather than linguistically motivated. He certainly had no trouble in sustaining a private practice under the English-language law courts after 1828: *Dictionary of South African Biography*, vol. III, p. 208.

which is required by the civil law to establish the guilt of an accused person'.[65]

Language was the most obvious culture clash in the 1820s libel trials, but almost as visible was the blurring of the lines between Roman–Dutch and English law, and the (ultimately futile) insistence of those on trial that they were subject to the laws of their 'own country'.[66] In the prize slave libel trial, the fiscal began his case against Cooke, Edwards and Hoffman by asserting that the accused had no right to be tried under English law, irrespective of whether they were English subjects.[67] In Edwards's exceptions to the legality of his second libel trial, he again insisted that 'I must be tried by an English law.' In response, the fiscal reiterated: 'the Contrary of this I have already proved to him on a former occasion, as every Man must be tried according to the Law of the Land in which he resides.'[68]

If Roman–Dutch law *was* still wholly in operation, however, the situation on the ground was far more murky than such assertions might lead one to expect. It was common for both sides to try as much as possible to find agreement between the two systems. Advocate Cloete, for the defence in the prize slave libel trial, claimed that the 'English laws on this head [defamation] agree so perfectly with the Roman and Dutch laws that either may be referred to.'[69] In Edwards's trial for libelling Somerset the prosecution disagreed that 'the two Laws correspond so well together with respect to libellous writings that it was all the same whether one had recourse to the one or to the other'. Yet, Denyssen continued, 'I shall not hesitate to appeal in this case to the English Laws although in other respects where I have found any essential difference between these Two Laws I shall set the English aside and follow the Dutch Law.'[70]

In reply, Advocate Christoffel Brand tried to argue that Edwards's case should be tried according to English law:

This has been frequently resorted to by this Court, and the Prisoner especially has a claim thereto, who as being an English Burgher, cannot be expected to be acquainted with the Roman Dutch Law, as in this case his plea, namely ignorance of the law, is in his favor.

Recognising that this was unlikely to occur, however, Brand went on to assure the court that 'We shall nevertheless not omit to confirm each point, as well of the Roman and Dutch Laws as of the English.'[71] In the repeated appeal to English authorities, Cape lawyers showed their

---

[65] Commissioners of Inquiry to Bathurst, 23 March 1825, *RCC*, vol. 20, pp. 374–9.
[66] *Mr Bishop Burnett, Cape of Good Hope*, p. 26. [67] *RCC*, vol. 17, p. 183.
[68] *RCC*, vol. 17, pp. 384, 385. [69] *RCC*, vol. 17, p. 197.
[70] *RCC*, vol. 17, pp. 399–400. [71] *RCC*, vol. 17, p. 435.

cognisance of the likely impact of metropolitan legal opinion via Colonial Office officials. The presence of Bigge and Colebrooke in the colony was a daily reminder of the transitional moment in which legal arguments were being made.

Brand was at pains to prove that under both English and Dutch law a sentence of transportation for libel was 'illegal'.[72] Denyssen's call for an exemplary sentence was, however, upheld by the court. This would prove a key area of Colonial Office concern in the case against Edwards for libelling Somerset. Bathurst had sought explicit information on the justification for this sentence, for 'punishment of transportation for seven years for a libel', as he put it, 'sounds very harsh to English Ears'.[73] As a misdemeanour rather than a felony, criminal libel was not a transportable offence under English law. The usual punishment imposed was a fine and imprisonment.[74] The Cape bench claimed that Edwards's guilt was 'much increased' by his behaviour in court, despite warnings that 'such conduct would be considered as an aggravation of his crime and consequently of his punishment'. Bigge and Colebrooke expressed grave 'doubts upon the application of this principle'. It would have been far preferable, as had been the case in the prize slave trial, for Edwards to have suffered imprisonment for contempt.[75]

It was common for British emigrants to argue, as did Bishop Burnett, that 'a British-born subject [was] entitled to be adjudged by the laws of his own country'.[76] During his trial, Burnett appealed in vain to decisions of the English courts 'by which it had been determined that memorials addressed to the king or parliament, complaining of injustice of oppression, and praying for redress, are not punishable as libels'.[77] James Stephen had indeed raised precisely the same issue in offering his legal opinion to Bathurst in *Fiscal v. Cooke, Edwards and Hoffman*, arguing that this 'right' to petition the king or his representatives 'is inherent in all his subjects, in whatever part of his dominions they may happen to reside'. In the colonies, argued Stephen, the 'constitutional mode of exercising this right' was precisely that which Cooke and Edwards had adopted – they had transmitted a complaint through the governor to the relevant department of 'His Majesty's Government at Home'. Stephen

---

[72] *RCC*, vol. 17, p. 444–445.
[73] Bathurst to Somerset, 19 Oct. 1824, BL, Bathurst Papers, 57/65.
[74] Harling, 'The law of libel', 120. Bathurst made no reference to the fact that the 1819 Blasphemous and Seditious Libels Act specifically laid down banishment (though not transportation) as the punishment for a second offence. As has been noted, however, the provisions of this Act remained largely a dead letter.
[75] Commissioners of Inquiry to Bathurst, 23 March 1825, *RCC*, vol. 20, pp. 374–9.
[76] *Mr. Bishop Burnett, Cape of Good Hope*, p. 26.   [77] *RCC*, vol. 24, p. 103.

conceded that Cooke's motives were 'obviously selfish' and that some of his complaints were 'absurd and futile'. In legal terms, however, this was irrelevant:

> it is the maintenance of the general principle of the right of petitioning, and not the merits of any individual case, which it seems necessary, on this occasion, to consider, and I cannot but think that, in the persons of Cooke and Edwards, that principle has been violated.[78]

Whereas Cooke's memorial led to an acquittal by the Cape judiciary, Burnett's did not. In answering Burnett's later complaints about the verdict tabled before the House of Commons, Chief Justice Truter claimed that Cooke's memorial 'admitted a construction of grievance and complaint', whereas Burnett's 'contained nothing but the most criminating invectives'.[79] Bigge and Colebrooke's investigation into criminal law and jurisprudence reported that a proclamation by 'the Dutch Commissioners' (Sebastian Cornelis Nederburgh and Simon Hendrik Frykenius) in 1792 declared the use of expressions in memorials and petitions that were 'inconsistent with the courtesy and respect due to the established authorities' to be prohibited. The authors of such memorials were subjected to a rising scale of punishments with banishment from the colony and a fine of 500 rixdollars for the third offence.[80] In being sentenced by the court to five years' banishment, Bigge and Colebrooke considered that Burnett 'undoubtedly was made to feel the difference between the system of law under which he had lived, and that to which he had thus voluntarily subjected himself'. Under such a system, a memorial could potentially be 'considered, and punished as a criminal act'[81] if deemed to proceed, in the words of the chief justice, from an 'offensive motive'. As Truter explained, 'the nature of the crime of libel, in the eye of the Colonial Law, is very different from what it is in the English Law' and according to a 'Dutch Jurist of great repute' carried a punishment that 'can be extended to corporal punishment and even to death itself'.[82]

However dimly they might view this definition of libel under Roman–Dutch law, Bigge and Colebrooke felt bound to assert that the sentence passed against Burnett was entirely legal. Furthermore, they endorsed the principle that British emigrants did not take their rights with them into a colony conquered from a foreign power:

---

[78] James Stephen to Wilmot Horton, 12 Aug. 1824, TNA, CO 48/95, Case of William Edwards.
[79] Truter to Somerset, 12 Oct. 1825, *RCC*, vol. 23, p. 272.
[80] *RCC*, vol. 33, pp. 19–20.   [81] *RCC*, vol. 24, p. 103.
[82] *RCC*, vol. 25, pp. 361 and 363.

We believe that the British settlers, with whom Mr. Burnett emigrated to this colony, were duly informed before their departure from England of the nature of the laws by which their conduct was to be regulated in it; and we are not aware that the right that Mr. Burnett claimed on his own behalf, and that of the other emigrants, of being tried by the British laws, had been conceded to British subjects in which a system of foreign law had been found to exist, and had been continued under the authority that His Majesty derived from conquest and cession.[83]

Yet Burnett's arguments underscored the popular perception of 'the rights of freeborn Englishmen' in the colonial realm, perceptions that had rhetorical weight in political struggles for all that they lacked constitutional foundation.

Debate inspired by these cases focussed on the fate of British emigrants subject to foreign laws in British colonies. It found vent in locations that ranged from the chamber of the House of Commons to the streets of Cape Town and the pages of the British and colonial press. As Radical MP Joseph Hume put it,

When an Englishman went to any of our colonies, he imagined that he carried with him the rights of a British subject, but in this expectation he was sorry to say that he would, for the most part, find himself entirely deceived. The will and pleasure of the governors of colonies became the law of the land, and if any individual was unfortunate enough to incur the displeasure of a governor, he was almost sure to be made the victim of the most arbitrary and tyrannical oppression.[84]

Yet Wilmot Horton made tactical use of the same argument for the opposite purpose. The law of conquest could be a useful way to shift blame from an autocratic governor onto an unfortunate, but necessary, reliance on a foreign legal system until such time as the necessary reforms could be properly implemented. 'It was unfair', he countered the opposition, 'not to distinguish, in such a complaint, between the acts of the governor and the defects of the Dutch law.'[85] Wilmot Horton referred repeatedly to the existence of the Commission of Inquiry and urged patience:

They were sent to the Cape for the purposes of introducing a change in the Dutch law, with a view to assimilate it to the law of England. And, could such an important change as this be effected in a moment?[86]

---

[83] *RCC*, vol. 24, p. 103.
[84] Hume presenting the petition of John Carnall, House of Commons Debates, 27 May 1825, vol. 13, cc. 903–9.
[85] Wilmot-Horton in reply to Brougham, House of Commons Debates, 16 June 1825, vol. 13, cc. 1167–73.
[86] Wilmot-Horton in reply to Hume, House of Commons Debates, 27 May 1825, vol. 13, cc. 903–9; see also *Times*, 28 May 1825.

Lord Edward Somerset was similarly vehement in Parliament in his brother's defence:

> Honourable gentlemen would naturally prefer the English law to the Dutch law; but they would recollect, that the governor of a colony must not govern it on the laws which he could wish, but on the laws which he found established in it.[87]

As we shall see in Chapter 8, Cape Town was plastered with broadsheets commenting on the government's actions against its critics during the 1824 libel trials. The way in which the Cape authorities were perverting English notions of the rule of law was a dominant theme in such placards, testifying to the strength of popular notions of rights and privileges. They warned against government autocracy: 'Englishmen assert your rights against the Spanish Inquisition' and 'The Inquisition is at Hand. An Englishman is dragged from his home to a Dungeon without Trial of Judge and Jury without any cause being assigned.'[88] They emphasised a contrast between the organic rights of 'freeborn Englishmen' and the corrupt officials of the previous regime. The first and last verses of one poem attacking Fiscal Daniel Denyssen, read as follows:

> Falsehoods detestable confes'd by all
> He who perverts Justice by it must fall
> What Title shall we call thee then great Man
> *Fix all* Prophet Daniel or *plain Dan*
> He is no less than Majesty itself
> Vain boast thy Robes will soon be on the shelf
> *Those great* those little *sable Man*
> Beware to oppress an Englishman.
> ...
> Once great Man the difference we see
> Between an honest Englishman and thee
> One falls unsullied never more to rise
> The Patriots crownd and hath receive the prize
> So never more infringe dear Dan
> The Birthright of an honest Englishman.[89]

Hudson's diary, where the only copies of these ephemeral protests mostly survive, is biased in favour of Somerset's critics, but Meurant's reminiscences highlight the way in which the governor's Cape Dutch allies were well aware that they were in the process of being displaced. At a high-end tavern 'noted as a rendezvous for supposed Government employés', a

---

[87] Lord Edward Somerset in reply to the petition of Bishop Burnett, House of Commons Debates, 8 May 1826, vol. 15, cc. 961–71.
[88] Hudson, Diary, 1 May 1824.   [89] Hudson, Diary, 29 March 1824.

'Under the cloak of liberty' 183

toast was raised as a 'counter-blast' to the English protests. It too would later be posted up as a placard on the streets of Cape Town:

> Alle die uit Engeland zijn gebannen, [*All who have been exiled from England*]
> Worden hier groote mannen; [*Become great men here*]
> En ons arme Hollandsche gezellen, [*And our poor Dutch companions*]
> Kan men de ribben op het lijf al tellen. [*Can count the ribs on their bodies.*]
> . . .
> O heere, wilt ons toch verlossen, [*O Lord will you not deliver us*]
> Van al die Engelsche ossen, [*From all the English oxen*]
> En leidt ons toch naar wenschen, [*And lead us yet to our desires*]
> Ons arme Hollandsche Christtenmenschen, Amen. [*We poor Dutch Christians, Amen.*][90]

Dutch law and the 'foreignness' of the Cape administration loomed large in wider commentary on the Edwards cases. When Edwards returned to New South Wales in 1824, the Sydney newspapers seized on Cape trials as an example of tyranny that served as useful propaganda in their own struggles to secure freedom of the press.[91] The *Sydney Monitor* emphasised the illegitimacy of Edwards's sentence, describing it as '*pure Dutch iniquity*' and the 'despotic Dutch law' of the 'notorious Lord Charles's administration'.[92] In Britain, the *Times* complained that accounts from the Cape described

> a tyranny so minute, so mean, so vindictive, so ungentlemanly, so opposite to whatever is understood by the word *English* . . . when is this brother of the House of Beaufort [Somerset] to be recalled? We answer, within one day after Parliament shall have been reformed. The existence, in truth, of such a Government, is enough to spread the passion for reform like wildfire through the land.[93]

Bathurst, hoping to deflect such criticism before it became a political liability, was characteristically inclined to offer Somerset some pragmatic advice. Whether or not a memorial could be

> prosecuted according to the Dutch Law . . . you must be aware that this is not the case according to the English Law, and in administering the Law in your Government, more particularly in what relates to the right of petitioning, the Dutch Law should be tempered by that of this Country. . . . I cannot persuade

---

[90] Meurant, *Sixty Years Ago*, pp. 28–9. With thanks to Hans Pols and Nigel Worden for their advice on my translation.
[91] Edgeworth, 'Defamation law and the emergence of a critical press', 50–82; J. J. Spigelman, 'Foundations of freedom of the press in Australia', *Australian Bar Review*, 23 (2002–2003), 89–109; Wright, 'Libel and the colonial administration of justice'.
[92] *Sydney Monitor*, 7 May 1828, 17 May 1828, 20 Dec. 1828.
[93] *Times*, 20 May 1825.

myself that under all the circumstances in which this case appears to have come before your Excellency, you have made a discreet exercise of your authority, if indeed you have not even exceeded it.[94]

Introducing 'Parr the forger'

On 11 May 1824, Edwards was convicted of criminal libel against Somerset. He immediately launched an appeal. Possibly aware of how far his own conduct had compromised his defence, he was now represented by Advocate Christoffel Brand, acting for Edwards 'in forma pauperis' as he had previously done in the case with Cooke. Brand had got Edwards off once before, but now the stakes were higher. Brand opened with Cicero's defence of Milo 'as he addressed the Roman Judges at the beginning of the Trial when he saw the Forum surrounded with glittering Arms'.[95] He was fully aware of 'the delicacy of my situation' in defending a man who had been 'accused of having insulted and defamed His Excellency, His Ministers, and His High Functionaries'. In full rhetorical flight, his evocation of the times was worthy even of the fiscal's denunciation of rebellion:

> I am aware that an advocate standing before the bar must not fear. I am aware that the function of an Advocate is too noble that he should feel so base a passion at the Bar, but Your Worships we are men, and we have connections. Besides the crime, the circumstances, the Persons concerned, the Colony, the times, and the political situation in which it is placed, are all causes which must contribute to fill my mind with anxiety, and which demand from me prudence and discretion.

Nonetheless, Brand asserted, he could prove the prisoner innocent, for dramatic new evidence had come to light.[96]

The appeal hearing saw a complete turnaround in the strategy of the defence. It now rested its case on the claim that the letters were a forgery. In this version of events, Edwards had been arrested without warning on the basis of two letters about which he knew nothing. His 'suspicion fell at once on a person who daily visited him, who had access to all his Papers,

---

[94] Somerset to Bathurst, 4 April 1825, *RCC*, vol. 21, pp. 1–2.
[95] *RCC*, vol. 17, p. 427. 'Although I fear, gentlemen of the jury (lit. judges), that it is a shameful thing for one beginning to speak on behalf of a very brave man to be afraid', *Cicero: Pro Milone*, edited with introduction and notes by F. H. Colson, in the Macmillan's Elementary School Classics series, 1893. There are numerous mistakes in the original Latin text in the court's transcription. Given Brand's education (see footnote 63) these are likely the responsibility of the clerk who took down the testimony verbatim. The reference is to the attempted defence of Marcus Tullius Cicero in the trial of Titus Annius Milo in 52 BC. Pompey the Great sought to intimidate the proceedings by surrounding the court with armed men.
[96] *RCC*, vol. 17, pp. 427–8.

who was fully capable, and able perfectly to imitate both his writings and his signature'. By this point, however, it was too late to do anything about it: Edwards was imprisoned in solitary confinement, denied access to the outside world and 'could take no measures to prove his suspicions'. It was for this reason that he was obliged to rest a 'provisional defence' on the witnesses he sought to call. Upon being made to plea, he had unequivocally declared himself neither the author nor the signatory to the letters. It had been Edwards's tactic during his first trial, claimed Brand, to continue this 'provisional' line of defence in court, 'thinking that he should thereby hush to sleep the real Criminal' while he sought the necessary evidence to prove his guilt.[97]

As he waited for the appeal to be heard, claimed Brand, Edwards had continually sought means to bring forth the real culprit. This, the advocate could now reveal, was Thomas William Parr: 'and when I mention his name, Your Worships will no longer doubt, for he was a convict and had been transported for forgery'.[98] Parr was visiting Edwards in jail 'not out of friendship, but for the Settlement of some business of his which the Prisoner had in his hands'.[99] He finally incriminated himself by offering to forge Edwards's signature on a memorial to the king for a free press then lying at the Commercial Hall.[100] In a subsequent conversation with Edwards, Parr allegedly admitted to having written the letters in Edwards's handwriting, caused them to be delivered to the governor and 'made himself master of the subject of the letters thro' the daily access which he had to the Prisoner; but that he had never thought that it would have been attended with such disagreeable consequences'. Edwards urged Parr to put this in writing. He claimed he would make no use of it until Parr had safely left the colony, as he planned to do in the coming weeks. In fact, however, Brand asserted that 'the Prisoner was determined as soon as ever he received it, to place it in the hands of His Majesty's Fiscal, and to make the suspected person pay for the Prisoner's long confinement'.[101] Despite repeated promises, Parr left the colony before providing Edwards with the confession he needed. Thus

---

[97] *RCC*, vol. 17, pp. 428–30. [98] *RCC*, vol. 17, p. 433.
[99] *RCC*, vol. 17, p. 431. We can speculate that Parr, who had been in New South Wales at the same time as Alexander Kaye, was probably aware of the notary's real identity. Employed in the survey department as a draughtsman and mineralogist, Parr had accompanied Surveyor-General John Oxley on an important survey expedition in 1817. Shortly after his arrival in Cape Town in April 1824, Parr employed Edwards as a notary following a shipboard dispute rich with scandalous accusations and counter-accusations about sexual and financial favours: see CA, NCD 27/1, no. 70, 1824.
[100] Edwards's name does indeed appear on the petition for a free press. Because he was in jail at the time, someone (whether or not it was Parr) must have signed it on his behalf.
[101] *RCC*, vol. 17, p. 432.

had Edwards become the victim of 'scandalous lies' so that he is 'now in danger of losing his honor and his liberty and of suffering an ignominious punishment'. Let not, Brand continued, the earlier conduct of the prisoner prejudice the court against him. His provocation had been extreme. Alluding to the fiscal's attempt to establish Edwards's past bad character by the previous court actions in which he had been involved, Brand reminded the court that these had no relevance in proving the present charges.

The defence also raised the all-important question of publication, as publication was 'the Chief requisite to constitute a Libel'.[102] Upon this point Brand cited Voet, Russell, Holt, Blackstone and English case law. Even if Blackstone argued that the mere sending of a libellous letter constituted publication, in the previous sentence the court had not convicted Edwards of publication, merely of authorship. Brandt then proceeded to attack the proof of authorship. Edwards had denied writing the letters. According to both Dutch and English authorities, the court had to prove the contrary in order to find him guilty. No sound evidence had been brought to prove that Edwards was the author, and comparison of handwriting could not be considered reliable. What, then, were the grounds that the fiscal advanced as to Edwards's authorship of the letters?: first, that, despite his outright denial of the charge, he had confessed to their authorship during his defence; second, that he had entered into a justification of the letters; and third, that the authorship could be deduced by comparing the content of the letters with the knowledge that Edwards had of all the circumstances contained within them.

In the first case, Brandt insisted that the court must rely on Edwards's unequivocal denial of his authorship in the formal examination. They could not subsequently infer confession from his defence. In the second place, a justification of the letters had no bearing on whether or not the original crime was committed:

In every instance the prisoner spoke by way of argument and for argument's sake, and where is the upright and well thinking judge who will convert an expression used by way of argument into a proof of confession or of guilt?

Brand emphasised once more that this arose from the confusion that the dual languages of the court had produced – 'the Prisoner spoke English and the records were held in Dutch not to have properly understood the prisoner'.[103] In the third instance, Edwards did not deny that the ideas contained within the letters corresponded with his own, but this did not constitute proof that he had written or published them.

[102] *RCC*, vol. 17, p. 435.   [103] *RCC*, vol. 17, p. 442.

How then did his ideas come to be expressed so closely in the letters themselves? It was because 'they were stolen from him... the fruits of a private conversation were torn from him in order therefrom to construct a libel in his name'. Anticipating arguments that would become increasingly voiced at the Cape, Brand hinted darkly at a government conspiracy, in this case involving 'Parr the forger' who may have been acting against Edwards as 'the means in the hands of others to crush him'. Sentiments against the government expressed in private in conversations with Parr had been transcribed into forged letters in Edwards's handwriting. Brand poured scorn on 'what scandalous means have been resorted to, in order to ruin the prisoner through the medium of a third person'. A private conversation, claimed Brand, was all that Edwards had been guilty of, and this could not constitute a libel. He therefore confidently expected an acquittal.[104]

Notwithstanding this confidence, he turned finally to the question of the sentence itself, finding no justification in either the Dutch or English law of transportation as punishment for libel. In both cases the precedents stipulated a monetary fine. The case boasted neither confession nor conviction, he concluded. A judge should not be compelled to 'suck the poison of confession and guilt from the prisoner's defence' in order to secure a guilty verdict. 'Judges, Judges', he concluded 'I look up to you as the Defenders of human Righteousness, I look up to you as to the Messengers, as the Representatives of Divine Justice, and I conclude ut in presentatione [to the presentation].'[105]

Hudson recorded that the evidence of forgery had 'astonished the whole of the Gothamites.... They are puzzled mightily how to proceed.'[106] But if the authorities were as puzzled as Hudson claimed, there was little evidence of it in court. Certainly they did not appear to put much weight in the evidence about Parr. In making answer to Brand's closing remarks, the fiscal identified only two arguments he considered the prisoner had made in his defence before the Court of Commissioners on 11 May. These were the non-existence of any proof that he was the author of the libels, and the 'improper application of the Dutch Law' with regard to the terms of his punishment.[107] These would be the focus of his reply. He reiterated briefly the grounds for proving that Edwards was the author of the letters: his 'style of writing, already very well known to

---

[104] *RCC*, vol. 17, pp. 442–4.   [105] *RCC*, vol. 17, p. 447.
[106] Hudson, Diary, 28 May 1824.
[107] Edwards drew on the work of 'Simon van Leeuwen's commentaries on the Roman Dutch Law, which has been translated into English by authority of the British Government... says that a Libel for the first time is only punished with a fine and for the second time with double the amount': *RCC*, vol. 17, p. 420.

this Worshipful Court'; the circumstances covered by the letters, which 'could not have flowed from any other channel than from the prisoner'; the identifiable handwriting and signatures; and finally in the 'Voluntary Acknowledgement of the prisoner himself that he is the Author of the two letters, which cannot be washed out by his subsequent denial when examined on interrogatories'.[108] Going back through Edwards's defence, he hammered home the point that the prisoner had confessed:

> The acknowledgement of the prisoner before the Court below was voluntary, unasked, unreserved and positive on pleading his exception of incompetency when he spoke of the pretended non existence of any Corpus delicti[109] and found good to expatiate on period for period first of the one letter and afterwards of the other, he took to himself everything that is written therein.[110]

The fiscal attacked Edwards's argument (in which he appealed to Gilbert's Law of Evidence) that such acknowledgement 'for the sake of argument' was not proof and that only the testament of depositions or examinations of witnesses could constitute proof. Instead, according 'to both English and Dutch Law proof may be derived from mere circumstances or from public or private documents'.[111]

Having deliberated, the court declared that

> the Appellant William Edwards not aggrieved by the Sentence of the Court of Commissioners dated the 11th Instant here in question and therefore confirm the said Sentence with the condemnation of the Prisoner and appellant in the costs and expenses of the prosecution.[112]

Edwards had been convicted, and that conviction was upheld, but despite the ostensibly successful outcome of the case the experience had not been a happy one for the authorities. In the first instance, the governor had to endure the indignity of all that was voiced in the trial. In a private letter to Bigge during proceedings, his outrage is palpable. The 'Maniac Edwards' was no less culpable than the 'two judges of the Supreme Court in the Colony and the prosecutor of the Crown sitting solemnly and tamely two successive days to hear this filthy language'. By their 'imbecility or timidity' they had 'exposed to insult, derision and contempt the conduct and character of the representatives of the King'. Were it not for the danger of revealing to 'the fractious that the House *is* divided

---

[108] *RCC*, vol. 17, pp. 447–8.
[109] Proof that a crime had been committed; literally 'body of crime'.
[110] *RCC*, vol. 17, p. 448.   [111] *RCC*, vol. 17, p. 449.   [112] *RCC*, vol. 17, p. 451.

against itself', Somerset told Bigge he would have had them 'dismissed for incapacity'.[113]

This, however, was only the beginning of the governor's problems, as soon became clear when he heard from his superiors in London. Somerset's account of the libels was sent to Bathurst on 21 May 1824, in the midst of the trial itself. After his conviction, on 18 June, Edwards also wrote to Bathurst, enclosing two petitions to the King and pleading a miscarriage of justice. Edwards represented himself as 'a humble Notary' who had fallen foul of the government for his actions in the prize slave affair. In acting for Cooke, he had only been doing his duty by exposing the cruel conduct 'towards an unfortunate race of men entrusted by our Sovereign to his care'. As a result, 'I was prosecuted for a libel in my complaint, this induced my adversaries to insult my loyalty, insult led to retaliation, retaliation to persecution and condemnation without evidence.' The blame for all rested firmly upon Somerset's shoulders:

> The Governor was my prosecutor, he has been my judge, and every stage of the proceedings has been marked with injustice and partiality. I therefore make bold to apply to your Lordship to procure a revision of the proceedings in the confidence that no other step may be necessary.[114]

Receiving news of a series of Cape libel trials, the secretary of state immediately felt doubts over the legality of Edwards's conviction. As with the libels upon Blair, there was no proof that Edwards's letters to Somerset had been published. Nor was it clearly explained how Edwards's conduct at the trial could have brought down upon him the 'heavy sentence' of seven years' transportation. Bathurst instructed Somerset to suspend execution of this 'severe sentence' until 'the whole of the proceedings were placed under his consideration'. It is clear that Bathurst considered the sentence so unwarranted that, having also been informed by Somerset that an appeal was in process, he anticipated that it would already have been 'reversed or modified by the Courts, or remitted by you [Somerset]' by the time the governor received his letter.[115]

Subsequent investigation into the trial made by the Commissioners of Eastern Inquiry, on Bathurst's orders, only confirmed these doubts. Bigge and Colebrooke fully believed Edwards to be guilty of sending the letters to Somerset, but this was not the point at issue. They recognised not only that the case was 'likely to attract notice and excite surprise in England', but also that the proof against Edwards was very slender

---

[113] Somerset to Bigge, 12 May 1824, marked private. Bigge–Somerset correspondence, Rhodes House, University of Oxford, MSS Afr, series 24.
[114] Edwards to Bathurst, 18 June 1824, *RCC*, vol. 17, pp. 498–9.
[115] Bathurst to Somerset, 29 Sept. 1824, *RCC*, vol. 18, p. 324.

indeed.[116] They reported the 'alarm' that had been excited amongst the 'English Inhabitants' of the colony by 'a principle by the Court of Justice that seemed to impart to a hypothetical argument the force and effect of a judicial confession and acknowledgement of guilt'. They blamed the confusion both on how Edwards had conducted his defence ('in a hurried manner and under the influence of great excitement') and the failure of Dutch-speaking members of the court to understand the English language. They also cast doubt upon the handwriting evidence. In short, they concluded 'that the evidence upon which he was convicted was in its nature presumptive, and that it did not constitute that legal and conclusive proof which is required by the civil law to establish the guilt of an accused person'. They agreed that the sentence was unusually severe, even for the Cape, and they expressed grave reservations over the legal reasoning that made conduct within the course of a trial an influence upon the sentence.[117]

Somerset faced reprimands from the secretary of state over the judiciary's conduct in Edwards's trial for libel, but the implications of his behaviour in the case went far beyond the treatment of one man. There was even more serious and wide-ranging import to be found in his associated actions towards the Cape press and the means he had taken to achieve its suppression.

[116] Bigge and Colebrooke to Bathurst, 23 March 1825, *RCC*, vol. 20, p. 374; Bigge and Colebrooke to Bathurst, 11 Oct. 1824, *RCC*, vol. 18, p. 441.
[117] Bigge and Colebrooke to Bathurst, 23 March 1825, *RCC*, vol. 20, pp. 375, 378–9.

7 'Unruly subjects'
Political removal and the problem of colonial constitutions

When Somerset first transmitted to Bathurst the libellous letters he had received from 'a person calling himself Wm. Edwards (which I suspect to be an assumed name)',[1] the governor claimed that he would have been 'well pleased to have treated the Author with Silent Contempt, particularly as he is by some considered as far from being in sane mind'. On the advice of Chief Justice Truter, 'the true interests of Government as well as the dignity of the station His Majesty has done me the honor to confide in me' compelled him to act.[2] Not only would this turn out to be one of the governor's more significant miscalculations, but other aspects of the advice given by Truter would also lead Somerset into choppy constitutional waters. The resultant political sensitivities were heightened further as the governor turned his attention from William Edwards to the newly established independent Cape press.

We know from Somerset's private correspondence with Bigge that the government's informers were hard at work during the course of Edwards's libel trials collecting incriminating information on the *South African Commercial Advertiser*:

After I left you on Tuesday I recd a great deal of Intelligence respecting the conductors of the Press – & perhaps *you* will not marvel to learn that Dr Philip is the Head Huntsman & I think Mr Fairburn, Mr Pringle & Paddy Wright are the whippers in – that they met at dinner once every week when their Paragraphs were concocted – the doctor gave out when he left town that he went out of the way to avoid the constant solicitations for a free Press – & he wishes to take no

---

Denyssen to Somerset, 14 Sept. 1824, CA, CO 212, Letters from the Office of the Fiscal, no. 88

[1] Somerset gave no explanation as to why he held these suspicions. Cape officials only seem to have connected Alexander Kaye and William Edwards a few months later. What is significant is that (with some justification) Somerset would consider it likely that Cape residents might be operating under a false identity.
[2] Somerset to Bathurst, 21 May 1824, *RCC*, vol. 17, p. 350.

part – those were matters not within his Calling! Villain! Hypocrite! when he himself is the primum Mobile.[3]

The governor was determined to move against the printer and his editors:

> I send you [Bigge] a paper given me just as I was leaving... by the Editor of the Cape Gazette – sent to them for insertion yesterday but which of course he did not insert – It is evidently the production of Pringle & Fairbairn – & shews how hard they are striving to get Edwards off. You may retain it till I have the pleasure of seeing you which will probably be tomorrow P. M. by which time I hope therefore B. B. [Bishop Burnett] & G. G. [George Greig] will be safe in the Trunk [jail].[4]

In Somerset's eyes, they were a nest of radicals – 'Greig's is indeed a regular Spa Fields letter' – and he urged Bigge to warn Bathurst against their cabal.[5]

The *South African Commercial Advertiser* had given significant space to reporting the prize slave trials. When Edwards's libels against Somerset came up for trial, the governor was determined to avoid similar publicity. The authorities sought assurances that the paper's contents would be kept apolitical and demanded security from printer George Greig of 10 000 rixdollars (£750) for the observance of these terms.[6] As a result, on 5 May 1824 (the day after Edwards's trial for libelling Somerset began) the paper's pages included a notice that

> His Majesty's Fiscal having assumed the Censorship of the *South African Commercial Advertiser*... we find it our duty as British Subjects to discontinue the Publication *for the present* in this Colony, until we have applied for redress and direction to His Excellency the Governor and the British Government.[7]

Three days later, printed handbills protesting the administration's actions against the press were being busily stuck up across the town advertising that a full account of the suspension of the paper by the authorities would be forthcoming. One cheekily appeared upon the wall opposite the fiscal's own office window, and scuffles ensued between Greig and the police who were trying to tear the notices down.

As a consequence, on 8 May the printers were in the very act of typesetting a protest broadsheet titled *Facts connected with the stopping of the Press*,

---

[3] Somerset to Bigge, 27 May 1824, Bigge–Somerset correspondence, Rhodes House, University of Oxford, MSS Afr, series 24.
[4] Somerset to Bigge, undated 'Sunday night' [1824], Bigge–Somerset correspondence.
[5] Somerset to Bigge, undated 'Sunday evening' [1824], Bigge–Somerset correspondence (the reference is to the 1816 protests at Spa Fields, Islington, London, seeking parliamentary reform).
[6] Cory, *Rise of South Africa*, p. 285.
[7] *South African Commercial Advertiser*, 5 May 1824.

and the censorship of the Fiscal, when the fiscal himself burst into Greig's premises on Longmarket Street. Carrying a warrant for the suppression of the press, he was accompanied by sheriffs and a commission from the Court of Justice. According to the terms of the warrant, Greig's conduct had 'proved subversive of that due submission to the lawful commands of the constituted authorities in this colony, without which peace and tranquillity cannot remain undisturbed'. He had 'openly transgressed the conditions' under which he was permitted to print his paper. Indeed he had 'wantonly and *seditiously* persisted in doing so', despite repeated warnings from the administration. The presses were to be sealed 'until His Majesty's pleasure shall be known', and Greig himself was 'to leave the colony within one month' on pain of arrest.[8]

With apparent sangfroid, Greig obediently showed the fiscal how to lock up the press. As Meurant, then a twelve-year-old apprentice, later remembered it, a farcical scene ensued with a member of the Court of Justice getting covered in printing ink and the fiscal nearly losing a hand as the iron plate on which the type was set was rolled into place. The fiscal, by now thoroughly vexed, was clearly keen to get the business over with. Having determined that there were no more presses, he then said, 'I think we should seal up the *types*.' Greig objected that it did not say so in the warrant. Denyssen conceded the point and departed, confident that he had stopped the production of a widely anticipated diatribe against the administration's tyranny.

The morning after the fiscal had sealed Greig's press, the streets in front of the printing office were filled with expectant crowds waiting for the promised explanation. To the outraged surprise of the government, bundles of the *Facts* pamphlet were thrown out of the upper-storey windows into the throng below. Scores were distributed gratis to the populace, delivering a scathing chapter-and-verse account of the events that had led to the 'stopping' of the *Advertiser*.[9]

In the course of the printers' help with executing the warrant the previous afternoon, the fiscal had dryly given his thanks, remarking 'we are not in the habit of sealing-up presses.' And therein lay his problem. For Denyssen clearly did not know that failure to seal the type meant that the *Facts* could still be produced. Notwithstanding the sealed press, the paper could be laid by hand upon the inked type. It was a laborious and somewhat imprecise method, but with the entire workshop toiling through the night, the job was done. The fiscal, now armed with orders

---

[8] Warrant for the suppression of the *Advertiser*, 8 May 1824, *RCC*, vol. 17, p. 301.
[9] Meurant, *Sixty Years Ago*, pp. 64–6.

to seal up the types and the composing rooms, arrived the next day to close the stable door, but public opinion had already bolted.[10]

'The expediency of a Governor': Making the decision to banish

It was no secret amongst the residents of Cape Town that this dramatic stand-off had been prompted by the need to stop verbatim reports of Edwards's latest trial being transmitted to an audience beyond the colony: 'Edwards's trial goes on and to convince every one how allarmed the parties are lest anything should get into circulation at home they have stopped the printing of the Cape Commercial Advertiser.'[11] And from that time forward, this is the way in which Edwards's story has usually been told. I want to take a somewhat different tack, setting the press struggle instead in the context of debates regarding sovereignty and the problems of constitutional law. Somerset's actions at the Cape were not only part of a much wider debate about freedom of the press, but also part of the broader crisis in legal pluralism discussed in the last chapter. C. A. Bayly reminds us that

> in the British tradition at least, the formal statements of constitutions or colonial minutes are a poor guide to real social and political change; there are distinct limitations to history based on what men tell their lawyers they are doing.[12]

Perhaps the dichotomy should rather be reversed. By tracking what men are told they should (and should *not*) be doing by their lawyers, here I take the messiness of real social and political relations as my guide to the history of constitutional change.

To understand this choice, let us begin by eavesdropping on a private conversation. Edwards's trial for libelling Somerset and his subsequent transportation are well known to historians. What remains unrecognised, however, is that this was not the first plan mooted to silence him. Once more, the fulsome published account in *Records of the Cape Colony* can direct us to a particular understanding of events. Unpublished sources provide a rather different facet to the whole.

Somerset's extensive unofficial correspondence with Bigge reveals a warm personal relationship between the two men, one that their relative positions as governor and Commissioner of Inquiry would not lead the historian to anticipate. Somerset's charm (when he chose to exercise

---

[10] Meurant, *Sixty Years Ago*, pp. 64–6.
[11] Samuel Hudson, Diary, 5 May 1824, Hudson Papers, CA, A602.
[12] Bayly, *Imperial Meridian*, p. 9.

it) was renowned. He once devoted an entire letter to Bigge (marked 'private') apologising, in humorous vein, for keeping the commissioners from their dinner.[13] Perhaps unexpectedly, Somerset clearly found in Bigge a confidante he badly needed. He wrote extremely candidly to the commissioner about his critics and their effect on his state of mind:

> To persons in opposition this holding of office may appear to have its sweets but to one who has been as unfortunate as I have been at the Cape – there is *no compensation* – that can make amends for what a man of feeling & honour is exposed to & is doomed to suffer in the performance of his Duty as a public Servant.[14]

In these circumstances, we are fortunate that Bigge was undertaking an extensive tour of the interior that kept him absent from Cape Town during many of the key developments in the Edwards–Somerset conflict. There was in Cape Town, Somerset explained to Bigge, 'a certain sort of Attorney call'd Edwards here who lays down the Law & defies all authority'.[15] Although we have only one side of their correspondence, it puts on record Somerset's requests for advice and his own private sentiments, these last through more than mere words. As the events provoked by Edwards unfolded, Somerset's correspondence with Bigge became increasingly strained and emotional. Descending into an illegible scrawl, at times the pen recording the relentless attacks by this notarial gadfly seems almost to spit with rage. On 29 April, Somerset wrote confidentially to Bigge with the news of Edwards's arrest:

> The great event of the week is the incarceration of Mr Wm Edwards. I enclose you copies of two letters he wrote to me. After the second – [Chief Justice] Truter said that I could not I *must* not remain tranquil & referring to the 29th article of my instructions proved to me that I had power to send him out of the colony. Mr [Justice] Kekewich (to whom I had also referred these letters) agreed with him but I differ from both as to the expediency of a Governor ever exerting his power as long as the hand of the law could apply a remedy. They both came round to my opinion except that Kekewich stated the alternative – 'suppose the court don't find him guilty?' I remarked that I concluded that that were scarcely possible but if it were we must wait 'till he did something more outrageous which I concluded would not be long. I sent his letters to the Fiscal yesterday morning & the proper forms were gone through and the court ordered his arrest.[16]

Somerset's off-the-cuff account raises several issues that would prove significant to events as they later unfolded. First, there is the question

---

[13] Somerset to Bigge, undated [c. 1823], Bigge–Somerset correspondence.
[14] Somerset to Bigge, 1 Dec. 1823, Bigge–Somerset correspondence (original emphasis).
[15] Somerset to Bigge, undated [Jan. or Feb. 1824], Bigge–Somerset correspondence.
[16] Somerset to Bigge 29 April 1824, Bigge–Somerset correspondence.

of the twenty-ninth article of his instructions. This gave the governor extensive and nebulous powers:

> to remove and send away from the said Settlement such persons as he shall suspect of adhering to the King's Enemies, and all such other persons, the continuing of whose residence he may have reason to *imagine* might be *inconvenient* or prejudicial to the peace, *good order* and security of the said Settlement.[17]

What was being suggested to the governor was extra-judicial banishment by executive decree, a Dutch colonial practice known by the illuminating term *politieke uitzetting* [political removal]. When Justices Truter and Kekewich suggested this course of action to Somerset, they coupled the security imperatives of acting against Edwards (imperatives that were later argued by the fiscal at Edwards's trial) with anxiety that they could not guarantee the necessary outcome in court. Ironically, it is clear from this account that Somerset was initially reluctant to go to these lengths in exercising his executive authority. He preferred to rely on 'the hand of the law' and, as the account he gave to Bigge quoted previously suggests, Somerset persuaded Justices Truter and Kekewich that it was preferable to put the troublesome notary on trial. Their advice as to how to deal with Edwards, however, was evidently not forgotten. The suggested course of action was employed against Greig only a week later. As we have seen, the judicial proceedings against Edwards would prove to be a distinct liability for the Cape administration, for all that the notary was convicted and transported. Somerset of course had no foreknowledge of this when he moved against Greig and the Cape press in the opening days of Edwards's trial. Nevertheless, he chose to deploy a different weapon from his disciplinary armoury.

Later, facing harsh criticism from London, both Somerset and his judiciary bent over backwards to retrospectively justify the legality of political removal, appealing to a range of legal authorities and precedents. This makes it difficult to get to the bottom of the original motivations and reasoning behind using it. We can likely depend upon the version of events that Somerset gave privately to Bigge, however. Not only was it written contemporaneously with the decision itself, rather than in the full glare of later reprimands, but it was also addressed to a correspondent to whom Somerset frequently turned for advice, both legal and personal. The suggestion that he use political removal against government critics, then, was first made to Somerset by Truter and Kekewich. The justices were

---

[17] Stephen to Wilmot Horton, 16 Oct. 1824, TNA, CO 48/96. This is the (distinctly jaundiced) transcription later provided to the Colonial Office by James Stephen. The emphasis is his.

concerned that the required outcomes could not be guaranteed through judicial process but must be sought in executive authority. They clearly anticipated weaknesses in evidentiary support with regard to Edwards, anxieties that later proved entirely justified. The case against Greig's newspaper was arguably even more shaky – one reason why Somerset may have chosen to employ executive powers instead. Either way, it was the broader constitutional implications of the advice that would prove of most significance. Although it was made on the basis of his British government instructions, it was offered to Somerset by two men trained in Roman–Dutch law and steeped in the practices of a previous colonial regime.

In the same letter to Bigge in which he reported the conversation with the Cape justice about using executive banishment against Edwards, Somerset noted that he was 'exceedingly anxious to consult you as to what I can legally do to stop Mr Greig'.[18] Bigge was absent from Cape Town, and we do not know whether he provided Somerset with the advice being sought. Events on the ground may have been moving too fast for that. Either way, what was initially contemplated against Edwards was in fact enacted against Greig: banishment from the colony by executive decree. The governor later withdrew his banishment order, although the closure of the newspaper and the confiscation of the press remained in effect. But the fact that it was never enforced was in a sense irrelevant to the debate that followed. In making that decision, Somerset not only unleashed a storm of public criticism, he also opened up a set of vexed jurisdictional issues over the question of British sovereignty in conquered territories.

Banishment and the law

Banishment was not considered problematic in itself. When Bishop Burnett was sentenced by the court to banishment for libel, for example, there was no question raised over the legality of this sentence per se, for all the controversy ignited over whether it was justified. As distinct from transportation, banishment had a place in both Dutch and British imperial systems, although it was more commonly used in the former. Although the terms are sometimes used loosely, even interchangeably, by historians (and by some contemporaries) in this context they were distinct.[19]

---

[18] Somerset to Bigge 29 April 1824, Bigge–Somerset correspondence.
[19] British parliamentary debates over the Blasphemous and Seditious Libels Act in December 1819 similarly made much of the differences between transportation and banishment. As the attorney general put it: 'Banishment was not so severe a punishment as transportation, because it enabled the the person on whom it was inflicted to select his

Somerset, for example, commuted the sentence of John Carnall (whom we will meet in Chapter 8) from transportation to one of banishment. Bishop Burnett successfully appealed the provisions of his sentence on the basis of the legal distinction between 'banishment' and 'transportation'.[20] Banishment came into European practice from Roman law, where it could be either judicial or executive. Under the Roman system it was 'entirely separate from penal servitude' and generally directed at those who were considered a threat to the political order.[21] As we have seen, the notorious Six Acts of 1819 included a provision for judicial banishment at a judge's discretion under the Blasphemous and Seditious Libels Act. The political sensitivity of such a measure, however, meant that it remained unutilised until it was repealed in 1830.[22]

The United Provinces did not, unlike Britain, have an established legal tradition of transporting felons to colonial outposts, although they enacted the right to banish people from their own provinces. The VOC maintained a complex and multifaceted intra-colonial system of forced migration that included slavery, transportation, banishment and exile.[23] Its legal system was distinct from that of the Netherlands, and the Company's Court of Justice in Batavia was the highest court in the empire. Under the VOC, free burghers were banished to other Company settlements or to Europe. Banishment was simple expulsion and did not involve recategorisation as a criminal. Unlike exile, it did not specify a destination. A distinction was also made between *bandieten* [convicts] and *bannelingen* [exiles], although in the case of those forcibly removed from Batavia to the Cape the categories could blur, with exiles frequently being criminalised unless evidence was provided to the contrary. Political and religious exile operated as a tool of diplomacy and conquest, and thus the Cape became the destination of both exiled political leaders and transported felons from Batavia, Ceylon and elsewhere in the Dutch East Indies. Penal transportation was used extremely rarely against high-ranking European Company servants or Europeans of burgher status, but

---

own place of retreat, and saved him from being forcibly detained among felons.' Others attacked it as a 'new punishment'. House of Commons debates, 21 December 1819, vol. 41, cc 435, 1421.

[20] House of Commons, *Papers Relating to the Case of John Carnall*, 1826–1827 (556). Report of the Commissioners of Inquiry into the case of Bishop Burnett, *BPP* 1826 (431), *Mr. Bishop Burnett*, p. 101.

[21] Benton, *A Search for Sovereignty*, p. 167. Like the Dutch, both the Spanish and Portuguese empires retained provision for banishment as either a judicial penalty or an executive act: R. G. Caldwell, 'Exile as an institution', *Political Science Quarterly*, 58:2 (June 1943), 239–62.

[22] Wickwar, *Struggle for the Freedom of the Press*, pp. 154–5.

[23] K. Ward, *Networks of Empire: Forced Migration in the Dutch East India Company* (Cambridge University Press, 2009).

was targeted at low-ranking Company servants, slaves, Chinese under Company jurisdiction and indigenous people.[24]

Thus both banishment and transportation were used against Cape inhabitants in the VOC period, and transportation melded into the new imperial networks of the British regime relatively seamlessly. In 1796, during the first British occupation, a soldier at the Cape court martialled for counterfeiting and sentenced to hang had his sentence commuted to transportation to New South Wales, where he served fourteen years as a convict. A few months later another soldier was transported for life.[25] Arrangements, however, remained ad hoc and informal. It was Somerset who, in 1815, took the matter up formally, requesting that convicts be sent from the Cape to New South Wales. The established destination of transported felons, Robben Island, was proving unworkable owing to lack of employment for labour on the island and the possibility of escape. Bathurst directed that convicts could be sent to New South Wales when necessary and informed Somerset that he had forwarded instructions to the governor of New South Wales, that they be received, and to the Transport Board to give the necessary orders to the masters of convict ships that they be taken on board. When Alexander Kaye docked in Cape Town with the convict ship *Atlas* in 1819, twelve extra convicts, sentenced to transportation at the Cape, were taken on board.[26]

Those sentenced to transportation under British rule were subject to the constraints of convicts within a penal system, however these might be defined.[27] They were generally held at Robben Island until such time as they could be transported to the penal settlements of New South Wales or Van Diemen's Land, although they could also serve out their sentence on Robben Island itself. Unlike transported convicts, those subjected to 'banishment' from the Cape (whether judicially or by executive order) were under no further constraint so long as they left the colony. The

---

[24] Ward, *Networks of Empire*, pp. 20, 22.   [25] Ward, *Networks of Empire*, p. 298.
[26] For the procedural questions raised by the transition to British systems of transportation at the Cape, see V. C. Malherbe, 'Khoikhoi and the question of convict transportation from the Cape Colony 1820–1842', *South African Historical Journal*, 17 (1985), 19–36.
[27] In England the 1679 Habeas Corpus Act prohibited transportation without trial. The 1718 Transportation Act (extended to Scotland in 1766) established transportation as a sentence that the courts could impose directly rather than as commutation of a sentence of death. Yet it failed to resolve 'the fundamental tension between transportation as a form of exile and transportation as a category of bondage' (Benton, *Search for Sovereignty*, p. 174). The result was ongoing confusion and debate regarding the legal rights held by transported convicts; see A. Atkinson, 'The free-born Englishman transported: Convict rights as a measure of eighteenth-century empire', *Past and Present*, 144 (1994), 88–115; B. Kercher, 'Perish or prosper: The law and convict transportation in the British Empire 1700–1850', *Law and History Review*, 21:3 (2003), 527–54; P. D. Halliday, *Habeas Corpus: From England to Empire* (Harvard University Press, 2010).

practice was effectively what we might term 'deportation'. When Burnett was banished from the Cape by the Council of Justice, he was free to go wherever he wished. Predictably, he chose to stir up trouble against the Somerset regime by proceeding to London and allying his cause with that of opposition Members of Parliament.[28]

The controversy at the Cape in the 1820s around the practice of banishment centred around its enactment by executive order rather than by judicial process. When Somerset informed Secretary of State Lord Bathurst of his action against Greig, he simply noted that he had taken the legal advice of the chief justice, and then cited the twenty-ninth article of his instructions.[29] Once it became clear that political removal was provoking criticism in London, however, Somerset called on his judiciary to provide the necessary legal foundations in Dutch colonial precedent. In a private and confidential letter to Bathurst dated 5 December 1824, he provided as much ammunition as possible 'in refuting any hostile arguments which may be urgent in the House of Commons'.[30] For his part, Bathurst turned to James Stephen to give his own views on the legality of Somerset's actions. As a consequence, we have on record a series of detailed opinions from both English- and Dutch-trained specialists on the moral justifications, the precedents and the constitutional basis of a practice that lay on the borderlands between the overlapping Dutch and British imperial systems.

For their part, Fiscal Denyssen and Chief Justice Truter expressed their utter confidence in the Dutch practice of political removal. All that was required was a 'tedious search' (as the fiscal put it) amongst the relevant documents to give chapter and verse of what they clearly regarded as common sense, that 'this right has always been exercised in the colony'.[31] In order to provide Bathurst with the means to combat criticism in the

---

[28] Given three-months grace to settle his affairs, Burnett appealed against his imprisonment for this period (arguing that confinement was appropriate only to 'transportation' and not to 'banishment') and was left at large. He went underground after rumours apparently reached him that the authorities contemplated transporting him to New South Wales rather than letting him proceed to England to make his complaints against the Somerset regime. Certainly papers found in his possession during the investigations into the placard affair (see Chapter 8) led the authorities to believe he was abusing his freedom, and orders were given to arrest him. In the account of events in his subsequent protests to Parliament, Burnett made much of the game of hide-and-seek he subsequently played with the authorities, including a daring escape disguised as his wife's 'Malay' slave woman, before he left the colony for London in December 1824: see *RCC*, vol. 24, pp. 72–106; Report of the Commissioners of Inquiry into the case of Bishop Burnett, *BPP* 1826 (431), *Mr. Bishop Burnett*.
[29] Somerset to Bathurst, 10 May 1824, no. 87, *RCC*, vol. 17, p. 306.
[30] Somerset to Bathurst, 5 Dec. 1824, Bathurst Papers, BL 57/54.
[31] Denyssen to Somerset, 1 June 1824, Bathurst Papers, BL, 57/54

'Unruly subjects' 201

House of Commons, Somerset forwarded two opinions from Truter and Denyssen to the secretary of state on 5 December 1824.[32] Truter's (dated 26 May) was brief, enclosing a list of 'burghers successively sent out of the Colony by the Dutch Government without any previous trial, on account of their pernicious conduct'. The fiscal, he assured the governor, would

> easily establish the same practice, under some modifications, in the Netherlands, where I have found that even the Supreme Courts of Law are or were prohibited from meddling with the political removal of Burghers from the Seat of their fixed domicile.

Although he was careful to acknowledge that ultimate 'Approval or Censure' should rest with the 'Home Government', Truter insisted that 'the nature of a Government over an infant State, distant from the Mother Country, seems to render that discretionary Power an indispensable attribute of the Public Administration.'[33]

Denyssen's opinion contained a detailed set of notes and enclosures (all duly transferred to Bathurst) charting the practice at the Cape and in the Netherlands against 'useless subjects' through the eighteenth and into the nineteenth century, and referring to the 1622 *Apologeticus* [*Defence*] of Hugo Grotius on the right of the authorities to exclude inhabitants from the community in 'troubled times'. On this basis he considered the action of political removal to be 'an indisputed right' exercised by the governors of the Colony during the VOC and Batavian period. It had never, he claimed, been considered an 'abuse of power', but was fully accepted by the inhabitants 'who declared themselves willing to submit to that authority, provided that same was not allowed to degenerate into oppression'. The sole moment of protest, in 1779, was not against the right per se of 'the removal of unruly subjects by Political decree' but against the forcible enlistment of free burghers into Company service.[34] In this the chief justice was being disingenuous. Kerry Ward has argued that the VOC network of forced migration was an important bone of contention in late eighteenth-century clashes between an increasingly self-confident Cape settler elite and the VOC. The case of Carel Fredrick Buytendagh, who was exiled to Batavia in 1779, became a rallying cry in the 'Patriot' movement against local Cape officials.[35]

---

[32] Somerset to Bathurst, 5 Dec. 1824, Bathurst Papers, BL 57/54.
[33] Letters of the Court of Justice, CA, CO 214, no. 30 (enclosure in Somerset to Bathurst, 5 Dec. 1824, Bathurst Papers, BL 57/54.).
[34] Denyssen to Somerset, 14 Sept. 1824, CA, CO 212, Letters from the Office of the Fiscal, no. 88 (enclosure in Somerset to Bathurst, 5 Dec. 1824, Bathurst Papers, BL 57/54.).
[35] Ward, *Networks of Empire*, pp. 287, 294. For a view that emphasises internal factional rivalries at the Cape, see Baartman, 'Fighting for the spoils'.

The fiscal placed the right of political removal upon the foundations of 'the common Law of the Netherlands' and on Dutch imperial practice at the Cape and elsewhere, it being an executive function and 'entirely unconnected with the exercise of judicial authority'. 'Such being the actual state of the Law', governors need not take recourse to the relevant section of their instructions from the British government, for in enacting political removal 'they are protected by the Law of the Colony', and

> British Governors are bound by their instructions to exercise the administration of justice and police as nearly as circumstances will permit in conformity to the Laws and Instructions that subsisted under the ancient Governor of this Colony.[36]

Having read the fiscal's opinion, Truter sent a more meditative endorsement of the right of the governor to 'order a noxious individual Resident or Burgher to leave the Colony, without a previous trial by some competent court' on 5 December 1824.[37] In arguments eerily familiar to modern readers, he claimed that 'turbulent times' justified the use of such extra-judicial measures.[38] Colonial societies, he concluded, stood in especial need of such provisions, as there were particular security risks 'where an influx of known and unknown Individuals and obscure characters form part of the population'.[39] It is perhaps significant that Somerset chose not to include this point in the despatch he sent to Bathurst that same day. Truter's reasoning was unlikely to offer strategic advantage against Whig and Radical critics concerned with the influence of personal despotism over the rule of law. Indeed, for all his confidence in passing on the researches into Dutch precedent to the secretary of state, Somerset was not as sanguine as he seemed. Writing privately to Bigge, Somerset sought advice on Truter's researches, which he considered wanting, mentioning the names of several opposition MPs and noting that to 'meet' them in 'Westminster Hall, I would rather Mr Truter had quoted one law than 28 precedents'.[40]

---

[36] Denyssen to Somerset, 14 Sept. 1824.
[37] Truter to Somerset, 5 Dec. 1824, CA, CO 214, no. 89. The fiscal, however, had earlier claimed that the practice was 'hardly ever resorted to' in the 'late United Netherlands' and was 'more frequent in this Colony': Denyssen to Somerset, 14 Sept. 1824, CA, CO 212, no. 88.
[38] Kostal discusses the broader question of the relationship between the rule of law and the emergency powers of martial law in 'extraordinary times' in his study of the 1865 Morant Bay rebellion in Jamaica: *Jurisprudence of Power*, ch. 1; see also N. Hussain, *The Jurisprudence of Emergency: Colonialism and the Rule of Law* (University of Michigan Press, 2003).
[39] Truter to Somerset, 5 Dec. 1824.
[40] Somerset to Bigge, 27 May 1824, Bigge–Somerset correspondence.

'Unruly subjects' 203

Somerset's anxiety proved fully justified. James Stephen's legal opinion to the Colonial Office was uncompromising. Somerset's action clearly got under his constitutional skin, to the point that he felt compelled to write a separate note to the undersecretary of state, apologising for his vehement tone. Stephen did not see it as his role to offer an opinion as to whether Somerset had made 'wise and judicious use of the powers with which his Instructions purport to invest him'; his focus was rather on the question of sovereignty itself. As he baldly put it, the 'Instruction is itself illegal, and that His Majesty had not authority to issue it in these terms'. During the period of military occupation, it might have been permissible under the 'Laws of War', but after the Cape was formally ceded to the crown, the inhabitants 'became entitled to the benefits of the British Constitution, so far as they could be imparted to them, compatibly with the maintenance of the Dutch code, and with the local circumstances of the colonists'. Neither on his own behalf nor through his governor could the king pronounce a sentence of banishment without trial at the Cape any more than he could do so in the United Kingdom. The right could not be enacted through an Order in Council, much less through the instructions to a governor. To 'invest the Governor of a Colony with powers so unusual and so formidable' would require the authority of the king in Parliament.[41]

Even supposing the Dutch law to have authorised such actions, 'that portion of the Dutch Code became ipso facto abolished' once the colony was ceded to Great Britain, as it was 'contrary to fundamental [British] principles' forbidding imprisonment or exile without trial. Here Stephen cited *Campbell v. Hall* (1774) in which 'Lord Mansfield asserts that the King, without the concurrence of Parliament, cannot make any change in the Laws of a conquered Country "contrary to fundamental principles."'[42] Of even greater direct relevance was the 1774 case of *Fabrigas v. Mostyn*, in which a verdict was given for £3000 damages against the governor of Minorca for banishment by executive order based

---

[41] Stephen to Wilmot Horton, 21 Sept. 1824, TNA, CO 48/96.
[42] *Campbell v. Hall*, a case in Grenada over export duties on sugar, was 'of lasting importance in British imperial history' in its implications for 'the powers of the Crown in relation to the law and government of conquered colonies': Ward, *Colonial Self-Government*, p. 10. Yet despite Mansfield's judgement, ambiguity remained well into the period under discussion, and the case became a constant reference point in debates over the applicability of British institutions in colonial settings: Epstein, *Scandal of Colonial Rule*, pp. 122–3. It preoccupied Jeremy Bentham, for example, in his 1803 attack on the legal foundations of New South Wales, 'on the right of the Crown to legislate without reference to Parliament', and on the legitimacy of what would become known as the crown colony system: Benton, *Search for Sovereignty*, p. 193; J. Bentham, *A Plea for the Constitution* ... (London: Mawman and Hatchard, 1803); Eddy, *Britain and the Australian Colonies*, p. 64.

on 'the previous law of the Island'. (Greig too made extensive reference to this case in his own protests to the Colonial Office.)[43] The Mostyn case, as Stephen recognised, 'decided by Judges so eminent as Lord Mansfield, Sir William Blackstone and Chief Justice De Grey, and corresponding so closely with the Case of Greig, hardly leaves room for additional argument'. In 'deference to the greatest authorities known to the Law of England', Stephen maintained the position that only the monarch in Parliament could legislate to reintroduce such a law: it would have ceased upon conquest as being 'malum in se' [wrong in itself] and contrary to 'fundamental principles'. Stephen made comparison here with the case of Sir Thomas Picton, appointed commandant and military governor of Trinidad after conquest from the Spanish in 1797. Picton was put on trial in 1806 (and on appeal in 1808) for the torture of the thirteen-year-old slave girl Luisa Calderón. At issue was whether, as a British governor, Picton had the right to sanction torture under Spanish law. The comparison is especially significant because the British had explicitly outlawed torture following their conquest of the Cape, but had not made similar provision against political removal.[44] 'Consequently', Stephen went on, 'I hold that an Instruction from the Crown, a commission under the Great Seal, or an order in Council, purporting to revive or recognize it, would be unconstitutional and void.'[45] Greig, he concluded, had every right to bring an action against the Governor for banishing him from the Colony.

'Neither better nor worse than other... Despotisms'

Somerset's response to the Cape press's attempts to report Edwards's trials thus highlights the vexed legal foundations of British colonial rule at the Cape in the years immediately prior to the new Charter of Justice. In her studies of colonial Georgia and New South Wales in this period, Lisa Ford argues that the 1820s and 1830s saw settler societies increasingly grappling with the problems of legal pluralism. Where once multiple understandings and practices had coexisted in flexible legal regimes 'encompassing natural law retaliation, common law culture, and customary indigenous law', now settler and indigenous violence was prompting a new and more rigid conception of settler sovereignty to emerge.[46] With its prior colonial heritage (including over a century of frontier conflict)

---

[43] House of Commons, Papers relating to Mr Greig and the *South African Commercial Advertiser*, 1827, p. 6; *RCC*, vol. 19, pp. 149–50.
[44] For a full account of the Picton affair see Epstein, *Scandal of Colonial Rule*.
[45] Stephen to Wilmot Horton, 21 Sept. 1824, TNA, CO 48/96.
[46] Ford, *Settler Sovereignty*, p. 3.

and the pluralities offered by the dictates of conquest law, the Cape offers a particular variant on this broader story. Yet parallels with the legal transformations of other settler societies seeking to drive out legal pluralism in this period are also profound.

Definitions of executive power were not simply arid technicalities. Translated into accusations of tyranny, they also offered powerful and emotive political rhetoric. In the light of what was to follow, it is ironic that Daniel Denyssen, of all people, saw this so clearly. In making his prosecution against Edwards for libelling Somerset, he contrasted the prisoner's intemperate language with the moderate response of the administration on the question of executive banishment. This power, he argued, had quite deliberately *not* been exercised against Edwards, for all its existence as a formidable weapon in the state's arsenal:

> it will be said in former times the Governor had the right to send such disturbers of the public peace out of the Colony. The same right, Your Worships, is given to the British Governors by their Instructions, and that His Excellency has not availed himself of this right in the prisoner's case is a proof of his moderation and a desire not to impede the ordinary course of law except there be an absolute necessity for so doing, which has always been the characteristic of His Excellency as well as of his Predecessors, but there might be a circumstance which could render the use of this power by the Governor indispensable.[47]

The secretary of state recognised that Somerset's actions had significance well beyond the Cape. That colony may have been of relative unimportance to MPs in comparison with the West and East Indies, but it was no less useful as a political traction point for that. Those who had argued or voted against press freedom in India and the Caribbean, argued Bathurst,

> may even be glad to avail themselves of this opportunity of redeeming the popularity which they may imagine they have lost in sympathy to a more arbitrary system in the other British Possessions, in which they are individually interested by showing an extraordinary zeal for a free Press at the Cape and anywhere else.[48]

Making reference in his private correspondence to events in the West Indies and India, Bathurst was well aware of what historians like C. A. Bayly and James Epstein have recently emphasised: that the early 1820s, to quote Bayly, 'represented the first international conjuncture of radical liberalism'.[49]

It is easy to see why India would have loomed large in Bathurst's mind in this context. The Cape developments had been preceded by

---

[47] *RCC*, vol. 17, p. 398.
[48] Bathurst to Somerset, 19 Oct. 1824, Bathurst papers, BL 57/65.
[49] Bayly, *Recovering Liberties*, p. 71. On the 'radical underworld' in the West Indies, see Epstein, *Scandal of Colonial Rule*, ch. 5.

remarkably similar government actions against the press for criticising Company officials in Bengal the year before. The sequential 1823 deportations of James Silk Buckingham, editor of the *Calcutta Journal*, and subsequently Sandford Arnot, his assistant editor, had provoked spirited debate over the question of press freedom, the relationship between the legislative and executive branches of government and the right to deport British subjects from India. With regard to the latter it is significant that Buckingham sought to protect his paper by placing the editorship in the hands of Francis Sandys, a man of both British and Indian descent. This proved some measure of defence, but though the government could not forcibly remove the Indian-born Sandys, it deported the assistant editor, Sandford Arnot, instead, and it subsequently revoked the newspaper's licence.[50] Once back in Britain, Buckingham conducted an elaborate publicity campaign, touring the provinces, suing the directors of the East India Company for lost income and arbitrary arrest and forming the subject of a bill in Parliament against the Company sponsored by reforming MPs on his behalf.[51] Thomas Pringle, having left the Cape for London in April 1826, was contributing articles critical of the Cape government to Buckingham's *Oriental Herald* by October of that year.[52]

The *South African Commercial Advertiser* made sure to keep its readers informed of Buckingham's campaign, choosing to provide an update on the first anniversary of its reinstatement following the ban of 1824.[53] 'No man – who values Liberty', they wrote of Buckingham,

can be indifferent to the case of a man who has fought his battles so sincerely, or who has suffered so much in the cause. We do not wish to speak severely of the India Government. We believe it is neither better nor worse than other subordinate Despotisms. It is a melancholy reflection, that so large a portion of the globe should be kept in slavery by the freest country in the world. We hope the emancipation of India and the Colonies is near at hand. In the mean time so distinguished a champion as Mr Buckingham should not be neglected.[54]

---

[50] A. F. Salahuddin Ahmed, *Social Ideas and Social Change in Bengal 1818–1835* (Leiden: Brill, 1965), p. 64.
[51] Bayly, *Recovering Liberties*, p. 76. [52] Vigne, *Thomas Pringle*, p. 182
[53] *Advertiser*, 2 Sept. 1826. Further details on the ongoing Buckingham case and on the freedom of the press in India appeared in the *Advertiser* on 5 Sept. 1826 and 30 Jan. 1827; see also *Statement of Facts Relative to the Removal from India of Mr. Buckingham late editor of the Calcutta Journal* (Calcutta, April 1823); *A Sketch of the History of the Indian Press* (London: William Low, 1829); *Mr Buckingham's Defence of his Public and Private Character* (Sheffield: John Blackwell, 1832); Salahuddin Ahmed, *Social Ideas and Social Change*. On the problems of defining the legal status of British subjects under the rule of the East India Company see Marshall, 'Britain and the world in the eighteenth century',1–15; S. Sen, 'Imperial subjects on trial: On the legal identity of Britons in late eighteenth-century India', *Journal of British Studies*, 45:3 (2006), 532–55.
[54] *Advertiser*, 2 Sept. 1826.

Similarly, in New South Wales, the *Australian* newspaper gave a long and sympathetic account of the suppression of the *Advertiser* and the tribulations of printer George Greig, in which they pictured him 'sighing over the stern secrecy of that tremendous despotism, within the range of which so many British subjects had unwarily suffered themselves to be entrapped'.[55] The *Australian*, established in the same year as the *Advertiser*, was also the first independent newspaper in its colony. When Edwards arrived in New South Wales under the Cape sentence of seven years' transportation for libel, the Sydney newspapers like the *Australian* and the *Monitor* seized on his case as an example of tyranny that served as useful propaganda in their own struggles to secure freedom of the press. These struggles involved both legislative initiatives and seditious libel actions that would see Edmund Smith Hall, editor of the *Monitor*, repeatedly imprisoned.

The fledgling independent press in New South Wales, however, had a significant advantage over that of the Cape not only in the person of Chief Justice Francis Forbes but also in a recently amended constitutional landscape. Forbes was reluctant to criminalise public scrutiny of official practice as a matter of routine. On the basis of the New South Wales Act of 1823, which gave the chief justice the right to disallow colonial legislation deemed repugnant to the laws of England, he repeatedly opposed the more draconian legislative measures sought by Governor Ralph Darling against the press. Specifically, these included the provision that the Supreme Court be given the right to banish those convicted of a second offence of criminal libel. Darling's attempts to get the provision onto the books in New South Wales were finally scotched by the 1830 repeal of the banishment clause from the 1819 Blasphemous and Seditious Libels Act, making any colonial measure concerning banishment a clear violation of English legal practice.[56]

'Two most delicate questions': the Colonial Office intervenes

The broader implication of these debates, in the Cape as much as in Australia, lies in 'the peculiar constitutional framework' in which they were fought out.[57] Given that the Cape libel trials, the suppression of the

---

[55] *Australian*, 2 Dec. 1824.
[56] Edgeworth, 'Defamation law', 50–82; Spiegelman, 'Foundations of freedom of the press',89–109; Wright, 'Libel and the colonial administration of justice'; Currey, *Sir Francis Forbes*.
[57] Edgeworth, 'Defamation law', p. 51, in relation to New South Wales.

Advertiser and the banishment of Greig all came in the midst of the Commission of Eastern Inquiry's investigations, the timing was particularly bad. Writing confidentially to Somerset, Bathurst lamented:

> I am very much afraid that what has passed lately at the Cape will bring on a jealous enquiry and revision of the powers vested in the Governors of the ceded Possessions and unless precautions are taken, it will end in their being curtailed in a manner very prejudicial to their real interests. There has been indeed a strong disposition to question these powers, on other occasions, in other Colonies.

Summing up Somerset's errors within this wider political context, he concluded:

> you have unfortunately stirred two most delicate questions to which every English feeling is most likely to be alive. The one, the freedom of the Press: the second, the power of expulsion without trial, without Conviction, by the exercise of your own individual Authority.[58]

Despite this private admonition, the secretary of state took a far less vehement position on the legality of Somerset's actions than did James Stephen. Bathurst was willing to concede that the power existed under Somerset's instructions, though he pointed out (clearly with reference to Stephen's advice) 'that the Right of the Crown to gain this Power is by some persons questioned'. It could only be justified 'by the suppression of some extreme case of danger where the ordinary Administration of the Law will not admit of timely assistance'. These, Bathurst considered, were not to be found in the criminal libel cases or the newspaper reports of court proceedings. Viewed from the metropole, Somerset's measure 'will appear harsh and arbitrary'. It was Bathurst's personal belief that powers of political removal could be legally justified, but that their importance lay more in the threat than in the execution:

> I believe in my conscience that the possession of such power in the Government of our distant possessions is necessary, but its salutary effect is rather in the knowledge that there is such power, than in its exercise, and one instance of its improvident use will go a great way to deprive our Foreign Governments of this valuable, if not necessary, Instrument of Authority.[59]

---

[58] Bathurst to Somerset, 19 Oct. 1824, Bathurst papers, BL 57/65. Lord Granville Somerset was in full agreement about the dangers of 'a case which involves so many popular Topicks'. He anticipated that in the forthcoming debates of the House of Commons, the 'great brawling will be about the Press'. Granville Somerset to Wilmot Horton, 13 Nov. and 5 Dec. 1824, Wilmot Horton Papers, Catton Collection, Derbyshire Record Office, D3155/WH 2876.

[59] Bathurst to Somerset, 19 Oct. 1824, Bathurst Papers, BL 57/65.

It is certainly true that the existence of such powers operated powerfully on the minds of Cape residents, as the placards about 'inquisition' quoted in the last chapter demonstrate. At Howel's booksellers and stationers, Hudson wrote:

> every person is hot upon the commitment of Edwards to the Trunk and I must confess it strikes me as an unprecedented proceeding to send a person to a Prison to punish him ere he is regularly been brought before any court but the Inquisitorial one of Lord Charles's guilty conscience.[60]

Hudson's diary suggests a general sense that anyone could be next:

> It appears that Messrs Pringle and Fairbairn waited upon Major Colebrook with their case ready to make affidavits that they as well as many others were proscribed persons designated as dangerous subjects and to be sent out of the Colony and this severity for daring to act like honest men.[61]

Certainly Pringle's correspondence confirms both the efficacy of the threat and his own genuine fears about the possibility of being subjected to transportation. Referring to information held by missionary and Liberal ally John Philip that would be damaging to the government, he told Whig MP Henry Brougham that 'it was considered dangerous to publish them at present, for the slight *libel* on Authority here is sufficient to obtain a sentence from our subservient Courts to send any man to Botany Bay – though every word of it be true.'[62]

In another letter to Brougham asserting his 'Whig principles', Pringle outlined his determination to publish an exposé of the Cape administration, whatever the consequences:

> If this Governor remain I must expect inveterate persecution – and if I publish what I intend respecting his administration I presume I must prepare for *prosecution*. And if this Court of Justice continue persecution for telling unpleasant truths of the Governor or the Govt is synonymous with sentence of banishment to Botany Bay. *That* is a fate I confess I deprecate and fear to run the risk of. I fear nothing else.[63]

If it was Bathurst's personal belief that powers of political removal could be legally justified, then in the report published on the administration of the colony in 1826, the Commissioners of Eastern Inquiry also endorsed the legality of the practice. They provided historical background that

---

[60] Hudson, Diary, 30 April 1824.   [61] Hudson, Diary, 16 May 1824.
[62] Pringle to Brougham, 18 Dec. 1824, Randolph Vigne (ed.) *The South African Letters of Thomas Pringle* (Cape Town: Van Riebeeck Society, 2011), p. 149.
[63] Pringle to Brougham, 20 Dec. 1824, *Letters of Thomas Pringle*, p. 153. Pringle here uses 'banishment' in its generic rather than specific sense and is actually referring to convict transportation.

was clearly reliant upon the researches of Truter and Denyssen. Despite their conclusion, however, they too expressed reservations, considering executive banishment more suited to those 'accustomed to an arbitrary form of government' and recognising that the influx of vociferous English settlers claiming 'the right of free discussion' at the Cape had rendered it politically unwise. Their recommendation was that the practice be confined to 'aliens, or persons who are not natural born subjects of His Majesty', and to those with limited property or limited length of residence in the colony.[64]

To help resolve the immediate problem raised by Somerset's misguided tactics against his opponents, Bathurst proposed bringing forward an initiative he had originally planned to execute only upon the recommendation of the Commissioners of Eastern Inquiry: that of an advisory council. It was a significant shift in Bathurst's thinking. He had rejected the Select Committee on Transportation's recommendation of an advisory council for the governor of New South Wales in 1812, citing concerns about both factional politics and suspect colonial social status, particularly in a colony 'composed of such discordant materials'.[65] Now he considered it 'prudent to establish it at once; as I am sure it will be of great use in the discussions which will take place, if such a system is already adopted'. Somerset's unguarded behaviour through the libel trials and the banishment debacle had led directly to this initiative, as Bathurst's private correspondence indicates:

Command of temper is the most serviceable of all qualities in men vested with Authority, and one of the great advantages of a Council is, that it comes in aid of a Governor by giving him time to reflect, when from human infirmity, he may lose that Command of which they who are opposed to him normally try, by provocations, to deprive him and Parliament will more willingly trust authority to a Governor, where they have this security against its abuse.[66]

It was Somerset's injudicious attempts to protect his own reputation (and Bathurst's efforts to neutralise the political opposition) that had proved decisive, and the Cape Advisory Council was sworn in on 4 May 1825, anticipating the recommendations of the Commission of Eastern Inquiry by over a year.[67]

[64] *Report of the Commissioners of Inquiry Upon the Administration of the Government of the Cape of Good Hope, BPP* 1826–1827 (282) . My thanks to Lisa Ford for alerting me to this provision.
[65] *HRA*, 1:7, pp. 669–76; T. P. Woods, 'Lord Bathurst's Policy at the Colonial Office, 1812–1821, with particular reference to New South Wales and the Cape Colony', unpublished DPhil thesis, Oxford University (1971), p. 181.
[66] Bathurst to Somerset, 19 Oct. 1824.
[67] Although it was the first step towards diluting gubernatorial autocracy, the intervention was limited. A 'toothless body of officials', in the words of Timothy Keegan, the Council

Increasing numbers of Britons in this period were emigrating to colonies recently conquered from foreign powers. Here they made frequent, strident and undoubtedly opportunistic claims to have brought their constitutional rights with them. The reality was far more murky, and, as we have seen, could lead them into profound difficulties. In mediating these disputes, administrators in London and on the ground were caught between managing the complexities of a highly contingent doctrine of conquest law and the political expediency of applying foreign regulations to volatile British settler populations. The ultimate result, we might argue, helped to recast legal plurality in a more hierarchical idiom and to tip the balance towards a more powerful articulation not just of British sovereignty but also of British law over a variety of colonial domains across the nineteenth century.[68]

Although the Charter of Justice that came into effect in January 1828 under Chief Justice Sir John Wylde did not result in the wholesale replacement of the Roman–Dutch system, the influence of a new coterie of officials would prove transformative. In 1849, with some twenty years in office behind him, Wylde underscored these developments in a judgement that brushed off the authorities of the previous legal regime like so many pesky flies:

Quote what Dutch or Roman books you please – musty or otherwise – and they must be musty if they lay down such doctrines. I belong to a higher court than they refer to – a court not to be broken up or paralysed by their authorities, much less by the maxims of philosophers dozing over the midnight lamp in their solitary chambers. My Queen has sent me here to administer justice under the Royal Charter.... [W]hen you speak of the Institutions of Holland, and of binding myself down by the practice of Dutch courts – I absolve myself from that bondage, I look to my Charter, to my oath and to my duty.[69]

The attitude and practice of men like Wylde were contributing factors in the development of South Africa's mixed legal system. This, along with the widespread removal of the Cape Dutch from influence, patronage and government employment (from men like Denyssen and Truter to far more lowly officials) was indicative of the regime change in colonial administration that followed the Commission of Eastern Inquiry.[70]

---

of Advice had no legislative powers: T. Keegan, *Colonial South Africa and the Origins of the Racial Order* (Cape Town and Johannesburg: Historical Publication Society, 1996), p. 100. The *Advertiser* (20 Dec. 1828) was similarly scathing of this institution 'with Lord Bathurst's character and name impressed upon it'. The governor had the power to act without his council, but had to report to the secretary of state when he disregarded its advice: Ward, *Colonial Self-Government*, p. 137.

[68] On this broader question, see Benton and Ross, 'Empires and legal pluralism'.
[69] An 1849 judgement quoted by Fagan, 'Roman-Dutch law', p. 56.
[70] Sturgis, 'Anglicisation at the Cape of Good Hope'; Peires, 'The British and the Cape'.

Scandals over gubernatorial excess in the early nineteenth century (be they Picton in Trinidad or Somerset at the Cape) remind us that assertions of supposedly inherent British rights were undercut by exerting colonial authority through alien judicial systems. If sovereignty was 'not a given... but would depend upon recurring proofs',[71] then the Cape libel trials raised questions that were deeply discomforting to the foundations of British rule. Scholars of legal pluralism have recently argued that jurisdictional conflicts involving settlers and indigenous peoples across the long nineteenth century helped to generate a 'more hierarchically structured legal order defined in part by the assertion (whether realised or not) of imperial jurisdiction'.[72] In the problems they raised over the relations between English and Dutch law and punitive practice, the Cape disputes of 1824 underscore the need to include a recognition that conflicts between variants of European law were as important as relations between colonisers and colonised in helping to stimulate that shift.

[71] Benton, *Search for Sovereignty*, p. 23.
[72] Benton and Ross, 'Empires and legal pluralism', p. 12.

8 'A conspiracy of the darkest and foulest nature'
The placard affair

In the final days of May 1824, Governor Somerset can be forgiven any feelings of complacency he might have entertained. With no foreknowledge of the constitutional anxieties his 'illegal' actions had unleashed at the Colonial Office, he had apparently prevailed against the 'Radicals'. In the wake of the disastrous outcome of the prize slave libel trials, he had suppressed the newspaper that had been giving such damaging publicity to the allegations against his regime. Its creators had helpfully closed their own paper rather than submit to what they described as 'censorship'. Its proprietor was temporarily silenced under threat of banishment. The necessary legal actions had been frustratingly protracted, but the insults by which Edwards had undermined the authority of the Cape government had eventually been brought to an end. Under sentence of transportation, the miscreant was safely in jail awaiting a ship to take him to New South Wales. Unfortunately for Somerset, the respite that followed Edwards's final conviction would last a scant three days.

'A suspicious Paper sticking upon the wall'

Without the *South African Commercial Advertiser* at its disposal, Cape public opinion could no longer be so easily transmitted beyond the boundaries of the colony. But it was by no means silenced. The city remained plastered with commentary on the recent libel cases and the government's actions against its critics, 'truly expressive of the indignation of the generality of the people'.[1] The Heerengracht (now Adderley Street) was a prominent place for posting such attacks upon authority. In his memoir of the period, the former printer's apprentice Louis Meurant described the canal that then ran down its length as fringed with trees and 'affording cover to spies'. It also afforded excellent cover for those wishing to fasten papers while remaining undetected, with the posts of the small bridges

---

Somerset to Bathurst, 12 Oct. 1825 ('private'), Bathurst Papers, BL 57/88.
[1] Hudson, Diary, 25 Feb. 1824, Hudson Papers, CA, A602.

that spanned the canal presenting a suitable surface.[2] At the corner of the Heerengracht and Longmarket Street was a spot known as 'Dreyer's Corner', after a large house that had once belonged to a gentleman of that name. The house boasted a high *stoep* and a rounded corner. Both smooth and high enough to avoid the papers being easily torn down, it offered a perfect canvas for the 'political squibs' that appeared there almost daily.[3]

Opposite Dreyer's Corner was James Howell's Circulating Library and Stationers, with the African Society House, a club dominated by the English-speaking elite, a few doors down. These were the 'places of public resort', where news was to be had, and consequently a favourite spot for placarding one's political opponents. As Meurant remembered it:

'Dreyer's corner' during the excitement which prevailed in consequence of the 'State Trials' was placarded almost every morning with squibs, and although the 'Dienders' (policemen) were ever on the watch, or pretended to be, the authors of the placards could not be discovered.[4]

Rumours of such activities were swapped at places of congregation such as Howell's bookseller and stationery shop. Hudson visited there almost daily:

At Howell's I heard that the rascaly spy that I had observed standing at the corner of the Bridge for several nights had stationed himself there last night when two persons passing and seeing a suspicious Paper sticking upon the wall went up to read it when the scamp jumped up and ran to the spot thinking no doubt they were going to stick up a placard. An exploration took place and he received a hearty drubbing which made him take to his heels with the fleetness that fear had given him added to the weight of his disgraceful office. May such base worms be trod under foot as they deserve.[5]

If William Edwards was incarcerated in Cape Town prison, he was (at least at first) by no means separated from these swirling currents of news. Although he would later endure a period of solitary confinement, he initially received frequent visits from his numerous supporters. Meurant remembered accompanying Edwards's servant Thomas Mahony (who was allowed to deliver his master's meals) to the jail, together with 'a small dog belonging to Edwards, which wore a broad leather collar'. Never was a dog so conscientiously exercised. For while Mahony and Meurant were searched entering and leaving the cell, the dog was not – and a regular correspondence was smuggled in and out hidden in the

---

[2] See Cory, *Rise of South Africa*, vol. II, p. 270.   [3] Meurant, *Sixty Years Ago*, p. 26.
[4] Meurant, *Sixty Years Ago*, p. 26.   [5] Hudson, Diary, 12 June 1824.

faithful canine's collar.[6] Evidence given by another of Edwards's servants, Daniel Lee, demonstrates both how his master was connected to what was quite literally the 'word on the street', and how the contents of libellous writings were spread around the town:

> I saw several people copying it [an anti-government broadsheet] which was stuck up opposite Mr. Hoffman's House, and I copied it from another copy, that was copied by me of the man who was standing there. I brought my copy to Mr. Edwards, who scolded me very much for having done so, saying that if such a thing was found on me, I should be put in the Trunk and that I could not get out so easily as the people who put these things up.[7]

Part and parcel of political culture in the early nineteenth-century British world, such 'street literature' is by its very nature ephemeral, and no originals from the Cape of this period survive.[8] We are fortunate that Hudson saw fit to transcribe so many examples into his private diary, although as an acknowledged critic of the 'Gothamites' his choices were never going to be disinterested.[9] Government officers were instructed to tear broadsheets down as fast as protestors could stick them up. As we saw in the previous chapter, scuffles between the opposing sides inevitably broke out. Ordinary citizens, whether motivated by outrage moral, political or both, also busied themselves in tearing down offensive material. One witness, giving evidence to the authorities on the practice, testified that he saw an insulting notice stuck up on the bridge crossing from Hout Street to the Commercial Hall and 'pulled the paper down from a persuasion it was very improper to be there'.[10] Although the original was later burnt, the information contained in this particular squib nevertheless survived, and a transcription of the contents would eventually find a place in London's National Archives.

Colonial Office records are punctuated with such scribbled copies on slips of paper. Their existence, and the carefully transcribed witness testimony on the contents of insulting placards, underscores not only how important it was for colonial authorities to keep abreast of such informal information networks, but also how difficult it was to control

---

[6] Meurant, *Sixty Years Ago*, p. 35.   [7] Testimony of Daniel Lee, *RCC*, vol. 18, no. 94.
[8] J. Vernon, *Politics and the People: A Study in English Political Culture c.1815–1867* (Cambridge University Press, 1993), p. 132.
[9] Although Hudson's diaries are biased towards transcribing English-language placards, he provides sufficient hints to indicate that the practice was also utilised against opponents (both personal and political) by the Cape Dutch. In the midst of the Edwards scandals he made note of a placard 'in Dutch advising Eckerman the Bo[a]rder to be a little more cautious in his public sittuation and to look back to former times when he was convicted of stealing a gold watch and various other Articles' (1 May 1824).
[10] Testimony of Archibald Shaw Robertson, *RCC*, vol. 18, p. 84.

them. Even ostensibly idle gossip with no obvious political import could be an important resource in imperial governance. Many of the examples to be found in Hudson's diary and in Colonial Office files are baffling, with only a general sense of their offensive allusions now remaining. Reminding us of the close-knit community in which they were created and used, they are filled with innuendos that would have been perfectly understandable to the intended audience.

Contemporary diarists, published reminiscences and witnesses brought before the fiscal's 1824 investigation of such practices all therefore agree: the streets of Cape Town were thickly papered with libellous writings, not just about the Somerset regime, but against all manner of targets, both personal and political. Yet amidst this paper avalanche of broadsheets, placards and squibs there was one that was sufficiently notorious to become known simply as '*the* placard'. No copy survives. Accounts of its content and wording vary in their details. Only one person admitted to having actually seen it. The official record made of his memory of the text reads as follows:

> A person living at Newlands makes it known or takes this opportunity of making it known to the Public authorities of this Colony that on the 5th instant he detected Lord Charles buggering Dr Barry; Lady Charles or her ladyship had her suspicions, or saw something that led her to suspicions, which had caused a general quarrel and which was the reason of the Marchionesses's going home – the person is ready to come and make oath to the above.[11]

The placard appeared on 1 June 1824, just days after Edwards had been found guilty of criminal libel and sentenced to transportation to New South Wales. Captain John Findlay, a forty-six-year-old Scot, was the only person able (or willing) to provide an eyewitness report. Coming onto the *stoep* of his lodging house in the Heerengracht early that morning, Findlay saw two others looking at the placard in question, 'one black of complexion and the other yellow'. One of these observers, a boy described of some sixteen years, told Findlay that it 'was something about Lord Charles'. Neither of these two witnesses could afterwards be traced. At this point Findlay was called back into the house by a servant as he had wandered into the street without his shoes. When he came out again the paper had disappeared. Thomas Kift Deane, one of the next people on the scene, 'about sunrise', overheard people on the street passing on the news of the placard's contents. Having left the house to see for himself, however, he found only an empty space with 'nothing but

---

[11] Testimony of John Findlay, TNA, CO 48/95. The transcription in *RCC* (vol. 18, p. 74) elides this section of Findlay's evidence, as it does all accounts of the wording and contents of the placard, with ∗∗∗.

4 or 5 wafers on it'.[12] The placard itself had vanished, but its contents were already spreading rapidly by word of mouth. Thomas Hammond, government printer, testified that it was soon 'the subject of conversation all over the town'.[13]

Most people brought as witnesses in the fiscal's investigation into the matter admitted they had heard about it and knew details of the contents before forty-eight hours had elapsed. Their evidence is a timely reminder of how the surviving archive can both privilege written over oral information networks and erase the intimate connection that continued to exist between them. A masculine bourgeois public sphere may have been emerging at the Cape in this period, with self-consciously 'rational' debate in the rooms of coffeehouses and the pages of independent newspapers,[14] but all sorts and conditions of men and women were discussing the placard affair and its implications. Although their rendering of the wording may have differed – 'Lord Charles buggering Dr Barry', 'an improper connection imputing improper intercourse or unnatural Crime, or words to that effect', 'contained something about Lord Charles & Dr Barry, who were seen together in a certain position' – in essentials their accounts were in agreement.

Respectable Cape Town wrestled with how to reconcile their sense of propriety with their evident eagerness to impart the salacious news. William Bridekirk, the government printer, described how Thomas Hammond, another member of his office, 'suggested the particulars delicately'. Pressed under examination as to what words he used, Bridekirk elaborated:

The words I cannot mention particularly, but the nature of the Libel Hammond mentioned, but not particularly. He named the persons Lord Charles and Dr. Barry but made a distant allusion, so that I could comprehend the meaning.[15]

Mr Saunders, who together with his wife kept a coffee-shop habituated by Barry, refused to discuss the details in the presence of his wife. His reticence was apparently wasted, for Mrs Saunders later told the printer Thomas Hammond 'as decently and politely as she could that Dr. Barry had mentioned it to her'.[16] Indeed Hammond later said that 'Dr Barry

---

[12] Testimonies of Thomas Kift Deane and John Findlay, *RCC*, vol. 18, pp. 72–5.
[13] Testimony of Thomas Hammond, *RCC*, vol. 18, p. 103.
[14] McKenzie, *Scandal in the Colonies*; 'The Franklins of the Cape: The *South African Commercial Advertiser* and the creation of a colonial public sphere 1824–1854', *Kronos: Journal of Cape History*, 25 (1998/1999), 88–102.
[15] Testimony of William Bridekirk, *RCC*, vol. 18, p. 101.
[16] Testimony of William Bridekirk, *RCC*, vol. 18, p. 102.

Figure 6 The African Theatre, where Lord Charles Somerset and Dr James Barry stared down their critics at the height of the placard scandal.

was said to have cried at Saunders, in consequence of the injury done to him'.[17]

Faced with this storm of public commentary, the administration moved fast. On the evening of the day the placard appeared, the printer William Bridekirk was called to open the Government Printing Office after hours. A proclamation was printed offering a reward for information leading to the arrest of those responsible. The second necessary step was a public show of unity. On the following day, Dr Barry joined Lord Charles and Lady Somerset in the box of the African Theatre (of which the Somersets were patrons) [Figure 6] in an ostentatious public appearance. On offer were 'the comedy "The Heir at Law" and the farce of "Lovers' Quarrels"'[18] but there was greater dramatic interest to be found amongst the spectators. As Hudson described it,

His Lordship, Lady Charles and Dr Barry were at the play last night and were received with enthusiastic applause by the audience. I am glad they were at the Theatre it was doing what they ought. Had he [Somerset] been as attentive to those constant visitations and made the public his friends that deep hatred would never have taken place.[19]

The third action by the authorities was to open an official investigation into the matter. Suspicion immediately fell upon the 'Radicals' in general and upon Edwards in particular. Every effort would be made by the state to prove both their direct authorship and their wider complicity in the scandal. By 4 June, testimony was being taken by the fiscal before W. Bentick, Sitting Commissioner of the Council of Justice.

If Edwards's trial had showed up the constitutional and procedural difficulties of Anglo–Dutch legal pluralism and linguistic confusion, the placard investigation underscores these in a rather lighter vein. Despite the fact that almost all the witnesses were British emigrants, the office of the fiscal and the Council of Justice remained staffed by Dutch-speaking clerks. Under the circumstances, accurate transcription presented some challenges. Taking down the testimony of Thomas Kift Deane and Captain Findlay before the fiscal, the Dutch scribe [Figure 7] was clearly at somewhat of a loss. With frequent false starts and crossings-out, he made several abortive attempts to spell the word 'buggering'. Having rejected 'Burgher', along with other possibilities, he eventually settled on 'bugguering'.[20]

---

[17] Testimony of Bernadus Josephus van der Sandt, *RCC*, vol. 18, p. 86.
[18] *Cape Town Gazette and African Advertiser*, 29 May 1824.
[19] Hudson, Diary, 3 June 1824.
[20] CA, CJ 3352. Inquiry into Placard scandal, 1824.

Figure 8 Anonymous portrait of a youthful James Barry, undated.

'A conspiracy of the darkest and foulest nature'   223

Like the exact nature of his relations with Somerset, which contemporaries universally recognised as close, Barry's sex remains shrouded in mystery. This is perhaps as it should be for someone who carved out his own persona with such a determined hand.[25] At times – for there is yet another impostor who will shortly reappear in these pages – the bemused historian is tempted to ask if anyone in the Cape Town of 1824 was *not* participating at some level in an elaborate masquerade. The most extensive recent biography, by Rachel Holmes, makes an intriguing case for the doctor's intersexuality, based in part on the clues that Barry himself left in his medical researches into hernia.[26] Whatever the truth, Barry was an arresting figure on the streets of Cape Town, an unabashed dandy invariably accompanied by his poodle, the first in a long line of canine familiars.

Barry's poodles were all called 'Psyche'. Holmes suggests that the first Psyche, acquired in Cape Town, might even have been a gift from Somerset himself. Although we have no evidence for this, it would be consistent with both the governor's sense of humour and the penchant for allusive nicknames that the 'Llama' shared with his political adversaries.[27] The story of Cupid and Psyche is a story of beautiful monstrosity, of intimacy in the dark, and the consequences of too much curiosity about a lover's appearance.[28] If the poodle's name was Somerset's (or Barry's) idea of a joke, then it was a dangerous one. Even Hudson, who had no

[25] The extraordinary life and unsolved mysteries of James Barry have unsurprisingly attracted significant attention in both history and fiction. Amongst several biographies are those of I. Rae, *The Strange Story of Dr James Barry* (London: Longmans, Green, 1958); J. Rose, *The Perfect Gentleman: The Remarkable Life of Dr James Miranda Barry, the Woman who Served as an Officer in the British Army from 1813 to 1859* (London: Hutchinson, 1977); and Holmes, *Scanty Particulars*. A recent investigation into Barry's origins is that by Hercules Michael du Preez, 'Dr James Barry: The early years revealed', *South African Medical Journal*, 98: 1 (2008), 52–62. Although many unanswered questions remain, the scholarly consensus is that Barry was born Margaret Bulkley, probably in 1789, in Cork, Ireland. This would make Barry thirty-five years old at the time of the placard scandal, some two decades younger than Somerset. Bulkley, the niece of the artist and Royal Academician James Barry (1741–1806) disappeared and reemerged as the medical student James Barry in Edinburgh in 1809.
[26] The lack of any archival references in her popular history unfortunately make Holmes's claims about Barry very hard to assess, but I am sympathetic to her suggestion that Barry would probably not have considered his sex the most important question to ask of what was a long and impressive career. Our apparent need to assign stable sexual categorisation is underscored by the decisions that need to be made when writing about the doctor. I have chosen to accord him his pronoun of choice.
[27] Thomas Pringle and John Fairbairn made frequent use of facetious nicknames in their correspondence. 'Llama' was clearly inspired by Somerset's sense of his own exalted position; the Commissioners of Eastern Inquiry were 'the Bogles', a Scots word for ghost. Pringle to Fairbairn, 5 April 1825; Vigne (ed.) *South African Letters of Thomas Pringle*, p. 178; Vigne, *Thomas Pringle*, p. 143.
[28] Holmes, *Scanty Particulars*, p. 82.

love for 'Scamp Charley',[29] was profoundly shocked by the accusations of 'buggering', a capital offence at the Cape.[30] We should certainly not underestimate how serious were the claims contained within the placard. But the question remains, serious for whom?

Just as Edwards and the more raffish elements of the colonial opposition were quickly edited out of the narratives of Cape liberalism, so too has the placard affair faded from explanatory frameworks charting imperial governance in this period. Although it has (perhaps inevitably) attracted the attention of popular histories, scholars appear to have been at rather a loss as to whether it has any significance beyond salacious gossip. G. E. Cory's *Rise of South Africa* provided the first and amongst the most detailed description of the events, though delicacy prevented his revealing the actual contents of the 'disgusting anonymous letter'. He ended his account of the placard affair by speculating that the entire incident might have been a government conspiracy to discredit Somerset's opponents. Writing in 1913, Cory was content to leave these thoughts as 'mere supposition', to mourn that more would have 'come to light had a thorough and perfectly impartial investigation been made', and to conclude that 'the placard remains a mystery'.[31] Yet the unanswered questions at the heart of the placard scandal were precisely its point and its power. In our own very different historiographical climate, the mystery re-emerges not as the frustrated end to enquiry that it was for Cory, but rather as the starting point of my analysis.[32]

Very little, if any, of the relevant facts can be proved one way or another. We do not know what form Somerset and Barry's undoubted intimacy might have taken, let alone whether it included a sexual dimension.[33] Nor do we know precisely what might have motivated the author. If Somerset had numerous enemies at the Cape, so too did the chronically

---

[29] Hudson, Diary, 14 May 1824.
[30] To be more precise, under Cape Dutch law (following that of the Netherlands) anal penetration with ejaculation inside the body needed to be proved to constitute a capital offence; S. Newton-King, 'For the Love of Adam', 21–42.
[31] Cory, *Rise of South Africa*, pp. 270, 274.
[32] In *Scandal in the Colonies* I emphasised how scandal, and the unpredictable ways in which scandals unfold, can be used as a route into understanding contemporary social and political relations regardless of whether it is possible (or indeed desirable) to uncover the 'truth' of the original transgression. On the importance of scandal as an analytical tool for understanding the operation of politics in this period see also, amongst a wide literature, A. Clark, *Scandal: The Sexual Politics of the British Constitution* (Princeton University Press, 2004). On scandal and colonial rule see N. B. Dirks, *The Scandal of Empire: India and the Creation of Imperial Britain* (Harvard University Press, 2006); Epstein, *Scandal of Colonial Rule*.
[33] For a discussion of the wide-ranging analytical possibilities of this concept, see T. Ballantyne and A. Burton (eds.), *Gender, Mobility and Intimacy in an Age of Empire* (University of Illinois Press, 2008).

'A conspiracy of the darkest and foulest nature' 225

belligerent Barry, who not only engaged in endless factional feuding with other members of the administration but also fought a duel with Somerset's aide-de-camp.[34] Only one person could be traced who claimed to have seen the placard itself. The offending notice disappeared almost immediately after it was posted, and the person who had torn it down was never found. Despite widespread suspicions and circumstantial evidence pointing to William Edwards and his supporters, its authorship remained unproven. No one was able to claim the substantial reward offered for information that would bring the perpetrators to justice. No one was charged or punished for the act itself. Indeed the very existence of the placard came into dispute. Despite Somerset's privately expressed frustration[35] (and the undoubted bias mentioned by Cory) the government investigation was exhaustive. The historian is unlikely to succeed where Fiscal Denyssen so manifestly failed.

For our purposes, the scandal's utility lies precisely in recognising its tenuous hold on reality and in tracing the tactics of the ideological warfare that broke out in its aftermath. My interest lies in the political management of the scandal rather than in the alleged sexual improprieties of Somerset and Barry or the identity of the persons who claimed to have brought them to light. We need to situate the placard scandal firmly within the unfolding struggle of oppositional politics in Britain and the Cape, which is indeed how it was seen by those most concerned at the time. There was a strong sense of titillation in the way the allegations were initially passed around the inhabitants of Cape Town. But what is equally notable, particularly given the racy contents of the placard, is how soon this faded and how quickly the terms of the debate shifted elsewhere.

In this account, I give only limited space both to the evidence brought to light against Edwards and his compatriots by the state and to the holes that were driven through this evidence by opposition forces. The vanished placard opened a space upon which an entirely other set of meanings, quite separate from alleged sexual impropriety between Barry and Somerset, could be inscribed. The significance of the placard scandal lies in how

---

[34] The chosen weapons were pistols and both escaped unscathed. The upshot of the duel between Barry and Abraham Josias Cloete was a lifelong friendship between the two former combatants: Holmes, *Scanty Particulars*, pp. 85–90.

[35] In typical racing parlance Somerset complained to Commissioner Bigge: 'I saw Mr Fiscal yesterday but no whip or spur can rouse him having got in a very strong degree that malady upon him so fatal at Newmarket called "The Slows" it is however unpardonable in the present case. . . . perhaps your suggestion may induce him to act with more vigour & celerity – a word from *you* to him is like a stroke *on the raw* to an Irish post horse.' (undated 'Sunday evening' [1824], Bigge–Somerset Correspondence, Rhodes House, University of Oxford, MSS Afr, series 24).

it illuminates the liabilities of informal and covert information-gathering that we encountered in Chapter 3. This formed part of a much broader debate about state-sponsored espionage that connected metropole and colonies in a powerful feedback loop. It was a debate that would see the unexpected re-emergence of Oliver the Spy, the most notorious covert operative of them all, onto the British political stage.

'Everything short of legal proof': making the case against Edwards

Whether culpable or not, Edwards was no fool. He knew that the terms of his imprisonment gave him sufficient access to the outside world for suspicion to immediately fall upon him as a conspirator. In the midst of the scandal, Hudson would write, 'I must think Edwards enjoys it as do what they will they cannot punish him more than their former sentence.'[36] Yet Edwards still seems to have feared the possible consequences, for as soon as the placard scandal broke he took what pre-emptive steps he could. On 2 June he wrote to a member of the Commercial Hall (the local merchants' association) denying any connection with the 'odious placard' that he urged 'emanates from some one who wishes to bring the press and the public feeling of this Colony into disrepute'. He enclosed a copy of this letter in another one to the fiscal, also denying authorship.[37] Four days later, as the state began to move against him, he wrote yet another denial to the fiscal in which he claimed that 'until I have washed out the very suspicion of a base assassin-like act I shall be unwilling to shew my face to my Mother and my Children or any friend and fit only to associate with the worst felons of New Holland'.[38]

An anonymous letter, sent to Barry's house on 4 June, asserted that Edwards and Greig were the men behind the placard. The following day, Fiscal Denyssen received a tip-off that the truth could be got out of Edwards's servant, Daniel Lee. Lee came to be vilified as the 'Judas' of the case, but his situation now reads eloquently of extreme vulnerability. An Irish indentured servant brought to the colony by the labour speculator John Ingram, he had been living with William Edwards for three months at the time of the placard scandal.[39] He was around twenty years of

---

[36] Hudson, Diary, 5 June 1824.
[37] Edwards to Twycross, 2 June 1824, encl. in Edwards to Denyssen, 3 June 1824, *RCC*, vol. 18, pp. 69–70.
[38] Edwards to Fiscal, 6 June 1824, *RCC*, vol. 18, p. 79.
[39] Daniel Lee's testimony of 5 June 1824 is to be found in TNA, CO 48/95 and his later testimony in *RCC*, vol. 18, pp. 88–95.

'A conspiracy of the darkest and foulest nature' 227

age and admitted he could 'write little in a passable manner'.[40] Under investigation by the fiscal he claimed that the alleged conspirators George Greig, Bishop Burnett and William Edwards

> would not lead me in all the Secrets and so I only know of it by having been employed by the authors as their messenger. They promised me to clear me of the passage money due to Mr. Ingram and they also promised to keep me in good clothing &c.[41]

Like the prize slaves we encountered earlier in this volume, these Irish indentured servants were a product of those who sought to profit from the perceived labour shortage at the Cape that followed the abolition of the slave trade. Ingram arrived with a boatful of men, women and children from the south of Ireland in late 1823, receiving in advance a set fee for each passenger.[42] The indentured servants had also to pay Ingram for the cost of their passage. In his capacity as notary, Edwards was responsible for drawing up a number of the necessary indentures, which is how he presumably first met Daniel Lee.[43]

The link between speculation in Irish indentures and the system of unfree labour at the Cape was well recognised. As Somerset put it,

> Mr Ingram's is an odd Trade – He has recd £15 per Head for 326 persons from Govt (£4900) – He has brought out 322 – including women & children & yet he asks £30 per tête to be paid to Him by each person – either down or to receive it out of their wages – but it is to be secured to him by the Hirer of the *white Slave* – A few more Ingrams wd balance the act of abolishing negroe Slavery.[44]

Like prize slaves, those Irish who arrived at the Cape as indentured servants were soon absorbed into the port city's underclass community of slaves, free blacks, Khoekhoen, soldiers and sailors. Cape Town's 'dangerous nest' of 'rascally drunken Irish scamps'[45] was frequently classed with the more raffish elements of the town's multi-ethnic 'canteen culture' by the respectable.[46] Somerset, for one, considered Ingram 'the

---

[40] Testimony of Daniel Lee, TNA, CO 48/95.
[41] Commissioners of Inquiry, TNA, CO 48/121.
[42] Newton-King, 'The labour market of the Cape Colony', pp. 188–90
[43] Protocol of the Notary William Edwards, CA, NCD 27/1, no. 1–105.
[44] 29 Jan. 1824, Bigge–Somerset correspondence.
[45] Hudson, Diary, 23 Jan. and 26 March 1824. Hudson came upon the 'beastly exhibition' of 'a man and woman in the very act of copulation' in the Parade one evening. It is significant that although he noted that the woman was 'Mocambique', he was unable to determine whether the man was 'one of the Irish settlers or a House Boy [slave]': Hudson, Diary, 12 April 1824.
[46] The term is Andrew Bank's, from *The Decline of Urban Slavery*, ch. 3. See also Ross, *Status and Respectability*, ch. 6.

228   Imperial Underworld

biggest rogue amongst them', and labour disputes between him and his party of emigrants soon attracted the attention of the authorities. Cape Town's Irish, therefore, had both a symbolic and literal connection to the city's disreputable elements, including slaves and indigenous people. This would prove of vital importance in how the placard scandal could be manipulated.

Daniel Shee was a Cape Town tailor who employed two of Ingram's apprentices, one of whom, Roger O'Grady, had come out to the Cape on the same ship as Daniel Lee and was around the same age. As the imprisoned Edwards's route to activities beyond the prison walls, Lee was an obvious weak point amongst the alleged placard conspirators and Shee saw an opportunity to profit.[47] The 'noseless tailor', as he was known, was already an infamous figure on the streets of Cape Town, notable for a disfigurement suffered some two months earlier. Hudson, predictably, gives us a spirited account:

> A curious circumstance took place on Friday evening between a Mr Shea a Taylor and Mr Tilly a saddler two notorious characters. Some dispute took place that led to great warmth and at last came to blows. The wife of Tilly came to the assistance of her husband who actually bit off the Taylors nose and spit it upon the stoop. A surgeon was sent for and great search was made for the separated piece of the snout but so long a time had elapsed from the time of separation that tis doubtful wether the parts will adhere. Add to this that the surgeon had actually sewed the part on in a quite reversed state to what it was originally and had to separate it a second time. This most assuredly is a joke upon Snips misfortune but that it was bit off is most certain.[48]

Shee urged O'Grady that 'the servant of Mr Edwards was the only person who could lead to the discovery of the person who posted up the paper against His Excellency', and set him to work.[49] O'Grady duly walked the streets until he met up with Lee and casually brought the placard into the conversation. In response to leading questions, Lee admitted that he could show O'Grady a copy of the placard, and the following evening the two men repaired to the Sun, a new public house near the Barracks. In Lee's words O'Grady had 'asked me to come and take a bottle of wine with him in the evening and talk about our Sweethearts'.[50] In reality, O'Grady sought to pump him on the subject of the placard. Whether his purse had been lined by Shee for the purpose is not recorded,

---

[47] Testimony of Daniel Shee, TNA, CO 48/95.   [48] Hudson, Diary, 14 March 1824.
[49] Testimony of Daniel Shee, TNA, CO 48/95.
[50] Testimony of Daniel Lee, *RCC*, vol. 18, p. 94.

but as soon as he found Lee to be 'a little warm from the wine', he tried to get him off the subject of love, and onto the subject of the placard.

At first things did not go so well: 'I could not get him to tell me any thing about it. He was continually introducing his sweetheart in the conversation, but I was always wanting him to tell me about the placard.' O'Grady, however, was not done yet. He waxed lyrical on the cleverness of the writer of the placard, and the courage of those that had put it up, and eventually Lee admitted that he could get hold of a copy of the placard and promised to get it for O'Grady the next day. He 'called for a bottle of old wine', Lee would later claim, 'whether we had a second bottle, I don't know, I was very tipsy and he was just as bad.'[51] Filled with wine and emotion, Lee's discretion clearly began to get away from him and he admitted to his – and Edwards's – complicity in sticking up the placard.[52] Lee then returned to the subject clearly uppermost in his mind, his 'sweetheart', to whom he wanted to write a letter. Lee's literary skills were clearly not of the first order. Urging his point, O'Grady promised he would write Lee's letter for him in exchange for a copy of the placard.

The authorities were as assiduous in collecting information on Lee's courtship as they were upon the placard itself. When O'Grady later denied having written the love letter in question, he was presented with a copy in challenge to his evidence. Duly transcribed and filed by Colonial Office clerks, it now sits within the voluminous pages of evidence about Edwards's activities at the Cape:

My dear the sky was blue the wind was still the moon was shining clearly when I laid you down on the top of the hill near cape town so dearly. I have won your heart it was my intent, for I loved you most sincerely. I kissed you o'er and o'er again on the top of the hill so dearly. I locked you in my fond arms my heart was for you beating, my blessing on that happy place near cape town so dearly, up stairs and down stairs and upstairs so bonnie o I never shall forget that happy night I spent on the hill so dearly I remain Your Lover, D Lee.[53]

Whether Daniel Lee's sweetheart ever received this heartfelt masterpiece remains unrecorded. If it was delivered, then her 'Lover, D Lee' asked for it back, for beneath the letter are meticulously noted the requisite layers of official information gathering:

---

[51] Testimony of Daniel Lee, *RCC*, vol. 18, p. 94.
[52] Testimony of Roger O'Grady, TNA, CO 48/95.
[53] Evidence produced by Daniel Lee, TNA, CO 48/95. Line breaks in original.

> Exhibited by D Lee & Stated to have been written by Mr Shee's man June 5th 1824
> E Bergh 3rd Ass[istant] Clerk
> Exhibited to R J O'Grady 5th June 1824
> E Bergh 3rd Ass[istant] Clerk.[54]

By the time the fatal evening was over, a witness testified that Lee was so drunk that 'he was carried home in a litter'.[55] The next morning, no doubt nursing a hangover, Lee was arrested and hauled off to jail to be questioned by the fiscal over several days. He would pay dearly for his bibulous indiscretion. Daniel Lee would later claim that the placard he was discussing with Roger O'Grady was not the one about sexual relations between Barry and Somerset, but another which text began 'Offenders and Blacklegs', information that O'Grady's testimony confirmed. Either way, it put Lee in the hands of the fiscal, and he soon began telling all he knew – or claimed to know – about the real object of their enquiries.

Lee's evidence was the cornerstone of the case against Edwards. In the fiscal's opinion, it was Edwards's 'vindictive spirit' that had 'prompted him after the pronunciation of the Sentence for his transportation to New South Wales... to suggest to his associates the idea of publishing the Placard'.[56] Denyssen alleged that once the deed was done, Edwards had second thoughts and sought to distance himself as far as possible from his own action. The fiscal's report to the Commissioners of the Council of Justice asserted that on the basis of the investigations he had conducted between 4 and 12 June, Edwards was guilty of having composed and published the placard, and Bishop Burnett, George Greig and one Benjamin Wilmot were his accomplices.

The Council of Justice, however, disagreed, considering the evidence on the basis of the witness statements to be circumstantial and concluding that there were insufficient grounds for mounting a criminal prosecution against any of the alleged perpetrators. In defiance of the fiscal's report, by a resolution of 14 June the court ordered that Edwards be released from the solitary confinement into which he had been placed and restored to his rights of visitor access; that Wilmot be released from prison; and that Daniel Lee also be released, having cooperated with the authorities as 'informer'. Furthermore, authorisation to arrest Greig and Burnett was denied.[57]

---

[54] Evidence produced by Daniel Lee, PRO CO 48/95.
[55] Testimony of Louis Meurant, CA, CJ 3352.
[56] Fiscal to LCS, 7 July 1824, *RCC*, vol. 18, p. 66.   [57] *RCC*, vol. 18, pp. 119–20.

It was a slap in the face for the fiscal, notwithstanding their urging him to continue with his enquiries. Despite the failure of the investigation to come to any conclusion, Somerset remained adamant, writing confidentially to Bathurst that

> the suspicions attached to Benjamin Wilmot and his associates Wm Edwards (a convict under sentence of transportation for 7 years to New South Wales), Greig (the printer) and Bishop Burnett (an individual who came out here on speculation) have amounted to everything short of *legal* proof.[58]

Somerset was keen to discredit Wilmot before he could arrive in England to make 'representations or rather *mis*representations to Your Lordship or Government or Parliament', and he was fully alive to the broader political implications of the placard investigation, warning Bathurst that 'the enemies of the peace and tranquillity of this colony may have it in their contemplation to employ this man'.[59] As Somerset makes clear, the importance of the incident was how it could be turned to political account. The outcome of the official investigation was inconclusive, but the battle over the meaning of the placard scandal was only just beginning.

A 'sham plot'?

In the initial stages, public sympathy was very much with Somerset and Barry. Written testaments of support for the governor flooded in, and a public subscription was opened at the Commercial Hall offering a reward leading to the arrest of the culprits, adding to the amounts already offered by both Somerset and Barry.[60] Given the near impossibility of proving the accusations the placard contained, it was far more likely to do damage to opposition forces than to the government itself. The first mention of the placard in Hudson's diary (a day after it was posted up) is redolent not only of the ambiguous position in which it placed colonial Whigs and Radicals but also the difficulty of assigning meaning to the event:

> A most diabolical Placard has been stuck up concerning his Excellency Lord Charles Somerset with unnatural practises with Dr Barry it has thrown the whole Cape in consternation. If true it is pregnant with Infamy to the parties if false is a most convincing proof what length the malignant will go to ruin the character of this disgraceful man. The indignation of the public is fully shewn by a most liberal subscription to find out the author of this scandalous libel. Tis said Ten Thousand Dollars is already subscribed as a reward to whoever will discover the

---

[58] Somerset to Bathurst, 31 June 1824, incl. letter from Daniel Denyssen, Bathurst Papers, BL 57/54.
[59] Somerset to Bathurst, 31 June 1824.   [60] Somerset to Bathurst, 31 June 1824.

Author. How galling it must be to the friends of Lord Charles and Dr Barry there are many who will rejoyce to see these Arrogants tumbled but if innocent the scheme is a diabolical one.[61]

As Edwards recognised in his protestations of innocence to the Commissioners of Inquiry, the placard was potentially far more damaging to his own cause than it was to those named within it:

> no one man is more anxious to have its Author (if it has one) detected. It blasted all my prospects & all my schemes, which made me first suspicious of it. It was calculated to rise those who were sinking & to sink those who were rising. If it sho^d prove a sham plot, it will be a sorry one for its authors.[62]

For all that he was already seeking to distance his political cause from men like Edwards, Thomas Pringle was in agreement. Writing to his ally in Parliament, Henry Brougham, Pringle later claimed:

> The great object of the 'Placard Plot' was obviously to ruin our characters and defeat our better aims by *connecting* us if possible with these persons ['Radicals and Desperadoes – Edwards and Burnett'] in the eyes of the Public. Their object has, through the blessing of God, totally failed. But had the Commissioners of Inquiry not been here it *might* have succeeded as far as to serve for the time the purposes of the Government.[63]

Paradoxically, therefore, the placard initially presented an advantage to the government, despite the damaging accusations. The opportunities were twofold. The administration used the placard not only as an excuse for issuing search warrants against their critics, but also as a way of discrediting the opposition's political credentials by reducing their attacks on the administration to the level of outrageous muckraking. It therefore provided strategic benefit both in practical terms (in justifying searches and seizures of papers) and in terms of the ideological conflict going on over the actions of the administration.

Search warrants ostensibly issued to investigate the placard offered the possibility of uncovering other compromising documents. Problems soon arose for the administration, however, when nothing incriminating was turned up. Those subjected to investigation protested vehemently in the established language of liberty and quickly recast the placard affair as yet another instance of the administration's tyranny. Somerset complained to Bigge that

[61] Hudson, Diary, 2 June 1824.
[62] Edwards to Commissioners of Inquiry, 21 June 1824, TNA, CO 414/9.
[63] Pringle to Brougham, 20 Dec. 1824, *Letters of Thomas Pringle*, p. 152.

> Greig came to me at the Office just as it was dark yesterday & with a great deal of flippant expressions of respect was exceedingly impertinent – *demanding as a free-born Englishman* to know what the information was & by whom given, what occasioned me to issue my warrant for searching his abode.[64]

Pringle was outraged when a rumour reached him that the fiscal possessed a warrant to search his papers and wrote to Denyssen protesting that such a warrant could be issued only upon information given on oath, and 'no such information could be *justly* given respecting me'.[65] The recent editor of Pringle's letters calls the failure to 'clear his name' of any association with the placard 'unforgiveable',[66] and there is no doubt that Somerset and his allies found it useful for suspicion to hang around their enemies. But having failed to find anything incriminating, their actions could be quickly turned to the opposition's tactical advantage. Briefing Henry Brougham on anything useful he could contribute to the parliamentary campaign against Somerset and the Tories, Pringle promised him

> some further facts respecting the 'Placard Plot'. But all I can ascertain further of any consequence is that a Search Warrant with blanks left for the names was at the same time furnished which he [the fiscal] was intrusted to insert or withhold according as circumstances might seem to warrant – and that *my name* and that of Dr Philip stood on the list.

Somerset had taken this precaution that he and the fiscal might deny that they had ever signed a warrant with Pringle's name upon it. 'Of this fact I have many reasons to believe the accuracy, having had it vouched for from more than one confidential source.' In Pringle's view this 'furnished the Governor and the Fiscal with a salve sufficient for their consciences when they denied on their honour to the Commissioners that any warrant had ever been issued in regard to me'.[67]

As an eloquent testament of public support, the ever-increasing reward for information (reaching the huge sum of around 21 000 rixdollars[68]) was also initially to Somerset's benefit. He was certainly quick to use it as evidence of the degree to which his critics were merely a vocal minority of Cape inhabitants. Yet the amount of money involved was also a double-edged sword in a context in which paid informers were

---

[64] Somerset to Bigge, undated [1824], Bigge–Somerset Correspondence (original emphasis).
[65] Pringle to Denyssen, 11 June 1824, *Letters of Thomas Pringle*, p. 103.
[66] *Letters of Thomas Pringle*, p. 103, n. 74.
[67] Pringle to Brougham, 18 Dec. 1824, *Letters of Thomas Pringle*, p. 149. On the issue of the warrants see also Pringle to John Fairbairn, 13 Aug. 1825, p. 211.
[68] The enormity of the sum to men like Daniel Lee or Shee the tailor can be gauged by the fact that skilled artisans in Cape Town such as masons earned around 30–40 Rds a month. Mason, *Social Death*. p. 120.

an increasing political liability. One of the strongest arguments made against state-sponsored espionage in Britain over the previous decade was the assertion that anyone recruited into this role was by definition unreliable. Only the most despicable characters of society, it was argued, would stoop to spying on their fellow subjects. The increasing acceptance of this view in British public opinion is underlined by the difficulties that the authorities ran into in treason trials when they sought to rely on evidence secured by spies, difficulties that eventually led to the collapse of the late-eighteenth and early nineteenth-century spy system.[69]

Like the failure of their warrants against men like Pringle and Greig to turn up incriminating evidence, relying on drunken gossip gathered in a tavern, the paid evidence of Irish indentured servants and a 'notorious character' like Shee therefore put the government on the back foot. Edwards challenged the fiscal to 'produce one respectable man to swear I am the author or publisher of any anonymous placard'.[70] Rumours were rife in the town that Daniel Lee had perjured himself and that he had been bribed by the fiscal and the governor to give evidence that would prove the guilt of Edwards, Burnett and Greig.[71] Edwards hastened to disown his servant. He claimed that Daniel Lee had robbed his house and that he was 'supplied with dainties & foreign wines in Prison by the Fiscal', and promised £500 and a 'place under Government' to perjure himself.[72] Giving further evidence before the fiscal, Edwards said that he had discovered that Lee had appropriated several pairs of his 'trowsers'.[73] Having caught Lee in the act of theft, he protested in a letter to the commissioners, 'is it likely I would trust a thief with a secret so ruinous to my character'.[74] Edwards further alleged that the witness testimony was full of contradictions and false charges.

The fact that Lee had been entrapped into a confession upon an occasion of public drunkenness was common knowledge throughout the town, prompting commentary that his testimony was worthless.[75] Hudson wrote that many now wanted to take their names off the subscription list offering a reward on the placard, as it was 'so great a temptation to the cupidity of many of the venal tribe at this place'. Word was beginning to spread that there may have been no placard at all and that it was simply a ruse to discredit Somerset's enemies.[76] Certainly this was an opinion

---

[69] Porter, *Plots and Paranoia*, p. 37.
[70] Edwards to the Council of Justice, 11 June 1824, *RCC*, vol. 18, p. 116.
[71] Testimony of Murdoch McLoud, CA, CJ 3352.
[72] Edwards to Truter, 15 June 1824, TNA, CO 414/9.
[73] Testimony of William Edwards, CA, CJ 3352.   [74] TNA, CO 414/9.
[75] Hudson, Diary, 7 June 1824.   [76] Hudson, Diary, 11 June 1824.

that Edwards was expressing to the Commission of Eastern Inquiry some three weeks after the event:

The moment I heard of it I suspected it was written by the man who told me of it, or by some agent of Gov^t. Now I begin to think it is altogether a hum! as I am told there is only one man who ever saw it & him a person in whose word I wo^d place no great reliance – the paper cannot be found & none can tell what it was but Capt Findlay – no one saw it put up – none saw it pulled down or can tell who did it, or what became of it & although above 20000 rds are offered as a reward, no probable proof of the fact can be found.[77]

Public sympathy that had initially swayed in favour of Somerset and Barry began to shift, influenced by the large sums of money involved and the dubious circumstances of the witnesses – circumstances that seemed to confirm all the worst assumptions about paid informants. The 'Rascal Blood Money hunter Shee', as Hudson described him,[78] complained to the authorities that his name was being bandied about in catcalls in the street: 'watch that damned perjurer Lee – whether he is going to the house of Shee.'[79] Giving evidence before the fiscal, Louis Meurant testified that placards concerning 'Shee's nose' were being posted up around the town.[80] 'It seems one was stuck up some days since concerning Shee the noseless Taylor', reported Hudson, 'desiring him to take care that his Ears were not clipped for his rascality.'[81]

Predictably it was the most vulnerable person involved, Daniel Lee, who suffered most cruelly in the wake of the placard affair. After Lee was released from jail, Ingram demanded that he be returned to his service. He claimed Lee had only been lent to Edwards and was still under indenture to Ingram himself. The fiscal heard Ingram 'in a most unfriendly manner' declare Lee a '*blackguard* and Informer'. Lee was understandably reluctant to return to Ingram's service 'for fear of accidents', but was eventually forcibly escorted by the undersheriff to Ingram's estate 'Sonnebloem', where his fears proved only too well founded. The following morning the fiscal received news that Lee had been attacked by masked vigilantes.[82] He had been 'so brutally beaten' that the fiscal had to take him into protective custody in the hospital.[83]

Using reward money as bait to flush out the perpetrators of the placard affair may have seemed a logical response by the authorities, but in the ideological warfare that broke out in the wake of the scandal, it was

---

[77] Edwards to Commissioners of Inquiry, 21 June 1824, TNA, CO 414/9.
[78] Hudson, Diary, 29 June 1824.   [79] Testimony of Daniel Shee, CA, CJ 3352.
[80] Testimony of Louis Meurant, CA, CJ 3352.   [81] Hudson, Diary, 15 June 1824.
[82] *RCC*, vol. 18, p. 190.   [83] Fiscal to Somerset, 7 July 1824, *RCC*, vol. 18, p. 67.

a particularly dangerous tactic. Somerset already had a tarnished reputation for spying. Both sides of Cape politics used varieties of informal information-gathering, and Somerset certainly extended such practices into what we might more properly call espionage, using paid informants and covertly obtaining copies of opposition correspondence. Whatever their suspicions, all of this was hard for the opposition to prove and correspondingly difficult for them to use politically. But the administration's actions in the wake of the placard scandal provided something concrete upon which to hang these general suspicions. Plus there was an added advantage in being able to lay the government's actions at the feet of the man then considered to be the blackest villain in the history of British espionage.

Re-enter Oliver the Spy

Many of Somerset's troubles can be traced to his own making, but he must have felt it spectacularly unfair that he should have been chosen as the one to shelter the most notorious informer and agent provocateur of the age. Oliver the Spy's 1817 exposure had been politically damaging to Home Secretary Lord Sidmouth and to the government in general. In the wake of the scandal, and the associated outrage over his role in the executions and transportations that followed the Pentrich treason trials, it suited the interests of many in power that Oliver should speedily be got out of the way. A quiet colonial backwater beyond the immediate attention of the parliamentary opposition must have seemed an excellent choice.

In 1819 Henry Goulburn, the undersecretary of state, wrote to Lord Charles Somerset directing that a grant of land be made to one 'Mr William Jones whose object in proceeding to the Cape of Good Hope is to settle in that Colony'.[84] Three months later, Goulburn wrote again, recommending the services of 'Mr Jones a builder'. Nothing incriminating was put in the official record, but Somerset would have been fully alive to the implications of some very powerful people taking such an interest in a seemingly obscure emigrant. '[T]aking a very considerable interest in his behalf', wrote Goulburn, 'I cannot resist taking the liberty of bringing his name under your notice in the hope that you may be able to assist him by your recommendation if not to employ him on behalf of the public.'[85] (Oliver had been, in whistle-blower Edward Baines's words,

---

[84] CA, GH 1/25, no. 298.
[85] CA, GH 1/25, no. 299. It was ironically the acting governor, Sir Rufane Donkin, who actually oversaw Jones's initial employment, as Somerset was then on leave in England.

'a respectable builder' before he embarked upon his notorious career.[86]) And thus the most infamous of all Britain's domestic spies was sent to the Cape Colony in the hope of getting him off the public agenda. As the political situation in the colony went rapidly downhill during Somerset's fractious second term, what must have seemed a good decision in 1819 blew up spectacularly in the government's face. Given what was about to unfold at the Cape, it is perhaps hard to think of the Home Office settling on a more unfortunate destination.

Oliver's fate after Pentrich has been largely ignored by historians outside South Africa. If mentioned at all in histories of British politics, it rates a colonial epilogue, seemingly no longer significant to the issue at hand. Some have even been taken in by the official version of Oliver's disappearance. It is perhaps no surprise that one of the few scholars outside South Africa to recognise Oliver's colonial career is another historian of British politics operating from a former colonial periphery. Unaware of the harassment to which Jones the builder was subjected at the Cape, however, Paul Pickering suggests he 'found relative anonymity and a quiet life as a government inspector' there. He concludes that Oliver 'had escaped his past'.[87] Bernard Porter's wide-ranging history of British espionage goes even further, failing to recognise Oliver's colonial fate entirely and claiming that 'nothing was ever seen or heard of him again'.[88] In fact, nothing could be further from the truth. The historiography on Oliver the Spy underscores the way what should be seen as interconnected has instead been apportioned into discrete and mutually exclusive literatures dealing with either Britain or its colonies. Contemporary debates made no such easy divide.[89]

This was a point carefully made by Somerset (and conveniently forgotten by Donkin) during investigation into Jones's somewhat dubious career as a government builder at the Cape: *RCC*, vol. 23, p. 475.
[86] Baines (snr), *History of the Reign of George III*, p. 87.
[87] Pickering, 'Betrayal and exile, pp. 201; 213, n 5.
[88] Porter, *Plots and Paranoia*, p. 51.
[89] E. P. Thompson's monumental *Making of the English Working Class*, which gives significant attention to Oliver, ignores his colonial career, as does most of the other work of British historians. An exception is Hammond and Hammond, *The Skilled Labourer*, which provides a short account of 'Oliver's later history' in an appendix, written after they were alerted by the librarian of the South African Public Library. Even for the Hammonds, however, this colonial afterlife is clearly outside their topic of analysis. This failure to see any political significance in Oliver after his departure from the mother country is particularly glaring when we consider how frequently he appeared in both the British press and in parliamentary debates of the early 1820s. Conversely, Oliver's presence in the colony has never been a secret for historians of South Africa (understandably, given how prominently he appears in the sources), though the significance of his alleged activities at the Cape to an understanding of British politics remains

Pickering's research into former British spies in colonial Australia in the following decade demonstrates that Chartist informers James Cartledge and William Griffin were much more successful in hiding their pasts when they were sent to new lives, in Van Diemen's Land and New Zealand respectively. The contrast to Oliver is even more striking, since they did not even bother to change their names. Pickering's explanation for why these later informers were never exposed is suggestive. On the one hand, he argues that the growing success of Chartist principles and practices in the Australasian colonies in this period may have made exposing a traitor counter-productive. On the other hand, a convict colony required particular delicacy in enquiring into antecedents where so many were seeking to reinvent themselves. With so many seeking a new beginning, he concludes, 'it would be a mistake to underestimate the importance of forgetting in this process.'[90]

The Cape had no such scruples, and, perhaps more importantly, Oliver was far too useful in his new political context to be forgotten. Britain's most notorious spy would not only have a prolonged colonial afterlife, but his supposed activities on the periphery would provide a powerful feedback loop for metropolitan political debate. 'Oliver' had arguably always been more useful as an opposition symbol than he had been to the government interests he served. In the wake of the placard scandal, this paradox would become even more evident.

When Leeds journalist Edward Baines published his history of Oliver's initial exposure in 1820, there were already rumours in Britain that the spy had landed on his feet:

he no doubt trusted to the disposition of ministers to remunerate services like his. The results have shown that he was right; it is asserted on good authority (though we cannot vouch for the fact) that he has since been appointed to a lucrative place at the Cape of Good Hope.[91]

How precisely such vague accusations were pinned down to an individual is unclear, but it was certainly the widely held belief in 1820s Cape Town that the government builder William Jones and the notorious Oliver the Spy were one and the same. Jones himself even wrote to Colonial Secretary Bird seeking 'some suggestions of yours that may tend to pacify

---

equally undeveloped: see A. F. Hattersley, *Oliver the Spy and Others: A Little Gallery of South African Portraits* (Cape Town: Maskew Miller, 1959).

[90] Pickering, 'Betrayal and exile', p. 213. Although it should also be said that attempts to reinvent a new identity in convict colonies frequently ran into difficulties. See McKenzie, *A Swindler's Progress*.

[91] Baines (snr), *History of the Reign of George III*, p. 87.

'A conspiracy of the darkest and foulest nature'   239

the public mind at present so much prejudiced against me'.[92] Given the deliberate efforts to conceal the spy's new identity, it is impossible now to be absolutely sure, though the balance of probabilities points firmly in that direction. More importantly, for both the individual himself and for the purposes of political rhetoric, the truth hardly mattered. The allegation was powerful enough. In the early 1820s, the *Times* newspaper kept news of Oliver before the British reading public, publishing a full account of his destination, new occupation (somewhat exaggerated) and his supposedly secret alias at the Cape:

> It is *because* this man is *Oliver*, the spy, that he rolls in affluence at the expense of the nation.... But we would fain ask, must this horrible engine be naturalized in the British constitution?... Mr. *Oliver*, supported as he is by the Government, contrives to maintain his footing in this ill-fated colony, though his *pseudonym* has long ceased to conceal him from the inhabitants, who are more than anxious to be rid of his society – thinking, perhaps, that there is another English colony towards the South, in which he has more legitimate claims to a settlement.[93]

If Somerset, as we know, was using paid informants against the Cape 'Radicals', then we can be reasonably sure that Oliver was not amongst them. His notoriety hardly made him useful as either a covert operative or a conduit for clandestine information. The former spy was being carefully watched well before the placard incident. 'Oliver the spy seems to have engaged the attention of the Public', wrote Hudson in April 1824, 'his name being chalked up at the corners of most of the principal streets in Cape Town'. For all that Hudson considered Oliver to be Somerset's 'Jackall',[94] it seems reasonable to assume that 'Jones' pursued his trade merely as a builder (and a not very successful one at that) at the Cape.[95] But this did not stop opposition voices seizing on his presence in the wake of the placard scandal and transforming him into one of the most powerful symbols of the tyrannical excesses of the Somerset regime. His presence at the Cape was a continual referent in the hunt for the instigators of the placard. 'O Oliver Oliver', raged Hudson in his diary, 'thy political espionage will not answer in Africa tho the great man may need thy aid and assistance to counteract the vile exposures of thy truly ruinous

---

[92] William Jones to Lieutenant Col Bird, 9 Nov. 1821, CA, CO 145.
[93] *Times*, 5 April 1822 (see also 10 Aug. 1821).
[94] Hudson, Diary, 3 April and 11 Dec. 1824.
[95] Insolvent Liquidation and Distribution Account of the estate of Harriet Dear Widow of the late William Jones, 1827, CA, MOIC 2/328, no. 1148. William Jones was questioned before the Commission of Eastern Inquiry as to the expense of building works at the Cape: *RCC*, vol. 21, pp. 91–4. Christopher Bird made dark hints before the commissioners regarding Somerset's continued reliance upon Jones despite the latter's evident incompetence and misuse of funds: *RCC*, vol. 21, p. 168.

short-term benefits, but when nothing incriminating was found it put the government on the defensive. Even worse, by offering large rewards in their attempt to flush out the alleged perpetrators and by relying on testimony gained in dubious circumstances by marginal members of Cape society, the administration mired itself in accusations of spying. By so doing, they touched a sensitive political nerve about espionage that could be easily taken up by the opposition in the House of Commons.

Released from solitary confinement by order of the Council of Justice, Edwards would make good use of his relative liberty. In June 1824, he married the twenty-three-year-old Elisabeth (later anglicised as 'Elizabeth') Catharina Rens without leaving the confines of the jail: the Matrimonial Court authorities attended the couple in Edwards's own cell. 'This is certainly a Lady's going to the tread Mill', commented Hudson in his diary.[112] The same entry noted the departure of Greig, Burnett and Wilmot for London. There, wrote Hudson, they 'no doubt will keep a little stir where their concerns become canvased in the proper place'.[113] In their response to the placard scandal, the administration had transformed a general sympathy for Somerset and Barry, as the victims of outrageous allegations, into a widespread resentment against government tyranny. This had immediate political purchase in the Somerset impeachment drama playing out in London, and it carried wider implication for the debate over the Cape's political future.

Most of the alleged placard conspirators, departing the Cape for Britain as Edwards languished in jail, would play their parts in this wider drama. Under sentence of transportation, Edwards could not. Elizabeth Edwards chose to share her husband's exile and would prove amongst his most ardent supporters in New South Wales. Two and a half months after their prison-cell marriage, the couple departed the colony on the convict transport *Minerva*. Whether Edwards was guilty or not, the placard affair would prove to be his last action in influencing the ongoing debates over the practices of Cape governance. But it would by no means be the last of his challenges to imperial authority.

[112] Hudson, Diary, 11 July 1824. The marriage was registered at the Matrimonial Court on 13 July 1824: CA, CO 4572, no. 145. In the placard investigations, however, Elizabeth Edwards gives evidence under that name on 29 June 1824: CA, CJ 3352.
[113] Hudson, Diary, 11 July 1824.

9 Bring up the body
The many escapes of 'Alexander Edwards'

In September 1824 the arrival of the *Minerva* in Simon's Bay, across the peninsula from Cape Town, finally offered the possibility of getting rid of William Edwards. Now incarcerated on Robben Island and awaiting transport to a penal colony, he had been at the Cape a scant year, albeit one packed with incident. But as if determined to exact the full measure of drama from the time remaining him, what should have been a routine embarkation went far from smoothly. Edwards first suffered a near-shipwreck on being transferred to the mainland.[1] Next, en route to the transport ship *Minerva*, he managed to escape from right under the authorities' nose.

On 17 September 1824 Edwards was loaded onto a cart, accompanied by his wife Elizabeth and her sister. In the charge of Third Under-Sheriff Stillwell and a constable, both on horseback, the party set off for Simon's Bay.[2] At Wynberg dwelt a friend of Edwards, a retired sea captain named John Carnall. There, claiming to be ill and using the ruse of needing the 'night chair', Edwards managed to escape from the privy via the back door.

The escape caused a sensation. Hudson noted with delight that 'Dog Dan' and 'the Leviathon his Protector and Lord must feel equaly galled at being so humbled by this blunt man of Law'.[3] The news no sooner reached Cape Town than the fiscal himself rushed out to join the pursuit. Carnall was arrested and imprisoned in the Cape *tronk*, as was Under-Sheriff Stillwell. Charges flew thick and fast – against Carnall's wife, against a lodger in Carnall's house, against his servants. As the

---

The *Sydney Gazette's* portmanteau solution to his disputed identity, 6 Jan. 1829.
[1] In a letter of complaint to the fiscal, Edwards wrote 'I was in danger of losing my life (perhaps no great loss) & that of my wife.' More to the point, he sought reimbursement from the government for the loss of clothes, bedding and 123 sovereigns. He received short shrift from the fiscal, being reminded that he had pled *in forma pauperis* in court and the existence of the money could not be independently confirmed: Edwards to Denyssen, 14 Sept. 1824, and reply, CA, CO 212, vol. 1, nos. 89 and 90.
[2] Meurant, *Sixty Years Ago*, p. 68, quoting the *South African Chronicle*, 18 Aug. [sic] 1824.
[3] Hudson, Diary, 18 Sept. 1824, Hudson Papers, CA, A602.

245

advocate defending Carnall later put it with withering sarcasm, even 'the horse ... on which Edwards made his escape was actually taken into custody'.[4]

The horse's fate is not recorded. As for Carnall, he was kept in 'solitary confinement', as he later complained, in a cell 10 by 12 feet, for over three months. The tedium was enlivened by Barry, who, incensed by the escape of the alleged placard conspirator, came to the jail in person to harangue the unfortunate Under-Sheriff Stillwell:

I cannot help thinking what a d____d fool you was to let Edwards run away; I always thought what a very unfit man you were to be a sheriff's officer. If you had been a soldier you would have been shot for it. You ought to think yourself d____d well off that you were not a soldier.[5]

Carnall was sentenced to be transported for five years, a sentence commuted by Somerset to banishment from the colony for the same period.[6] He promptly made his way to London where his petition against ill-treatment, backed up by a traditionally lurid prison diary, provided further grist to the mill of opposition politicians seeking Somerset's impeachment.[7]

The authorities eventually discovered Edwards secreted behind the thatch partitions in an upper room of Carnall's house, concealed by his wife, apparently prostrate on a sickbed.[8] A violent struggle ensued. Edwards tried to slit his own throat with a razor but with his right hand pinioned by his captors, 'he was not able with his left to inflict a mortal wound'.[9] Observers saw an undoubted element of farce in Edwards's inventive escape at the Cape, his recapture and perhaps even in his bungled and theatrical attempt upon his own life. Yet viewed from the perspective of later events, the episode casts a much darker shadow. Sending a report to Governor Brisbane in New South Wales, Bigge noted that Edwards 'has since declared that he will never return alive to New South Wales or be landed there as a Convict'.[10]

[4] House of Commons, *Papers Relating to the Case of John Carnall*, 1826–1827, p. 18.
[5] *Papers Relating to John Carnall*, p. 10.
[6] Sentence upon John Carnall, 8 Nov. 1824, CA, CJ 818, no 21. For the distinction between 'transportation' and 'banishment' see Chapter 7.
[7] Carnall was eventually granted a full pardon by the king on 27 Aug. 1827: see despatch, 6 Sept. 1827, CA, GH 1/64. See also K. Bergemann, 'The murderers, the soldiers and the wrongfully accused: The role of transportation and banishment at the Cape in the first half of the nineteenth century', BA (hons) thesis, University of Cape Town (2007).
[8] *Papers relating to John Carnall*, p. 8.
[9] Somerset to Bathurst, 13 Oct. 1824, CA, GH 23/7, no. 119.
[10] Bigge to Brisbane, 24 Sept. 1824, *HRA*, 1:15, p. 269.

When he died on Norfolk Island on 9 June 1828, Edwards's suicide had been preceded by at least two previous attempts at ending his own life, and there may have been more. Although historians have differed as to whether convict suicide can be regarded as escape, to kill oneself as a prisoner under sentence is at least a measure of resistance against the carceral power of the state.[11] In repeated and diverse ways, Edwards's body and identity emerge as a route through which we can track another series of contentious debates being fought out in this period over the nature of the British colonial order. These involved not only the most appropriate mechanisms of surveillance, but also the limits of state authority in a penal colony that was taking on many of the characteristics of a 'free' society.[12] Edwards's serial escapes raised a series of related questions about the place of 'gentlemen' convicts in an authoritarian system, the jurisdictional ambiguities surrounding secondary punishment on penal stations and the overarching problems presented by the fluid identity of colonial subjects. Imperial reforms had tightened up systems of penal discipline to make transportation 'an object of real terror'. Yet with the connivance of sympathetic lawyers and newspaper editors, convicts like Edwards found ways to exploit the forces of law and public opinion in bringing accusations of 'tyranny' against colonial administrators. By doing so they exposed the limits of state control during the constitutional transitions of the 1820s.

The 'gentleman convict'

William and Elizabeth Edwards arrived in Sydney on 19 November 1824. It was almost exactly three years since a notice of Edwards's initial escape from the colony had appeared in the *Sydney Gazette* on 8 December 1821

---

[11] L. Ross, 'The final escape: An analysis of suicide at the penal settlement of Port Arthur', *Journal of Australian Colonial History*, 7 (2005), 181–202.

[12] A debate between John Hirst and David Neal in the 1980s thrashed out questions around whether New South Wales could be characterised as some version of a free or a slave society: D. Neal, 'Free society, penal colony, slave society, prison?', *Historical Studies*, 22:89 (Oct. 1987), 497–518; J. B. Hirst, 'Or none of the above: A reply', *Historical Studies*, 22:89 (Oct. 1987), 519–24; also Neal, *The Rule of Law*, and J. B. Hirst, *Convict Society and its Enemies: A History of Early New South Wales* (Sydney: Allen & Unwin, 1983). More recently, historians and legal scholars including Grace Karskens and Bruce Kercher have emphasised that the 'freedoms' that many interpretations identify were emerging in the 1820s and 1830s and had a much longer history. I would concur, as my discussion of the legal complications raised by the Kables' 1788 court case suggests, but I would still argue that in the establishment of a colonial press and in the constitutional changes of the New South Wales Act and subsequent legislation, a genuine shift can be seen in a longer story of the relationship between colonial freedoms and the carceral state. See Kercher, *An Unruly Child* and G. Karskens, *The Colony: A History of Early Sydney* (Sydney: Allen & Unwin, 2009).

signed by William Hutchinson, principal superintendent of convicts.[13] Immediately upon the *Minerva*'s arrival in Sydney from the Cape, the authorities identified Edwards as Loe Kaye. I discuss at some length later in this chapter the means by which they did so, but Hutchinson certainly played a prominent role. Once he was identified as a runaway convict, Edwards was sent some 400 kilometres north of Sydney to the penal station of Port Macquarie, 'as a place of greater security for desperate offenders'.[14] Elizabeth Edwards was permitted to reside with her husband at Port Macquarie, an 'indulgence' later made much of by Governor Darling in rebutting accusations of prejudice against the couple, though it was not in fact uncommon. Two children were born to them: a son in May 1825 and a daughter in December 1826. Elizabeth Edwards complained that her health suffered from the heat of the region, and in July 1827 the family was permitted to leave for the cooler climate of Bathurst, around 200 kilometres west of Sydney across the Blue Mountains. But problems soon arose again. As Governor Darling described it, the 'Magistrates . . . soon found it necessary to apply for his removal, as, having been bred an Attorney, he was intriguing with the Prisoners, and occasioning much trouble and dissatisfaction in the District'.[15] Edwards and his family were ordered to Wellington Valley, with permission for his wife and children to receive free rations from the government stores. Known colloquially as 'the Valley of Swells', this was a remote frontier outpost some 150 kilometres north-west of Bathurst, designed to separate 'gentlemen convicts' from the rest of the population.[16] Shortly before his planned departure for there, however, Edwards escaped to Sydney on 1 January 1828.

Ordering Edwards to Wellington Valley was characteristic of a broader shift in policy towards this troublesome category of convicts in the aftermath of the Bigge reports. As David Andrew Roberts's study of the Wellington Valley settlement argues, the debate over educated prisoners threw up a rich amalgam of assumptions about class, rank and power. With education that made them articulate and connections that could be manipulated to the embarrassment of colonial administrations, high-status convicts were dangerous forces in an interconnected world of imperial politics and the growing emancipist lobby of the 1820s.

---

[13] *Sydney Gazette*, 8 Dec. 1821.
[14] Brisbane to Somerset, 31 March 1825, Brisbane Letter Book, SLNSW, A1559, vol. 2, p. 169.
[15] Darling to Huskisson, 11 May 1828, *HRA*, 1:14, p. 165.
[16] D. A. Roberts, '"The valley of swells": "Special" or "educated" convicts on the Wellington Valley settlement 1827–1830', *History Australia*, 3:1 (2006), 11.1–11.20.

As Home Secretary Robert Peel recognised, problems arose 'from the extreme difficulty of finding a severe and disgraceful punishment applicable to a criminal, whose education and previous habits of life make it revolting to the general feeling, to class him with the ordinary victims of the law'. It is significant that Peel's words were written just as William Edwards was making waves in Australia upon his return from the Cape. These were exactly the kinds of activities the authorities sought to limit and, predictably, Kaye/Edwards (and his legal expertise) turned up in their discussions. When Peel wrote to Wilmot Horton criticising the idea of a purpose-built penitentiary for the elite in Britain, his imagined 'prisoner in the Gentleman's Magazine or by whatever name your new prison would be called' made reference to examples like 'young Kaye, the solicitor, who lately decamped'. In an unknowingly prescient comment he also anticipated Kaye's ultimate fate. Wilmot Horton had raised concerns that educated convicts might disturb the peace of the colony (and one cannot help thinking that two years of dealing with attacks like Edwards's on colonial administrations had influenced his views). Peel's solution to this imagined troublemaker was simple: 'If he does disturb it, send him to Norfolk Island.'[17]

Governor Ralph Darling was at first unconvinced about the policy of segregating 'Gentlemen Convicts' by sending them to settlements in the remote interior. Insistent attacks upon his administration, however, made him change his mind.[18] Darling is a far less extreme example of gubernatorial mismanagement than Somerset, but he was a similarly unfortunate choice for a colony entering a period of political tension between rival local factions – in this case the emancipists and exclusives. Wealthy emancipists and their allies claimed that they had as much right to civil responsibility as their equivalents in the mother country. The exclusives considered that former convicts should suffer permanent political disqualification based on their prior conviction. The more extreme amongst them insisted upon a hereditary inferior status.[19] The administrations of Somerset and Darling reached such heights of controversy that a Tory administration in London would replace both governors in turn with the avowed Whig Richard Bourke, clearly chosen in part to soothe ruffled local feathers when he was sent to the Cape in 1826 and subsequently to New South Wales in 1831.

In Darling's case it was less his propensity to act like a throwback to the eighteenth-century aristocracy than his rigidly hierarchical and militaristic outlook that contributed to these problems. As a Tory general,

---

[17] Peel to Wilmot Horton, 8 Feb. 1826, TNA, CO 201/175.
[18] Roberts, 'The valley of swells'.   [19] Neal, *Rule of Law*, pp. 12, 18–19.

Darling would not brook opposition, he was often inflexible and he was deeply unsympathetic to a rising wave of resentment against the political restraints of a penal colony. In his defence, he was undoubtedly also subjected to a continued and inventive tide of abuse from critics of the system over which he presided.[20] When Darling arrived in December 1824, these emancipist sentiments had found expression in the establishment just two months earlier of the *Australian* newspaper by two Sydney barristers, William Charles Wentworth and Robert Wardell. Two years later, Edward Smith Hall founded the *Monitor* newspaper, which (at least at first) was an even more outspoken mouthpiece in the same political interest.[21] Both papers would face repeated charges of criminal libel in the years to come, to the point that Hall spent significant periods of time editing his newspaper from a cell in Sydney jail.

Apart from their personal abilities, from 1824 the emancipist lawyers and newspaper editors held an important advantage in the person of the new chief justice, Sir Francis Forbes. Although Darling flatly accused Forbes of conspiring with government critics like Wentworth and Wardell to undermine him, the chief justice's position came more from Forbes's insistence of holding executive power to newly minted constitutional dictates. The judicial reforms that had followed the Bigge report found expression in the New South Wales Act of 1823, which Forbes had partially drafted. Forbes had in fact foreseen that conflict between Governor and Chief Justice would be inevitable under the terms of the act, and tried to tone down its provisions.[22] He was overruled, and the final version effectively gave the chief justice a veto over colonial legislation proposed by the governor, as all legislation had to be signed off by him as being not 'repugnant' to the law of England. As we saw in Chapter 7, it was this provision that allowed Forbes's insistence that Darling's actions against the New South Wales press were unconstitutional to prevail.[23]

Penal colony or not, the emancipists sought 'the rights of free-born Englishmen' for all (males) no longer under sentence. This was the general thrust of their political platform, whereas the specifics focussed around a proper system of trial by jury and an elected legislature, demands that Wentworth expressed in a widely read 1819 manifesto

---

[20] For a more sympathetic view of the governor see Fletcher's suggestively titled book *Ralph Darling: A Governor Maligned*.
[21] E. Ihde, *A Manifesto for New South Wales: Edward Smith Hall and the Sydney Monitor 1826–1840* (Melbourne: Australian Scholarly, 2004). The newspaper's political views shifted in the 1830s, in part as a result of financial pressure.
[22] Kercher, *An Unruly Child*, p. 84.
[23] Darling and Forbes would come into conflict again over the 1828 Australian Courts Act that further strengthened the power of the judiciary over the executive.

published in the midst of the Bigge enquiries.[24] In the absence of an elected legislature, the emancipists turned the newspapers and the law courts into a quasi-parliament. In cases prosecuted before the courts and reported in an emergent colonial press, the necessity and direction of constitutional change was a constant undercurrent, even in the most localised and ostensibly trivial contests.[25] Wardell and Wentworth were widely recognised as lawyers of spectacular ability, and they ran rings around their government opponents, using the impressive trappings of legal power against the state itself.[26] Did the ordinary liberties of the British people apply in a penal colony? This was the central political issue of the 1820s and 1830s. In this fundamentally law-infused world, it was a question that all sorts and conditions of men posed in legal and constitutional terms. In early colonial New South Wales, 'litigation was often politics carried out under another name.'[27] As the authorities recognised, it was a world of opportunity for a man like William Edwards.

'I shall be out of the reach of the Philistines'

On 11 January 1828 a prominent government notice appeared in the *Sydney Gazette*, offering £50 reward and a ticket-of-leave (which permitted convicts to earn their own living and live independently, subject to official surveillance over continued good behaviour) to any person who apprehended 'Alexander Lookaye *alias* Edwards' who had escaped from Bathurst. He was described as a native of North Wales, a lawyer of forty-four years, 5 foot 8¼ inches in height and 'rather bald, with brown hair, hazel eyes, and dark complexion'.[28] Edwards was said to be either in Sydney or on the road to it. The *Australian* would later deem the reward excessive and see it as a sign of conspiracy against the erstwhile

---

[24] W. Wentworth, *A Statistical, Historical, and Political Description of the Colony of New South Wales and its Dependent Settlements in Van Diemen's Land* (London: G. and W. B. Whittaker, 1819). It was issued in revised and enlarged editions in 1820 and 1824 and was widely read in Australia, Britain and beyond. Hudson purchased a copy at the Cape in 1824 (see his Diary, 10 Sept. 1824, Hudson papers, CA, A602). He was favourably impressed, particularly commenting on the accuracy of Wentworth's account of Governor Bligh, whom Hudson remembered without fondness from the time he had hosted the former governor at his Cape boarding house.
[25] Neal, *Rule of Law*.
[26] A. Atkinson, *The Europeans in Australia, A History*, 2 vols. (Oxford University Press, 2004), vol. II, *Democracy*, p. 55.
[27] Neal, *Rule of Law*, p. 88; Kercher, *Unruly Child*, p. 84. The term 'law-infused world' is L. Benton's: *Humanity* editors, 'Of pirates, empire, and terror: An interview with Lauren Benton and Dan Edelstein', *Humanity: An International Journal of Human Rights, Humanitarianism, and Development*, 2:1 (Spring 2011), 75–84.
[28] *Sydney Gazette*, 11 Jan. 1828.

whistle-blower on state corruption.[29] In fact, as the research of David Andrew Roberts into convict regulations shows, it is more likely to be part of a general punitive response to a wave of illegal convict movement from Bathurst in this period. The background to this pattern was the redeployment of convict gang and pastoral labour to outlying districts in the wake of the Bigge reports. When Edwards started using his legal skills to 'intrigue' with the prisoners of the Bathurst district, he was doing so in a tense situation with limited resources of law enforcement that had already been identified as a potential security risk by the colonial government. Post-Bigge measures designed to increase state control over convict discipline had proved profoundly destabilising, which was precisely the opposite of their intent. As Roberts argues, the Bathurst district had seen a rise in a connected series of incidents that involved convict disorder, bushranging activities and increased frontier violence against Aboriginal people.[30]

Edwards would not remain at large long. On the morning after the notice was posted, Saturday 12 January, 'private information' led the chief constable ('well armed') to the Sheer Hulk Public House in the Rocks. Here, in the heart of a neighbourhood notorious amongst the elite for its rowdy convict and emancipist community, Edwards was apprehended.[31] Edwards explained that he had left Bathurst for Sydney to seek a meeting with the chief justice. He wished to investigate rumours that a pardon had been issued in London but was being denied him by the local authorities.

In response, the authorities would later claim that far from coming to Sydney to speak to Chief Justice Francis Forbes, Edwards had been apprehended in the midst of planning another escape by sea to Batavia. These accusations were not made public at the time. They were first documented in response to a petition that Elizabeth Edwards sent to the secretary of state regarding her husband's mistreatment. By the time this petition had got to London and received a response from Darling in reply to a request from the secretary of state, Edwards had been dead for well over a year. Darling sent a copy to the secretary of state of a letter 'found with some trifling Papers, Copies of Letters and Memoranda'

[29] *Australian*, 16 Jan. 1828. On the *Monitor*'s highly gendered view of convict escape, in which male (though not female) convicts were given some leeway in resisting improper treatment, see E. Ihde, '"Bold, manly-minded men" and "sly, cunning base convicts": The double standard of escape', *Journal of Australian Colonial History*, 7 (2005), 123–38.

[30] D. A. Roberts, 'A "change of place": Illegal movement on the Bathurst frontier 1822–1825', *Journal of Australian Colonial History*, 7 (2005), 97–122.

[31] The maritime-orientated community of the Rocks was frequently implicated in convicts escaping by sea: G. Karskens, *The Rocks: Life in Early Sydney* (Melbourne University Press, 1998), p. 183.

that purported to show Edwards's true intentions in coming to Sydney in January 1828.[32] In a letter to an accomplice dated 6 January 1828, Edwards described himself as 'stowed on the Frederick, where it is quite impossible for me to be found', and he sought to make arrangements for his wife to follow him to Java after he had made his escape.[33] 'When this is delivered to you', he concluded, 'I shall be out of the reach of the Philistines.'[34]

It is not known why Edwards left the comparative safety of the *Frederick* and went ashore, but six days after this letter was written he was arrested.[35] Continuing to claim that his presence in Sydney was not an escape attempt, he was brought up for examination before the magistrates.[36] The Police Office was apparently 'thronged' with interested spectators, eager to know whether 'he were really guilty of any offence beyond absconding'. Edwards tried to raise the vexed issue of his identity, and even entered upon an explanation of the Dutch law that had transported him. It was an ironic reversal of his dealings with the authorities at the Cape: the police magistrate stopped him with the riposte that 'it was quite unnecessary for him to render any explanation of that description; he was now under *British* law.' The following day he was 'sentenced by the Magistrate to be removed, for better security, to such place in the Colony as his Excellency the Governor may think fit and proper to direct'.[37] In giving his account, Edward Smith Hall of the *Monitor* found it 'a hard case' and recommended that Elizabeth Edwards 'have her husband brought before the Chief Justice by *Habeas Corpus*, to procure him a patient hearing, which it seems was denied him before the Bench'.[38]

With his almost uncanny attachment to jurisprudential controversy, Edwards had just walked straight into yet another vexed debate in imperial governance. In this case the question was over the authority to transport offenders to penal stations. It was not the first time that issues regarding the procedures of secondary punishment had been raised in his case. In 1825, Governor Brisbane wrote to Commissioner Bigge (then at the Cape) to notify him of Edwards's fate in New South Wales. The 'case excited a good deal of interest here, and feeling, in his behalf', and Brisbane had acted against the advice of his own attorney general

---

[32] Darling to Murray, 23 Nov. 1829, *HRA*, 1:15, p. 264.
[33] The *Frederick* was delayed, finally leaving for Batavia on 29 Jan.: *Monitor*, 28 Jan. 1828; *Australian*, 30 Jan. 1828.
[34] Edwards to Dickson, 6 Jan. 1828 (enclosure in Darling to Murray, 23 Nov. 1829), *HRA*, 1:15, p. 265.
[35] *Australian*, 16 Jan. 1828.   [36] *Monitor*, 14 Jan. 1828; *Sydney Gazette*, 14 Jan. 1828.
[37] *Australian*, 16 Jan. 1828; *Monitor*, 21 Jan. 1828.   [38] *Australian*, 21 Jan. 1828.

on the matter. Nevertheless, concluded Brisbane, in identifying Edwards as a 'runaway from this Colony' he felt justified in sending him to Port Macquarie: 'I have acted upon my own responsibility, and my own construction of the Act of Parliament; and I am happy in thinking that the Council entertain the same opinion.'[39]

Brisbane's comment that Attorney General Saxe Bannister disputed his power to send convicts to places of secondary punishment reflected a heated debate then playing out between the various arms of the colonial government. Some ten days before Brisbane wrote this letter to Bigge, Forbes had received a petition from a group of convicts at Port Macquarie protesting the legality of their transportation there. The petition sought Forbes's intercession with the governor to curb the power of the magistracy to send convicts to penal stations. As Lisa Ford and David Andrew Roberts suggest, the petition 'signals a growing awareness amongst the most isolated and abject of convicts not only that gaps between the local practices and metropolitan penal law existed, but that they opened a space for contestation'.[40] For a man like William Edwards, legally trained and a veteran of challenging the boundaries of colonial jurisprudence, an awareness of the possibilities for challenging the system would be even stronger.

The New South Wales Act of 1823 had sought to bring constitutional order to the colony in the wake of the Bigge reforms. The problem with bringing the ad hoc arrangements of the penal colony under the sway of proper British legal procedure, was, as Ford and Roberts succinctly put it, that the result effectively 'turned local informality into illegality'. Indeed the process was 'so systematic that some portions of the Act had to be ignored'.[41] In particular, the Act addressed the legality of magistrates sentencing convicts to penal settlements and the procedures by which they should do so. There was a spike in absconding from Port Macquarie in the wake of the Act. Local legislation sought to formalise and particularise the power of the magistracy, but, as the 1825 petition shows, such initiatives failed to end a legal ambiguity that convicts were quick to exploit.

By the time a writ of *habeas corpus* was brought before the Sydney Supreme Court in March 1828 to produce the body of William Edwards, the authorities had tried to address this inconsistency. A flurry of legislation and enquiries into magisterial power at the local level was followed by the passage of the Transportation Act (6 Geo. IV. c.69) received in the

---

[39] Brisbane to Bigge, 21 March 1825, Brisbane Letter Book, SLNSW, A1559, vol. 2, p. 169.
[40] Ford and Roberts, 'Legal change', 176.   [41] Ford and Roberts, 'Legal change', 180.

colony in 1826. It shored up magisterial power over non-capital crimes committed by convicts, as well as confirmed the power of the governor to appoint sites of secondary punishment. Enough questions had been raised, however, to leave a strong legacy of jurisdictional doubt, and these would flavour the discussions over who had the right to send Edwards to Norfolk Island. In addition, proper attention to procedural niceties could still be shaky at the magisterial level, providing potential pressure points for litigants. At issue, argued Edwards's counsel, was not only the sloppy practice of the magistracy (they had not passed a sentence, but merely 'recommended' the matter to the governor) but also the fact that the governor did not possess this power, 'except in pursuance of the sentence of a competent Court'.[42] Forbes was in agreement that the '*quasi* sentence', as he put it, was not 'sufficiently explicit', and he issued a writ of *certiorari* ordering the lower court to go through the process again. Nevertheless it was, he claimed, 'clearly within the jurisdiction of the Magistrates, and one on which they had authority to order punishment'. The legal wrangling had significance far beyond the individual circumstances of Kaye/Edwards. Paul Halliday's monumental study of *habeas corpus* across Britain and its empire includes the case to demonstrate how the New South Wales Supreme Court endorsed the 'enormous discretion that local statutes accorded magistrates' even when their practice of legal procedure was at fault.[43] This systematic failure by the Supreme Court to intervene in cases deemed under magisterial authority did much to strengthen punitive master and servant laws in both New South Wales and Van Diemen's Land.

Brought before the bench of magistrates once more, the prisoner handed in a written address to the bench, 'imploring them to deal with him as with runaways in ordinary cases,[44] and to order the most debasing punishment to be inflicted on his person, but not to separate him from his wife and children'. His pleas were to no avail. On 2 April 1828, after 'remaining in consultation for some time', Edwards was sentenced by the bench 'to be transported to such penal settlement as His Excellency

---

[42] *Sydney Gazette*, 10 March 1828.
[43] Halliday, *Habeas Corpus*. Halliday notes that the case 'echoed hundreds of seventeenth-century cases where JPs made insufficient warrants' in the mother country (p. 296).
[44] David Andrew Roberts's analysis of illegal convict movement on the Bathurst frontier documents a general tolerance of temporary absenteeism as routine and habitual convict behaviour, so long as convicts returned. Those convicted of attempting to escape were generally punished locally, though some were sentenced to be transferred to Port Macquarie. Transportation to Norfolk Island was indeed, as Edwards argued, not a common outcome. Rather, as Darling reported to London, it was a response to his perceived repetitive challenges to colonial authority. Roberts, 'A "change of place"', 108, 112–14.

256   Imperial Underworld

the Governor should think proper to appoint, for the term of three years, and to be kept to hard labour during that period'.[45]

Edwards's final escape

If hard labour was part of Edwards's sentence, the state received very little out of him. Probably this was less important than the hope that sending him to a 'place of greater security' would also remove him from the glare of publicity. By committing suicide shortly after his arrival on the island, Edwards frustrated either such intention. It was the third known attempt he had made on his own life, and there may have been more.

Edwards made his second suicide attempt [Figure 9] upon being ordered to Port Macquarie shortly after his return to Sydney:

> Upon his return to the Barrack at Hyde Park, he paced the room for some moments, apparently considerably agitated, and was soon observed to seize a tin vessel; this he half filled with water and then mixed up a powder, which he took from his pocket.... The draught was taken, and followed by the words '*Farewell, Port Macquarie!*'

Holding the poison to his mouth, he railed against the late superintendent of convicts for identifying him as Kaye, saying 'that he thought Mr. Hutchinson would have been the last person in the world to come forward against him'. He began writing a letter to his wife, but had got no further than the first line when he collapsed from 'excessive agitation'. Rushed to the hospital, 'where he became dangerously ill', he was forced to take an antidote. The *Gazette* warned that it was only a matter of time before he would make another attempt and urged leniency on the authorities on the grounds of what we might call mental illness:

> There cannot be the least doubt but that his mental suffering is excessive, and could any leniency be exercised by the Government towards such an object of extreme commiseration, it might tend to heal the mind, and prove effectual in preserving existence. Should he even be the character represented, perhaps it would be more charitable to mitigate woe, than render punishment ultra-excessive. We by no means wish to advocate the cause of Edwards; it is humanity forces us to speak.[46]

When Edwards did finally succeed in taking his own life, it was with a great deal of determination. He may or may not have exercised his

---

[45] *Sydney Gazette*, 2 April 1828; also accounts in *Monitor* and *Australian*, both 2 April 1828.
[46] *Sydney Gazette*, 2 Dec. 1824.

Figure 9 The convict barracks at Hyde Park, Sydney, where Alexander Loe Kaye worked as a clerk during his first period in New South Wales. As William Edwards he attempted suicide while confined here in 1824.

undoubted skills in persuading others to turn a blind eye. Certainly the *Monitor* was suspicious:

> The hut in which he was found hanging, was only eight feet high from the ridgepole; and the hut was crowded with three men besides himself. It must therefore be considered a very marvellous circumstance, that a man unperceived by his comrades, should have terminated his existence by hanging himself.[47]

The *Gazette* claimed that Edwards had planned his suicide as soon as he knew that Norfolk Island was to be his destination. Far from having been done away with by his cell-mates (as the *Monitor* had implied) he had secretly manufactured a cord in preparation. 'Whilst in prison [awaiting shipment to Norfolk Island] he made several attempts to destroy himself by poison, and starvation; having at one time, swallowed a quantity of laudanum, and, at another, fasted for fourteen days.'[48]

Edwards was 'decently interred, and the burial service read at the grave' as a consequence of being declared temporarily insane.[49] This reflected shifting attitudes towards suicide that had also seen recent changes to the law in Britain (and thus in Australia). As both a sin and a felony in criminal law, suicide was punishable in both the legal and religious realms. Suicides underwent posthumous trial by a coroner's jury and, if found guilty, heirs faced confiscation of their property. The corpse was denied burial in consecrated ground and could even be interred under a crossroads with a stake through the heart. Coroners' juries were increasingly reluctant to enforce these rules, however, and so frequently returned verdicts that found the deceased innocent of the crime of self-murder by reason of temporary insanity.[50] In 1823 the custom of profane burial was abolished by an act of Parliament. The rules on forfeiture of property would follow only in 1870.

Despite these changes, studies of convict suicide have emphasised the continued and widespread belief in this period that suicide was an offence against the dictates of Christianity. The data on convict suicide is patchy. Systematic underreporting by the authorities in institutions is likely, given that convicts were cheating justice of its due by taking their fate into their own hands and out of the control of the administrators.[51] Lynette Ross's study of suicide at Port Arthur underlines both the difficulties of interpreting the meanings of such acts and the wide variety of circumstances in which convicts took their own lives. Some appear to have been public

---

[47] *Monitor*, 20 Dec. 1828.   [48] *Sydney Gazette*, 6 Jan. 1829.
[49] *Sydney Gazette*, 8 July 1828.
[50] P. Jalland, *Australian Ways of Death: A Social and Cultural History 1840–1918* (Oxford University Press, 2002), p. 274.
[51] Ross, 'The final escape', p. 198.

and overt acts of resistance, as when a convict refused food in protest and starved himself to death. Some appear much more impulsive and opportunistic, as when convicts threw themselves overboard. Other acts were done in private, and elaborate precautions were taken to ensure they remained undisturbed while the deed was carried out. The form of convict suicide that attracted the most attention was when convicts attacked one another in order to end their own lives by judicial murder. Execution by hanging provided the advantage of death without the danger of eternal damnation.[52]

The problem in assigning meaning to Edwards's suicide mirrors the challenge of coming to an understanding of his curious career as a voice for colonial reform. The intolerable strain under which he had been placed is undeniable, and his death followed a pattern of previous suicide attempts. Yet even on Norfolk Island, suicide was very rarely chosen as a course of action by convicts under sentence. Reading the mental state of the past is more than usually difficult in the case of Edwards, whether in life or in death. Even those who encountered him during his periods of freedom struggled with whether to dub him a 'maniac', a 'champion' or a 'desperado'. Somerset claimed of Edwards that 'he is by some considered as far from being in sane mind'.[53] Those who witnessed his sufferings as a convict used words such as 'madman', or urged leniency in order 'to heal the mind'. It is clear that many who encountered him face-to-face were at a loss as to whether to judge him sane or mad.

Can we do any better on the basis of the surviving manuscript evidence? If Edwards made paranoid claims of being surrounded by shadowy conspiracies and constantly plotting enemies, then so did Governors Somerset and Darling. In the light of what we know of the faction-filled world of imperial politics, it seems only fair to judge persecution anxiety an entirely rational response. If the written records Edwards has left us seem undeniably tinged with a strand of ranting incoherence, even the most cursory glance at press, courtroom or parliamentary records reminds us that impassioned and convoluted political rhetoric was very much an accepted genre of his period. Were Edwards to be judged insane on these grounds, then so must most early nineteenth-century colonial

---

[52] L. J. Clarke, '"Lost to all humanity"? Suicide, religion and murder pacts in convict Van Diemen's Land', unpublished BA (hons) thesis, University of Tasmania (2002). Murder–suicides did occur in the Australian convict system, yet they also gave rise to a lurid mythology that more recent research has debunked. As mentioned in the Introduction, one of the most enduring stories about the horrors of Norfolk Island was that of the 'suicide lotteries' in which men would draw straws and offer themselves up for death.

[53] Somerset to Bathurst, 21 May 1824, *RCC*, vol. 17, p. 350.

governors, lawyers, newspaper editors and MPs. In the final analysis, what led Edwards to kill himself is perhaps as unknowable as the vagaries of his mental state or the underlying motivations of his challenges to imperial authority. What is easier to untangle, however, are uses to which his death would be put. In death, as in life, Edwards remained a name to conjure with.

'Edwards, alias Lookaye': a convenient untruth?

The news of the 'melancholy catastrophe' reached Sydney in July 1828. Papers that had tracked his adventures across four eventful years now gave brief notice of the death of 'Edwards, alias Lookaye'. 'Thus terminated the life of this unhappy man', concluded the *Sydney Monitor*. 'If he be not the person he denied he was, never was a British subject more oppressed. If he were, he had met a severe punishment for his fraud.'[54] As always, his disputed identity was the heart of the problem. The ongoing mystery made it impossible for either side in the struggle over political rights in New South Wales to label Edwards definitively as either shameless fraudster or political martyr.

In the forces gathering against Governor Darling, Edwards's sufferings played a relatively muted part in comparison to other allegations of tyranny.[55] William Wentworth claimed to the secretary of state that Edwards had been 'driven' to suicide by Darling's 'barbarous and illegal conduct'.[56] Writing shortly after Edwards's death, Edward Smith Hall was incensed by assertions that Darling's supporters had made about the governor's 'humane character'. In rebuttal, the *Monitor* painted the picture of a man whose humanity had been corrupted by his excessive attachment to military discipline. 'In judging of Governor Darling as to his general character for tenderness of heart and sympathy, let us consider various other acts of his Government', wrote Hall. The catalogue of crimes took more than two full pages of closely packed newsprint to detail.[57] In 1835 the case of 'Alexander Edwards' would be mentioned,

---

[54] *Monitor*, 21 July 1828.
[55] Amongst the key accusations was the 'Sudds and Thompson' affair centring around the punishment of two privates, Joseph Sudds and Patrick Thompson, for theft and the death of the former in custody.
[56] Wentworth to Sir George Murray, 1 March 1829, enclosure in Darling to Murray, 28 May 1829, *HRA*, 1:14, p. 857; *Report from Select Committee on the Conduct of General Darling, while Governor of New South Wales*, BPP 1835 (580), pp. 162–3. See also 'Vindex', *Australian*, 14 Jan. 1831, who catalogued Edwards's mistreatment by the regime, while still recognising that he was (and the writer claimed to have known him well) 'a troublesome, perverse, officious, and dangerous character'.
[57] *Monitor*, 20 Dec. 1828.

albeit briefly, in the impeachment charges that were finally brought against Darling in Parliament.[58] Yet for all his appearance in these arguments, Edwards's identification as Kaye would always undercut his usefulness to opposition voices, in New South Wales no less than had been the case at the Cape or in Britain after his convict background surfaced there. Even Hall saw the dilemma. The *Sydney Monitor*, Edwards's staunchest public supporter in New South Wales, acknowledged that if the two were indeed one and the same, then punishment (albeit less severe than the savage fate of transportation to Norfolk Island) was owed for his 'fraud'. For the authorities, of course, it more than justified any actions taken against him.

Edwards went to his death claiming that his identification as Alexander Kaye was a government conspiracy backed by the powerful Beaufort family. As always, the point at issue was not only of vital significance to him personally, but also carried broader political implications of corruption and patronage. Profound disquiet existed at the highest level over the legality of Edwards's transportation from the Cape for libelling Somerset. As we have seen, Bathurst had instructed Somerset to release Edwards and send him to England. In the context of sustained criticism of the Cape regime in London, the secretary of state was determined to investigate the botched legal proceedings of the libel trial. Yet any injustice that Edwards had claimed was clearly irrelevant if he was in reality the escaped convict Alexander Kaye. It was from the Cape that Bathurst first received news of Edwards's disputed identity, along with the information that he had already left that colony and could not be returned to London as the secretary of state required. Bathurst now sent instructions to New South Wales to have the matter investigated there. The implications that Edwards's identity would have for his fate were baldly stated in the directions to Governor Brisbane of June 1825:

As there is reason for believing that a person calling himself William Edwards, may have recently arrived at New South Wales from the Cape under a Judicial Sentence of Transportation – I have to desire that you will take measures for releasing such person from any restraint, under which he may be placed, and for facilitating his return to England, unless it should appear, upon enquiry, that William Edwards should be identified as the Convict Alexander Low Kay.[59]

So if Edwards could prove he was not Kaye, then he would be released and the authorities would facilitate his return to England. On the other hand,

---

[58] House of Commons, Debates, 30 July 1835, vol. 29, cc. 1254–75, hansard.millbanksystems.com/commons/1835/jul/30/general-darling#S3V0029P0_18350730_HOC_59.

[59] Bathurst to Brisbane, 20 June 1825, *HRA*, 1:11, p. 671.

if Kaye and Edwards were one and the same, the entire embarrassing problem would go away. The upshot of Somerset's bungling would for once have been beneficial to the Colonial Office, for it could be cast in an entirely new and positive light. Instead of a miscarriage of justice easily exploited by the parliamentary opposition, they could offer up to public opinion the case of a notorious escapee who had been returned to serve out the remainder of a perfectly unexceptional sentence. Was the identification of Edwards as Kaye a convenient untruth? Given the profound advantages that existed for so many people in declaring the two men one and the same, it is worth taking some time to consider both the general manner of convict identification and the plausibility of accusations of conspiracy in this particular case. The convict system was in part dependent upon its ability to fix identity and track individuals. But Edwards was by no means alone in the way he exploited the manifold difficulties presented by doing so.

The records of the convict system pin down its subjects to the barest set of observations, attempting to fix identity through measurable observations such as height, and the colour of eyes, hair and 'complexion'.[60] Such descriptions were needed to verify identity, keep track of movement and punishment and prevent escape. But they are also the product of a whole series of interpersonal and bureaucratic interactions, including misinformation, bribery and simple human error. Frank Clune's account gives some credence to the differences in the convict records made of Edwards and Kaye. My own judgement would be that they are too subtle to be in any way conclusive.[61] Differences in eye colour and complexion are subjective descriptions, dependent upon both personal choice and external factors such as the light conditions during observation. As Clare Anderson's study of the Indian transportation system puts it succinctly, the authorities were faced with the problem of 'the subjectivity of clerks' descriptions, coupled with the instability of bodily appearance'. Convict record keeping, as she argues, sought the 'textualization of the criminal

---

[60] In the case of Kaye/Edwards: SRNSW, Principal Superintendent of Convicts, Convict indents, NRS 121 88: 4/4006, p. 397, 4/4003A, p. 110, A/4009A, p. 123.

[61] The ¾-inch difference in the heights of 'Edwards' in 1824 and 'Kaye' in 1819 is insubstantive and may have been the result of human error. Variations occur even in the measurement of those we know should have been the same. 'Kaye' was recorded with a height of 5 feet 7¾ inches when transported in 1819 on the *Atlas*, but he had measured 5 feet 7½ inches in the Gloucester Gaol records less than a year earlier: Gloucester Archives, Gaol Calender, Q/Gc 5/2. If we compare these data with the description recorded of the Cato Street Conspirator George Edwards (with whom we know William Edwards was wrongly confused at the Cape) there are also similarities. TNA HO 44/4/69 ff247–8. Cato Street conspiracy: R. F. Chambers, Union Hall, with descriptions of John Peeling alias Privett and George Edwards. My thanks to David Andrew Roberts for this reference.

Bring up the body 263

body' in a continual battle between the state and convicts themselves.[62] Observation and record keeping had a practical purpose; it was also intended to subject the prisoner's body to the humiliation of surveillance by the state.[63]

Embracing efficient practices of data collection did not prevent advantage being taken of the system. In 1800 Governor King uncovered a scheme whereby corrupt government clerks were being bribed to alter a convict's term of transportation.[64] The *Australian* was concerned that official records were far too easily accessible to 'any decently dressed person' and could be altered 'to meet a political end'.[65] In 1832, two brothers, Patrick and Owen Flanagan, switched identities in an attempt to gain early release from the Moreton Bay penal settlement. Patrick was the taller by an inch, according to the records, but Owen was still able to secure a certificate of freedom by impersonating his brother.[66]

Even the most meticulous and humiliating methods of bodily record-keeping could be manipulated by determined convicts. Anderson's study of *godna*, the system of tattooing Indian convicts with identifying information, emphasises that what might be easily regarded as the ultimate 'inscription of colonial power on the body' was nonetheless marked by repeated challenges and was uneven and diverse in practice.[67] Furthermore, for all the vast empirical data collected by the convict system, it is clear from the disputes over Kaye and/or Edwards that in the 1820s gossip, hearsay and qualitative information loomed just as large in official practice as did the collection of supposedly concrete statistical information. It was upon these kinds of information that the authorities based their conclusions about Kaye and Edwards.

Edwards's association with Kaye appears to have happened independently at the Cape and in New South Wales. It surfaced at the Cape just after he was embarked upon the *Minerva* as she rested in Simon's Bay.[68] The earliest evidence we have for the link between Kaye and Edwards is

---

[62] C. Anderson, *Legible Bodies: Race, Criminality and Colonialism in South Asia* (Oxford and New York: Berg, 2004), pp. 3, 9.
[63] Linus Miller (an American citizen transported to Van Diemen's Land in 1840 after being captured trying to overthrow British rule in Canada) gave a searing account of the dehumanising nature of these experiences in his memoirs: *Notes of an Exile to Van Diemen's Land* (New York: Fredonia, 1846).
[64] Hirst, *Great Convict Escapes*, p. 221. [65] *Australian*, 16 Dec. 1824.
[66] Once Owen was free, the real Patrick came forward to demand release on the basis of misidentification. Owen was eventually caught and sent back to serve out his sentence. Patrick, despite his collusion, was allowed to keep the certificate of freedom. Hirst, *Great Convict Escapes*, p. 222; *Sydney Gazette*, 22 Dec. 1832.
[67] Anderson, *Legible Bodies*, p. 2.
[68] *Cape Town Gazette*, 25 Sept. 1824, notes that Edwards was 'safely embarked' upon the *Minerva* 'on Thursday last' (i.e., 23 Sept.)

dated one day later, 24 September 1824, in a letter from Commissioner John Thomas Bigge to Governor Brisbane of New South Wales. At this point Bigge *suspected* (but did not know for sure) that 'Edwards was a Convict, when he was formerly in New South Wales, and that he made his escape from Transportation'. He based this supposition on two grounds. First there was the fear that Edwards had expressed at being returned to New South Wales, a fear to which Bigge ascribed 'the late desperate attempt that he made upon his own life, he first assigned as a reason the separation from his Wife, yet he has since declared that he never will return alive to New South Wales or be landed there as a Convict'.[69]

If Edwards's fear of Botany Bay was the first reason for Bigge's suspicions, the second was a letter that Bigge described as 'written in answer to an enquiry by a respectable Individual in this place, concerning the Character and History of Edwards'. Written from 'J. F.' in Chester to 'F. R.' at the Cape, an extract was duly included in Bigge's brief to Brisbane:

There was an Attorney at Flint, of the name of Shackville [actually Shackfield], who had only one Daughter,[70] who married a Mr. *Alexander Lowe Kay* who was a short time a Banker in Flint, afterwards in a public office in Chester, and after a number of notable exploits there and in other places, was ultimately transported to Botany Bay for stealing a Horse and Gig. I have never heard of him since.

William Edwards, claimed Bigge, had seemed to confirm aspects of the letter in his own descriptions of his past. He 'has always avowed his connection with North Wales, and has stated that his Wife's Name was Sackville and that she was connected with the Noble Family of Dorset'. Outlining the reasons for Edwards's transportation to New South Wales, Bigge warned Brisbane to expect a troublemaker who had complained to Earl Bathurst of the illegality of his sentence from the Cape. In order for Brisbane to 'form a judgment of the desperate character of Edwards', Bigge enclosed a printed account of his escape, recapture and attempted suicide.[71]

A few weeks later, Bathurst was sent the news of Edwards's alleged identification as Kaye by both the Commissioners of Inquiry and Somerset himself. Neither gave specifics to the secretary of state as to the source of the information they had obtained, but both provided detailed versions of Kaye's background.[72] Although the accounts have some errors, they

---

[69] Bigge to Brisbane, 24 Sept. 1824, enclosure in Darling to Murray, 23 Nov. 1829, *HRA*, 1:15, p. 269.
[70] It was in fact Susannah Shackfield's *uncle* (not her father) who was the attorney. He died in 1794.
[71] Bigge to Brisbane, 24 Sept. 1824.
[72] Bigge and Colebrooke to Bathurst, 11 Oct. 1824; Somerset to Bathurst, 13 Oct. 1824, *RCC*, vol. 18, pp. 442, 494.

are substantially correct, and it is significant that Somerset and the commissioners all get the name 'Alexander Low [or Lowe] Kay' more or less right, suggesting that the source of their information was England rather than New South Wales, where the name was more usually given as 'Lookaye' or 'Lockaye'.

Edwards was identified as Kaye as soon as he docked in New South Wales. Less than twenty-four hours after the arrival of the *Minerva*, Brisbane's private secretary, Major T. Ovens, sent word to Somerset enclosing a 'hasty Statement' by the late principal superintendent of convicts, William Hutchinson, that identified Edwards as Kaye.[73] According to the *Australian* newspaper, it was William Hutchinson who 'was the first to recognize him on board the Minerva'.[74] This was presumably on the basis of physical resemblance. Only three years had passed when the *Minerva* docked in Sydney, and it is unlikely that Kaye had changed so much as to be unrecognisable.

A week later, on 27 November, Edwards was examined before magistrates at the Police Office in order to confirm in a more official manner what was already suspected. Various witnesses were brought forward to testify as to his previous identity. 'He at length acknowledged having been in the Colony, but declined stating when, or in what capacity, as he said he was bound by oath not to reveal the circumstances connected therewith.'[75] Nonetheless, his identity was declared confirmed, and he was ordered to be sent to Port Macquarie.

We appear therefore to be faced with two separate and independent moments in which Edwards was identified as Kaye. One arose in Cape Town, where unverified rumours from unnamed sources surfaced towards the end of his time there. From what we know of the ways in which seemingly separate colonial outposts were connected by the transfer of information, this should not surprise us. We know that former convicts were coming through Cape Town, that gossip connected Cape Town with communities in Britain and that people could be recognised and their past lives revealed to their new neighbours. Some of these identifications were patently false (William Edwards was *not* George Edwards, the Cato Street conspirator). Others were not. The second moment of

---

[73] Somerset to Bathurst, 27 Aug. 1825, enclosed letters from T. Ovens and W. Hutchinson, both 20 Nov. 1824, *RCC*, vol. 23, pp. 24–6.

[74] Several Australian newspapers (*Australian*, 16 Dec. 1824; *Sydney Gazette*, 7 May 1828; *Monitor*, 12 May 1828) named Hutchinson as the man who identified Edwards, though in strict accuracy it should be noted that the letter enclosed to Somerset signed by Hutchison merely describes the career of Lockaye. It was Ovens who made the connection between the two in the covering letter.

[75] *Australian*, 2 Dec. 1824; *Sydney Gazette*, 2 Dec, 1824.

identification came in Sydney, with the recognition by Hutchinson. The former chief superintendent of convicts would have had ample opportunity to observe Kaye who had worked for a period as a clerk in the prisoners' barracks. The idea that he was recognised by sight is entirely plausible. This was followed by an official investigation, with numerous witnesses giving testimony of their personal dealings with the accused and their recognition of Edwards as Kaye. But, given what we also know of imperial information exchange, were the identification at the Cape and the identification in Sydney two separate processes?

When the *Minerva* docked in Sydney it carried not only Edwards but also two letters concerning him addressed to Governor Brisbane. One was the letter from Bigge quoted earlier, identifying Edwards as 'Alexander Low Kaye'. The other was a letter from Somerset dated 16 September 1824 that has not survived.[76] Can we speculate that the identification in Sydney followed from the identification at the Cape? To put it more bluntly, was the political embarrassment of Edwards neutralised by false (and extremely convenient) information cooked up by the Cape authorities that discredited him as an escaped convict? Although we cannot know this for certain, it seems unlikely. Too many people, and from too many varied backgrounds, appear to have recognised Edwards as Kaye when he landed in Sydney. The initial identifications of 1824 were not the final word on the matter. As I will detail, a second more extensive investigation was made in 1826. Finally, a detailed report into the question and all the steps that had been made to prove Kaye and Edwards to be the same person was provided by Governor Darling in 1828. To accept a government conspiracy would be to accept the complicity not just of Somerset, Bigge, Colebrooke, Brisbane and Darling, but also of a whole host of minor officials, free settlers, emancipists and convicts. We also need to take into account the strength of the opposition forces in New South Wales and the ingenuity of Edwards in exploiting potential allies. In this context, some hint of government dirty tricks would surely have been discovered. From the way in which supposedly confidential directives from London about Edwards's case found their way into the domain of public opinion in Sydney, the colonial administration clearly leaked like a sieve. The opposition papers were not backward in making allegations on the slimmest of pretexts, as we saw in the accusations that Edwards was a spy for Bigge. Yet for all this popular support, Edwards was never able to bring forward any substantive witnesses who could

---

[76] Brisbane acknowledged the letter, confirming that it had arrived on the *Minerva*, in a letter the following year: Brisbane to Somerset, 31 March 1825, Brisbane Letter Book, SLNSW, A1559, vol. 2, p. 169.

prove that he was not Kaye or to provide Kaye with any kind of independent existence. We must also remember the convoluted versions of Alexander Kaye's past life that repeatedly bled through the fantasies concocted by William Edwards, too many and too varied to be dismissed simply as coincidence.[77]

When Bathurst's June 1825 instructions to release Edwards unless he was Lockaye finally arrived in New South Wales, Governor Darling went through the whole process of investigation again. Fulsome evidence was taken at the Sydney Police Office over two sessions in March 1826. The report declared that the affidavits of ten people, both convicts and free settlers, served to conclusively prove that the two were one and the same. Central to the testimony was not only the fact that Edwards was recognised by a series of witness, but also the physical signs of a former injury. In 1821 Kaye's collarbone had been fractured by the fall of a cedar log. Drs Bowman and Allan both recognised Kaye from the prisoner's duties in conveying the sick between the convict barracks and the hospital. They also gave medical evidence to the effect that Kaye's injury could be observed upon the body of Edwards. Those who gave evidence against Edwards were all, with the exception of the doctors, former convicts, but the committee named them 'men of property' and 'good conduct', who had no ulterior motives and who had all been 'so frequently in contact with the Prisoner that it is impossible they can be under a mistake as to his identity'.

Edwards had little to say to rebut the evidence brought by the state, concentrating rather on attacking the witnesses' characters. For his part he brought forward three men to testify on his behalf, identified only as 'Best, McCormick and Keans' by the committee's report, whose evidence was both vague and lacking in foundation. 'We cannot help saying in conclusion', ended the committee's report, 'that we consider the conduct of Lockage one of the most impudent impositions ever attempted.'[78]

'Her conjugal anxiety': Elizabeth Edwards takes up the cause

Edwards's identity was endlessly debated in the Sydney press, and each stage in the legal processes that ended with his being sent to Norfolk

---

[77] Those reading closely may have picked up, for example, that Edwards admitted to being from Flint, where Kaye had lived; that his wife was related to the Sackvilles (in fact Shackfields); and that he had been treated by Dr Bowman in Sydney, the same man who later testified to having treated Kaye: see *HRA*, 1:15, p. 270.

[78] Report on the Identity of Alexander Lockage, 13 March 1826, enclosure in Darling to Bathurst, 29 April 1826, *HRA*, 1:12, pp. 242–3.

Island provoked commentary. The doubts that hung over the legality of his Cape sentence were common knowledge, even though never publicly acknowledged by the authorities. As we have seen, in 1825 Bathurst had instructed Governor Brisbane to release Edwards from his Cape sentence, unless he was proved to be Kaye. Possibly as a result of leaks from this despatch, rumours about a pardon were evidently running riot through the town. The *Sydney Gazette* went so far as to remind its readers that Edwards 'is not retained in the Colony as a prisoner under his latter [Cape] sentence, but under his original term of transportation to this Colony for Life, when he is said to have escaped as Lookaye'.[79] Yet doubts continued to be aired. When the *Monitor* gave notice of his transportation to 'Norfolk alias Gomorrah Island' it commented that 'This man's fate is a hard one, if he be not the original Edwards or Lookaye.'[80]

Edwards's case was now taken up by his wife. Elizabeth Rens, it was widely agreed by the colonial authorities, was the 'dupe' of her bigamous husband.[81] Bigge described her as both 'infatuated' and 'respectably connected', and claimed she had brought a fortune of 6000 rixdollars to the marriage. When she insisted on leaving the Cape for New South Wales, she did so very much against the advice of the authorities there.[82] Once in New South Wales, she proved her husband's most persistent supporter. 'Great exertions have been made to persuade my excellent Wife that I am that Lockaye', wrote Edwards to an accomplice on the eve of his planned escape to Java. Perhaps remembering his previous marriage, he went on: 'my conduct towards her, so different from his [Kaye], has been her best security of its falsity, and nothing my enemies can do will ever prevail on her to credit the Slander.'[83] With Edwards sentenced to Norfolk Island, she not only petitioned the secretary of state for his release, but also brought a case before the Supreme Court, seeking their intervention and raising the question of his disputed identity yet again.[84] The judges refused her, claiming that they had no grounds upon which to intervene and recommending she take her case to the governor. Furthermore, they argued, her husband's identity was irrelevant. The prisoner had admitted to being Edwards. He had absconded from a sentence of transportation as Edwards and must be punished accordingly. Edward Smith Hall found in their reaction yet another instance of the harsh treatment that Edwards

[79] *Sydney Gazette*, 16 May 1828.   [80] *Monitor*, 31 May 1828.
[81] The term is Darling's: Darling to Murray, 23 Nov. 1829, *HRA*, 1:15, pp. 256–7.
[82] Bigge to Brisbane, 24 Sept. 1824, enclosure in Darling to Murray, 23 Nov. 1829, *HRA*, 1:15, p. 269.
[83] Edwards to J. Dickson, 6 Jan. 1828, enclosure in Darling to Murray, 23 Nov. 1829, *HRA*, 1:15, p. 265.
[84] *Sydney Gazette*, 2 May 1828 (original emphasis).

had received at every stage from the authorities. In a note from the editor he commented, 'Infinitely more consideration has been given to felons; but Edwards can write, and is a politician.'[85]

The description of Edwards as a 'politician' is instructive and needs to be seen within the context of the growing political voice of the emancipists in the constitutional debates of the 1820s. Edwards proved himself adept in his manipulation of the law, a potential rallying point for opposition forces in both the Cape and New South Wales. These ranged from ordinary convicts seeking redress in the courts of Bathurst to newspaper editors like Edward Smith Hall who insisted that exposing state corruption was honourable conduct.[86] If, as I have argued, William Edwards was a small-time lawyer who did not embark intentionally on the path of colonial 'reformer' in 1824, then by 1828 he had accomplished much in remaking himself in this image. He had made a name for himself in reforming circles in the colonies and in Britain. His case had been taken up by Whig and Radical MPs. If he could disprove his fatally discrediting identification as escaped convict Alexander Kaye, it might be taken up in these circles again.

Edwards was clearly involving himself in the broader debates over imperial reform by the time he was sent to Norfolk Island. We see this in the pamphlets he had written during his life and through which, by means of sale by subscription, Elizabeth Edwards tried to raise money after her husband's death. The twenty-seven items she advertised in the *Australian* newspaper in May 1828 were a combination of Edwards's personal and political interests, clearly linking his individual case to wider questions being debated around imperial policy. Many of the items are copies of letters preserved in the *Historical Records of Australia*: petitions to the Supreme Court and the British Parliament and correspondence to the governor and the secretary of state. All follow the theme of 'refuting the pretence that I am Lookaye'. But the list of publications also provides evidence of broader issues including, amongst others, 'A review of Wentworth's New South Wales', 'A Reply to Reports of Mr Bigge; with some observations on his motives and prejudices', 'A Calculation of the Profits and Losses of Penal Settlements, as they are contrasted with what they ought to be', 'On Character in Europe and the Colonies' and 'A Review of both the Administrations of General Darling in Mauritius'.[87] Whether

---

[85] *Monitor*, 3 May 1828.
[86] Elizabeth Edwards's letter to Huskisson claimed they had been ordered to Wellington Valley because 'my Husband (who was obliged to earn our Bread by his Pen) had been solicited to write the Brief of a Man Committed for Trial': Elizabeth Edwards to Huskisson, 15 April 1828, *HRA*, 1:14, p. 166.
[87] *Australian*, 28 May 1828.

these papers were published by subscription is unknown. Certainly Elizabeth's plans to support herself by these means came to nothing, and in September 1828 the *Monitor* carried a public notice addressed 'To the Humane and Benevolent', seeking financial help from the public for Mrs Edwards and her two children to return to the Cape.[88]

Clearly the public proved insufficiently humane and benevolent in the case of Elizabeth Edwards. Two months later Darling wrote to the secretary of state that he had authorised the expenditure of £80 as the means for the widow and her children, 'being totally destitute', of returning to the Cape.[89] Although this may have been disinterested benevolence, it may also have been politically astute. In the midst of an increasingly fraught debate over Darling's administration, in which the Sydney newspapers were playing a starring role, the authorities in New South Wales would no doubt have found it convenient for Elizabeth, along with her collection of papers, to be removed from the colony. Although this is rank speculation, it is even possible that Edward Smith Hall might have advised Elizabeth to advertise the existence of the papers to pressure the administration with this end in mind.

The Supreme Court had dismissed Elizabeth's case challenging the transportation to Norfolk Island. But the secretary of state was more circumspect when he eventually received her petition alleging a conspiracy that reached from New South Wales to the Cape and the very heart of the British establishment: 'Nothing will assist General Darling which will give us a fair Trial; he thinks by persecuting my wretched Husband to please the Beaufort Family, and procure himself a powerful Patron'. Elizabeth claimed she had 'accidentally learnt that our Gracious Sovereign had more than two Years ago Commanded the Governor to release my Husband, on proving that he was not Lookaye.' She claimed that

> Mr Suell [Shewell] an English Gentleman informed me of a Person, who had recently conversed with the real Lookaye, working for Government on the Roads.... I have since found that the Person who saw Lookaye has been silently released from Prison, and Lookaye removed from the place where he was seen.[90]

---

[88] *Monitor*, 15 Sept. 1828.
[89] Darling to Murray, 10 Nov. 1828, *HRA*, 1:14, pp. 445–6. For Murray's authorisation, Murray to Darling, 24 June 1829, *HRA*, 1:15, pp. 20–1. In 1830 Elizabeth inherited a quarter portion of her deceased mother's modest estate. She died aged seventy-nine in 1872, having never remarried. Cape Town Archives Repository, Inventories of the Orphan Chamber MOOC 8/45.63. Jacomina Mosterd, 4 November 1830. My thanks to Judy Buxton for this reference.
[90] Elizabeth Edwards to Huskisson, 15 April 1828. Darling, in countering this claim to the secretary of state, replied that Shewell's affidavit had no credibility as it had been written in Lockaye's own hand and signed by a man in jail with him at the time: Darling to Murray, 23 Nov. 1829, *HRA*, 1:15, pp. 256–7, 263.

Darling, claimed Elizabeth Edwards, was entirely prejudiced against the couple and had denied them a proper hearing at every turn. She called on Huskisson to bring Darling to account and require from him 'some other reason than a wish to please the Beaufort Family, why he has so cruelly persecuted us'.[91]

'The case... ceases to have any interest or importance': the view from the Colonial Office

Although the Supreme Court's concern was the proper operation of the law, the secretary of state had to give more explicit attention to the wider political resonances of the case. Sir George Murray (who had replaced William Huskisson) insisted that Darling go point-by-point through the allegations in Elizabeth Edwards's petition and provide answers to each. Although not inclined to put much faith in the couple's assertions, he was not satisfied that the enquiry into Edwards's identity had been properly conducted. Specifically, Murray insisted to Darling that the matter of Edwards's identity must be tried before the Supreme Court rather than merely under magisterial authority. Once more, he instructed that Edwards be released if he proved not to be Kaye, underscoring the dim view that London took of the Cape sentence of transportation for libelling Somerset. Murray was evidently aware that Darling would have a visceral reaction both to the memorial and to being asked to justify himself in relation to it. He explicitly warned against any but a strictly neutral response, clearly anticipating a characteristic show of temper that would have been politically ill-advised. Ironically, given that the letter was undoubtedly mostly the production of William Edwards, Murray tried to excuse it to Darling (and prevent a heavy-handed response) as written by a woman suffering the disadvantages of 'her sex, her foreign birth, her conjugal anxiety, and her unmerited afflictions'.[92]

By the time Darling received these instructions, Edwards's suicide made a retrial before the Supreme Court redundant, but the ongoing debate over Darling's administration made it no less important that the governor clear his name with regard to previous treatment of Edwards and his family. Murray's expectations as to Darling's frame of mind were amply justified. The governor began his response by expressing his regret

---

[91] Elizabeth Edwards to Huskisson, 15 April 1828.
[92] Murray to Darling, 1 May 1829, *HRA*, 1:14, p. 731. It was not the first time that letters were evidently dictated to Elizabeth Edwards. Her letter to Attorney-General Saxe Bannister from Port Macquarie (20 Dec. 1825, *HRA*, 1:15, pp. 266–7) slips up by referring to William Edwards as 'I'. See also H. Heney, *Dear Fanny: Women's Letters to and from New South Wales 1788–1851* (Canberra: ANU Press, 1985), pp. 90–1.

that he had to go over the matter yet again, when it had already been decisively proven by the affidavits of 'Men of the first respectability' giving evidence before 'the Chairman of the Quarter Sessions and two other Magistrates'.[93] He was clearly exasperated that he was being called to make such a detailed account, naming Elizabeth 'a very ignorant Woman, and there is little doubt [she] has been the dupe of her husband, who has concealed from her the Events of his Life previous to their marriage'. The petition written under his wife's name was characteristic of Edwards himself, 'whose Education and acquirements seemed to have rendered him an Adept in distorting and misrepresenting facts'. Far from having treated the couple with harshness, Darling claimed he had bent over backwards to accommodate them. It was at this point that Darling produced the evidence of Edwards's alleged attempt to escape to Java, which, he argued, fully justified the decision to send him to Norfolk Island.

For all that he went meticulously point-by-point through the allegations in Elizabeth's letter, Darling complained that the government continually found itself 'grossly imposed upon, and had wasted much time in attending to Individuals of Lockaye's description'. If Edwards had 'succeeded in duping the Government and again effected his escape, it would have been very justly blamed for its Credulity'. Darling considered that 'while the Government is charged with the Custody of Men of Lockaye's Character, it is a paramount duty to defeat and put down every attempt, which may be made to embarrass or impose upon it'. Darling's final verdict on the impostor's fate was that he deserved all he got:

As to the result, though the depravity of the Man's mind may be lamented, there is nothing which can excite Compassion for the Individual or palliate his Proceedings. He possessed Talents, which he always employed to the very worst purpose, and, when deprived of the means of being mischievous, Life appears to have been no longer desirable.[94]

Darling's refutation arrived on Murray's desk with an accompanying report from Under-Secretary Robert Hay on what Hay called 'the much debated case of the convict Lookaye or Edwards'.[95] The commentary was kept informal, and, as such, it did not merit inclusion in the transcriptions of *Historical Records of Australia* – yet another example of how unofficial conduits of information constantly glossed and managed official ones. Hay explained that he did not feel it worth writing a formal report:

[93] Darling to Murray, 23 Nov. 1829, *HRA*, 1:15, pp. 256–7.
[94] Darling to Murray, 23 Nov. 1829.
[95] Report by Hay, 14 Oct. 1830, regarding despatch from Darling, 23 Nov. 1829, TNA, CO 201/203.

because I think that nothing is left to discuss. The evidence is all on one side, and seems to me to place the identity of Lockaye and Edwards beyond all reasonable doubt. Whether this evidence could have been shaken by Lookaye had he lived, it is too late to enquire.

Hay was almost admiring of the impostor's talents. Commenting on Darling's claim that the petition was essentially Edwards in drag, he considered that a

> more touching and apparently simple specimen of feminine affection and conjugal tenderness can scarcely be met with.... If they were fabrications, it is indeed a pity that a man possessing so much dramatic power should not have used it to a better purpose.

Now that Edwards had killed himself, the question of his identity (and therefore his punishment) required no immediate action on the part of the authorities in London: 'The case ... ceases to have any interest or importance except as far as it may be thought to affect the character of General Darling.'

This was the real thrust of the unofficial report. Could what had happened in the case of Edwards damage Darling's administration (and by implication the Colonial Office) politically? In Hay's judgement it could not. Darling's point-by-point refutation of Elizabeth Edwards's accusations fully exonerated his conduct. In making such a conclusion, Hay considered two issues. One was the facts at hand. The other was the relative standing of the assertions and the need of the secretary of state to accept the word of the governor of the colony over that of 'one of the convicts under his command'. Luckily, in this instance, 'it is not necessary to rest the case on the superior claims of the Governor to credit.' The facts bore out his version of events as well.

Hay reminded the secretary of state that the governor had to be supported at all times against such ceaseless erosion of his authority, and that this was a particular problem in a penal colony. His conclusion provided an assessment of local peculiarities from which I have already quoted:

> In short I have no doubt that this case is a specimen of that strange system of artifice of which all writers on the colony have given such copious accounts, and that persons who have never lived in a convict settlement are totally unprepared to detect, or even to imagine the possibility of such plausible and audacious frauds as are daily practised there. It would be a very dangerous precedent to give countenance to such people, or to their complaints, except on the most clear and indisputable grounds, and a Governor in such a situation stands in need of all the support which he can possibly receive from this country.[96]

---

[96] Report by Hay, 14 Oct. 1830.

In summary, whether written by William or by Elizabeth Edwards, there was no truth in the accusations against the governor. In seeking to neutralise any further use to which the case might be put, only one part of the public despatch might have negative political consequences. This was the closing remark in Darling's letter in which 'Edwards is mentioned in terms which would probably be represented by the Governor's opponents as harsh & unfeeling. That however is scarcely a matter for animadversion by the Secretary of State.'[97] Nothing further, in consequence, need therefore be done by the Colonial Office, and certainly the secretary of state agreed, as the summary bears a pencil remark directing that 'No answer to the Governor seems necessary.' From first to last, as Hay's final report makes abundantly clear, the significance of Edwards lay in the use that could be made of his case by the political opponents of controversial governors.[98]

This correspondence was the last time that Edwards engaged the substantive interest of the Colonial Office, and there are two final points to be made about Hay's report. The first is his agreement with Darling about the constant pressure being exerted upon colonial authorities by convicts pushing at every possible chink in the system's armour. No one who had not lived in such a system, argued both Darling and Hay, could understand the continual barrage that disrupted their attempts to impose order on the colony and the time and energy wasted in countering these 'Adepts in Fraud and Villainy'. No wonder such men were turned 'harsh and unfeeling' as a result. But the second point to be made is this: for all the sympathy of the Colonial Office with Darling, it still deemed it necessary that the governor be called to account in answering such complainants.

Such contradictory forces were, as James Stephen put it just months before Edwards killed himself, part of a 'great anomaly in the condition of this Colony... its character as a Penal Settlement'.[99] The inconsistences presented by the rule of law in a penal colony were those being ruthlessly exploited by the group of politically astute lawyers and newspaper editors (often one and the same) who stood in the vanguard of the emancipist cause in the 1820s. 'The People are taught by the Papers', complained Darling, 'to talk about the rights of Englishmen and the free institutions of the Mother Country, Many of them forgetting their

---

[97] The phrase referred to is where Darling writes that Edwards killed himself because 'when deprived of the means of being mischievous, Life appears to have been no longer desirable': Darling to Murray, 23 Nov. 1829, *HRA*, 1:15, pp. 256–7, 261.
[98] Report by Hay, 14 Oct. 1830.
[99] James Stephen's annotations on the amendments required to the 1823 New South Wales Act, 1 March 1828, TNA, CO 201/195.

actual Condition'.[100] Cases like that of Edwards provided grist to the mill of their campaign against gubernatorial autocracy and their lobbies for constitutional change. Where Edwards ultimately failed them as a *cause célèbre*, however, was in the impossibility of settling once and for all the question of his identity. Even death would not end Edwards's capacity to stir controversy or to raise his own posthumous voice in the clamorous debate over who he really was.

In the repeated investigations made into the escapee's identity, during his life and after his death, both the evidence marshalled to prove Edwards and Kaye one and the same and his corresponding denials underscore the transitional nature of the period and the paradoxical consequences of the Bigge reports in the Australian colonies. An emphasis on 'objective' and measurable physical characteristics were increasingly parts of the state's apparatus against dissent, but gossip and interpersonal information networks remained just as vital to the business of government. Similarly, the harsher disciplinary system of convict punishment enacted in the wake of the Bigge reports did not negate the wider opportunities for legal challenges that were opened up by the same reforms.

[100] Darling to Hay, 9 Feb. 1827 (secret and confidential), *HRA*, 1:13, p. 99.

Epilogue
An infamous end

Perched on the very edge of Norfolk Island's shore, periodically threatened with erosion by the storms coming off the South Pacific Ocean, the island's historic cemetery is now one of its most popular tourist destinations. Amongst the picturesque and carefully maintained graves of executed convict rebels and *Bounty* mutineers, no marker now exists bearing either of his names. The absence of any surviving memorial seems only too appropriate. As the *Monitor* reminded its Sydney readers in 1828, 'the mystery of Edwards, alias Lookaye, must remain for ever.'[1]

The mystery might endure, but death did not end the 'tragedy of Alexander Edwards'.[2] There was one final act yet to be played. Six months after his demise, the pages of the *Monitor* included a startling revelation:

The singular character of Edwards, induced the Commandant to exercise 'his pleasure' on his body. On visiting the Hospital the next day, Edward's head was found sawn in two and a large slice thereof, was placed on the stump of a tree, the Surgeon being *at work*. His body was open, and his limbs scattered about as in a dissecting house. Thus, if he had been sentenced to die and to be dissected, the end of this unfortunate man, a man of literary talents, and of an unconquerable spirit of independence, could not have been more infamous.[3]

The paper's outrage was swiftly attacked by counter-arguments. Alluding to a popular eighteenth-century satire, the pro-Darling *Sydney Gazette* dismissed its rival's account as 'big with horrors', one that 'far out-tragedises even *Chrononhonthologos*, the most tragical tragedy that ever was tragedised'.[4] Instead of frightening 'all the old women and young children in Sydney' with gruesome details, wrote the *Gazette*, the *Monitor* should give the proper facts. An inquest, they argued, must certainly

---

[1] *Monitor*, 12 Jan. 1829.   [2] *Sydney Gazette*, 6 Jan. 1829.   [3] *Monitor*, 20 Dec. 1828.
[4] *Sydney Gazette*, 6 Jan. 1829; H. Carey, *Chrononhonthologos: The most tragical tragedy that ever was tragediz'd by any company of tragedians* (London, 1734) was a satire on Robert Walpole and Whig politics. Coincidentally, the protagonists face an invasion by the Antipodeans.

have been held, for it had returned a verdict of insanity (necessary for Edwards to be buried in consecrated ground). And if a dissection was indeed carried out, 'it was only what the deceased had himself ordered'.[5] In this version of events, the intention of the perpetrators was not disciplinary. Rather, it was to apply the principles of scientific observation to questions that remained unanswered. Could the marks known to be carried upon the living body of Alexander Kaye be found within the corpse of William Edwards?

The *Gazette* backed up its story by reproducing a letter ('politely transmitted to us') from the man himself, dated *Phoenix* hulk, 28 January 1828. As it was effectively a suicide note, it was, 'out of delicacy to my wife', to be delivered only after Edwards's death. In it Edwards noted that he had been advised that the request needed to be made in writing to be legal. The letter, to one Dr Gibson of Sydney, requested that he, in attendance with Dr Murray, superintendent of the *Phoenix*, and 'my friend' Dr Shortt, attend to the following: that 'my body be opened . . . as soon after my death as you possibly can' and that investigation be made, specifically:

whether the irregularity in my shoulder is such in its appearance as to have been an injury received in my earliest days . . . and whether there is any scar on my arms, or body, particularly the marks of flagellation on my back. If you find no such scars or marks, nor any broken bones in the members I have mentioned, you will simply say so, and thereby clear my innocent children from the odium of having sprung from a felon.[6]

The existence of these marks upon his body had been part of the identification of Edwards as Kaye by Drs Bowman and Allan in the investigation of 1826.

It was, speculated the *Gazette*, 'in consequence of this request' that the dissection had taken place. If, however, the dissection had been upon Edwards's written request, continued the paper, then the results were quite otherwise than the letter suggested they would be. In fact, the case was proved even more strongly in death than it had been in life:

---

[5] *Sydney Gazette*, 6 Jan. 1829.
[6] *Sydney Gazette*, 6 Jan. 1829. The addressee was presumably Dr Andrew Gibson, a surgeon of the 39th Regiment, then serving in Sydney. Francis Shortt, who claimed to have been a surgeon in the Royal Navy, was a merchant at the Cape before arriving in Australia in 1822. Frank Clune mentions another letter, dated 22 Jan. 1828, expressing similar sentiments, also requesting dissection and addressed to Laurence Halloran, another Cape connection (and Francis Shortt's father-in-law) then living in Sydney. Halloran sent it to Colonial Secretary Alexander Macleay, who apparently took no action. See *Rascals, Ruffians and Rebels of Early Australia* (Sydney: Angus & Robertson, 1987), pp. 176–8. Unfortunately all attempts at verifying Clune's unreferenced source by finding the original correspondence have failed.

the result has been that the unfortunate man is clearly proved to have been Lookaye, upon the kind of evidence on which he has chosen to rest his identity; inasmuch as the ribs were found to have been formerly fractured, the collar bone to have been broken, and, in short, the whole of those marks by which his identity was to have been established, though imperceptible in a great measure during life, more clearly distinguishable on dissection.[7]

The *Monitor* remained unconvinced, still determined to see proof of government tyranny. Having admitted that the 'letter carries internal marks of authenticity', they reproduced it in order that their readers might decide for themselves.

Yet this was not the end of the matter. First, the *Monitor* questioned why Edwards, if he were really Lockaye, would call for his body to be cut up after death when it would only testify against him? If, on the other hand,

he were not Lookaye, but Edwards, and consequently a man of truth, and not an impostor, *then* the letter he wrote was natural, and the rational act of a rational man. Otherwise, it was the act of a madman. Of a madman, however, who could not bear to live because of his degradation; yet had reason enough it seems to point out to his enemies, the only infallible means of discovery; and which means, by presently destroying himself, he placed in their power.

Those whom Edwards had requested do the dissection could not testify. Shortt had recently died, and the others had never seen the body. The *Monitor* cast doubt on whether the testimony of those on Norfolk Island could be believed. His body 'fell into the hands of a stranger, an officer of that Government Edwards so bitterly complained of'. Could such a witness be without bias? The *Monitor* thought not.[8]

The records from Norfolk Island in this period are unfortunately incomplete, and no official account of Edwards's dissection has survived.[9] Although the *Monitor*'s information came from a witness on the island, it cannot be said to be impartial. In March 1829 the matter of Edwards's dissection got caught up in a dispute between Lieutenant Charles Cox of the 39th Regiment and Captain Thomas Edward Wright, commandant

---

[7] *Sydney Gazette*, 6 Jan. 1829.   [8] *Monitor*, 12 Jan. 1829.
[9] Although outward letters in the NSW colonial secretary's correspondence have survived for this period, inward ones have not. The surgeon in question would have been Philip Harmot Hartwell, who was appointed in late 1827 (McLeay to Wright, 13 Dec. 1827, SRNSW, NRS 988, Colonial Secretary: Letters sent to Norfolk Island). Hartwell, who was ill during most of his service there, did not last long on the island, nor did he long survive Edwards. He died on 3 Nov. 1828, aged forty-five years. Unlike Edwards's grave, his memorial survives in the cemetery of Norfolk Island. His 'handsome' tombstone, 'erected by the Civil Officers of this est[ablishment] as a tribute of respect', has been beautifully restored and maintained: Aaron Price, 'History of Norfolk Island c. 1774–c. 1852', SLNSW, DL MS, pp. 247–9.

of Norfolk Island. Cox was court martialled for challenging Wright to a duel and for other instances of insubordination. In response, Cox brought forward a series of counter-charges against Wright's illegal actions during his command.[10] Amongst these were the 'improper acts' that followed the death of Edwards:

> on his being found suspended from a ridge-pole of his hut, had no inquest held on his body, though the same was requested by Lieutenant Cox in his magisterial capacity; and that the body was dissected in an exposed and indelicate manner, that is to say, 'cut up' in the cell yards, in lieu of being anatomized in the hospital.[11]

Together with another member of the regiment, Cox was part of what Darling called 'a foul conspiracy' that involved Edward Smith Hall and William Charles Wentworth. Their intent was to expose official misconduct on Norfolk Island to public scrutiny. Cox is the most likely source of the lurid and unattributed account of Edwards's dissection that Edward Smith Hall reproduced in his paper some three months before the court martial.

It is curious that neither the dissection nor its supposed outcome was mentioned in the lengthy account that Darling wrote to the secretary of state in November 1829 to exonerate his conduct towards Edwards. This is especially so because much of the justification of his actions rested on claims that Edwards and Kaye were one and the same. It may be that the 'exposed and indelicate' circumstances of the dissection's procedure made him reluctant to mention it. Nevertheless, if the *Gazette*'s assertion that the outcome of the dissection decisively proved Edwards to be Kaye, it seems odd that Darling made no reference to it, given how important it was to the authorities in both London and Sydney to lay this matter to rest. Nor did Darling make mention of the suicide letter from Edwards that was reproduced in the *Gazette*.

The work of Helen MacDonald and Hamish Maxwell-Stewart emphasises both the horror that continued to hang over the practice of dissection in the 1820s and the opportunities that a colonial and penal setting offered would-be men of science seeking access to bodies. Before the British Anatomy Act of 1832, dissection was carried out as an added form of punishment on the executed bodies of murderers; hence the disgust in

---

[10] *Monitor*, 6 and 23 March 1829. Edwards's case was largely incidental to a much larger and more tangled set of circumstances involving disputed authority on the island. Cox's court martial proceedings were closely followed by ones against Wright himself. The original catalyst for the latter was a convict mutiny led by Patrick Clynch in 1826 and Clynch's subsequent execution in 1827 for attempting to murder Wright: see *Australian*, 14 Oct. 1829; M. G. Britts, *The Commandants: The Tyrants who Ruled Norfolk Island* (Norfolk Island: Kapak Publishing, 1980).

[11] *Monitor*, 23 March 1829.

the Sydney press over Edwards's fate. These were the only corpses made legally available to medical men. Under the 1752 'Act for better preventing the horrid Crime of Murder', dissecting and gibbeting were listed as additional punishments meted out to murderers alone.[12] Dissection was fully intended to 'result in the mutilation of the dead'[13] and finds its place in the last of Hogarth's celebrated series of engravings *The Four Stages of Cruelty* (1751).[14] In *The Reward of Cruelty*, the condemned murderer's body is pictured in the anatomy theatre where it is being literally torn to pieces, complete with a dog in the foreground feasting upon the remains as they fall from the table. The dog excepted, the image is reminiscent of the charnel house evoked within the pages of the *Monitor*, an account that firmly demonstrated the continued association of dissection with punishment rather than with the ordered procedures of science. Regulations written in 1812 by the College of Surgeons in London attempted to impose more order (and consequently more respectability) upon the practice. It was a response to the riotous scenes that had marred the dissection of John Bellingham, executed for assassinating Prime Minister Spencer Perceval.[15]

The 1832 Act was passed in part in response to public concern about the illegal trade in corpses by 'resurrectionists'. The infamous Edinburgh murderers and body-traders Burke and Hare were arrested in 1828, the year of Edwards's death. News of 'The Late Horrible Murders in Edinburgh, to Obtain Subjects for Dissection' (as the Sydney headlines put it) arrived in New South Wales in May 1829, only months after Edwards's dissection had provoked outrage in the same papers.[16] Burke himself became one of the last murderers to be sentenced to both death and dissection, an occasion attended by a near riot when insufficient tickets were issued for admission. (Hare escaped conviction by turning king's evidence.)

If the 1832 Act was intended to provide medical men with increased legal supplies of bodies for dissection, widespread popular anxiety about dissection remained. The Act itself euphemistically referred to 'anatomical examination' rather than 'dissection', and its provisions meant that it was mostly the poor whose bodies were subjected to the practice.[17] In a

---

[12] H. MacDonald, *Human Remains: Episodes in Human Dissection* (Melbourne University Press, 2005), p. 12.
[13] MacDonald, *Human Remains*, p. 17.
[14] Hamish Maxwell-Stewart, *Closing Hell's Gates: The Death of a Convict Station* (Melbourne: Allen & Unwin, 2008), p. 97.
[15] MacDonald, *Human Remains*, p. 18. [16] *Sydney Gazette*, 12 May 1829.
[17] Hospitals and workhouses could now make bodies available for 'anatomical examination' if they were not claimed by relatives within a certain period. Because claiming a

penal colony with large numbers of individuals under the carceral control of the state, opportunities for surgeons were wider. Even in Britain, the rules were frequently evaded and, as Maxwell-Stewart suggests, 'Fewer questions were asked about the bodies of the dead in New South Wales and Van Diemen's Land.' The bodies of executed convicts were dissected even when they were not convicted murderers, which was technically illegal.[18]

Helen MacDonald notes that although there were numerous mentions of dissection in association with execution in Van Diemen's Land, there was little public discussion of the practice. The outrage expressed over the treatment of Edwards appears to have been unusual. Although the Australian colonies had the ability to replicate British laws, the 1832 Anatomy Act was not amongst these. Convicts continued to be dissected, as did numerous Aboriginal people, despite the fact that only convicted murderers could legally be subjected to this practice. Surgeons jealously guarded their access to corpses, and many colonists profitted (financially and professionally) from a growing international trade in body parts. As the science of race expanded in the second half of the nineteenth century, scientific greed for indigenous human remains proceeded hand-in-hand with violent settler greed for land across the British Empire.[19] Crime and punishment were not the only means of gaining access to the dead. Frontier warfare and colonial expansion were increasingly more significant.[20]

As always in the case of Edwards, the alleged dissection remains far more obscure than the motivation of the *Monitor* in providing a lurid description of it for political ends. Anatomical examination is a way of 'capturing the subject, of knowing it as a set of related systems' while denying its ultimate humanity.[21] Yet the treatment of Edwards's corpse reveals itself as an almost absurdist attempt to render concrete in death what had proved itself infinitely malleable in life. If he was indeed subjected to it, as seems likely, then the treatment of his remains represents both the ultimate attempt to fix his identity in biometric terms and a patent failure to put an end to the human speculation and allegations of

body meant that burial costs needed to be paid, the bodies of the poor became fair game for dissection: MacDonald, *Human Remains*, p. 40.

[18] Maxwell-Stewart, *Closing Hell's Gates*, pp. 97, 100.
[19] T. Griffiths, *Hunters and Collectors: The Antiquarian Imagination in Australia* (Cambridge University Press, 1996); A. Bank, 'Of "native skulls" and "noble Caucasians": Phrenology in colonial South Africa', *Journal of Southern African Studies*, 22:3 (Sept. 1996), 387–403; MacDonald, *Human Remains* and *Possessing the Dead: The Artful Science of Anatomy* (Melbourne University Press, 2011).
[20] MacDonald, *Human Remains*, p. 95.
[21] Maxwell-Stewart, *Closing Hell's Gates*, p. 99.

conspiracy that had marked his imperial career. The alleged dissection of the man known variously as Alexander Kaye and William Edwards was the last act in a personal and political drama that had set the claims of individual liberty and reform against the demands of state surveillance and security [Figure 10] for the best part of the previous decade.

Edwards took his own life in 1828. It was a year of significant legal and constitutional transformations in both the Cape and New South Wales. Sir John Wylde, former judge advocate of New South Wales and son to the man from whose service Alexander Kaye had escaped in 1821, arrived as the Cape's first British chief justice. He would preside over the implementation of the new Charter of Justice recommended by the Commission of Eastern Inquiry, revolutionising a Cape legal system whose shortcomings had been so clearly illuminated by its handling of cases like Edwards's. In New South Wales, the 1828 Australian Courts Act sought to resolve some of the inconsistencies in colonial authority that convicts like Edwards had tried to exploit in that colony, weaknesses that had become evident as a result of the legislation enacted following Bigge's investigations at the beginning of the decade. In both the Cape and New South Wales, relations between judicial and executive powers were a central concern in these constitutional changes, just as they had been a central factor in Edwards's legal travails in the Antipodes. Finally, 1828 also saw a triumph for the humanitarian lobby in the promulgation of Ordinance 50 at the Cape, the 'Magna Carta of the Hottentots', which liberated the Khoekhoen from a raft of restrictions imposed by the colonial state. None of these developments were of course *caused* by Edwards, the last least of all, but nor can it be argued that those like him were mere distractions to those involved in bringing these initiatives in governance to fruition.

If scholars are increasingly emphasising the role of interpersonal networks and individual motivations in understanding the transitions of this period, their more usual focus generally lies elsewhere. Colonial officials and humanitarian activists are more commonly studied as the prime instigators of imperial reforms than are unstable mavericks. As long ago as 1927, historian W. M. Macmillan recognised that 'the apparently meaningless clash of personalities in the episodes of this time really marks a significant stage in South African development'.[22] This is where we must seek the significance of those like Edwards and the scandals they instigated. They were both actors in their own right and ammunition for other interests in a wider political struggle that encompassed both colonies and metropole. This is why such an obviously marginal figure – an

---

[22] *The Cape Colour Question: A Historical Survey* (London: Faber & Gwyer, 1927), p. 188.

Figure 10 Norfolk Island's convict settlement in 1838. A decade after William Edwards's suicide, the disciplinary architecture planned for 'Norfolk's fell isle' is taking shape.

obscure notary, later exposed as an escaped convict – could have such an impact across such a wide range of localities and why his accusations against prominent colonial officials were taken so seriously and by such powerful people.

In understanding the legal and constitutional transitions of the period between Waterloo and the Reform Act, it is tempting to translate the vicissitudes of colonial regimes into abstract terms – into liberalism versus authoritarianism, if you will. But the scandals that Edwards exposed and that were so inextricably part of this transition did not play out in entirely in these terms. Such controversies were orchestrated and defended by individuals who hooked their personal interests and reputations into powerful abstractions such as liberty, tyranny, despotism and sedition. Disentangling the selfless from the self-serving motives in such instances is usually an exercise in futility. William Edwards and his ilk – the 'clever fellows' of Colonial Secretary Richard Plasket's warning to London on the pitfalls of colonial governance – are no less a part of this story than more conventional reformers and lobbyists. Their protests, and the actions taken against them, blurred the edges between hard law, popular debate and the politics of reform in the course of the Crown commissioners' investigations. Ostensibly localised scandals about particular individuals could provide powerful traction and exert tactical influence in much wider and interlinked battles over imperial policy and metropolitan politics across distinct geographic locations. Looking at the forces unleashed by such self-interested and unpredictable historical actors – focussing on what was the murky underworld of imperial reform – allows us to take a fresh look at this paradoxical moment in the transformation of the British colonial order.

Bibliography

ARCHIVAL SOURCES: MANUSCRIPT

UNITED KINGDOM

British Library, London (BL)
  Bathurst Papers, Loan 57
Derbyshire Record Office
  Catton Collection: Wilmot Horton Papers
    D3155/WH 2751
    D3155/WH 2774
    D3155/WH 2876
    D3155/WH 3028
Bodleain Library, Rhodes House, University of Oxford
  Bigge–Somerset correspondence, MSS Afr, series 24
Gloucester Archives
  Q/Gc 5/2: Gaol Calendar
  Q/Sib.3: Quarter Sessions Indictment Book 1808–1819
  Q/SI (a) 1818 D: Quarter Sessions Indictment Roll
The National Archives (TNA), formerly Public Record Office, Kew
  Admiralty (ADM)
      ADM 101/6/2: Atlas Surgeon's Journal
  Colonial Office (CO)
      CO 48/89: Mr D'Escury and Lord Charles Somerset
      CO 48/95: Case of L. Cooke and W. Edwards, Libel on the Governor
      CO 48/96: Case of Greig and Fairbairn, Censorship of the Press
      CO 48/121: Commissioners Bigge, Colebrooke and Blair
      CO 201/175: Offices: House of Commons, Admiralty, Crown Agents, Commander in Chief, Board of Trade, East India 1826
      CO 201/195: Offices: House of Commons, Admiralty, Crown Agents, Commander in Chief, Board of Trade, East India 1828
      CO 201/203: Despatches
      CO 323/144: Private letters to Mr. Hay – Cape, Sierra Leone, Africa
      CO 324/146: Letters from Secretary of State (domestic)
      CO 414/6: Commission of Eastern Inquiry: Prize Negroes and Free Blacks
      CO 414/9: Commission of Eastern Inquiry: Laws and Courts of Justice. Police and Gaols. Missionary Institutions
  Records of the Chancery Court, Palatinate of Lancaster (PL)

PL 14/84: Chancery Court: Pleadings and miscellanea
National Library of Wales
SA/1820/39: Welsh Probate Records, Parish of Flint, Flintshire, Diocese of St Asaph

SOUTH AFRICA

Western Cape Archives Depot, Cape Town (CA)
Accessions (A)
    A602: Papers of Samuel Eusebius Hudson
Court of Justice (CJ)
    CJ 632 Records of the case against John Carnall
    CJ 818 Proceedings of the Court of Justice, 1824
    CJ 3352 Inquiry into Placard scandal, 1824
Colonial Office (CO)
    CO 212: Letters from the Office of the Fiscal
    CO 214: Letters from Court of Justice
    CO 145: Private correspondence
    CO 414/9: Commissioners of Inquiry, Correspondence
    CO 3924/185: Memorials received
    CO 4572: Minutes of Proceedings of Matrimonial Courts
Government House (GH)
    GH 1/25: Papers received from Secretary of State, General Despatches
    GH 1/64: Papers received from Secretary of State, General Despatches
    GH 28/10: Enclosures to Despatches
    GH 23/7: Official correspondence, 1824–5
Insolvency Papers (MOIC)
    MOIC 2/328: Insolvent Liquidation and Distribution Account of the estate of Harriet Dear Widow of the late William Jones. 1827
Notarial Protocols (NCD)
    NCD 26/1: Protocol of the notary David Passmore Taylor
    NCD 27/1: Protocol of the notary William Edwards
Library of Parliament, Cape Town
    Class a. 916.87, no. 9202: Dudley Perceval, Letters from the Cape of Good Hope 1825–1828

AUSTRALIA

State Library of New South Wales (SLNSW)
A1559: Brisbane Letter Book
MS 247–249: Aaron Price, 'History of Norfolk Island c. 1774–c. 1852'
Bonwick Transcripts BT Box 1 – Evidence of William Hutchinson, 10 Nov 1819
State Records of New South Wales (SRNSW)
Colonial Secretary
    NRS 988 4/382: Letters sent to Norfolk Island
Principal Superintendent of Convicts: Indents

NRS 12188 4/4003A: Alphabetical List of Convicts on Transports, 1788–1800.
NRS 121 88 4/4006: Bound Indents, 1818–1819
NRS 121 88 A/4009A: Bound Indents, 1823–1826

PRINTED PRIMARY SOURCES

OFFICIAL PUBLICATIONS

BPP 1822 (448) *Report of the Commissioner of Inquiry into the State of New South Wales*
BPP 1823 (33) *Report of the Commissioner of Inquiry, on the Judicial Establishments of New South Wales, and Van Diemen's Land*
BPP 1823 (136) *Report of the Commissioner of Inquiry on Agriculture and Trade in New South Wales*
BPP 1826–27 (42) *Slaves, Cape of Good Hope: Prize Slaves*
BPP 1826–7 (282) *Cape of Good Hope. Reports of the Commissioners of Inquiry; I. Upon the administration of the government of the Cape of Good Hope: II. Upon the finances of the Cape of Good Hope*
BPP 1826 (431) *Mr. Bishop Burnett, Cape of Good Hope*
BPP 1826–7 (470) *Cape of Good Hope: South African Commercial Advertiser*
BPP 1826–7 (556) *Cape of Good Hope. Papers relating to the case of Mr. John Carnall*
BPP 1829 (292) *Report of the Commissioners of Inquiry upon the Slave Trade at Mauritius*
BPP 1835 (580) *Report from Select Committee on the Conduct of General Darling, while Governor of New South Wales.*
Governor and Legislative Council, Cape of Good Hope, *Report of the Law of Inheritance Commission for the Western Districts*, G 15–65 (Cape Town, 1866)

ARTICLES, BOOKS, COLLECTIONS OF LETTERS, DIARIES AND PAMPHLETS

Anon., *Spies and Bloodites!!! The Lives and Political History of those Arch-Fiends Oliver, Reynolds, & Co. Treason-Hatchers, Green-Bag-Makers, Blood-Hunters, Spies, Tempters, and Informers-General to His Majesty's Ministers*... (London, 1817)
Anon. [William Wilberforce Bird], *State of the Cape of Good Hope in 1822*, facsimile edn (Cape Town: Struik, 1966)
Arnot, S. *A Sketch of the History of the Indian Press* (London: William Low, 1829)
Baines, Edward (jnr), *The Life of Edward Baines, Late M. P. for the Borough of Leeds by his son, Edward Baines* (London: Longmans, 1851)
Baines, Edward (snr), *History of the Reign of George III, King of the United Kingdom of Great Britain and Ireland* (Leeds: Long, Hurst & Co., 1820)
Bentham, Jeremy, *A Plea for the Constitution Shewing the Enormities Committed to the Oppression of British Subjects... In and by the Design, Foundation and Government of the Penal Colony of New South Wales: Including an Inquiry into*

Bibliography

the Right of the Crown to Legislate without Parliament in Trinidad and Other British Colonies (London: Mawman and Hatchard, 1803)

Blackstone, William, *Commentaries on the Laws of England*, first published 1765; facsimile of 9th edn, 1783 (New York and London: Garland Publishing, 1978)

Buckingham, James Silk, *Mr Buckingham's Defence of his Public and Private Character* (Sheffield: John Blackwell, 1832)

Buckingham, James Silk and Adam, John, *Statement of Facts Relative to the Removal from India of Mr. Buckingham late editor of the Calcutta Journal* (Calcutta, 1823)

Carey, Henry, *Chrononhonthologos: The most tragical tragedy that ever was tragediz'd by any company of tragedians* (London, 1734)

Historical Records of Australia (HRA), Series 1, Governor's despatches to and from England, Frederick Watson (ed.), 26 vols. (Sydney, 1914–25)

Historical Records of New South Wales (HRNSW), F.M. Bladen and Alexander Britton (eds.), 7 vols. (Sydney, 1892–1901)

House of Commons Debates: http://hansard.millbanksystems.com/commons/

Lenta, M., and B. le Cordeur (eds.), *The Cape Diaries of Lady Anne Barnard 1799–1800*, 2 vols. (Cape Town: Van Riebeek Society, 1998–1999)

Lewin Robinson, A. M. (ed.), *The Letters of Lady Anne Barnard to Henry Dundas from the Cape and Elsewhere, 1793–1803, Together with her Journal of a Tour into the Interior and Certain other Letters* (Cape Town: Balkema, 1973)

Meurant, L. H., *Sixty Years Ago; or Reminiscences of the Struggle for the Freedom of the Press in South Africa*, orig. publ. 1885, facsimile edn (Cape Town: Africana Connoisseurs Press, 1963)

Miller, Linus W., *Notes of an Exile to Van Diemen's Land* (New York: Fredonia, 1846)

Morrell, Philip (ed.), *Leaves from the Greville Diary: A New and Abridged Edition* (London: Eveleigh Nash & Grayson, 1929) Philip, John, *Researches in South Africa, Illustrating the Civil, Moral, and Religious Condition of the Native Tribes*, 2 vols. (London: James Ducan, 1828)

Pringle, Thomas, *Narrative of a Residence in South Africa* (London: Moxon, 1835)

Records of the Cape Colony: from February 1793 to April 1831 (RCC), George McCall Theal (eds.), 36 vols (London, 1897–1905)

Taylor, H., *Autobiography of Henry Taylor* (London: Longmans, 1885)

Vigne, Randolph (ed.), *The South African Letters of Thomas Pringle* (Cape Town: Van Riebeeck Society, 2011)

Wentworth, William, *A Statistical, Historical, and Political Description of the Colony of New South Wales and its Dependent Settlements in Van Diemen's Land* (London: G. and W. B. Whittaker, 1819)

NEWSPAPERS

Australian (Sydney)
Bataviasche Courant
Cape Town Gazette and African Advertiser
Chester Chronicle

Daily Mirror (Sydney)
Gloucester Journal
Hobart Town Gazette
Hull Packet and Original Weekly Commercial, Literary and General Advertiser
South African Commercial Advertiser
Sydney Gazette
Sydney Monitor
Times (London)

REFERENCE WORKS

Australian Dictionary of Biography
Dictionary of South African Biography
Oxford Dictionary of National Biography (Oxford University Press, 2004)
Cokayne, E., with Vicary Gibbs, H. A. Doubleday, Geoffrey H. White, Duncan Warrand and Lord Howard de Walden (eds.), *The Complete Peerage of England, Scotland, Ireland, Great Britain and the United Kingdom, Extant, Extinct or Dormant*, new edn, 6 vols. (Gloucester: Alan Sutton, 2000)

SECONDARY SOURCES

Adderley, Rosanne Marion, *'New Negroes from Africa': Slave Trade Abolition and Free African Settlement in the Nineteenth-Century Caribbean* (Indiana University Press, 2006)
Allen, Richard B., 'Licentious and unbridled proceedings: The illegal slave trade to Mauritius and the Seychelles during the early nineteenth century', *Journal of African History*, 42 (2001), 91–116
Anderson, Clare, *Legible Bodies: Race, Criminality and Colonialism in South Asia* (Oxford and New York: Berg, 2004)
Anderson, Clare, 'Multiple border crossings: "Convicts and other persons escaped from Botany Bay and residing in Calcutta"', *Journal of Australian Colonial History*, 3:2 (2001), 1–22
Anderson, Clare, *Subaltern Lives: Biographies of Colonialism in the Indian Ocean World 1790–1920* (Cambridge University Press, 2012)
Asiegbu, Johnson U. J., *Slavery and the Politics of Liberation 1797–1861* (London: Longmans, 1969)
Athulathmudali, Lalith W., 'The law of defamation in Ceylon: A study in the interaction of English and Roman-Dutch Law', *International and Comparative Law Quarterly*, 13:4 (Oct. 1964), 1368–1406
Atkinson, Alan, *The Europeans in Australia: A History*, 2 vols. (Oxford University Press, 1997 and 2004)
Atkinson, Alan, 'The free-born Englishman transported: Convict rights as a measure of eighteenth-century empire', *Past and Present*, 144 (1994), 88–115
Baartman, Teunis, 'Fighting for the spoils: Cape burgerschap and faction disputes in Cape Town in the 1770s', unpublished PhD thesis, University of Cape Town (2011)

Ballantyne, Tony, *Orientalism and Race: Aryanism in the British Empire* (New York: Palgrave, 2002)
Ballantyne, Tony, *Webs of Empire: Locating New Zealand's Colonial Past* (Wellington: Bridget William Books, 2012)
Ballantyne, Tony, and Antoinette Burton (eds.), *Gender, Mobility and Intimacy in an Age of Empire* (University of Illinois Press, 2008)
Bank, Andrew, *The Decline of Urban Slavery at the Cape 1806–1843* (Rondebosch: Centre for African Studies, 1991)
Bank, A., 'The Great Debate and the origins of South African historiography', *Journal of African History*, 38 (1997), 261–81
Bank, A., 'Liberals and their enemies: Racial ideology at the Cape of Good Hope, 1820–1850', unpublished PhD thesis, University of Cambridge (1995)
Bank, Andrew, 'Of "native skulls" and "noble Caucasians": Phrenology in colonial South Africa', *Journal of Southern African Studies*, 22:3 (Sept 1996) 387–403
Barker, Anthony J., 'Distorting the record of slavery and abolition: The British anti-slavery movement and Mauritius 1826–1837', *Slavery and Abolition*, 14:3 (1993), 185–207
Barker, Anthony J., *Slavery and Antislavery in Mauritius 1810–1833: The Conflict between Economic Expansion and Humanitarian Reform under British Rule* (London: Macmillan, 1996)
Bashford, Alison, and Stuart Macintyre (eds.), *The Cambridge History of Australia* (Cambridge University Press, 2013), vol. I, *Indigenous and Colonial Australia*
Bayly, C. A., *Empire and Information: Intelligence Gathering and Social Communication in India, 1780–1870* (Cambridge University Press, 1996)
Bayly, C. A., *Imperial Meridian: The British Empire and the World 1780–1830* (London: Longmans, 1989)
Bayly, C. A., *Recovering Liberties: Indian Thought in the Age of Liberalism and Empire* (Cambridge University Press, 2012)
Bell, Sydney Smith, *Colonial Administration of Great Britain* (London: Longmans, 1859)
Bennett, J. M. 'The day of retribution: Commissioner Bigge's inquiries in colonial New South Wales', *American Journal of Legal History*, 85 (1971), 85–106
Bennett, J. M., *Sir Francis Forbes: First Chief Justice of New South Wales 1823–1837* (Sydney: Federation Press, 2001)
Benton, Lauren, 'Abolition and imperial law 1790–1820', *Journal of Imperial and Commonwealth History*, 39:3 (Sept. 2011), 355–74
Benton, Lauren, *Law and Colonial Cultures: Legal Regimes in World History 1400–1900* (Cambridge University Press, 2002)
Benton, Lauren, *A Search for Sovereignty: Law and Geography in European Empires 1400–1900* (Cambridge University Press, 2010)
Benton, Lauren and Richard Ross, 'Empires and legal pluralism: Jurisdiction, sovereignty, and political imagination in the early modern world', in Lauren Benton and Richard Ross (eds.), *Legal Pluralism and Empires 1500–1850* (New York University Press, 2013)

Bibliography

Bergemann, Karl, 'The murderers, the soldiers and the wrongfully accused: The role of transportation and banishment at the Cape in the first half of the nineteenth century', unpublished BA (hons) thesis, University of Cape Town (2007)

Botha, H. C., *John Fairbairn in South Africa* (Cape Town: Historical Publication Society, 1984)

Bourne, J. M., *Patronage and Society in Nineteenth-Century England* (London: Edward Arnold, 1986)

Britts, M. G., *The Commandants: The Tyrants who Ruled Norfolk Island* (Norfolk Island: Kapak Publishing, 1980)

Brown, Christopher Leslie, *Moral Capital: Foundations of British Abolitionism* (University of North Carolina Press, 2006)

Butler, Jeffrey, 'Review of Anthony Kendal Millar, Plantagenet in South Africa', *American Historical Review*, 71:2 (1966), 638–9

Caldwell, Robert G., 'Exile as an institution', *Political Science Quarterly*, 58:2 (June 1943), 239–62

Causer, Timothy, '"Only a place fit for angels and eagles": The Norfolk Island penal settlement 1825–1855', unpublished PhD thesis, University of London (2010)

Clark, Anna, *Scandal: The Sexual Politics of the British Constitution* (Princeton University Press, 2004)

Clarke, Luke Joachim, '"Lost to all humanity"? Suicide, religion and murder pacts in convict Van Diemen's Land', unpublished BA (hons) thesis, University of Tasmania (2002)

Clune, Frank, *Scallywags of Sydney Cove* (Sydney: Angus & Robertson, 1968); republished as *Rascals, Ruffians and Rebels of Early Australia* (Sydney: Angus & Robertson, 1987)

Cochrane, Peter, *Colonial Ambition: Foundations of Australian Democracy* (Melbourne University Press, 2006)

Cory, G. E., *Rise of South Africa: A History of the Origin of South African Colonisation and of its Development towards the East from the Earliest Times to 1857* (London: Longmans, Green, 1913)

Crais, Clifton, *White Supremacy and Black Resistance in Pre-Industrial South Africa: The Making of the Colonial Order in the Eastern Cape 1770–1865* (Cambridge University Press, 1992)

Currey, C. H., *Sir Francis Forbes: The First Chief Justice of the Supreme Court of New South Wales* (Sydney: Angus & Robertson, 1968)

Dirks, Nicholas B., *The Scandal of Empire: India and the Creation of Imperial Britain* (Harvard University Press, 2006)

Dooling, Wayne, 'The good opinion of others': Law, slavery and community in the Cape Colony c. 1760–1840', in Nigel Worden and C. Crais (eds.), *Breaking the Chains: Slavery and its Legacy in the Nineteenth-Century Cape Colony* (Johannesburg: Witwatersrand University Press, 1994)

Dooling, Wayne, *Slavery, Emancipation and Colonial Rule in South Africa* (Scottsville: University of KwaZulu-Natal Press, 2007)

du Preez, Hercules Michael, 'Dr James Barry: The early years revealed' *South African Medical Journal*, 98: 1 (2008), 52–62

Eddy, J. J., *Britain and the Australian Colonies 1818–1831: The Technique of Government* (Oxford: Clarendon Press, 1969)

Edgeworth, Brendan, 'Defamation law and the emergence of a critical press in colonial New South Wales 1824–1831', *Australian Journal of Law and Society*, 6 (1990–1991), 50–82

Edwards, Isobel, *The 1820 Settlers in South Africa: A Study in British Colonial Policy* (London: The Royal Society, 1934)

Elbourne, Elizabeth, *Blood Ground: Colonialism, Missions, and the Contest for Christianity in the Cape Colony and Britain 1799–1853* (London: McGill-Queen's University Press, 2002)

Elphick, Richard and Hermann Giliomee, 'The origins and entrenchment of European dominance at the Cape 1652–c. 1840', in R. Elphick and H. Giliomee (eds.), *The Shaping of South African Society 1652–1840*, 2nd edn (Cape Town: Maskew Miller Longman, 1989), 521–66

Elphick, Richard and Robert Shell, 'Intergroup relations: Khoikhoi, settlers, slaves and free blacks, 1652–1795' in R. Elphick and H. Giliomee (eds.), *Shaping of South African Society*, 2nd edn (Cape Town: Maskew Miller Longman, 1989), 184–239

Emsley, Clive, 'An aspect of Pitt's "Terror": Prosecutions for sedition during the 1790s', *Social History*, 6:2 (May 1981), 155–84

Epstein, James, 'The radical underworld goes colonial: P. F. McCallum's travels in Trinidad', in Michael T. Davis and Paul Pickering (eds.), *Unrespectable Radicals? Popular Politics in the Age of Reform* (Aldershot: Ashgate, 2008), pp. 147–65

Epstein, James, *Scandal of Colonial Rule: Power and Subversion in the British Atlantic during the Age of Revolution* (Cambridge University Press, 2012)

Erasmus, H. J., 'The interaction of substantive law and procedure' in Reinhard Zimmermann and Daniel Visser (eds.), *Southern Cross: Civil Law and Common Law in South Africa* (Oxford: Clarendon Press, 1996), pp. 141–62

Evans, Raymond, '19 June 1822: Creating "an object of real terror" ~ The tabling of the first Bigge Report', in Martin Crotty and David Andrew Roberts (eds.), *Turning Points in Australian History* (University of New South Wales Press, 2009)

Fagan, Eduard, 'Roman-Dutch law in its South African historical context', in Reinhard Zimmermann and Daniel Visser (eds.), *Southern Cross: Civil Law and Common Law in South Africa* (Oxford: Clarendon Press, 1996), pp. 33–64

Fletcher, Brian, *Ralph Darling: A Governor Maligned* (Oxford University Press, 1984)

Ford, Lisa, *Settler Sovereignty: Jurisdiction and Indigenous People in America and Australia 1788–1836* (Harvard University Press, 2010)

Ford, Lisa and David Andrew Roberts, 'Expansion 1820–1850', in Alison Bashford and Stuart Macintyre (eds.), *The Cambridge History of Australia* (Cambridge University Press, 2013), vol. I, *Indigenous and Colonial Australia*, pp. 121–48

Ford, Lisa, and David Andrew Roberts, 'Legal change, convict activism and the reform of penal relocation in colonial New South Wales: The Port Macquarie

penal settlement 1822–1826', *Australian Historical Studies*, 46:2 (2015), 174–91
Fremantle, A. F, 'The truth about Oliver the Spy', *English Historical Review*, 47 (1932), 601–16
Freund, William M., 'The Cape under the transitional governments 1795–1814', in R. Elphick and H. Gilliomee (eds.), *The Shaping of South African Society 1652–1840*, 2nd edn (Cape Town: Maskew Miller Longman, 1989), pp. 324–57
Griffen-Foley, B., 'Digging up the past: Frank Clune ~ Australian historian and multi-media personality', *History Australia*, 8:1 (2011), 127–50
Griffiths, Tom, *Hunters and Collectors: The Antiquarian Imagination in Australia* (Cambridge University Press, 1996)
Halliday, Paul D., *Habeas Corpus: From England to Empire* (Harvard University Press, 2010)
Hamilton, Carolyn, Bernard K. Mbenga, and Robert Ross (eds.), *The Cambridge History of South Africa* (London: Cambridge University Press, 2010), vol. I, *From Early Times to 1885*
Hamilton, Carolyn, Bernard K. Mbenga and Robert Ross, 'The production of preindustrial South African history', in Hamilton, Mbegna and Ross (eds.), *The Cambridge History of South Africa* (Cambridge University Press, 2010), pp. 20–1
Hammond, J. L., and Barbara Hammond, *The Skilled Labourer* (London: Longmans, 1919)
Harling, Philip, 'The law of libel and the limits of repression 1790–1832', *Historical Journal*, 44:1 (March 2001), 107–34
Harling, Philip, *The Waning of 'Old Corruption': The Politics of Economical Reform in Britain 1779–1846* (Oxford: Clarendon Press, 1996)
Harries, Patrick, '"The hobgoblins of the Middle Passage": The Cape and the Trans-Atlantic slave trade', in U. Schmieder and K. Füllberg-Stolberg (eds.), *The End of Slavery in Africa and the Americas: A Comparative Approach* (Münster: LIT Verlag, 2011), pp. 27–50
Harries, Patrick, 'Negotiating Abolition: Cape Town and the Trans-Atlantic Slave Trade', *Slavery and Abolition*, 34:4 (2013), 579–97
Hattersley, A. F., *Oliver the Spy and Others: A Little Gallery of South African Portraits* (Cape Town: Maskew Miller, 1959)
Heney, Helen, *Dear Fanny: Women's Letters to and from New South Wales 1788–1851* (Australian National University Press, 1985)
Hirst, J. B., 'Or none of the above: A reply', *Historical Studies*, 22:89 (Oct. 1987), 519–24
Hirst, J. B., *Convict Society and its Enemies: A History of Early New South Wales* (Sydney: Allen & Unwin, 1983)
Hirst, Warwick, *Great Convict Escapes in Colonial Australia*, rev. edn (Sydney: Kangaroo Press, 2003)
Holdridge, Christopher, 'The escape of William Edwards: Respectability, intrigue and invented identity in the early British Cape and Australia', unpublished BA (hons) thesis, University of Cape Town (2008)

Holmes, Rachel, *Scanty Particulars: The Strange Life and Astonishing Secret of Victorian Adventurer and Pioneering Surgeon James Barry* (London: Penguin, 2002)

Hughes, Robert, *The Fatal Shore: A History of the Transportation of Convicts to Australia 1787–1868* (London: Collins, 1986)

Humanity editors (unattributed), 'Of pirates, empire and terror: An interview with Lauren Benton and Dan Edelstein', *Humanity: An International Journal of Human Rights, Humanitarianism, and Development*, 2:1 (Spring 2011), 75–84

Huselbosch, Daniel Joseph, 'The ancient constitution and the expanding empire: Sir Edward Coke's British jurisprudence', *Law and History Review*, 21:3 (2003), 439–82

Huselbosch, Daniel Joseph, *Constituting Empire: New York and the Transformation of Constitutionalism in the Atlantic World 1664–1830* (University of North Carolina Press, 2005)

Hussain, Nasser, *The Jurisprudence of Emergency: Colonialism and the Rule of Law* (University of Michigan Press, 2003)

Ihde, Erin, '"Bold, manly-minded men" and "sly, cunning base convicts": The double standard of escape', *Journal of Australian Colonial History*, 7 (2005), 123–38

Ihde, Erin, *A Manifesto for New South Wales: Edward Smith Hall and the Sydney Monitor, 1826–1840* (Melbourne: Australian Scholarly, 2004)

Jalland, Pat, *Australian Ways of Death: A Social and Cultural History 1840–1918* (Oxford University Press, 2002)

Karskens, Grace, *The Colony: A History of Early Sydney* (Sydney: Allen & Unwin, 2009)

Karskens, Grace, 'The early colonial presence 1788–1822', in Alison Bashford and Stuart Macintyre (eds.), *The Cambridge History of Australia* (Cambridge University Press, 2013), vol. I, *Indigenous and Colonial Australia*, pp. 91–120

Karskens, Grace, *The Rocks: Life in Early Sydney* (Melbourne University Press, 1998)

Karskens, Grace, '"This spirit of emigration": The nature and meanings of escape in early New South Wales', *Journal of Australian Colonial History*, 7 (2005), 1–34

Keegan, Timothy, *Colonial South Africa and the Origins of the Racial Order* (Leicester University Press, 1996)

Kercher, Bruce, *Debt, Seduction and Other Disasters: The Birth of Civil Law in Convict New South Wales* (Sydney: Federation Press, 1996)

Kercher, Bruce, 'Perish or prosper: The law and convict transportation in the British Empire 1700–1850', *Law and History Review*, 21:3 (2003), 527–54

Kercher, Bruce, *An Unruly Child: A History of Law in Australia* (Sydney: Allan & Unwin, 1995)

Kostal, R. W., *A Jurisprudence of Power: Victorian Empire and the Rule of Law* (Oxford University Press, 2005)

Lachlan Macquarie: The Father of Australia (Ronin Films, 2010). www.roninfilms.com.au/feature/6093/lachlan-macquarie-father-of-australia.html (viewed 17 Jan. 2014)

Laidlaw, Zoë, 'Breaking Britannia's bounds? Law, settlers and space in Britain's imperial historiography', *Historical Journal*, 55:3 (2012), 807–30
Laidlaw, Zoë, *Colonial Connections 1815–1845: Patronage, the Information Revolution and Colonial Government* (Manchester University Press, 2005)
Laidlaw, Zoë, 'Investigating empire: Humanitarians, reform and the Commission of Eastern Inquiry', *Journal of Imperial and Commonwealth History*, 40:5 (2012), 749–68
Lambert, David, and Alan Lester (eds.), *Colonial Lives across the British Empire: Imperial Careering in the Long Nineteenth Century* (Cambridge University Press, 2006)
Legassick, Martin, and Robert Ross, 'From slave economy to settler capitalism: The Cape Colony and its extensions 1800–1854', in Carolyn Hamilton, Bernard K. Mbenga and Robert Ross (eds.), *The Cambridge History of South Africa* (Cambridge University Press, 2010), vol. I, From Early Times to 1885, pp. 253–318
Lester, Alan, *Imperial Networks: Creating Identity in Nineteenth-Century South Africa and Britain* (London: Routledge, 2001)
Lester, Alan, and Fae Dussart, *Colonization and the Origins of Humanitarian Governance: Protecting Aborigines across the Nineteenth-Century British Empire* (Cambridge University Press, 2014)
Levell, David, *Tour to Hell: Convict Australia's Great Escape Myths* (University of Queensland Press, 2008)
Loveland, Ian, *Political Libels: A Comparative Study* (Oxford: Hart, 2000)
MacDonald, Helen, *Human Remains: Episodes in Human Dissection* (Melbourne University Press, 2005)
MacDonald, Helen, *Possessing the Dead: The Artful Science of Anatomy* (Melbourne University Press, 2011)
Macintyre, Stuart, and Anna Clark (eds.), *The History Wars*, new edn (Melbourne University Press, 2004)
Macintyre, Stuart, *Concise History of Australia* (Cambridge University Press, 1999)
MacKenzie, John M. (ed.), *Imperialism and Popular Culture* (Manchester University Press, 1986)
MacKenzie, John M., '"To enlighten South Africa": The creation of a free press at the Cape in the early nineteenth century', in C. Kaul (ed.), *Media and the British Empire* (Basingstoke: Palgrave, 2006), pp. 20–36
MacKenzie, John M., *Propaganda and Empire: The Manipulation of British Public Opinion 1880–1960* (Manchester University Press, 1984)
Macmillan, M. W., *The Cape Colour Question: A Historical Survey* (London: Faber & Gwyer, 1927)
Malherbe, V. C., 'Khoikhoi and the question of convict transportation from the Cape Colony 1820–1842', *South African Historical Journal*, 17 (1985), 19–36
Marshall, P. J., 'Britain and the world in the eighteenth century: The turning outwards of Britain', *Transactions of the Royal Historical Society*, 11 (2001), 1–15
Mason, John Edward, 'Hendrik Albertus and his ex-slave Mey: A drama in three acts', *Journal of African History*, 31 (1990), 423–45

Mason, John Edwin, *Social Death and Resurrection: Slavery and Emancipation in South Africa* (University of Virginia Press, 2003)
Maxwell-Stewart, Hamish, '"Those lads contrived a plan": Attempts at mutiny on Australia-bound convict vessels', *International Review of Social History*, 58 (2013), 177–96
Maxwell-Stewart, Hamish, *Closing Hell's Gates: The Death of a Convict Station* (Sydney: Allen & Unwin, 2008)
McCreery, Cindy and Kirsten McKenzie, 'The Australian colonies in a maritime world', in Alison Bashford and Stuart Macintyre (eds.), *Cambridge History of Australia* (Cambridge University Press, 2013), vol. I, *Indigenous and Colonial Australia*, pp. 560–84
McKenzie, Kirsten, 'The Franklins of the Cape: The South African Commercial Advertiser and the creation of a colonial public sphere 1824–1854', *Kronos: Journal of Cape History*, 25 (1998/1999), 88–102
McKenzie, Kirsten, 'My own mind dying within me: Eliza Fairbairn and the reinvention of colonial middle-class domesticity in Cape Town', *South African Historical Journal*, 36 (May 1997), 3–23
McKenzie, Kirsten, '"My voice is sold & I must be a Slave": Abolition, industrialisation and the Yorkshire election of 1807', *History Workshop Journal*, 64 (2007), 48–73
McKenzie, Kirsten, *Scandal in the Colonies: Sydney and Cape Town 1820–1850* (Melbourne University Press, 2004)
McKenzie, Kirsten, *Swindler's Progress: Nobles and Convicts in the Age of Liberty* (University of New South Wales Press, 2009)
McLachlin, N.D. 'Bathurst at the Colonial Office, 1812–1827: A Reconnaissance' *Historical Studies: Australia and New Zealand* (1967–69), vol. XIII
Meiring, Jane, *Thomas Pringle: His Life and Times* (Cape Town: Balkema, 1968)
Meltzer, L., 'Emancipation, commerce and the rise of John Fairbairn's Advertiser', in N. Worden and C. Crais (eds.), *Breaking the Chains: Slavery and its Legacy in the Nineteenth-Century Cape Colony* (Johannesburg: Witwatersrand University Press, 1994), pp. 169–99
Millar, Kendal, *Plantagenet in South Africa: Lord Charles Somerset* (Cape Town, 1965)
Neal, David, 'Free society, penal colony, slave society, prison?', *Historical Studies*, 22:89 (Oct. 1987), 497–518
Neal, David, *The Rule of Law in a Penal Colony: Law and Power in Early New South Wales* (Cambridge University Press, 1991)
Newton-King, Susan, 'For the love of Adam: Two sodomy trials at the Cape of Good Hope', *Kronos: Southern African Histories* 28 (2002), 21–42
Newton-King, Susan, 'The labour market of the Cape Colony', in Shula Marks and Anthony Atmore (eds.), *Economy and Society in Pre-Industrial South Africa* (London: Longman, 1980), pp. 171–207
Niekerk, J. P. van, 'British, Portuguese, and American judges in Adderley Street: The international legal background to and some judicial aspects of the Cape Town Mixed Commissions for the suppression of the transatlantic slave trade in the nineteenth century', *Comparative and International Law Journal of Southern Africa*, 37 (2004), 3 parts, 1–39, 197–225, 404–35

Olivier, N. J. J., 'Laster' in G. G. Visagie, L. F. van Huyssteen, C. R. de Beer, N. J. J. Olivier, W. du Plessis, J. Th. de Smidt and H. C. Gall (eds.), *Die Siviele Appèlhof en die Raad van Justisie, Hofstukke en Uitsprake wat Betrekking het of Siviele Sake, 1806–1827: 'n Evaluering van Capita Selecta uit Bepaalde Gebiede van die Reg aan die Kaap* (Die Kaapse Regspraak-Projek, final research report. University of the Western Cape, Potchestroomse Universiteit vir Christelike Hoër Onderwys, Leiden University, 1992)

Outing, Roger, *The Standard Catalogue of the Provincial Banknotes of England and Wales* (Honiton: Token Publishing, 2010)

Peires, J. B., 'The British and the Cape' in R. Elphick and H. Gilliomee (eds.), *The Shaping of South African Society 1652–1840*, 2nd edn (Cape Town: Maskew Miller Longman, 1989), pp. 472–518

Pickering, Paul, 'Betrayal and exile: A forgotten Chartist experience', in Michael T. Davis and Paul Pickering (eds.), *Unrespectable Radicals? Popular Politics in the Age of Reform* (Aldershot: Ashgate, 2008), pp. 201–17

Porter, Bernard, *The Absent-Minded Imperialists: Empire, Society and Culture in Britain* (Oxford University Press, 2004)

Porter, Bernard, *Plots and Paranoia: History of Political Espionage in Britain 1790–1988* (London: Routledge, 1989)

Rae, Isobel, *The Strange Story of Dr James Barry* (London: Longmans, Green, 1958)

Ranchod, Bhadra, *Foundations of the South African Law of Defamation* (Leiden University Press, 1972)

Rayner, Mary, 'Wine and slaves: The failure of an export economy and the ending of slavery in the Cape Colony, South Africa 1806–1834', unpublished PhD dissertation, Duke University (1986)

Reidy, Michael Charles, 'The admission of slaves and "prize slaves" into the Cape Colony 1797–1818', unpublished MA thesis, University of Cape Town (1997)

Ritchie, John, *Punishment and Profit: The Reports of Commissioner John Bigge on the Colonies of New South Wales and Van Diemen's Land 1822–1823 – Their Origins, Nature and Significance* (Melbourne: Heinemann, 1970)

Roberts, David A., 'A "change of place": Illegal movement on the Bathurst frontier 1822–1825', *Journal of Australian Colonial History*, 7 (2005), 97–122

Roberts, David A., '"The valley of swells": "Special" or "educated" convicts on the Wellington Valley settlement 1827–1830', *History Australia*, 3:1 (2006), 11.1–11.20

Roberts, Michael, 'Lord Charles Somerset and the "Beaufort Influence"', *Archives Year Book for South African History*, 2 (1951)

Robinson, A. M. L., *None Daring to Make Us Afraid: A Study of English Periodical Literature in the Cape Colony from its Beginnings in 1824 to 1835* (Cape Town: Maskew Miller, 1962)

Rose, June, *The Perfect Gentleman: The Remarkable Life of Dr James Miranda Barry, the Woman who Served as an Officer in the British Army from 1813 to 1859* (London: Hutchinson, 1977)

Ross, Lynette, 'The final escape: An analysis of suicide at the penal settlement of Port Arthur', *Journal of Australian Colonial History*, 7 (2005), 181–202

Ross, Robert, *The Borders of Race in Colonial South Africa: The Kat River Settlement, 1829–1856* (Cambridge University Press, 2014)

Ross, Robert, *Cape of Torments: Slavery and Resistance in South Africa* (London: Routledge, 1983)

Ross, Robert, 'Donald Moodie and the origins of South African historiography', in Robert Ross (ed.), *Beyond the Pale: Essays in the History of Colonial South Africa* (Johannesburg: Witwatersrand University Press 1993), pp. 192–212

Ross, Robert, 'Paternalism, patriarchy and Afrikaans', *South African Historical Journal*, 32 (May 1995), 34–47

Ross, Robert, *Status and Respectability in the Cape Colony 1750–1870: A Tragedy of Manners* (Cambridge University Press, 1999)

Rugarli, Anna Maria, 'Eyes on the prize: The story of the prize slave present', *Quarterly Bulletin of the South African Library*, 62:4 (2008), 161–72

Russell, G., *The Theatres of War: Performance, Politics and Society 1793–1815* (Oxford: Clarendon Press, 1995)

Salahuddin Ahmed, A. F., *Social Ideas and Social Change in Bengal 1818–1835* (Leiden: Brill, 1965)

Saunders, Christopher, '"Free, yet slaves": Prize negroes at the Cape revisited', in Nigel Worden and Crais (eds.), *Breaking the Chains* (Johannesburg: Witwatersrand University Press, 1994), pp. 99–115

Saunders, Christopher, 'Liberated Africans in Cape Colony in the first half of the nineteenth century', *International Journal of African Historical Studies*, 18:2 (1985), 223–39

Schuler, Monica, *'Alas, Alas Kongo': A Social History of Indentured African Immigration into Jamaica 1841–1865* (Baltimore: Johns Hopkins University Press, 1980)

Scully, Pamela, *Liberating the Family? Gender and British Slave Emancipation in the Rural Western Cape, South Africa 1823–1853* (Portsmouth: Heinemann, 1997)

Sen, Sudipta, 'Imperial subjects on trial: On the legal identity of Britons in late eighteenth-century India', *Journal of British Studies*, 45:3 (2006), 532–55

Shell, Robert, *Children of Bondage: A Social History of the Slave Society at the Cape of Good Hope 1652–1838* (Johannesburg: Witwatersrand University Press, 1994)

Smith, Keith, 'Securing the state, the institutions of government, and maintaining public order', in William Cornish, J. Stuart Anderson, Ray Cocks, Michael Lobban, Patrick Polden and Keith Smith (eds.), *The Oxford History of the Laws of England* (Oxford University Press, 2010), vol. XIII

Smith, Ken, *The Changing Past: Trends in South African Historical Writing* (Ohio University Press, 1988)

Spigelman, J. J., 'Foundations of freedom of the press in Australia', *Australian Bar Review*, 23 (2002–2003), 89–109

Spigelman, J. J., 'The Macquarie Bicentennial: A reappraisal of the Bigge reports', History Council of New South Wales Annual History Lecture 2009 (Sydney: History Council of New South Wales, 2009)

Stephens, John, *England's Last Revolution: Pentrich 1817* (Buxton: Moorland, 1977)

Sturgis, James, 'Anglicisation at the Cape of Good Hope in the early nineteenth century', *Journal of Imperial and Commonwealth History*, 11 (1982), 5–32

Theal, George McCall, *History of South Africa from 1795–1872* (London: Allen & Unwin, 1915)

Thompson, E. P., *The Making of the English Working Class* (London: Penguin, 1980), first published 1963

Toit, André du, and Hermann Giliomee, *Afrikaner Political Thought: Analysis and Documents* (Cape Town: David Philip, 1983), vol. I, 1780–1850

Tomlins, Christopher, *Freedom Bound: Law, Labor, and Civic Identity in Colonizing English America 1580–1865* (Cambridge University Press, 2010)

Turner, Edward Raymond, 'The Secrecy of the Post', *English Historical Review*, 33:131 (July 1918), 320–2

Vernon, James, *Politics and the People: A Study in English Political Culture c. 1815–1867* (Cambridge University Press, 1993)

Vigne, Randolph, *Thomas Pringle: South African Pioneer, Poet and Abolitionist* (Woodbridge, Suffolk: James Currey, 2012)

Walvin, James, 'Freedom and slavery and the shaping of Victorian Britain', *Slavery and Abolition*, 15:2 (1994), 246–59

Ward, John M., *Colonial Self-Government: The British Experience 1759–1856* (London: Macmillan, 1976)

Ward, Kerry, *Networks of Empire: Forced Migration in the Dutch East India Company* (Cambridge University Press, 2009)

Watson, R. L., *Slave Emancipation and Racial Attitudes in Nineteenth-Century South Africa* (Cambridge University Press, 2012)

Watson, R. L., *The Slave Question: Liberty and Property in South Africa* (Johannesburg: Witwatersrand University Press, 1990)

White, R. J., *From Waterloo to Peterloo* (London: Heinemann, 1957)

Wickwar, W. Hardy, *The Struggle for the Freedom of the Press 1819–1832* (London: Allen & Unwin, 1928)

Williams, E. T., 'The Colonial Office in the thirties', *Historical Studies, Australia and New Zealand*, 2:7 (May 1943), 141–60

Wilson, K., 'Rowe's Fair Penitent as global history: Or, a diversionary voyage to New South Wales', *Eighteenth-Century Studies*, 41:2 (2008), 231–51

Wilson, K., *The Island Race: Englishness, Empire and Gender in the Eighteenth Century* (London and New York: Routledge, 2003)

Wolter, Michael, 'Sound and fury in colonial Australia: The search for the convict voice 1820–1840', unpublished PhD thesis, University of Sydney (2014)

Woods, T. P. 'Lord Bathurst's Policy at the Colonial Office, 1812–1821, with particular reference to New South Wales and the Cape Colony' unpublished DPhil thesis, Oxford (1971)

Worden, Nigel, 'Artisan conflicts in a colonial context: The Cape Town blacksmith strike of 1752', *Labour History*, 46:2 (May 2005), 155–84

Worden, Nigel, 'Demanding satisfaction: Violence, masculinity and honour in late eighteenth-century Cape Town', *Kronos* 35 (2009), 32–47

Worden, Nigel, *Slavery in Dutch South Africa* (Cambridge University Press, 1985)

Wright, Barry, 'Libel and the colonial administration of justice in Upper Canada and New South Wales c. 1825–1830', in H. Foster, B. Berger and A. Buck

Index

Bathurst, Henry, third Earl Bathurst (*cont.*)
  on the curtailment of colonial government powers, 208
  deference to Somerset in their correspondence, 77
  description of Somerset as a 'Jockey', 77
  doubts concerning the legality of Edwards's libel sentence, 189
  dual administration system of, 79–80
  on the errors made by Somerset, 208
  exasperation with Somerset, 66, 77
  farewell to the colonial governors, 78
  Greville's description of, 64–6
  haphazard way of handling papers and correspondence, 67
  humorous nature of, 66
  instructions to Somerset to release Edwards, 261, 268
  interest in the Edwards–Somerset libel case, 179
  key elements in managing the interpersonal relations of colonial governance, 76–7
  on the legality of political removal, 209–10
  on the legality of Somerset's executive power, 208
  pragmatic nature of, 66
  private correspondence of, 79
  proposal for an advisory council, 210
  relationship with colonial officials, 78
  reprimand of Somerset, 70–1, 76
  skill as a manager, 66
  warning to Somerset concerning the apprentice slave system, 150
Bayly, C. A., 10, 194, 205
'Beaufort influence', 75, 76, 96
Bennett, J. M., 9–10, 98, 99, 101
Bentick, W., 219
Benton, Lauren, 111
Bigge, John Thomas, 5, 19, 25, 39, 60, 98, 109, 115, 134, 170, 171–2, 188–9, 197, 246, 251, 266
  complaints of Somerset to, concerning Denyssen and Greig, 225, 232
  concern over the harsh sentencing of Edwards, 179
  correspondence with Somerset, 25
  as an information-gathering bureaucrat, 6
  instructions concerning convicts and convict transportation, 53
  investigation into criminal law and jurisprudence, 180
  investigation into Edwards' allegations against Somerset, 61–2
  investigation into the identity and background of Edwards, 60
  investigations in Van Diemen's Land, 5, 51
  and the issue of 'salutary terror', 53
  opinion of the Burnett memorial libel case, 180–1
  poor reputation of, in Australia, 52
  recommendation of the implementation of English law in Trinidad, 175
  report on the Courts of Justice, 175
  on Somerset's actions having significance in colonies other than the Cape, 205
  warm personal relationship with Somerset, 194–5
  See also Bigge, John Thomas, reports concerning Australian colonies; Bigge, John Thomas, reports concerning New South Wales; prize slave scandal and investigations
Bigge, John Thomas, reports concerning Australian colonies, 25–6, 52
  criticism of the reports, 98
  key outcome of the Bigge reports, 54
  motives behind the commission, 53
  recommendations concerning convicts, 54–5
  recommendations leading to greater colonial rights and constitutional development, 55
Bigge, John Thomas, reports concerning New South Wales, 51
  general reports, 9–10, 23
  judicial reforms following the reports, 250
  report on judicial establishments, 35–6
  report noting escapes from New South Wales, 35
biography, transnational, 11
Bird, Christopher, 41, 177
  conflicts of, with Somerset, 61
Bird, William Wilberforce, 105, 107, 116, 138, 161
  Groene Rivier property, 124
  personal benefits from the prize slave system, 121
  protestations of his innocence in the prize slave scandal, 127
  strategies to profit from the prize slave system, 123, 124
Birkwood, W. J., 123
Bishop, Sophia, 221
Blackstone, William, 57, 145, 186, 204
Blackwood's Edinburgh Magazine, 47

Index

Blair, Charles, 19, 105, 106, 107, 116, 119, 129, 130, 134–5, 139, 144, 146, 151
  accusations against, as a political liability for Somerset, 151
  denial of cruelty towards Cousins, 135
  dispute with Corbitt over Malamo, 135–6, 137
  gossip concerning Blair's 'transactions', 126–7
  as the 'great Prize Negro Merchant', 125
  personal benefits of the prize slave system, 121
  protestations of his innocence in the prize slave scandal, 127
  return to England (1820), 123
  sale of his Stellenberg estate, 124, 125
  strategies to profit from the prize slave system, 123, 124
  temper of, 130, 135
  See also prize slave libel trial, of Edwards and Cooke; prize slave scandal and investigations concerning
Blanketeers March (1817), 46
Blasphemous and Seditious Libels Act (1819), 168–9, 179, 198
  parliamentary debates concerning, 197–8
  repeal of the banishment clause of, 207
Bourke, Richard, 81, 249
Brand, Christoffel Joseph, 176, 177, 178
  defence of Edward during his appeal of the Edwards–Somerset libel conviction, 184, 185–7
  defence of Edwards during the prize slave libel trial, 145
  on the sentence of transportation for libel as 'illegal', 179
  use of Cicero's defence of Milo in defending Edwards, 184
Bridekirk, William, 217, 219
Brisbane, Thomas, 246, 261, 266
  involvement of, with Edwards and subsequent political debate concerning, 253–4
Britain
  conceptions of freedom in, and subsequent opposition to slavery, 155
  concepts of good governance in, 101
  conservative reaction to revolutionary challenges in North America and Europe, 10
  controversial nature of colonial administrators in, 10
  emigration initiatives of, 46
  generational shift in eighteenth-century notions of governance, 71
  government reform investigations into the Cape and Australian colonies, 6
  national identity of, 3
  'Old Corruption' in, 5, 14, 43, 92, 121
  overhaul of imperial administration, 4
  political and social upheavals after Waterloo, 45–6, 53
  transformations from the eighteenth to the nineteenth century, 75
  See also British colonial subjects
'British and the Cape, The' (Peires), 51–2
British colonial subjects, 181, 211
  definition of, 167
  legal rights/status of, 167, 176, 211, 251
  See also settler societies
Brougham, Henry, 15, 16, 48, 66, 91, 209, 241, 242, 243
  on Oliver the Spy and the placard scandal, 241
Brown, Christopher Leslie, 155, 158
Bryant, Mary, 35
Buckingham, James Silk, deportation case of, 206
  reported in the *Advertiser*, 206
buggery, 224
Burbidge, Peter, 28, 30
Burdett, Francis, 91
Burnett, Bishop, 16, 17, 95, 96, 156, 166, 192, 230, 241–2, 243
  banishment for libel, 197, 198
  daring escape, 200
  on Oliver the Spy, 240–1
  trial for a memorial libeling the Cape judiciary, 179
Buxton, Thomas Fowell, 49, 113
Byron (George Gordon, Lord Byron), opinion of the Hortons, 68

Calcutta Journal, 206
Calderón, Luisa, 204
Caldwell, Maria, 67
Campbell v. Hall (1774), 203
Canning, George, 82, 89
Cape Advisory Council, 210–11
Cape Colony, 4, 9
  activists/reformers in, 48
  alliance in, between the Cape Dutch gentry and the ruling British administration, 43, 151, 158
  British subsidised emigration scheme for settlers (the '1820' settlers) in, 46, 47, 274–5
  the 'Cape Patriot movement' in, 43, 201

306   Index

Denijssen (Denyssen), Daniel, 43, 44–5, 145, 151, 152, 161, 172, 177, 178, 193
　attacked in satirical placards, 182
　call for an exemplary sentence in the Edwards-Somerset libel case, 179
　as 'Dog Dan', 44
　Edwards's attacks on his service and loyalty, 45, 108
　on executive power, 205
　legal opinion concerning banishment, 200–2
　letter defending himself against Edwards's charges, 152, 153
　an opponent of Anglicisation, 45
　proficiency in the English language, 177
　prosecution of Edwards in the Edwards–Somerset libel case, 187–8, 205
　prosecution of Edwards in the placard scandal, 226
　retirement of, 45
　Somerset's complaints concerning, 225
dissection, 280–1
　of convicts and Aboriginal people in colonial Australia, 281
　horror of, 279–80
Dixon, Charles, 123–4
Donkin, Rufane, 41, 61, 96, 236–7
　cost-cutting during his tenure as governor, 92
　opinion of Somerset, 91
　squashing of espionage operations when governor, 92, 93
Dooling, Wayne, 112
'Dreyer's Corner', 214
Dutch East India Company (*Vereenigde Oostindische Compagnie* [VOC]), 43, 144–5
　forced migration network of, 201
　legacy of, at Cape Colony, 153
　legal system of, 198, 199
Dutch Reformed Church, 49
Dyke, R., 97

Eddy, J. J., 11, 66, 69, 75
Edwards, Elizabeth. *See* Rens, Elizabeth Catharina (Elisabeth Edwards)
Edwards, George, 84, 85, 87, 241, 265
　as an agent provocateur, 85
Edwards, William (Alexander Loe Kaye), 3, 11, 12, 22–3, 39, 48, 59, 63, 105, 130, 249, 282, 284
　accusations of spying against, 98, 99
　application to remain in Cape Colony, 84
　applications to work for the Commission of Eastern Inquiry, 26, 27, 39, 63, 83, 113
　anecdote concerning an old slave's view of England's goodness, 154–5
　arrests of, 20, 21, 125, 157, 162, 253
　arrival at the Cape Colony, 113
　assertions of his genteel social credentials, 26–7
　attack on the character and actions of Denyssen, 151–2
　at Bathurst, New South Wales, 248, 252
　under the influence of the anti-government opposition, 155, 156
　on the betrayal of British reformist ideals, 153
　boasts concerning money, 38
　as a British 'patriot', 153, 157
　burial of, 258
　charges against Somerset, 16, 61
　children of, 248
　colonial contexts in which Edwards came to prominence, 18
　colorful escapades of, 8
　complaints concerning legal pluralism, 175
　reported connection to the Bigge commissions, 100–1
　continuing protests against the Cape administration, 8, 151–2
　controversies concerning, 13
　as a covert agent for Bigge, 6
　difficulty in establishing the status and identity of, 12–13
　reported dissection of Edwards's body, 276, 278–9, 280
　escapes of, 245–6, 247, 248
　evidence compiled against, 9
　exposé by (with Cooke), of the treatment of former prize slaves, 8, 20, 79
　genuine outrage over the situation of prize slaves at the Cape, 157
　and *habeas corpus* legal arguments on behalf of, 254–5
　identification as an escaped prisoner, 248
　'imperial careering' of, 11
　independent spirit of, 2
　'infamous Character' of, 75
　legal training of, 8
　letters to Bathurst concerning his conviction for libel, 189
　link to Bigge's activities in New South Wales and Australia, 98, 100–1
　on the manipulation and betrayal of the Abolition Act by corrupt officials, 153–4

Index

marriage of, 244
in Mauritius, 63
mental suffering and possible madness of, 256, 259
motives of, 23
move from Java to Mauritius, 26
near-shipwreck of, 245
notary and legal work of, 38, 83–4
notoriety of, 3, 27, 34
as a 'politician', 269
problems in assigning meaning to the suicide of, 259–60
reasons for Edwards's attack on Somerset, 19
reasons for Edwards's leaving the *Frederick*, 253
recapture after his escapes, 246, 252
recurring bouts of 'Java fever' suffered by, 26
reward offered for the capture of, 251
scandals instigated by, 71
sentencing for leaving the *Frederick*, 253, 255
suicide of, 2–3, 247, 256–8, 282
suicide attempts of, 246, 247, 256
taking of the name William Edwards (transition from Kaye to Edwards), 8, 27–8
various publications of, 269–70
at Wellington Valley, 248, 269
See also Edwards, William, false accusations against as agent provocateur George Edwards; Edwards, William, investigations concerning the identity of; Edwards, William, and the placard scandal; Edwards, William, as a political activist; Edwards, William, trial of for horse stealing; Edwards, William, trial of for libeling Somerset; prize slave libel scandal, Edwards' pre-trial involvement in; prize slave libel scandal and investigations; prize slave libel trial, of Edwards and Cooke

Edwards, William, false accusations against as agent provocateur George Edwards, 84, 88
defence of, 85
testimony of witnesses for, 85–6
use of a notary to defend himself, 87

Edwards, William, investigations concerning the identity of, 260, 265, 267, 275
and the accessibility and manipulation of convict records, 263

Bigge's suspicions concerning the identity of Edwards, 264, 266
broader political implications of, 261–2
complaints concerning the investigation of Edwards' identity, 272
Darling's investigation into the matter, 267
debates in the Sydney press, 267–8
earliest evidence for the link between Edwards and Kaye, 263–4
Hay's opinion of the investigation, 272–3, 274
height differences between Edwards and Kaye, 262
identification of Edwards as Kaye on arrival in Cape Colony, 265, 266–7
identification of Edwards as Kaye on arrival in New South Wales, 265–7
identification of Edwards as Kaye by the Commissioners of Inquiry and Somerset, 264–5
investigations into the identity/background of, 23, 60
primary thrust of the investigation, 273
and the secretary of state's response to Elisabeth Edwards' petition concerning, 271
and use of convict records to determine identity, 262–3

Edwards, William, and the placard scandal
accusation by Edwards's servant (Daniel Lee) against Edwards, 226–7, 230
the Court of Justice's dismissal of the case, 230
denial by Edwards of any involvement, 226
Denyssen's proposed motives for Edwards's involvement, 230
Edwards's challenge to the fiscal to produce a respectable witness, 234
Edwards's opinion of the scandal given to the Commission of Eastern Inquiry, 234–5
Edwards and other 'radical', as persons of suspicion in, 219, 225
failure of the investigation to come to any conclusion, 231
recognition by Edwards of the damage done to him by the scandal, 232
Somerset's reaction to the dismissal of charges against Edwards, 231
unreliability of the evidence against Edwards, 234

Edwards, William, as a political activist,
      37, 38, 269
   and the cause of the Khoekhoen, 50
   difficulty establishing Edwards's motives
      for, 160
   doubts concerning Edwards's motives
      amongst anti-Somerset activists, 159
   insistence by Edwards on his identity as
      a lawyer, 38
   involvement in Cape Colony politics,
      18–19
   lack of clues as to the origin of his
      activism, 37–8
   negligible influence of Philip on, 49
   while incarcerated, 214–15
Edwards, William, trial of, for horse
      stealing, 20
   acquittal of, after the first arrest and
      trial, 21
   guilty verdict after the second arrest and
      trial, 21
   sentence of, 21, 27
Edwards, William, trial of for libeling
      Somerset, 160–1, 166, 167
   the Act of Accusation made against
      Edwards at, 168
   arguments concerning which laws
      (Dutch or English) should apply at the
      trial and sentencing, 178–9
   appeal by Edwards of his conviction, 184
   arrest of Edwards, 162, 195
   conviction of Edwards, 184
   Court of Justice ruling that Edwards had
      confessed, 177–8
   defence claim that the letters of Edwards
      were forged, 184, 186–7
   difficulty in determining the intent of
      Edwards's letters regarding, 161
   Edwards's list of witnesses, 170–2
   incarceration of Edwards, 209, 214–15,
      245
   judicial actions brought against Edwards
      by Somerset because of the letters,
      161–2
   letters sent to Somerset by Edwards
      regarding the 'house molestation'
      charges, 160–1
   muzzling of the Cape press from
      covering the trial, 170
   possible motivations for Edwards's
      letters to Somerset, 162–3
   presentation by Edwards's defence that
      William Parr was the true culprit,
      185–6
   proposed punishment of Edwards and
      the doctrine of Roman law, 173–4
   the prosecution's case against Edwards,
      172–3, 205
   the prosecution's response to Edwards's
      defence appeal, 187–8
   questions concerning the legitimacy of
      the sentence of transportation, 187,
      268
   representation by Brand during
      Edwards' appeal, 184–5, 186–7
   self-defence of Edwards at the initial
      trial, 170
   upholding of Edwards's sentence on
      appeal, 188
   witness of the manumitted slave
      'Carolina', 171–2
Ellé, Jean, 20, 103, 104, 107, 113, 130
   apprenticeship to Samuel Murray, 106,
      123
   involvement in the prize slave scandal,
      109
   wages as a cook, 106
   See also prize slave scandal and
      investigations
Epstein, James, 156, 205
espionage/spies, 83, 243–4
   anti-spying paranoia and the concept of
      English liberty, 87
   arguments against state-sponsored
      espionage in Britain, 234
   and British military success in India,
      93
   government spies, 87
   as part of a wider reformist agenda, 90–1
   political liability of, 93
   state-sponsored espionage as a foreign
      invention, 88
   use of informers against popular
      radicalism, 87
   See also espionage/spies, in the Cape
      Colony; Royal Mail, the, and
      espionage practices
espionage/spies, in the Cape Colony, 92,
      93, 191–2
   the opening of private correspondence
      by Somerset's informers, 95–6
Evans, Raymond, 52
Evans, Thomas, 31, 32
executive power, 205
   Denyssen's opinion of, 205
   See also banishment, and the law
expression, freedom of, 21

Fabrigas v. Mostyn (1773), 203
Facts connected with the stopping of the
      press, and the censorship of the fiscal,
      192, 193

Index

Fairbairn, John, 13, 14, 15, 47, 48, 49, 94, 95, 209
  as co-editor of the *Advertiser*, 47–8
  use of nicknames by, 223
  doubts concerning Edwards's motives, 159
Farquhar, Robert T., 113, 114
Fatal Shore, The (Hughes), 2
Faure, Abraham, 49
'felony attaint', legal doctrine of, 58
Findlay, John, 216
fiscal, 152
  duties of, 44
  Edwards's speech against, 148–9
  placard of deriding the fiscal, 148
  unpopularity of, 148
Flanagan, Owen, 263
Flanagan, Patrick, 263
Forbes, Francis, 58, 207, 252
  conflicts with Darling, 250
  insistence on holding executive power to newly minted constitutional dictates, 250
Ford, Lisa, 164, 204, 254
Four Stages of Cruelty (Hogarth), 280
France, 87
Francis, D. P., 97
Frykenius, Simon Hendrik, 180
Fyans, Foster, 2

Garrow, William, 31
Gibson, Andrew, 277
Gloucester Journal, 32
Goldsmith, Charles, 30
Goulburn, Henry, 236
governance. *See* imperial governance
Great Reform Act (1832), 18
Greig, George, 13, 15, 16, 21, 47, 48, 49, 85, 92, 192, 204, 207, 230, 240
  actions of Somerset against, 196, 197
  complaints concerning search warrants issued against him, 232–3
  on the government's handling of the placard scandal, 242
  Somerset's animosity towards and distrust of, 192
  as a suspect in the placard scandal, 226, 227
Greville, Charles, 64–6, 68
Griffin, William, 238
Grotius, Hugo, 201

habeas corpus
  legal arguments concerning Edwards and, 254–5
  periodic suspension of, 11

Habeas Corpus Act (1679), 199
Hall, Edward Smith, 250, 260, 268, 269, 270
Halloran, Laurence, 277
Hammond, Thomas, 217
Hammonds, Barbara, 237–8
Hammonds, J. L., 237–8
Harling, Philip, 168
Hartwell, Philip Harmot, 278
Hastings, Warren, 145
Hay, Robert, 67, 69
  and the Colonial Office report on Edwards, 37
  opinion of the investigation into Edwards' identity, 272–3, 274
Hero (ship), 26, 84
Hirst, John, 247
History of the Reign of George III (Baines), 90
History of South Africa (Theal), 14
Hoffman, Jan Bernard, 121, 140
  evidence to the Commissioners, 121–2
Hogarth, William, 280
Hollett, William, 124
Holmes, Rachel, 223
Holy Alliance, the, 15
honour, 78–9, 166
  See also prize slave scandal and investigations, themes of honour in
Hopley, W. M., 97
Horton, Anne Beatrix, 68
  Lord Byron's praise of her beauty, 68
Horton, Robert Wilmot, 63, 68, 69, 71, 74, 75, 81, 92, 150, 249
  on the Cape government being 'under public opinion', 73
  as the 'chief protagonist of Anglicisation', 153
  exasperation at having to defend Somerset, 73
  invaluable service to the Colonial Office, 68
  on the law of conquest and colonial governance, 181
Howell, James, 97, 214
Howell's Circulating Library and Stationers, 214
Hudson, Samuel, 22, 96, 97, 132, 182, 187, 209, 245, 251
  account of Shee's disfigurement, 228
  on the Cooke–Edwards libel trial, 147, 148
  on the departure of Greig, Burnett and Wilmot from the Cape to London, 244
  on English and Dutch placards, 215

310   Index

Hudson, Samuel (*cont.*)
  gossip concerning Blair's 'transactions', 126–7
  on the incarceration of Edwards, 209
  on Oliver the Spy, 239–40
  placard deriding the fiscal, 148
  on rumours and gossip at Howell's book shop, 214
Hughes, Robert, 2
  account of 'suicide lotteries', 2
Hughes, Thomas, 32
humanitarianism, British, 121
Hume, Joseph, 48, 66, 72, 181, 240
Humphreys, Samuel, 30
Hunt, George, 84, 86–7
Huskisson, William, 271
Hutchinson, William, 33, 34, 36, 248
  as the person who identified Edwards as Kaye, 224, 248, 265
  imperial governance, debates concerning, 11, 247, 253–4
  factionalism in colonial administrative politics, 41, 62, 91
  implications of obscure/local scandals on imperial power relations, 75–6
  importance of theatre to the governmentality of imperial society, 156–7
  interpersonal controversies that mark imperial governance, 23
  systemic problems of, 61
  transformation after the Napoleonic Wars, 39
  transition from a Dutch to British imperial system at Cape, 22

Imperial Meridian (Bayly), 10
indentured servants, Irish, 227
  link between indentured servants and the system of unfree labour at the Cape, 227
  as part of the Cape underclass, 227, 228
India, 205
  British actions against the press in, 206
  British military success in, 93
information-gathering/collection, 23, 80, 101, 243
  and informal intelligence networks, 62, 215
  potential stigma of espionage in, 243
  role of gossip and interpersonal correspondence in, 62–3, 93
  'word on the street' and the means of spreading libelous writings, 215–16
Ingram, John, 226, 227, 235

Jane (ship), 34
Java. *See* Batavia (Java)
Jones, William. *See* Oliver, William (real name W. J. Richards, aka William Jones)
Jury, James, 85

Kable, Henry, 58
Kable, Susanna, 58
Karskens, Grace, 247, 252
Kaye, Alexander Loe (William Edwards), 162, 199
  arrival in Sydney, 33–4
  assigned to solicitor Thomas Wylde, 34
  as a banker, 30, 31
  birth and baptism of, 7, 28
  escapes of, 6, 34
  imprisonment in King's Bench prison after a fuel bill dispute, 31–2
  inaccurate reports that he was sent to Van Diemen's Land after his conviction, 33
  indictment for assault, 32
  involvement in attempted mutiny on the convict transport *Atlas*, 33
  involvement in property speculation, 28
  marriage of, 30
  movements within the convict system of New South Wales, 34
  notary and legal work of, 19, 20, 28
  precarious financial position of, 31
  press reports of his trial for horse stealing, 32
  time in Batavia (Java), 35
  trial and conviction for horse stealing, 6, 31–2
  variants of his surname, 28, 31
  See also Edwards, William, investigations concerning the identity of
Kaye, Charles (brother of Alexander Loe Kaye), 29, 30
Kaye, Edward Shackfield (son of Alexander Loe Kaye), 31
Kaye, Margaret (mother of Alexander Loe Kaye), 28, 29, 31
Kaye, Mary (sister of Alexander Loe Kaye), 29, 30, 162
  low opinion of her brother Alexander, 29–30
Kaye, Thomas (brother of Alexander Loe Kaye), 19
  death of in the British–American War (1814), 29
Kaye, Thomas (father of Alexander Loe Kaye), 28, 29, 31
  bankruptcy of, 29

Index

Kekewich (Justice), 195, 196
Kercher, Bruce, 247
Khoekhoen ('Hottentots')
  rights of parents over children, 118
  legal status, 118
Kostal, R. W., 202
Krumpholtz, Philip, 86

Lady Campbell (ship), 25
Laidlaw, Zoë, 11, 62, 77
law, 202
  constitutional law, 164
  decline in seditious libel prosecutions in English law, 169
  Dutch law and the 'foreignness' of the Cape administration, 183
  law of conquest, 166, 181
  law as a threat to tranquility, 165
  'Laws of War', 203
  maritime law regarding prize slaves, 104–5
  See also banishment, and the law; defamation/defamation law; legal pluralism; libel; Roman–Dutch legal system, in the Cape
Law of Libel (Holt), 145
Le Victor (ship), 111
  capture of, 103
  See also *Le Victor*, alleged slave passengers of
Le Victor, alleged slave passengers of
  Denis, 103
  Jean-Pierre, 103
  Louisa, 103
  See also Ellé, Jean
Lee, Daniel, involvement in the placard scandal, 226–7, 228, 230, 235, 241–2
  arrest of, 230
  attempted coercion of Lee by O'Grady, 228–9
  beating of, 235
  coerced confession while drunk, 234
  Edwards's dismissal of, 234
  rumours of concerning bribery to commit perjury, 234
Leeds Mercury, 89
legal pluralism, 166, 194, 211
  blurring of the lines between Roman–Dutch and English law in libel cases, 178
  complaints concerning indiscriminate application of Roman, English, and Dutch law, 175–6
  concern across the British empire in relation to, 164
  debates concerning the Edwards–Somerset libel trial, 178–9
  problems with, in settler societies, 204–5, 212
  and the relationship between civil and common law, 174
libel, 174
  blurring of the lines between Roman–Dutch and English law in libel cases, 178
  criminal libel, 141, 167, 179
  decline in seditious libel prosecutions in English law, 169
  difficulty in defining, 164
  the risk of libel trials, 168
  seditious libel actions, 166
  under Dutch–Roman law, 166, 169, 187
Libel Act of 1792 (Fox's Act), 168
liberalism, 224
  radical liberalism, 205
liberty and security, relationship between, 22
Liverpool (Robert Banks Jenkinson, second earl of Liverpool), 82, 84
Loe, Margaret (aunt of Alexander Loe Kaye), 28, 31
  death of, 30
London Missionary Society, 48, 49
Louis decision, 111
Luddites, attacks of, 46

MacDonald, Helen, 279, 281
Macmillan, W. M., 15, 282
  view of Edwards as a 'bounder', 15
Macquarie, Lachlan, 52, 54, 99, 101
'Macquarie Bicentennial', 52
Mahony, Thomas, 214
Malamo, dispute over between Blair and Corbitt, 135–6, 137
Mansfield (William Murray, first earl of Mansfield, Lord Chief Justice), 166, 203, 204
Mascarenes Islands, 113
Mason, John, 137, 138
Mauritius, 5, 113
Maxwell-Stewart, Hamish, 33, 279
McCallum, P. F., 156
McLachlin, N. D., 69
Melville (Henry Dundas, first Viscount Melville), 145
Métairie, Claude Guillaume, 103, 104
Meurant, Louis, 92, 193, 214, 235
  on Edwards's speech against the fiscal, 148–9
  on spies in the Cape Colony, 93
Miller, Linus, 263

Minerva (ship), 98, 244, 245, 248, 265, 266
Mixed Commissions, the (1819), 111
Murray, George, 271
Murray, Samuel, 106

Napoleonic Wars, 111
  shifting of the legal system after, 111
  social and economic upheaval following, 10–11
Narrative of a Residence in South Africa (Pringle), 14, 92, 97
Neal, David, 247
Nederburgh, Sebastian Cornelis, 180
New South Wales, 5, 199
  administration of, 9, 51
  and British emigration policy, 46
  centralisation of population in, 54
  as a colony of settlement rather than of conquest, 57
  dissection of prisoner bodies in, 281
  establishment of a Legislative Council for, 55
  establishment of a Supreme Court for, 55
  free immigrant population of, 53
  as a free or 'slave' society, 247
  independent press of, 207
  legal issues concerning its character as a penal settlement, 58–9
  litigation in, 251
  migrant and emancipist population of, 54
  rights of convicts not in accordance with English law, 58
New South Wales Act (1823), 55, 57, 58, 207, 250, 254
Norfolk Island, 1–2, 54, 255
  cemetery of, 276
  first suicide reported on, 2
  lurid reputation of, 2
  as 'the modern Gomorrah', 1
  myth of murder–suicide lotteries in, 2, 259
  as 'Norfolk's fell Isle', 1
notaries, use of, 87

O'Grady, Roger, 228, 230
  attempted coercion of Lee in the placard scandal, 228–9
  wrote love letter for Lee in exchange for information, 229–30
Oliver, William (real name W. J. Richards, aka William Jones), 88, 89, 236, 238, 243
  exposure as a government agent, 88, 89
  fate after the Pentrich uprising, 237
  hatred of, by the English populace, 91
  historiography on, 237–8
  as 'Oliver the Spy', 88, 89, 236
  See also Oliver, William (real name W. J. Richards, aka William Jones), in the Cape Colony
Oliver, William (real name W. J. Richards, aka William Jones), in the Cape Colony, 238–9, 240
  Burnett's view of, 240–1
  Edwards's view of, 240
  and opposition attacks on Britain's Tory government, 241
  and the placard scandal, 241
  as Somerset's 'Jackall', 239
  as a symbol of the excesses of the Somerset regime, 239
  usefulness as a covert operative, 239
Olivier, N. J. J., 174
Order in Council (1808), 115
Ordinance 19, 117
Ordinance 50, 50, 282
Ordinance 60, 159
Oriental Herald, 206
Ovens, T., 265

Parr, Thomas William, 185–6
Parker, George, 85
paternalism, 139
  in the Cape slave system, 137
  and family structure in Cape slave society, 137–8
  pervasiveness throughout the prize slave investigations, 135
patronage/patronage networks, 121, 128
Peel, Robert, 249
Peires, Jeff, 51–2
penal colonies
  ad hoc legal arrangements in, 254, 274–5
  emancipist sentiments concerning, 250–1
  reform of, 50–1
Pentrich uprising (1817), 46, 88
  allegations against Oliver concerning, 89
  fate of the leaders of, 88
Perceval, Dudley, 41, 80
  duties of, 80
  ennui of, 80
  letter book of, 80
  opinion of Somerset, 41–2
  reports to London concerning the Cape Colony, 81

Index

on the weaknesses in Somerset's character, 81
Perceval, Spencer, 41, 80
'Peterloo' massacre (1819), 46
Philip, John, 14, 15, 16, 48, 49, 94, 95, 209
  return to London as a lobbyist, 49
  as superintendent of the London Missionary Society in the Cape, 48–9
Pickering, Paul, 87, 237, 238
Picton, Thomas, 204
Pigou, H. M., 106–7, 133, 134
  See also prize slave scandal and investigations
Pitt, William (the younger), 87
'spy system' of, 243
placard scandal, 22, 225, 242
  advantageous opportunities for the government created by, 232
  attempts by witnesses to reconcile their own propriety with the salacious content of the placard, 217–19
  as a dirty tricks campaign manufactured by the authorities, 243
  first appearance and disappearance of the placard, 216–17
  G. E. Cory's account of, 224
  immediate responses of the colonial administration, 219
  inability to prove facts, 224–5
  initial public sympathy for Somerset and Barry, 231–2
  legal pluralism and the comic aspects, 219
  in the oppositional politics of the Cape, 225
  origins of, 216
  political implications of, 231, 241, 242–4
  response in London, 240
  reward offered for information concerning, 233, 234, 235–6
  Somerset and Barry's appearance together in the wake of, 219
  text of the offending placard, 216
  use of search warrants during, 232–3
  witnesses to the placard, 217
  See also Edwards, William, and the placard scandal; Lee, Daniel, involvement of in the placard scandal; O'Grady, Roger, attempted coercion of Lee in the placard scandal
placards, 209, 215
  against the Cape authorities' perverting English concepts of law, 182

examples in Dutch, 183
examples in English, 182
prominent place for the posting of, 213
as 'word on the street' and the means of spreading libelous writings, 215–16
See also 'Dreyer's Corner'; placard scandal
Plasket, Richard, 165, 284
  on the law as a threat to tranquility, 165
politieke uitzetting [political removal]
  Bathurst's belief concerning, 209–10
  Somerset's attempts to justify the legality of, 196–7
  Somerset's use of against Greig, 196
  See also banishment, and the law
Port Macquarie, 248, 255
Porter, Bernard, 237
Porter, William, 45
Powley, F. G., 97
Pringle, Thomas, 13, 14, 15, 17, 47, 48, 49, 158, 206, 209
  assessment of Edwards as an 'adventurer', 14
  on the 'Cape Reign of Terror', 14, 92
  co-editor of *Blackwood's Edinburgh Magazine*, 47
  co-editor of the *South African Commercial Advertiser*, 47–8
  complaints concerning search warrants issued against him, 232–3
  determination to publish an exposé of the Cape administration, 209
  disjunctures between the published work and private correspondence, 17
  doubts concerning Edwards's motives, 159
  fear that his private correspondence was under surveillance, 94
  fear of the possibility of incarceration, 209
  financial ruin of, 14
  on the intimidation of the Cape population by Somerset's administration, 97
  letter to Brougham, 15, 16
  letter to Fairbairn, 16
  low opinion of Edwards, 14, 15, 17
  on the object of the 'Placard Plot', 232
  opinion of the Commissioners of Inquiry, 97
  return to Britain, 49
  as secretary of the Anti-Slavery Society in London, 49
  use of nicknames by, 223
  'Whig principles' of, 209

314   Index

prize slave libel scandal, Edwards's
    pre-trial involvement in, 124, 158
  compiling of testimony by, concerning
    Blair's corruption, 108
  dismissive attitude of, towards Blair's
    supporters, 132–3
  and the drawing up of Cooke's
    complaint, 107
  information provided by, to the
    Commissioners of Eastern Inquiry,
    114
  letter of, to the Commissioners of the
    Court of Justice, 151–2, 155, 156
  manipulation of the scandal by Edwards
    for local/metropolitan audiences, 131
  memorial of, brought to the Lords
    Commissioners of His Majesty's
    Treasury, 130–1
prize slave libel scandal and investigations,
    97, 120, 131, 138
  Blair's primary defence, 127–8
  charges brought against Cooke and
    Edwards by Denyssen, 108
  circumstantial evidence presented at, 128
  colonial and imperial context of, 109
  Colonial Office reaction to, 109
  informal nature of the investigation,
    128–9
  investigations concerning Blair's control
    over the distribution of prize slaves,
    122, 132
  origins of the scandal, 106–7, 133–4
  the prize slave system at the Cape
    Colony, 110–11
  protestations by Blair and Bird of their
    innocence in the scandal, 127
  testimony during, as almost exclusively
    by British subjects, 138–9
  testimony of prize slaves during, 120
  See also prize slave libel scandal and
    investigations, themes of honour in;
    prize slave libel trial, of Edwards and
    Cooke
prize slave libel scandal and investigations,
    themes of honour in, 131, 132
  Edwards' imagined dialogue between
    Cooke and Ellé, 134
  the honour culture between the Dutch
    and the British, 133
  the manner in which honour and status
    were conceived in Cape slave society,
    134–5
  the pervasiveness of paternalism
    throughout the investigations, 135,
    139

prize slave libel trial, of Edwards and
    Cooke, 77, 131, 139, 144, 148, 159,
    166
  acquittal of Edwards and Cooke, 149,
    160
  Brand's defence of Edwards, 145
  Cloete's defence of Cooke, 144–5
  basis of the indictment, 139
  as both a *cause célèbre* and a form of
    public entertainment, 147
  charges against Cooke, 108, 140
  charges against Edwards, 108, 140
  Cooke's defence against the charges,
    142–3
  Denyssen's arguments against the
    defences of Cooke and Edwards,
    143–4
  Edwards's attack on the Cape regime
    and the fiscal during, 140, 148–9
  Edwards's charged with contempt of
    court, 140
  Edwards's defence, 143
  Edwards's vehement protest against the
    fiscal during, 140, 148
  failings of the Cape administration
    brought to light during, 146–7
  grandstanding of Edwards during, 131
  implications of the acquittal for the Cape
    administration, 149
  key element of, concerning the uses of
    the memorial, 141–2
  key points of, concerning the memorial,
    142
  libel as a breach of the peace, 139
  newspaper reports of, 147
  as a political liability for the Somerset
    administration, 149, 150, 151
  the prosecution's case against Edwards
    during, 77–8
  ruling of concerning allowing witnesses
    to the truth or falsehood of the
    memorial, 142
  Somerset's complaints concerning, 147
  unusual nature of (as a *criminal* libel
    case), 141
  See also Stephen, James, opinion on
    Fiscal v. Cooke, Edwards and Hoffman
    case
prize slaves, 110, 116, 120, 151
  complaints of, 116–17
  corruption in the prize slave system, 132
  length of apprenticeship for, 121
  maritime law regarding prize slaves,
    104–5
  mistreatment of, 151

Index

the prize slave system in imperial context, 110
as slaves seized by the British navy, 19, 20, 105
as a source of real income, 122
treatment as real property, 125–6
as under the authority of the local Customs Department, 105
See also Africans, liberated; prize slave scandal and investigations
public opinion
and the Cape government being 'under public opinion', 73
concerning the Colonial Office, 70, 73–4
Publications Act (1819), 168, 169

Racehorse (ship), 103
Records of the Cape Colony (Theal), 17, 194
Reminiscences (Meurant), 92
Rens, Elizabeth Catharina (Elizabeth Edwards), 244, 245, 247, 253
attempts by to raise money after Edwards's death, 269–70
authorisation by Darling of money for after Edwards's death, 270
Bigge's description of, 268
case brought by Elizabeth to the Supreme Court concerning Edwards's identity, 268–9, 270
inheritance from her mother, 270
petition regarding her husband's mistreatment and sentence, 252–3, 268
the secretary of state's response to her petition, 270–1
time with her husband at Port Macquarie, 248
Researches in South Africa (Philip), 50
Reynolds, Thomas, 89
Richards, W. J. *See* Oliver, William
Riches, Isaac, 85, 86
Rise of South Africa (Cory), 224
Ritchie, John, 98
Robben Island, 199, 245
Roberts, David Andrew, 52, 248, 252, 254
on illegal convict movement on the Bathurst frontier, 255
Roberts, Michael, 75
Roman–Dutch legal system in the Cape, 57, 164, 166, 174, 175
and laws concerning marriage and inheritance, 175
protests against Dutch law in the sentencing of Edwards for libel, 183

Wylde's opinion of, 211
See also banishment, and the law
Ross, Lynette, 258
Ross, Robert, 9
Royal Mail, 94
Royal Navy, 111

Samboo, testimony of, 119
Sandys, Francis, 206
Saunders, Charles, 116
Scallywags of Sydney Cove (Clune), 13
scandals, as a way of understanding social and political relations, 224
settler societies, 211
and the problems of legal pluralism, 204–5, 212
settler rights, 167
Shackfield, Edward (father-in-law of Alexander Loe Kaye), 31
Shackfield, Susanna (wife of Alexander Loe Kaye), 30, 31
Shee, Daniel, 228, 235
disfigurement of, 228, 235
Shortt, Francis, 277, 278
Shuttleworth, Thomas, 29, 30
Sidmouth (Henry Addington, first Viscount Sidmouth), 89, 236
Sitwell (Under-Sheriff), 245, 246
Six Acts (1819), 11, 84, 168, 198
slaves/slavery
Christian slaves, 117
as slave-owners' *volk* [people], 137–8
difficulty of eliminating the slave trade in the Cape Colony, 114
illegal slave trade in the south-west Indian Ocean, 113
number of captured slaves entering the British colonial system, 104–5
office of the Guardian of, 120
in parliamentary debates, 108–9
preparation for liberation, 115
shifting master–slave relations, 137
slave children (*see also* Malamo), 119
value of slaves captured at sea, 104
See also prize slaves; slavery, abolition of
slavery, abolition of, 19, 20, 104, 151
abolition as central to the conception of Britishness, 154
adherence to the cause of in Britain, 158
Edwards's view of the Abolition Act, 153–4
Somerset, Lord Charles, 8, 9, 14, 16, 25, 31, 57, 70, 96, 132, 146, 151, 200, 236, 262, 266
animosity towards Edwards, 195

316   Index

Somerset, Lord Charles (*cont.*)
  autocratic powers of, 41, 196
  belief that Bird had gathered conspirators ('the Aviary') against him, 61
  collapse of the parliamentary proceedings against, 82
  colourful background of, 39
  complaints concerning Greig, 232
  complaints concerning the inaction of Fiscal Denyssen in prosecuting cases, 225
  correspondence with Bigge, 25, 194–5
  chronic habit of misreading Britain's changing political climate, 243
  discrediting of Wilmot by, 231
  effect of the Edwards–Somerset libel trial on, 188–9
  executive actions of, having significance in colonies other than the Cape, 205
  extravagance of, 92
  and the factionalism of colonial administrative politics, 41, 62, 91
  failure to recognise the changing political climate surrounding him, 73
  gubernatorial mismanagement, 249
  as liability to the Tory administration, 41
  miscalculation in bringing libel charges against Edwards and Cooke, 149
  mistress of, 171–2
  nickname ('Llama'), 223
  as 'one of the villains of South African history', 41
  opinion of Pringle, Philip and Wright, 94–5
  Perceval's opinion of his character, 81
  period of time spent as governor of the Cape, 39
  persecution of Pringle by, 14
  popularity with the Dutch elite of the Cape, 41
  proclamation concerning chattel slavery (1823), 117–18, 119
  questions concerning an adequate defence of against allegations, 73–5
  reaction to Edwards's letter to the Council of Justice, 155
  return to London to answer his critics (1826), 81
  and the right of banishment by executive order, 21
  on the significance of the placard scandal for its political ends, 242–3
  suspicion that Edwards used a false name, 191
  use of paid informers by, 93–4
  vexatious nature of his second term as governor, 60–1, 213
  vicissitudes of, 17
  warm personal relationship of, with Bigge, 194–5
  See also Edwards, William, trial of for libeling Somerset; placard scandal; *politieke uitzetting* [political removal]; Somerset, Lord Charles, relationship of with the press; Somerset, Lord Charles, specific allegations of corruption made against
Somerset, Lord Charles, relationship of with the press
  attempted executive banishment of Greig by Somerset, 197, 200
  determination to move against Greig and his editors, 192
  suppression of the Cape Colony's first newspaper, 13
  use of government informers to gather information on the press, 191–2
Somerset, Lord Charles, specific allegations of corruption made against, 61
  attacking the liberty of the press, 61
  deportation without trial, 61
  distributing liberated Africans, 61
  See also 'Sorcerer Colt'
Somerset, Lord Edward, 18, 31
  defence of his brother before Parliament, 182
Somerset, Lord Granville, 71, 73, 75, 208
  advice to Horton on handling Edwards's anti-government crusade, 71
  on the character of Lord Charles Somerset, 74
  on the conduct of Cape politics, 149–50
  on the problems for the Colonial Office and the Tories due to the Somerset critics, 72–3
  reply of to Horton's complaint, 73–4
Somerset, Henry, 61
'Sorcerer Colt' (horse), 61
South Africa, 14, 53
  See also Cape Colony
South African Commercial Advertiser, 13, 22, 47, 95, 164, 192, 207, 213, 241
  account of the prize slave libel trial in, 21
  comical aspects of the fiscal's suppression of, 193
  confrontation with the colonial government, 21

on the government's handling of the placard scandal, 242
official suppression by the fiscal, 192–3
report of the Buckingham deportation case in, 206
suppression of publication by the Somerset administration during the Edwards–Somerset libel trial, 192
South African Journal [*Het Nederduitsch Zuid-Afrikaansche Tijdscrift*], 49
sovereignty, 164, 203, 211, 212
in conquered territories, 22, 197
Spa Fields riots (1816), 46
trials in the wake of, 89
Spies and Bloodites!!! (anonymous), 88, 89
State of the Cape of Good Hope (W. W. Bird), 115
Statistical, Historical, and Political Description of the Colony of New South Wales (Wentworth), 98, 251
Stephen, James, 58, 68–9, 80, 143, 146, 157, 200, 208, 274
on the condition of the Cape penal colony, 274
opinion concerning Somerset's use of executive banishment, 203–4
opinion in the *Fiscal v. Cooke, Edwards and Hoffman* case, 179–80
Stockenstrom, Andries, 16
Sudds, Joseph, 260
suicide, as a punishable offence, 258
Sydney Gazette
on the *Australian*'s attempts to discredit Edwards, 100
on the dissection of Edwards's body after his death, 276–7, 278
report on escaped prisoners, 34
reporting Edwards' connection to the Bigge Commissions, 100–1
Sydney Monitor, 207, 250
on the corruption of Darling, 260–1
on dissection of Edwards's body, 276–8
gendered view of convict escapes in, 252
on the injustice of Edwards's sentence for libel, 183
obituary of Edwards in, 260

Taylor, David Passmore, 84, 85
Taylor, Henry, 78
admiration of Bathurst's managerial skills, 66
Telfair, Charles, 114
'Belle Ombre' estate of, 114
Theal, George McCall, 14, 17

theatre, importance of, to the governmentality of imperial society, 156–7
Thompson, E. P., 88, 89
Thompson, Patrick, 260
Tory Party/Tories, 241
Reformist Tories, 127
ultra-Tories, 82
transportation, 53
differences between transportation and banishment, 197–8
and English law, 199
on the sentence of transportation for libel as 'illegal', 179
use of, against Cape inhabitants during the VOC period, 199–200
Transportation Act (1718), 199
Transportation Act (1826), 254–5
Treaty of Amiens (1802), 43
Truter, Johannes Andreas (Sir John), 43–4, 57, 86, 177, 196
legal opinion concerning banishment, 200–2
opinion of Cooke's and Burnett's memorials, 180
poor advice given to Somerset by, 191
proficiency in English, 177
retirement of, 45
Turner, William, 89
Turning Points in Australian History (Crotty and Roberts), 52

van der Stel, Willem Adrian, 145
Van Diemen's Land, 5, 199
administration of, 51
and British emigration policy, 46
as a colony of settlement rather than of conquest, 57
dissection of Aboriginal and prisoner bodies in, 281
van Leeuwen, Simon, 187
van Niekerk, J. P., 111
van Ryneveld, William, 107, 144

Ward, Kerry, 201
Wardell, Robert, 98, 250, 251
Warden, John, 124
Waterloo, Battle of, 18
Watson, R. L., 154
Wellington Valley (the 'Valley of Swells'), 248
Wentworth, D'Arcy, 98
Wentworth, William Charles, 98, 250, 251
West Indies, 205

Whig Party/Whigs, 165, 168, 241
Wickwar, W. Hardy, 169
Wilberforce, William, 49, 155
Williams, James Onslow, 125–6
Wilmot, Benjamin, 230, 231
Wilson, Kathleen, 156

Wright, Thomas Edward, 278
Wright, William, 94
Wylde, John, 34, 45, 211, 282
   on Roman–Dutch law, 211
Wylde, Thomas, 34
   death of, 34